BUSINESS ETHICS IN FOCUS

HF5387 .B87234 2007

0134 110255863

Business ethics in focus

c2007.

BUSINESS ETHICS IN FOCUS

LAURA A. PARRISH
EDITOR

Nova Science Publishers, Inc.
New York

Copyright © 2007 by Nova Science Publishers, Inc.

All rights reserved. No part of this book may be reproduced, stored in a retrieval system or transmitted in any form or by any means: electronic, electrostatic, magnetic, tape, mechanical photocopying, recording or otherwise without the written permission of the Publisher.

For permission to use material from this book please contact us:
Telephone 631-231-7269; Fax 631-231-8175
Web Site: http://www.novapublishers.com

NOTICE TO THE READER

The Publisher has taken reasonable care in the preparation of this book, but makes no expressed or implied warranty of any kind and assumes no responsibility for any errors or omissions. No liability is assumed for incidental or consequential damages in connection with or arising out of information contained in this book. The Publisher shall not be liable for any special, consequential, or exemplary damages resulting, in whole or in part, from the readers' use of, or reliance upon, this material.

Independent verification should be sought for any data, advice or recommendations contained in this book. In addition, no responsibility is assumed by the publisher for any injury and/or damage to persons or property arising from any methods, products, instructions, ideas or otherwise contained in this publication.

This publication is designed to provide accurate and authoritative information with regard to the subject matter covered herein. It is sold with the clear understanding that the Publisher is not engaged in rendering legal or any other professional services. If legal or any other expert assistance is required, the services of a competent person should be sought. FROM A DECLARATION OF PARTICIPANTS JOINTLY ADOPTED BY A COMMITTEE OF THE AMERICAN BAR ASSOCIATION AND A COMMITTEE OF PUBLISHERS.

LIBRARY OF CONGRESS CATALOGING-IN-PUBLICATION DATA
Business ethics in focus / Laura A. Parrish (editor).
    p. cm.
 Includes index.
 ISBN-13: 978-1-60021-684-8 (hardcover)
 ISBN-10: 1-60021-684-6 (hardcover)
 1. Business ethics. 2. Consumer behavior--Moral and ethical aspects. 3. Marketing--Moral and ethical aspects. 4. Social responsibility of business. I. Parrish, Laura A.
 HF5387.B87234 2007
 174'.4--dc22
                           2007007834

Published by Nova Science Publishers, Inc. ✦ *New York*

CONTENTS

Preface		vii
Expert Commentary	Business Ethics and the Corporate World *Almerinda Forte*	1
Expert Commentary	Challenging Issues Regarding Social Responsibility *Waymond Rodgers*	13
Expert Commentary	The Role of Virtue in Business *Surendra Arjoon*	17
Short Communication	On the Rationality of Stakeholder Orientation. *Caroline Gauthier*	21
Chapter 1	Consumer Ethics Research Review *Karen S. Callen-Marchione and Shiretta F. Ownbey*	27
Chapter 2	Ethical Issues in Training for Disaster Preparedness to Serve Frail Older People: An Innovative Approach to Graduate Health Management Education *Sarah B. Laditka, James N. Laditka, Margaret M. Houck, Carol B. Cornman and Courtney B. Davis*	49
Chapter 3	Facilitating Harm *Gregory Mellema*	69
Chapter 4	Macro versus Micro Ethical Dilemmas: Understanding Ethics on a Smaller Scale *Susan Fredricks and Andrea Hornett*	79
Chapter 5	Context and Whistle-blowing *Janne Chung, Gary S. Monroe and Linda Thorne*	93

Chapter 6	Ethical Views of Japanese Managers: Insights from the Rationality of Ends/Market Orientation-Grid *Sigmund Wagner-Tsukamoto*	113
Chapter 7	Money Profile and Unethical Behavior: A Study of Full-Time Employees and University Students in China *Du Linzhi, Thomas Li-Ping Tang and Yang Dongtao*	135
Chapter 8	Levinas and Corporate Responsibility: A New Philosophical Perspective *Conceição Soares*	149
Chapter 9	Relevance Lost in Corporate Responsibility Research: Getting Behind the Smokescreens Through Academia–NGO Collaboration *Niklas Egels-Zandén*	227
Chapter 10	The Employment Relationship – The Meaning and Importance of Voluntariness *Anders J. Persson*	247
Chapter 11	Do Business Schools' Theories Negatively Influence Students' Ethical Positions? *Waymond Rodgers, Birgitta Påhlsson and Arne Söderbom*	259
Chapter 12	Misery as Corporate Mission: User Imagery at the Nightclub the Spy Bar *Niklas Egels-Zandén and Ulf Ågerup*	275
Chapter 13	Responsible Communication as an Integrator: Discourses Linking Values to Actions *Tarja Ketola*	289
Index		305

PREFACE

Business ethics is a form of the art of applied ethics that examines ethical rules and principles within a commercial context, the various moral or ethical problems that can arise in a business setting, and any special duties or obligations that apply to persons who are engaged in commerce.

Business ethics can be both a normative and a descriptive discipline. As a corporate practice and a career specialisation, the field is primarily normative. In academia descriptive approaches are also taken. The range and quantity of business ethical issues reflects the degree to which business is perceived to be at odds with non-economic social values. Historically, interest in business ethics accelerated dramatically during the 1980s and 1990s, both within major corporations and within academia.

For example, today most major corporate websites lay emphasis on commitment to promoting non-economic social values under a variety of headings (e.g. ethics codes, social responsibility charters). In some cases, corporations have redefined their core values in the light of business ethical considerations (e.g. BP's "beyond petroleum" environmental tilt).

This new book presents and discusses new and important issues in the field.

Expert Commentary - Many executives assert that ethical behavior of employees, good corporate governance and transparency of corporate dealings are the three most dominant features of corporate responsibility. Prior research has indicated that several dominant ethical positions drive how individuals and organizations view corporate responsibility. These positions are ethical egoism, deontology, utilitarianism, relativist, virtue ethics, and ethics of care (stakeholders' perspective). Awareness of these six ethical positions may improve educational training of individuals regarding corporate social responsibility.

Short Communication - This note explains that involving stakeholders into the firm's control helps the shareholders to implement stakeholder-friendly innovations in a way that increases value. It therefore provides a rational for including stakeholders on the board or building formal partnerships with them. It deals with a main issue in Business Ethics: Providing a rational for adopting an ethical behaviour.

Chapter 1 - Frequently, consumers are portrayed as being victims of marketers rather than consumers exhibiting unethical consumer behavior. This stereotypical portrayal of marketers may have contributed to the extensive research that has been conducted investigating marketers' ethical decision making. Marketers have been found to behave unethically, but consumers have also been found to be accepting of unethical consumption activities. Unethical behavior by either the marketer or the consumer will lead to unproductive exchanges. Shoplifting has been the focus of much of the research that has been conducted investigating consumer ethics. Most people would probably agree that shoplifting is wrong; however, determining the rightness or wrongness of other non-normative consumer behavior may be cause for debate. Non-normative consumer behavior is consumer misconduct in the acquisition, usage, or disposition of goods and services. For example, some consumers may consider fraudulent returns inappropriate while others may approve of it under certain circumstances such as the need to purchase interview clothing when no money has been budgeted for new clothing. Further research is needed investigating non-normative consumer behavior that may be found inappropriate by some and appropriate by others depending on the circumstances.

Chapter 2 - The aftermaths of September 11, 2001, and Hurricane Katrina underscore the urgent need to enhance education in emergency preparedness for students of health administration. The authors' purpose is to describe an interactive assignment for teaching ethics to doctoral students of health administration. The assignment, Student-Developed Educational Modules in Preparedness, was designed as a train-the-trainer process: the authors' goal was to teach doctoral students to serve as preparedness educators for masters students. Their experiential assignment required doctoral students to develop a class module for master's students of health administration, on disaster preparedness for disabled older people in the community, with an emphasis on ethical considerations. The authors piloted this training in a doctoral seminar in the fall of 2006 (n=14 students) at the University of South Carolina. The training consisted of three 90 minute weekly classes. Students completed a pre-assignment survey before the first class and a post-assignment survey immediately after the third class. In session one, the authors provided an overview of disaster preparedness for older populations, and some of the ethical considerations. In class two, students worked in four small groups of 3 or 4 students, to develop teaching materials. In class three, students presented their teaching materials. The results of eight paired Likert scale questions on the pre- and post-assignment surveys showed significant and meaningful improvement in students' perceptions of their learning in disaster preparedness for vulnerable groups, preparedness for frail older people living in the community, and in their confidence in their ability to develop and teach disaster preparedness to students of health administration (all $p<.05$). The students developed several educational approaches to promote a consideration of the ethical dimension of preparedness. From the perspective of teaching about ethics, in their responses to open-ended questions, a number of students wrote that the assignment highlighted the importance of disaster preparedness for frail older people and the ethical implications of disaster planning, and the importance of teaching master's students of health administration about this topic. The Student-Developed Educational Modules in Preparedness approach appears to be an effective way to engage doctoral students in discussing, considering, and teaching about ethical dimensions of managing complex disasters.

Chapter 3 - Discussions of moral issues typically concentrate upon situations that are the result of what individuals have done. Much less typical are discussions that focus upon moral agents assisting others in producing wrongdoing. As a result, situations where some agents make it possible or likely for others to cause harm are not as well understood as those standardly treated in the literature. But as the dynamics of decision making in institutions such as corporations become more complex, those producing harm are frequently aided in various ways by what others have done. Codes of criminal conduct specify what qualifies as aiding or abetting in crime, but in the moral realm there remains much uncertainty and confusion about the moral status of one who helps make possible the wrongdoing of another.

In this paper the author concentrates upon the notion of facilitating harm. Roughly speaking, one facilitates harm when one makes it more likely that another is able to produce harm. Elsewhere the authors has have analyzed the stronger notion of enabling harm. One enables harm, according to his analysis, just in case one makes it possible for the actions of another to produce harm, and one is aware that one is doing so. And just as facilitating harm is a weaker notion than enabling harm, it is a stronger notion that condoning harm. One who merely condones harm is aware of the relevant actions of another but does not do anything to make the harm produced by the other more likely to occur (or, for that matter, anything to make the harm less likely to occur). Thus, facilitating harm is less serious, morally speaking, than enabling harm, but more serious than condoning harm (where all of these are varieties of complicity in wrongdoing).

Chapter 4 - Learning ethics can be assisted by a focus on everyday mundane matters. Experience with students and prior research suggests that students readily engage in ethical discernment when they can comprehend a connection between the situation and themselves or their families. This chapter presents research with both graduate and undergraduate business and communications students who change their responses to ethical dilemmas when the scenarios are repeated with the addition of a relationship or connection.

Respondents change their proposed course of action when family is present. Consistent with Gilligan (1982), females perceive relationships and take action more readily. However, males will choose an ethical approach to a situation when family relationships are specifically introduced. The conclusion is that with a perceived relationship, ethical choices are made.

The use of 'micro' ethical scenarios, everyday dilemmas, may offer the basis for a more effective ethical pedagogy than reliance on the 'macro' scenarios or less immediate and more abstract situations from the news or from traditional ethical pedagogy. In addition, more research is needed on ethical reasoning and the non-cognitive motivators of ethical discernment.

Chapter 5 – The authors' study uses an experiment to investigate three important contextual factors associated with individuals' tendency to whistle-blow: internal versus external whistle-blowing, rule-based or principle-based climate, and power of the wrongdoer. As predicted, individuals are more likely to whistle-blow internally than externally and they are more likely to whistle-blow in a principle-based organizational climate compared to a rule-based organizational climate. Furthermore, individuals are more likely to whistle-blow on a less powerful wrongdoer compared to a more powerful wrongdoer, but only if the complaint recipient is within the organization. The paper concludes with a discussion on the implications of these findings for theory and practice.

Chapter 6 - The paper positions empirical views of Japanese managers in the groceries / retail sector with the novel theoretical tool called the 'rationality of ends/market orientation-grid.' The grid distinguishes different managerial predispositions, ranging from self-interested opportunism and self-interested egoism to self-interested altruism and authentic altruism. These rationality features are related to a continuum of market features which range from perfect competition to imperfect competition. Based on the theoretical application of the rationality of ends/market orientation-grid, the researcher found that most observed business ethics behavior in the Japanese groceries / retail sector did not step outside charitable altruism and the compliance with legal regulation that reflected organizational slack. Ethical innovation or ethical stakeholder management showed up only in minor degrees. This leaves room for future business ethics programs. Based on the theoretical analysis and the empirical findings made, the paper makes certain business ethics recommendations for managers in this respect.

Chapter 7 - With two questionnaires named Money Ethics Scale (MES) and Propensity to Engage in Unethical Behavior Scale (PEUBS), which are designed by ourselves, this study investigates randomly 204 managerial staffs and 395 university students, to analyze their money profiles, and the relation between money profiles and unethical activity. The results show that Achieving Money Worshiper and Careless Money Admirer have more possibility to involve unethical activity than Apathetic Money Handler and Money Repeller when they are faced with work stress, but Apathetic Money Handler and Money Repeller have more possibility to involve unethical activity than Achieving Money Worshiper when they are faced with unethical organizational context; University students have more possibility to involve unethical activity than Managerial staffs when they are faced with work stress, conformity and organizational context.

Chapter 8 - Today in the mature economies and democracies of the West, with the increasing pace of globalisation, businesses as corporations have assumed unprecedented importance both nationally and internationally. Like all agents, they are capable of acting in ways with consequences said to be beneficial as well as harmful to society. Their increasing overwhelming prestige, power and resources have led some critics to argue that such entities should be held responsible for the latter. In other words, we need a notion of corporate responsibility both in the legal and moral domains. However, in such societies, the notion of responsibility is primarily that of individual responsibility which seems to run counter to that of corporate responsibility. As a result, the defenders of the *status quo* have seen fit to maintain that the concept of corporate responsibility is unintelligible and that the difficulties in rendering it intelligible and applicable, both morally and legally, are insurmountable.

This thesis is an attempt to overcome such objections and to construct a plausible defence of the notion of corporate responsibility. To do this, the following strategies are used:

1. The author argues that some of the major criticisms of corporate (legal) responsibility can be overcome; in other words, that it makes sense to hold certain people within the structure of a corporate hierarchy to be responsible for manslaughter, and that even the notion of *mens rea*, a fundamental requirement for attributing responsibility in the law of homicide within the framework of individual responsibility applies. The author uses the tragedy of the sinking of the Herald of Free Enterprise, to illustrate the points under discussion.

2.a. However, the author also claims that such a defense of corporate legal/moral responsibility may be too limited, too piecemeal and therefore not enough. The deep hostility and resistance to it will weaken only if the cultural ethos within which the theory of individual responsibility itself is embedded weakens, both at the level of theory and practice. In other words, the author argues that a shift in moral paradigm is urgently needed.

b. On the former level, an outline of an alternative perspective on responsibility must first be made available. To this purpose, the authors relies on some of the key insights of the philosophy of Levinas, especially his fundamental notion of infinite responsibility for the Other, to construct a plausible account in outline of corporate responsibility.

c. In the context of practice, the author sets out some evidence to show that, of late, society, for example, in the UK (standing as surrogate for many economically advanced Western countries) – at the level of committed individuals, of NGOs and even of the government appear to be turning away from the theory of individual responsibility and reaching out or groping towards (though, perhaps, not consciously) what may be the central value of Levinasian philosophy, that is, infinite responsibility for the Other.

As a way of focusing this set of themes, the author has chosen one case study – (a) the circumstances and events relating to the sinking of the Herald of Free Enterprise to stand as surrogate for problems in the domain of corporate legal and moral responsibility. The chapter attempts to demonstrate the relevance of Levinasian philosophy to these problems. Further Levinasian concepts are invoked to elucidate them.

It concludes in the light of all the arguments presented that the Levinasian philosophy which sees ethics as first philosophy, that the Levinasian concept of infinite responsibility for the Other, which is interpreted and defended in this chapter as an attempt to forge an *aretaic* ethic based on secular saintliness/holiness constitute a genuine new moral paradigm, and that this new paradigm may be relevant to the pre-occupations of the increasingly globalised world in the twenty-first century.

Chapter 9 - Paraphrasing Johnson and Kaplan's (1987) well-known argument that management accounting research has lost its relevance, this chapter argues that research into corporate responsibility in developing countries faces a similar dilemma. Due to an unwillingness to consider alternative research methods, corporate responsibility research has lost its relevance in terms of being able to describe corporate practice accurately and credibly. Instead, corporate responsibility research has ended up describing the smokescreens (created by transnational corporations and their suppliers) that serve to hide actual factory conditions. To restore relevance to corporate responsibility research, this chapter proposes an alternative research method based on academia–NGO collaboration in collecting empirical data in developing countries. The pros and cons of the developed research method are discussed, as are possible ways to overcome the difficulties of academia–NGO collaboration. Finally, the chapter concludes by discussing how managers can use the developed method both to improve and scrutinize their own monitoring.

Chapter 10 - This paper explores the viewpoint that the voluntariness of the contracting parties in an employment relationship has substantial value. One overarching issue concerns the meaning of voluntariness in the employment context, and another issue is its normative importance. With respect to the former issue, the paper proposes conditions that are required for the contracting parties' voluntariness. However, the author argues that exactly where the line should be drawn between voluntary and non–voluntary agreements in this context is indeterminate. Concerning the latter issue, the paper claims that even if we were able to draw such a line, it would tell us nothing about the voluntariness condition's normative importance, or about how much normative weight we shall assign to its fulfilment in the workplace context. Finally, the paper argues that the normative theory most suitable for support of the voluntariness condition is of a contractualist brand.

Chapter 11 - This article develops and applies a decision making framework for understanding and interpreting ethical theories that impact the most on organizations. This framework classifies six major ethical positions that reflect issues in accounting and management courses. As such, the *Throughput Modeling* approach indicates how the ethical theory supporting the "rational choice theory can be influenced and perhaps enhanced by other ethical theories. In part, employees' behavior may be guided into improved ethical decision making that can be made defensible, and how special problems facing them can be dealt with via a decision-making pathway leading to an action.

Chapter 12 - Despite extensive corporate responsibility research into both *what* and *how* firms produce, research is lacking in one product category in which the *what* and *how* linkage creates questionable corporate practice – luxury products. Luxury is in some cases created by companies controlling the so-called user imagery of their customers, i.e., encouraging 'desirable' individuals to consume their products and obstructing 'undesirable' individuals from consumption. This chapter critically analyses the implications of this corporate practice based on a study of Sweden's most luxurious nightclub. The study's results show that the nightclub has organised its activities to allow categorisations of individuals into 'desirable' and 'undesirable' customers. Furthermore, the study shows that a creation of 'misery' for the vast majority of individuals (the 'undesirable') is essential for creating 'enjoyment' for the selected few (the 'desirable'). The chapter concludes by discussing implications for practitioners interested in altering this situation.

Chapter 13 - Corporate responsibility incorporates economic, social and ecological issues, and sees these three areas as essential parts of business operations – not just separate charity gestures, which would earn society's acceptance to a company's real business. All business operations should be responsible. This means that the values, discourses and actions of the company should be consistent with each other. Coordinating and integrating these three levels of responsibility is a challenging task.

Empirical research shows that there is a wide gap between corporate values and actions, which companies tend to bridge with their discourses. However, often companies utilize these discourses to deny, excuse and justify those of their actions that are inconsistent with their values.

Based on empirical findings, there are at least three kinds of linking pin roles for discourses in companies that claim to value responsibility. Corporate discourses may be (1) *schizophrenic:* the discourses praise responsible values while deny and excuse irresponsible actions; (2) *desperate:* the discourses assert commitment to responsible values while justify irresponsible actions; or (3) *sublimating*: the discourses advocate responsible values and admit irresponsible actions in order to enable them to be turned into responsible actions.

This chapter argues that (1) schizophrenic and (2) desperate discourses exemplify irresponsible communication, which leads to separating corporate values and actions further apart while (3) sublimating discourses exemplify responsible communication, which leads to integrating values and actions into responsible business operations.

In: Business Ethics in Focus
Editor: Laura A. Parrish, pp. 1-11

ISBN: 978-1-60021-684-8
© 2007 Nova Science Publishers, Inc.

Expert Commentary

BUSINESS ETHICS AND THE CORPORATE WORLD

Almerinda Forte [*]

St. John's University, Division of Administration and Economics, Jamaica, NY, USA

Business ethics, especially among top managers, has become a topic of concern to the public and business community. As a result, much attention has focused on the development of moral reasoning in corporate individuals. Past research examining individual and business decision behavior, indicates that several variables such the level of moral reasoning, perceived ethical climate, education, age, management level, work tenure, industry types and gender have a significant impact on individual decisions. The following outlines the major findings by researchers investiaging these variables.

James Rest developed the Defining Issues Test (DIT) from Kohlberg's six stages of moral judgment. The reasoning and the level of one's moral evelopment can be determined by this test (Rest, 1979). The DIT seeks the reasons behind the decisions and is used to determine the level of the respondent's oral development. The DIT presents the test-taker with a series of scenarios and offers the test-taker solutions based on different rationales. Even though two individuals may arrive at the same answer, their reasoning can reflect a substantial difference in moral development and level of critical thinking, which the DIT reveals. The scenarios and responses present fundamental, underlying structures of social thought instead of the fine descriptions of specific concepts and ideas. The long form of the DIT contains six moral dilemmas, each with a set of forced choice questions. An index measures the relative importance placed on principled moral thinking. The scores are computed to indicate the placement of the respondent on a scale analogous to Kohlberg's six stages. The short form of the DIT contains three ethical scenarios, each accompanied by a set of questions. A Likert-type scale records the scores on the test. The subject ranks different issues presented for each dilemma or scenario by level of importance. This ranking provided the researcher with the subjects' preference for certain modes of thinking or stage structure. The higher stage preferences are weighted and averaged by the researcher A "P-Score," i.e., a principled score, calculated from the averages, indicates the extent to which a subject reasons in terms of

---

[*] Associate Professor and Chairperson, Division of Administration & Economics, 8000 Utopia Parkway, Jamaica, NY 11439. (718) 990-2039 (voice)…..fortea@stjohns.edu

principled ethical stages. The higher the P-score (which ranges from 0-90), the more moral reasoning the individual uses. The DIT also has an index of overall moral judgment development, consisting of a composite of all stage scores. Rest (1982, 1988) believed that the first three stages are not as significant as the latter three, and that each of the latter three stages operate with different importance for different individuals

Principled moral reasoning as measured by "P" scores was the dependent variable used in Forte's (2001) study. Forte's (2001) study found a mean "P" score of 35 with a standard deviation of 14.8. What should be noted is that this score is below the "P" score of 40 that Rest (1979) records as the average adult score. No definite reason can be given as to why the "P" scores of this sample fell slightly below the average adult "P" scores. Perhaps the results reflect the business environment. Bigel (1998) and Pennino (2001) found similar results in "P" scores researching business individuals.

In 1968, Harvard University's research division of the Graduate School of Business published two books on organizational work climates: Tagiuri and Litwin's *Organizational Climate, Exploration of a Concept*, and Litwin and Stringer's of *Motivation and Organizational Climate*. Litwin constructed a questionnaire to measure organizational climate. Working independently, Tagiuri investigated how executives perceived the environment in which they functioned. Litwin and Tagiuri reached the same conclusion: organizational climate influences the behavior of people in an organization (McKenna, 1993, p. 37).

Litwin and Stringer developed an instrument to collect perceptions of organizational environment. They contended that the realities of an organization are understood only as they are perceived by members of the organization (p. 42). Litwin and Stringer defined organizational climate operationally as the sum of perceptions of individuals working in the organization (p. 66).

Of importance to this research was their conclusion that organizational climate properties can be perceived by members of an organization and reported on by them through an appropriate questionnaire (p. 187).

Climate, according to Litwin and Stringer, influences organizational decisions by creating certain kinds of beliefs about what kind of consequences will follow from various actions (Litwin & Stringer 1968, p. 188). These authors conclude that members of organizations can offer an accurate perception of their firms' ethical climate.

Victor and Cullen in 1987 and 1988 studied the linkage between corporate ethical standards and organizational behavior. They designed an instrument that measured perceptions of ethical climate by members of an organization. Victor and Cullen prototyped organizations into categories of distinct ethical climate types (Caring, Law and Code, Rules, Instrumental, and Independence). The instrument they developed is a 36 statement survey questionnaire. Victor and Cullen not only concluded that corporations have distinct ethical climate types, but they also found that climate types influence managerial behavior and that climate types influence what ethical conflicts are considered and the process by which the conflicts are resolved.

Rest found that many studies "revealed that increased education is associated with higher levels of moral judgment" (Rest and Narvanez, 1994, p. 28). Years of formal education is a greater predictor of ethical reasoning and moral development than chronological age (Rest, 1986, p. 33). Rest summarized that "the evidence at hand suggests that adults in general do not show much advance beyond that accounted for by their level of education" (Rest, 1979, p.

113). Rest continued, "It is not specific moral experience as much as a growing awareness of the social world and one's place in it that seems to foster development in moral judgment. The people who develop in moral judgment are those who love to learn, who seek new challenges... are reflective... set goals... take risks... .(Rest, 1986, p. 57).

Mature managers may have more positive attitudes toward moral issues in business because of their more developed moral awareness. This explanation seems to be in accordance with Kohlberg's model of moral reasoning suggesting that individuals develop their capacity for moral reasoning over time. (Kuyala, 1995, p. 72) Touche Ross (1988) and Kelley et al. (1990) also reported a positive relationship between age and ethical behavior.

Lewin and Stephens (1994) state that post-conventional individuals are particularly likely to become leaders (Kohlberg et al., 1983), and as such have a special opportunity for organizational impact. Post-conventional or principled individuals believe that principles outweigh specific rules and interests, and view principles as universal, generalizable, and compelling. Principled individuals are very much concerned with right and wrong and with the dignity of the individual. Therefore, principled CEOs leaders at the highest levels will establish a climate of ethicality throughout their organizations and develop policies and processes that embody principles of respect for the individual. They will attempt to prevent wrongs committed in the name of the organization and not merely crimes of the organization (Lewin and Stephens, 1994, p. 198).

Drucker emphasizes that managers are responsible for the development and implementation of ethical decision making. He states, that "no one should ever become a manager unless he or she is willing to have his character serve as the model for subordinates" (David, Anderson, Lawrimore, 1990, pp. 31 & 32).

Sacasas and Cava (1990) state that good ethics requires that leadership become convinced of and committed to the notion that successful corporate governance requires more than just profit maximization.

Kelley, Ferrell, and Skinner in 1990 surveyed 1,500 marketing researchers. They found that respondents in their present positions for at least ten years reported their behavior to be more ethical than employees in their present positions for three to five years. Kelly, Ferrell, and Skinner suggested that employees after three to five years on a job may experience work frustrations. This may cause them to compromise their ethical values to advance their careers.

Posner and Schmidt (1984, 1987) suggested that the distinction between personal and organizational values of an employee becomes fuzzy over time. This happens not only the higher one advances up the organizational ladder, but also the longer one is employed by a particular organization. Posner and Schmidt alluded to a socialization process which influences this behavior. Harris in 1990 surveyed 148 individuals employed by the same organization at different management levels. He found that managers employed by the organization for at least ten years, which also included senior managers, were less tolerant of fraudulent practices than other employees.

On the other hand, Bigel (1998) investigated the ethical orientation of financial planners. Bigel hypothesized in his study that ethical orientation would increase with career tenure. This study showed a statistically significant decrease in ethical orientation from experienced (5-10 years) to established (10.1 + years). This finding was contrary to his hypothesized direction.

Numerous studies have been conducted on various professional fields such as accounting, nursing, teaching and medicine. These studies found that some of the service professions are prone to different levels of moral reasoning. This might suggest that there is something inherent in the industry's process that causes individual thought mechanisms to develop or not to develop to higher modes of moral development.

Forte (2001) did not find a statisical significance between industry types and the moral reasoning of individual managers.

Armstrong (1984, 1987) explored accountants' ethical reasoning and moral development. The results of Armstrong's research showed that CPAs and accounting students tended to be at lower levels of ethical reasoning than comparable groups of college-educated adults or college-age students.

Lampe and Finn (1992) studied accounting and CPAs in public firms but excluded partners. They compared subjects' DIT results to responses on a questionnaire containing seven short ethical scenarios. The results of Lampe and Finn's research found that both accounting students and practitioners tend to have lower DIT P scores than college-aged students, college-educated adults, and other professional groups such as law and medicine.

Studying the development of moral reasoning in nurses are Crisham, 1981a; Felton & Parsons, 1987; Gaul, 1987; Ketefian, 1981, 1989; Ketefian and Ormond, 1988; Mayberry, 1986. The moral reasoning of nurses was measured by the Defining Issues Test (DIT), or the Nursing Dilemma Test (NDT), developed by Crisham (1981b), which parallels the DIT. Crisham's research suggests that moral reasoning of nurses tends to increase with more formal education. The research showed that nurses' scores are usually equal to or sometimes higher than scores of other groups with similar academic credentials.

In the area of education, Diessner (1991) reviewed 30 studies and concluded that most teachers reasoned only at the conventional level. He used Kohlberg's interview format to measure the moral reasoning of teachers. Diessner found that most preservice and inservice teachers could recognize but were unable to produce postconventional thinking. The research also indicated that moral thinking is subject to change depending upon school leaders or the atmosphere of the schools in which the teachers serve.

Husted (1978) studied the moral reasoning ability of 488 medical students by utilizing the DIT test. The research found that medical students showed a preference for reasoning at stages 5 and 6.

While the mean "P" scores for females were higher than the mean "P" scores for males in Forte's (2001) study, no statistically significant correlations were found between gender and "P" scores. This finding is consistent with research conducted by Rest (1979) (1988), Derry (1989) and Harris (1990) and Pennino (2001). Rest found minimal differences between the moral reasoning scores of men and women. However, when differences did exist, females scored higher. Rest found that differences due to gender were not powerful when correlated with "P" scores. (Harris also found no differences between genders). Harris states, that with the exception of the self-interest construct, females, as a group, are not different from males in their degree of tolerance/intolerance to fraud, coercion, influence dealing, and deceit (1990, p. 744). Derry also found no moral reasoning differences between males and females. Derry's theory is that if general difference exist between men and women, they do not carry over into strong organizational cultures where both women and men are trained to think and judge as corporate members (Derry, 1989, p. 859). Pennino (2001) also did not find any difference between the moral reasoning of men and women.

Gilligan (1979, 1982) suggested that gender differences exist in the ways that men and women approach and solve ethical problems. She has argued that males typically take a justice orientation towards conflicts, emphasizing the importance of rights, justice, and obligations in the resolution of conflicts. Females, according to Gilligan, have a caring orientation, which emphasizes the importance of human relations and the welfare and well being of all parties involved. Gilligan also stresses that both males and females are capable of considering both perspectives, but one perspective or orientation predominates.

RECOMMENDATIONS

The following recommendations are divided into two sections: recommendations for the field and recommendations for future research.

Recommendations for the Field

1. Managers and executive level employees of any age, especially older managers, may benefit from training devoted to shaping managers' ethical thought processes and decision making.
   Business education should continue to strongly emphasize business ethics in business curricula. All business subjects, such as accounting, management and marketing should challenge students with ethical dilemmas and situations requiring moral reasoning. Students should be made aware of the importance of ethical reasoning in corporate America.
2. Ethical soundness should be reinforced by engaging top management in social and ethical audits of the company. In addition, periodic ethical seminars should be organized to ensure ethical thought processes and decision making.
   Business educators must stress that a successful corporate leader has the ability to establish a climate of ethicality throughout their organization. They accomplish this by developing policies and processes that embody principles of respect for all individuals. Students can experience this through role playing and related activities.
3. Corporations should examine closely their perceived organizational work climate by analyzing the policies, code of ethics and all other processes that embody principles of respect for all individuals of their firms. These policies should be under continual review and dissemination.
4. Corporate leaders, as D'Aquila (1997) suggests, should always try to hire managers and staff employees who are well educated and well experienced in their field. Since managers, especially top managers, set the tone of the organization's ethical work climate, this hiring practice would insure a more ethically sound work climate.
5. Managers or executive level employees should keep in mind that gender and the industry experience of a new manager may have an impact on his/her moral reasoning; knowing this, firms should take measures to offer new hired managers an extensive orientation program which clearly outlines the policies, code of ethics and all other processes which they expect each manager to subscribe.
6. Based on the varied results between work tenure and the moral reasoning of individual managers, all executive and managerial level employees would benefit

from training to enhance their ethical sensitivity. However, dramatic intervention might be necessary if the actual culture of the organization encourages managers to think less ethically. In those cases, a change in management as well as training could be necessary.

7. Rest (1986) and Trevino (1992), however, claim that there is something inherent in the educational process that causes individual thought mechanisms to develop to higher modes of moral development. Education, whether through traditional schooling or training, enhances the ability of individuals to operate at higher levels of principled moral reasoning.
8. Rest (1979) (1980), Darry (1989), Harris (1990), Pennino (2001) and Forte (2001) did not find significant differences between males and females in strong organizational structures, perhaps because men and women are trained to think and judge as corporate members. Managers should therefore determine whether specific ethical dilemmas or decisions require solutions from managers with more of a justice or caring orientation.
9. Managers or executive level employees should keep in mind that gender and the industry experience of a new manager may have an impact on the potential success of the new manager's ability to help set or change the organizational ethical tone desired of that corporation.
10. Managers or executive level employees should keep in mind that age, work tenure, management levels, education and the five ethical climate types may have little or no impact on his/her moral reasoning.

Recommendations for Future Research

Future research may be directed in addressing and answering the following issues and questions.

1. Forte's (2001) study should be replicated in order to ascertain whether there have been any changes in the moral reasoning of business managers of selected industries with a different sample as well as over a period of time.
2. A study should also be conducted to investigate this issue from a global perspective. A sample of business managers in selected industries drawn from a group of Canadian, British, Italian, German, or any other foreign country should provide interesting results.
3. An analysis should be conducted of other professional organizations and groups, such as accountants, lawyers, doctors, and educators in order to see if the results would be replicated or if these professions differ from the results found in Forte's (2001) study.
4. It would also be revealing to study individual managers from selected industries on a longitudinal basis to determine how changes in their levels, positions, and industries might impact their moral reasoning. Periodic examination over a number of years could prove insightful into determining how changes affect moral reasoning.
5. Further research is needed to investigate why the perceived ethical climate of some industries attract certain age groups while repelling others. For example, why is an

individual in Forte's (2001) study with a mean age of 44 attracted to a Caring perceived organizational ethical climate type, and what experiences has a 55 year old individual experienced which may have affected his/her perception of their organizational ethical work climate causing a deviation from one perceived organizational climate type to another.
6. Additional research across industry types should be conducted to assess what, if any, differences occur in moral reasoning among those industries and identify possible characteristics and reasons.
7. Future research is needed to investigate further the relationship between tenure and perceived ethical climate type. Because of the different findings of Kelley, Ferrell, Skinner and Bigel a closer examination seems to be warranted.
8. Future research should investigate whether managers and executive level employees gravitate to the perceived ethical climate type of their ethical tendency. This is important since members of a corporation may move to a more comfortable ethical climate if they feel uncomfortable in one organization. On the other hand, if these members remain with the organization, they may change the ethical orientation of the organization.
9. Future research should investigate the relationship between industry types, gender, and moral reasoning. Managers who move from organization to organization travel with their professional baggage from previous positions, which may influence their moral reasoning. It would be beneficial to understand as much as possible the subtle variations that could affect a manager's moral reasoning.
10. Additional research dealing with age and the moral reasoning of individual managers is needed. A sample with more of a variance in age than Forte's (2001) study may be drawn to measure a statistical significance, if any, observed.
11. A sample with more of a variance in education than Forte's (2001) study may be drawn to measure a statistical significant between education and P scores.
12. Given the varied research between managerial and executive women and men exist or do not exist. As Morrison (1997) recommended, research should address specific factors and examine them from a qualitative approach rather than a quantitative approach. Interviews could also prove useful in enhancing the findings of this research. Further studies should be undertaken to ascertain whether corporate culture, the nature of the management position or other variables cause men and women to demonstrate similar or difference decision making processes when dealing with ethical dilemmas and moral reasoning in the work place.
13. Additional studies should be undertaken to assess if a relationship between management levels and moral reasoning might exist. A sample with more of a variance in management levels may be drawn to measure a statistical significance between managerial levels and P scores. A statistical significance between management levels and P scores did not result in Forte's (2001) study possibly because the majority of the respondents were upper management. Dun & Bradstreet provided the researcher with a list consisting of a proportional stratified random sample of Fortune 500 firms but the majority of the respondents came from upper management.
14. Additional research across perceived ethical climate types should be conducted to assess what if any differences occur in moral reasoning among these types.

15. Future research should investigate the relationship between tenure, education, gender and industry types and perceived organizational ethical climate types. It would be beneficial to understand as much as possible how these variables affect variations in perceived ethical climate types.
16. Future research should investigate the relationship between age, work tenure, management levels, education, and the five ethical climate types and moral reasoning. It would be beneficial to understand as much as possible how these variables affect the subtle variations in a manager's moral reasoning.
17. Future research should investigate the relationship between the perceived organizational ethical work climate type among individual industry types.

CONCLUDING COMMENTS

The value of ethical reasoning is that it is a premise upon which our country and our business enterprises are founded. High moral reasoning and the continued development of ethical standards are goals to which our government, businesses, and educational system must ascribe.

BIBLIOGRAPHY

Armstrong, M. (1984). *Internalization of the Professional Ethic by Certified Public Accountants: A Multidimensional Scaling Approach*. Unpublished: University of Southern California, Doctoral Dissertation.

Armstrong, M. (1987). Moral development and accounting education. *Journal of Accounting Education*, 27-43.

Bigel, K. (1998). *The Ethical Orientation of Financial Planners Engaged In Investment Activities: A comparison of Practitioners Based on Professionalization and Compensation Sources*. Unpublished doctoral dissertation, New York University.

Crisham, P. (1981a). *Moral Judgment of Nurses in Hypthetical and Nursing Dilemmas*. Unpublished doctoral dissertation, University of Minnesota..

Crisham, P. (1981b). Measuring moral judgment in nursing dilemmas. *Nursing Research*. 30 (2), 104-110.

D'Aquila, J. (1997). *Internal Control Environment Forces and Financial Reporting Decisions Made by Financial Accountants*. Unpublished doctoral dissertation, New York University.

David, F.R., Anderson L.M., & Lawrimore, K.W. (1990). Perspectives on Business Ethics in Management Education. *SAM Advanced Management Journal*, Autumn, pp. 26-32.

Derry, R. (1989). An empirical study of moral reasoning among managers. *Journal of Business Ethics*, 8, pp. 855-862.

Derry, R. and R.M. Green. (1989) Ethical Theory in Business Ethics: A Critical Assessment. *Journal of Business Ethics*, 8, 521-533.

Diessner, R. (1991). *Teacher education for democratic classrooms: Moral reasoning and ideology critique*. 16th Annual Conference of the Association for Moral Education, Athens, GA.

Drucker, P. (1973). *Management*, New York, N.Y.: Harper & Row.

Felton, G.M., & Parsons, M.A. (1987). The impact of nursing education on ethical/moral decision making. *Journal of Nursing Education*, 26, 7-11.

Forte, A. (2001). *Business Ethics: A Study Of The Moral Reasoning Of Selected Business Managers*. Unpublished doctoral dissertation, New York University.

Gaul, A.L. (1987). The effect of a course in Nursing ethics on the relationship between ethical choice and ethical action in baccalaureate Nursing students. *Journal of Nursing Education*, 26, 113-117.

Gilligan, C. (1982). *In a different voice: Psychological theory and women's development*. Cambridge MA: Harvard University Press.

Gilligan, C., & Attanucci, J. (1988). Two moral orientations: gender differences and similarities. *Merrill-Palmer Quarterly*, 34(3), 223-237.

Gilligan, C. (1979). Women's place in man's life cycle. *Harvard Educational Review*, 29, 119-133.

Gilligan, C. (1977). *In a different voice: Women's conceptions of the self and of morality*. Cambridge, MA: Harvard Educational Review 47: Harvard University.

Harris, J.R. (1990). Ethical values of individuals at different levels in the organizational hierarchy of a single firm. *Journal of Business Ethics*, 9, 741-750.

Husted, S.D. (1978). *Assessment of moral reasoning in pediatric faculty, house officers and medical students*. Proceedings of the 17th Annual Conference on Research in Medical Education, 17, 439-441.

Kelley, S.W. Ferrell, O.C., & Skinner, S.J. (1990). Ethical behavior among marketing researchers: An assessment of selected demographic characteristics. *Journal of Business Ethics*, 9, 681-688.

Ketefian, S. (1981). Moral reasoning and moral behavior among selected groups of practicing nurses. *Nursing Research*. 30, 171-176.

Ketefian, S. (1989). Moral reasoning and ethical practice. In J. Fitzpatrick, R. L. Taunton, and J. Benoliel (Eds.), *Annual review of nursing research* (pp. 173-195). New York: Springer.

Ketefian, S., and Ormond, I. (1988). *Moral reasoning and ethical practice in nursing: An integrative review*. New York: National League for Nursing.

Kohlberg, L. (1981). *The Psychology of Moral Development Volume One*. Harper and Row.

Kohlberg, L. (1970). *Moral Stages and Moralization. Moral development and behavior* New York, N.Y.: Holt, Rinehart & Winston.

Kohlberg, L. (1984). *The Psychology of Moral Development Volume Two*. San Francisco: Harper & Row Publishers.

Kohlberg, L. (1969). Stage and sequence: the cognitive - developmental approach to socialization. *Handbook of Socialization Theory and Research*. Goslin D. (ed), Chicago, Rand McNally, pp 347-480.

Kohlberg, L. (1969). Stage and Sequence. *Handbook of Socialization Theory and Research Chicago*, IL: Rand McNally.

Kohlberg, L. (1976). Moral stages and moralization; the cognitive developmental approach. *Moral Development and Behavior*. Lickona, T. (ed). New York: Holt,Rinehart, & Winston, pp 31-55.

Kohlberg, L. (1984). *The Relationship of Moral Judgement To Moral Action, Morality, Moral Behavior and Moral Development*. New York: John Wiley & Sons.

Kohlberg, L. (1982). *Essays On Moral Development: The Philosophy of Moral Development*. San Francisco, CA: Harper & Row.

Kohlberg, L. (1958). The Development of Modes of Moral Thinking and Choice in the Years 10 to 16. Unpublished Doctoral Dissertation, The University of Chicago.

Kohlberg, L., Levine, C., and Hewer, A. (1983) *Moral stages: a current formulation and a response to critics*. Basel: Karger.

Kuhn, D., Langer, J. & Kohlbeg, L. (1971). *Relations Between Logical and Moral Development*. Recent Research In Moral Development. Holt: New York, NY.

Kujala, J. (1995). *Moral issues in business: Top managers' perceptions of moral issues in stakeholders relations*. University of Tampere, Finland, School of Business Administration.

Lampe, J., & Finn, D. (1992). A model of auditors' ethical decision process. *A Journal of Practice and Theory,* Supplement, 1-21.

Lewin, A.Y., & Stephens, C.U. (1994). CEO attitudes as determinants of organization design: An integrated model. *Organization Studies, 15* (2), 183-212.

Litwin, G.H. and Stringer, R.A. (1968). *Motivation and Organizational Climate*. Harvard Business School.

Mauro, N.J. (1987). *Business Ethics, Managerial Decision Making, and Corporate Culture and Values*. Unpublished doctoral dissertation, New York University.

Mayberry, M.A. (1986). Ethical decision making: A response of hospital nurses. *Nursing Administration Quarterly*, 10 (3), 75-81.

McKenna, J.N. (1993). *Ethical Dilemmas In Financial Reporting Situations and The Preferred Mode of Resolution of Ethical Conflicts As Taken By Certified and Noncertified Management Accountants In Organizations With Perceived Different Ethical Work Climates*. Unpublished doctoral dissertation, New York University.

Morrison, J. (1997). *Managerial Job Satisfaction: An Examination of the Impact of Selected Psychological, Personal, and Industrial Variables on the Job Satisfaction of Executive and Managerial Corporate Women*. Unpublished doctoral dissertation, New York University.

Pennino, C. (2001). *The Relationship Between Managerial Decision Style, Principled Ethical Reasoning, and Selected Variables in Business Organizations.* Unpublished doctoral dissertation, New York University

Posner, B.Z. & Schmidt, W.H. (1987). Ethics in 'American companies: A managerial perspective. *Journal of Business Ethics, 6*, 383-391.

Posner, B.Z. & Schmidt, W.H. (1984). Values and the American manager. *California Management Review, 20* (3), 202-216.

Rest, J.R. (1983). Morality. *Handbook of Child Psychology*, edited by P. Mussen, 4th Edition, Vol. 3 on Cognitive Development, pp. 556-629. New York, NY: John Wiley and Sons.

Rest, J.R. (1979). *Development In Judging Moral Issues*. Minneapolis, Minnesota: University of Minnesota Press.

Rest, J.R. (1982, February). *A psychologist looks at the teaching of ethics*. Hastings Center Report pp. 29-36

Rest, J.R. (1986a). *DIT Manual* (Third Edition, 8/90 Revision). Minneapolis, MN: Center for the Study of Ethical Development.

Rest, J.R. (1988). Why Does College Promote Development In Moral Judgement? *Journal of Moral Education, 17* (3), 183-193.

Rest, J.R. and Narvaez, D. (1994). *Moral development in the professions: Psychology and applied ethics.* Hillsdale, N.J. Lawrence Erlbaum Association, Publishers.

Rest, J.R. (1986). *Moral development: Advances in research and theory.* New York, NY: Praeger Publishers. Katholieke Universiteit Levven, Belgium Doctoral Dissertation.

Sacasas, R., & Cava, A. (1990). Law, ethics and management: Towards an effective audit. *Business Forum, 15* (1), 18-21.

Tagiuri, R. and Litwin, G.H. (1968) *Organizational Climate, Exploration of a Concept.* Harvard University Law School.

Touche Ross (1988, January). *Ethics in American Business: An Opinion Survey of Key Business Leaders on Ethical Standards and Behavior.*

Trevino, L.K. (1986). Ethical decision making in organizations: A person-situation interactionist model. *Academy of Management Review*, 11, 601-617.

Trevino, L.K. & Nelson, K.A. (1995). *Managing Business Ethics: Straight Talk About How To Do It Right.* New York: John Wiley and Sons.

Trevino, L.K. (1992). Moral reasoning and business ethics: Implications for research, education, and management. *Journal of Business Ethics*, 11, pp. 445-459.

Victor, B. and Cullen, J. B. (1987). A theory and measure of ethical climate in organizations. *Research In Corporate Social Performance and Policy* 9, 51-71.

Victor, B., & Cullen, J.B. (1988). The organizational basis of ethical work climates. *Administrative Science Quarterly March*, pp 101-125.

In: Business Ethics in Focus
Editor: Laura A. Parrish, pp. 13-15

ISBN: 978-1-60021-684-8
© 2007 Nova Science Publishers, Inc.

Expert Commentary

CHALLENGING ISSUES REGARDING SOCIAL RESPONSIBILITY

Waymond Rodgers[*]
A. Gary Anderson Graduate School of Management, University of California, Riverside, USA

The 21st Century presents many challenges in terms of our treatment of the environment and people that form a global community. The value placed on ethics has grown significantly as a result of numerous business scandals that today are still being felt for the irrefutable damage caused to employees, customers, community, investors and all businesses. For example, one quarter of all Global Fortune 500 companies now generate some kind of report that chronicles their environmental, social or sustainability efforts (Oracle, 2005). Ethics and social responsibility is concern with individuals' and organizations' moral judgments about right and wrong. Decisions taken within an organisation may be made by individuals or groups, but whoever makes them will be influenced by the culture of the organization. The decision to behave ethically is a moral one; customers, employees, suppliers, and managers must decide what they think is the right course of action. This may involve refusing the corridor that would lead to the largest short-term earnings.

Our basis of interaction with others is oftentimes stomped by a lack of knowledge of another particular ethical position. Unfortunately, problems can escalate due to us communicating with others on different wave lengths. For example, executives claimed (Oracle, 2005) that the three most critical aspects of corporate responsibility are: ethical behavior of staff, good corporate governance, and transparency of corporate dealings. For institutional investors, transparency of corporate dealings was even more imperative. A total of 68 percent stated that it was one of the three most essential aspects to corporate social responsibility, followed by high standards of corporate governance (62 percent) and ethical behavior of staff (46 percent) (Oracle, 2005). Prior research (Rodgers & Gago, 2001, 2003, and 2004) has indicated that several dominant ethical positions govern how we conduct our lives, relate to others in the community, and deal with our environment. That is,

---

[*] Waymond.Rodgers@ucr.edu

understanding six dominant ethical positions may abate potential disasters about to percolate in our quest of problem solving and decision making (Rodgers, 2006).

Six major ethical positions (Rodgers & Gago, 2001), namely ethical egoism, deontology, utilitarianism, relativist, virtue ethics, and ethics of care (stakeholders' perspective) guide us through live when we are confronted with an assortment of dilemmas in making a decision. Provided that we agree and relate to one another based upon one of the six dominant ethical positions could alleviate potential misunderstandings in the future. I will next explain briefly the six dominant ethical positions that govern our actions.

Ethical egoism position underscores that individuals are always motivated to act in their perceived self-interest. Individuals perceive obtaining a goal in terms of wants, desires and/or needs. For example, satisfying my desires to obtain employment may lead me to dismiss other people feelings and rights to the degree that someone may become harmed to a horrendous level.

Deontological position usually contains or implies the words "should," "ought," or "it is (or was) right or wrong to…" This position provides the rules or laws that we use in order to conduct a transaction with another party. The agreed upon code of conduct or rules is the blueprint that dictate our rights in a particular situation. For example, ethical standards are fundamental to how an organization operates, and include workplace policies, hiring, training, business conduct guidelines, and ethical and legal standards.

The *utilitarian position* is concerned with consequences, as well as "the greatest good for the greatest number of people." Therefore our actions are supported and justified by the notion that many will benefit in the future. Further, the utilitarian position states that individuals and organizations should ask themselves what are the consequences of a particular act in a particular situation for those affected in a particular group. If its consequences bring more total good than those of any alternative course of action, then this action is the right one and the most appropriate one for individuals or organizations to perform.

The *relativist position* assumes that people use themselves or the people around them as their basis for defining ethical standards. Hence, given the information or environmental setting, individuals' position can change as a result of what they believe will increase their wants, desires, and/or needs. For example, the guide for business conduct abroad is what is legally and morally accepted in any give country where an organization operates.

The *virtue ethics position* is the cultivation of virtuous traits of individuals' character as viewed as society morality's primary function. That is, a person or organization's principles are not affected by, or shaped by, the people involved, or what might result if a particular course of action is followed. An organization images and relations with the community is a dominant theme of this perspective. Virtues are personal qualities that provide the basis for people or an organization to lead a good, noble, or prosperous existence.

Finally, the *ethics of care* (stakeholders) position focuses on a set of character traits that are deeply highly regarded in close personal relationships, such as sympathy, compassion, fidelity, love, friendship, and the like. This position is beginning to emerge as society is demanding more from companies in terms of the treatment of customers, suppliers, employees, shareholders, community and the request for a sustainable environment. For example, corporate social governance policies and practices promote thoughtful and independent representation of stakeholders' interests.

CONCLUSIONS

Many organizations and individuals are newly discovering the importance of ethics, corporate social responsibility and the multiple ways in which they are part of this wider ecosystem. The amplified presence of corporate social responsibility in daily enterprise operations is being driven by an assortment of issues, such as the erosion of trust in big corporations, the globalization of business, the corporate-governance movement, the rise in importance of corporate socially responsible funds and steep competitive pressures.

In some cases, perhaps, it is a reaction to excesses of the prior decade. Due to a recent survey by Oracle Corporation and the Economist Intelligence Unit (Oracle, 2005), 84 percent of executives and investors surveyed felt corporate responsibility practices could positively impact a company's bottom line. These findings give emphasis to the overall importance and shift in thought around social responsibility. That is, it is now recognized that it is advantageous for organizations and individuals to be ethical. An ethical image for an organization can foster goodwill and loyalty among customers, suppliers, employees, shareholders and the community.

Many people as possible ought to be educated about the ethical issues that touch their lives. More precisely, the public needs these individuals to be educated. Knowing and understanding the six dominate ethical positions (ethical egoism, deontology, utilitarianism, relativist, virtue ethics, and ethics of care) can meet the challenges and obstacles in building, managing and measuring corporate responsibility programs and responsibilities within organizations. Building on these six dominant positions, the next dimension of this strategy is to influence the educational process by impacting these concepts on the classroom and curriculum, supporting classroom-based discussions of ethics and corporate responsibility through extra-curricular activities.

REFERENCES

Oracle Corporation. 2005. Oracle and Economist Intelligence Unit Announce Results From Corporate Responsibility Survey. *Business Ethics: The magazine or corporate responsibility*. http://www.csrwire.com/synd/business-ethics/article.cgi/3527.html.

Rodgers, W. 2006. *Process Thinking: Six pathways to successful decision making*. New York: iUniverse, Inc.

Rodgers, W. & Gago, S. 2001. Cultural and ethical effects on managerial decisions: Examined in a Throughput Model. *Journal of Business Ethics*, 31: 355-367.

Rodgers, W. & Gago, S. 2003. A model capturing ethics and executive compensation. *Journal of Business Ethics*, 48: 189-202.

Rodgers, W. & Gago, S. 2004. Stakeholder influence on corporate strategies over time, *Journal of Business Ethics*, 52: 349-363.

Expert Commentary

THE ROLE OF VIRTUE IN BUSINESS

Surendra Arjoon
Department of Management Studies, University of the West Indies,
St. Augustine, Trinidad

Typically, when one speaks of ethics in business, the leading contenders are utilitarian and deontologist or duty-based theories: the former emphasizes cost and benefit relationships, while the latter espouses general principles that regulate human behavior. Such approaches focus on the moral actions and decisions of agents and are characterized as act-based, rule-based or principle-based ethics. In the last decade in particular, there has been much interest generated in developing virtue theory as being fundamental to a theory of business and management, with applications in a wide spectrum of issues including leadership, corporate governance, corporate social responsibility, education and training, ethical decision-making and business strategy. The emphasis has been on an Aristotelian concept of virtue ethics which focuses on the character of moral agents (and so is categorized as agent-based ethics) and focuses on the question: "What kind of person or organization one ought to become in order to consistently do the right thing?" Recent trends in the literature suggest that, rather than pitting one theory against the other, there have been attempts to integrate complementary aspects of the various theories, especially as there is no dispute that they all contain some elements of truth about the moral life. For example, a deontologist would be of the view that virtues provide the means to act upon moral imperatives, and for utilitarians, virtues are dispositions that produce desirable consequences. For ethics to be practical both act-based (what is the right thing to do) and agent-based (having the dispositions to do the right thing) approaches need to be considered. For example, such considerations are required in determining whether or not a rule should be applied or when there are conflicting rules and principles. These two approaches are indispensable in addressing the two main challenges of ethical behavior: knowing what the right thing to do is (act-based) and doing the right thing (agent-based).

A virtuous agent, human or organizational, is one that exhibits robust character traits so that one fulfills one's function excellently, that is, in an ethically upright manner. A typical list of human and organizational virtues include practical judgment, self-control, fairness, integrity, empathy, warmth, courage, conscientiousness, zeal, industriousness, responsibility, loyalty, trust, and truthfulness. Given the increasing incidence of corporate moral deviance, several legal and ethical compliance measures have been introduced for promoting more effective corporate governance. One of the main challenges in implementation is to recognize the optimal balance between rules-based mechanisms (codes, legal and regulatory standards, reporting systems, etc.) and principled-based mechanism (ethical principles, relationships, etc.). Both mechanisms are complementary; the former emphasizes a specific set of procedural requirements, details, detection, enforceability and accountability, while the latter emphasizes communication, prevention, values and behavior. However recent studies have shown that the leading risk factor in business turns out to be the corporate culture or organization DNA (values that guide corporate vision and conduct). In particular, the attitude or collective tone at the top is found to be the most critical factor in determining organizational culture.

The debate on corporate governance, however, has overlooked the importance of effective governance at the personal level where the ultimate solution for restoring and promoting ethical behavior lies. It is, in fact, the virtues that are at the heart of corporate culture since they provide the basic guiding values of a strong corporate culture. The practice of the virtues implies the application of core values and principles toward attaining the goals of the organization. An example of a company that has built a strong corporate culture over the years is Synovus Financial Corporation which has been, since its inception in 1998, on the Fortune magazine list of the "100 Best Companies to Work For in America," and was also named one of "America's Most Admired Companies" in 2005. Synovus, a diversified financial services holding company with over $30 billion in assets, has developed a "Culture of the Heart" program which emphasizes the great importance of the value of every employee and has been able to attract the best people (creative, talented, energetic). In an interview[1] in 2002, Jim Blanchard the then CEO, explained, "As leaders of Synovus, we said we were not going to allow a mean-spirited, manipulative, commanding sort of leadership to exist in this company any longer. And we were going to remediate anybody who was like that – if they were willing to try. But if they couldn't or wouldn't change, then we would ask them to go somewhere else."

A related issue is the person-situation-virtue ethics debate. Essentially, the apparent controversy advanced by situationist social psychologists is that it is situational features that are solely or largely responsible for promoting unethical behavior. As well, any talk of virtue or developing robust character traits should be abandoned. In order to support their views, situationists cite a number of experiments with varied situational factors such as obedience to authority, bystander studies, degree of hurry, and group or mood effects. However, while the experiments were not primarily designed to investigate character traits, what the experiments do show is that most ordinary people are neither virtuous nor vicious. Situational features do indeed play an influential role in shaping behavior, but it is precisely the development of the virtues, defined as stable dispositional traits, that is critical to inoculate an agent from engaging in morally deviant behavior.

Codes have been the primary mechanism used to instill and promote ethical behavior in business and the professions. The contents of codes vary greatly from stressing general principles to emphasizing specific standards, and may include rules and value statements.

---

[1] An interview with John Maxwell (2003) "Ethics 101. What Every Leader Needs to Know, "New York: Time Warner Book Group. See also www.synovus.com for details on the "Culture of Heart" program.

Despite their many strengths and drawbacks, the main concern about codes is that they do not and cannot cover most decision-making situations and behavior, and therefore may not prescribe the best ethical cause of action in concrete situations. In order to promote a culture of trust and accountability, it is also necessary to focus on the moral character of the decision-maker, and not simply a reliance on codes. The acquisition of virtues therefore, is critical in addressing unethical behavior, and at the same time, promoting ethical behavior. Being a teleological theory, virtue enables us to know what is the most appropriate goal or ideal to pursue, and at the same time, provides motivation toward choosing the most appropriate means to achieve the goal.

There is an ongoing debate on what constitutes a profession. A profession is generally characterized by a code of ethics, provision of a public service, specialized knowledge and expertise, some autonomy and discretionary authority and perhaps self-regulation. The main concern of professional ethics is not whether certain jobs or occupations constitute a profession, but the focus is on the provision of a service in a competent and dedicated manner that directly or indirectly promotes the common good. In other words, all (legitimate) ordinary work performed excellently or virtuously, constitute professional work. While the characteristics of a profession, as indicated above, do help in promoting a professional attitude and conduct, many of the aspirations in guiding professional behavior cannot be strictly enforced or regulated. The relationship between professional behavior and ethics lie not only in ethical principles which guide such behavior, but also in attaining robust character dispositions or virtues. Virtues are therefore necessary in the development of professional ethical behavior, and provide the foundation of professional ethics.

One therefore, has a grave moral responsibility to develop one's character through the development of the virtues. Otherwise, it is easy to understand why many of us including executives at major corporations, slide down the path of 'slippery slope' along which many unethical acts occur without our awareness of the moral agent, in spite of the best intention to do the right thing (take the "Slippery Slope Quick Test" below). The inclination to do wrong, while not part of our nature, but rather stems from a defect in human nature, is fuelled by 'rotten apples' (one succumbs to the temptation in the work environment), 'rotten barrel' (the work environment provides many opportunities for deviant behavior), and the 'rotten core' (features of the market system that encourages and promotes deviant behavior, e.g., emphasis on short term profits).

I promote my self-interest first before the company's profits	*1*	*2*	*3*	*4*
I strive for efficient operations at all cost	*1*	*2*	*3*	*4*
The main motivation for performing my job is money	*1*	*2*	*3*	*4*
I would offer or accept a bribe if it is the only means available to win a contract	*1*	*2*	*3*	*4*
I would perform an illegal act to promote my own career	*1*	*2*	*3*	*4*
Business has its own morality	*1*	*2*	*3*	*4*
The well-being of my colleagues is not my concern	*1*	*2*	*3*	*4*
I usually tend to take the most expedient route, even if it involves lying, to meet deadlines	*1*	*2*	*3*	*4*
I often speak ill of others, especially in assigning blame, even if it is my fault	*1*	*2*	*3*	*4*
I believe that there should be different standards of behavior for those at the top	*1*	*2*	*3*	*4*

Take the "Slippery Slope Quick Test"
How Far Am I down the Slope?

Circle the number that corresponds to the number that most appropriately reflects your opinion or belief. The lowest end of the scale (1) represents "completely agree" and the highest end (4) represents "completely disagree."

Interpretation of Scores

Total the scores of all questions.

Score	
30-40	You can consider yourself a virtuous person but beware the slide down the slope is subtle. Your challenge is to develop mechanisms to continue moving up the slope.
20-30	Although this score reflects that you may be a relatively good person and attempt to stay out of trouble, you have the tendency to take the easiest route and begin to repeatedly fail to do what is right. Your dominant defect should be identified and measures taken to address it.
10-20	You should make sure that you have a good lawyer.

In: Business Ethics in Focus
Editor: Laura A. Parrish, pp. 21-26

ISBN: 978-1-60021-684-8
© 2007 Nova Science Publishers, Inc.

Short Communication

ON THE RATIONALITY OF STAKEHOLDER ORIENTATION

Caroline Gauthier[*]
Grenoble Ecole de Management, France

ABSTRACT

This note explains that involving stakeholders into the firm's control helps the shareholders to implement stakeholder-friendly innovations in a way that increases value. It therefore provides a rational for including stakeholders on the board or building formal partnerships with them. It deals with a main issue in Business Ethics: Providing a rational for adopting an ethical behaviour.

Keywords: shareholder-orientation, stakeholder-orientation, ethics

1. A NEED FOR THEORETICAL FOUNDATION

Analysing and dealing with the needs and demands of stakeholders seems to have become a major concern of modern business. There are numerous textbooks and articles promoting the idea that organisations must manage their stakeholders or face dyer consequences (see Journal of Business Ethics e.g.). Many companies are currently establishing some form of stakeholder management process. There are also numerous examples of firms holding an annual 'Report to Stakeholders' meeting in addition to the traditional Annual General Meeting of shareholders (Jonker & Foster, 2002). However, when one takes a critical look at many examples of the implementation of stakeholder management, "it is hardly scratching the surface of ongoing business practice" (Clarke & Clegg 1998). While the stakeholder model has much potential, it is argued here that before heading further

---

[*] Grenoble Ecole de Management –DFR MKT - 12, rue Pierre Sémard – BP127 - 38003 Grenoble cedex 01 – France - caroline.gauthier@grenoble-em.com

down this track there is a need for the theoretical foundations to be clarified to provide the basis for sound practical advice (Jonker & Foster).

Involving stakeholders – Some practices
The Sita Group, branch of Suez, expert in waste management, invites every year its stakeholders at the board of directors' committee. Environmental and social associations' members (Robin des bois, France Nature Environment, PNUE…), trade-union leaders, rating agencies and clients discuss and comment the Sita's strategy of sustainable development (www.suez.com). The industrial group Lafarge works in partnership with the World Wide Foundation. They announce the following joint ambitions: "Pursuing reductions of emissions, Measuring and driving our biodiversity performance, Promoting sustainable construction, Deploying our action in the field" (www.lafarge.com).

According to Freeman's now-classic definition, "A stakeholder in an organization is any group or individual who can affect or is affected by the achievement of the organization's objectives" (Freeman, 1984, 46). Although debate continues over whether to broaden or narrow the definition (see Mitchell & al., 1997), most researchers have used a variation of Freeman's definition of a stakeholder (e.g., Clarkson, 1995; Frooman, 1999; Rowley, 1997). The work of Freeman (1984) articulates a "Stakeholder Model" to replace the "Managerial Model" of the firm. The latter, which served managers well for many years, focused on the role of employees, suppliers, shareholders and customers. Managers could achieve their objectives by understanding these groups and their changing needs and expectations. However, changes in the external environment of the firm have become so turbulent and relevant to the achievement of a firm's objectives that managers need to develop ways of understanding and addressing these issues as well. He proposed a new conceptual model of the firm that essentially incorporates the external environment (natural environment, local populations, NGO, civil society…). Successful managers must understand and respond to the needs and aspirations of those groups in this environment.

Benefits from involving Stakeholders – The case of Kalundborg's Ecopark
Industrial symbiosis in the Kalundborg district (Denmark) is based on cooperation between five industrial companies and the municipality of Kalundborg. The five companies are: the Asnaes Power Station, the plasterboard manufacturer Gyproc, the pharmaceutical and biotechnology company Novo Nordsik, the soil remediating company A/S Bioteknisk Jordrens, and the Statoil refinery. The companies exchange waste as by-products, the waste from one enterprise becoming a raw material for one or several partners. The result is a reduction of both resource consumption and environmental impacts. The main objective is to reduce costs, but helps reducing the environmental impact of the companies activities. Water consumption has been reduced by 25% in the last ten years, 45000 tons of oil and 15000 tons of coal have been saved every year. The project's total cost was 75 millions of Euros, but generated more than 160 millions savings. From Jorgen Christensen, one of the leaders, the project could not have existed without (1) a long-term vision of cost reduction, (2) a excellent involvement of each firm's stakeholders.

Donaldson and Preston (1995) presented a still relevant taxonomy of stakeholder theory types - normative, descriptive/empirical and instrumental - and used the taxonomy to guide their discussion of the stakeholder literature.

Much of the literature in stakeholder management is from the normative realm, which concerns how managers should deal with corporate stakeholders. The theory is used to interpret the function of the firm, including the identification of moral and philosophical guidelines for the operation and management of firms. Normative concerns dominate the classic stakeholder theory statements (e.g., Boatright, 1994; Clarkson, 1995; Evan & Freeman, 1983; Goodpaster, 1991).

The descriptive literature describes specific corporate characteristics and behaviours. For example, the stakeholder theory has been used to describe the nature of the firm (Brenner & Cochran, 1991), the way managers think about managing (Brenner & Molander, 1977), how board members think about the interests of corporate constituencies (Wang & Dewhirst, 1992), and how some firms are actually managed (Clarkson, 1991; Halal, 1990; Kreiner & Bhambri, 1991).

The instrumental literature identifies the connections between stakeholder management and the achievement of traditional corporate objectives, like profit or growth. Many instrumental studies use conventional statistical methodologies (e.g. Aupperle, Carroll & Hatfield, 1985; Preston & Sapienza, 1990; Preston, Sapienza & Miller, 1991). Other studies are based on direct observation and interviews (e.g. Kotter & Heskett, 1992; O'Toole, 1991). These studies have tended to generate implications suggesting that adherence to stakeholder orientation achieves corporate performance objectives as well or better than rival approaches. In general, instrumental stakeholder theorists stop short of exploring specific links between cause (stakeholder management) and effect (corporate performance) in detail (Donaldson, Preston, 1995). Synthesizing ethics and economics, Jones (1995) presents the most well-articulated instrumental theory. He makes a case for the general proposition that if firms contract (through their managers) with their stakeholders on the basis of mutual trust and cooperation, they will have a competitive advantage over firms that do not. However they do not prove their results.

2. REINTERPRETATION OF THE AMBEC AND BARLA'S MODEL

Agency theory argues that firms are structured to minimize the costs (maximize the profits) of getting some participants (the agents) to do whatever other participants desire (the principals). Participants agree to cooperate with each other, through contracts, to minimize the costs of search, coordination, information, and so on. Integrating the stakeholder concept with agency theory may be attempted then.

Hill & Jones (1992) enlarged the standard principal-agent paradigm of financial economics, which emphasizes the relationship between shareowners and managers, to create "stakeholder-agency theory". According to this, managers can be seen as agents of the other stakeholders. However Hill & Jones could not find any equilibrium in stakeholder-agent relationships (see also Tirole, 2001, Cespa and Cestone, 2002).

Later on, Ambec and Barla (2002) use this theory to give a theoretical fundation to the Porter Hypothesis (Porter, 1995 ; Porter et Van der Linde, 1995). In this paper, we apply Ambec and Barla's model to our question to legitimate the stakeholder orientation approach. Using a model of renegotiation, they formalize the idea that regulation creates external pressure to overcome organizational inertia.

In this paper, we consider that stakeholders do create the external pressure. Two games are compared: the shareholder orientation game and the stakeholder orientation one. We can show that this both games tend to a perfect Bayesian Nash equilibrium. Comparing the results, we get:

Result 1. *A stakeholder-oriented strategy may reduce informational rents, relatively to a shareholder oriented one.*

Result 2. *A stakeholder-oriented strategy may decrease the private total profit when the technology causes environmental damage.*

Result 3. *Relatively to a shareholder-oriented one, a stakeholder-oriented strategy has a positive impact on investment in R&D as the marginal benefit to investment increases.*

Result 4. *The likelihood of obtaining a more productive and without environmental damage strategy is high.*

Result 5. *The marginal productivity gain induced by more productive technologies is high.*

Result 6. *The stakeholder-oriented strategy has a relatively small impact on the profit generated by the polluting technology compared to its effect on the output decision.*

Then we get the main result:

Result 7. *Stakeholder-orientation can increase simultaneously environmental-friendly innovations and firms' expected profit.*

The theoretical approach developed here is intended to strengthen the case for using the stakeholder orientation as a central paradigm for business and society. It may help explain why some "altruistic" behaviors turn out to be productive, and why organizations that commit in these behaviours survive and often thrive.

3. ANNEX - THE MODEL

Consider the three following agents: the shareholders *SH*, the environmental-friendly stakeholders *ST* and a manager *M*. Shareholders *SH* share the same objective: increase the firm's expected profit or value. The stakeholders *ST* can be polluted individuals who care about the pollution emitted by the firm or, more generally, the damage on the environment (e.g. biodiversity). We abstract from their benefit for consuming the product related to the consumers' surplus (e.g. by assuming that the good in sold in a competitive market and/or to outside markets).

The shareholders *SH* plan to implement a cleaner but also more productive technology. They contract with *M* who is in charge of managing the project.

They invest an amount *I* in the project. The outcome of the project is a technology with constant production cost $\alpha \in \{l, h\}$, with $\Delta\alpha = h - l > 0$. The cost is *M*'s private information. The probability of $\alpha = l$ is $p(I)$, with $p(0) = 0, p'(0) > 0, p''(0) < 0$ and

$p(\infty) = 1$. For simplicity, we assume that the technology l causes no environmental damage, whereas the technology h causes damage $d(q)$ with q the production level. We assume that $d(0) = 0$, $d'(q) > 0$ and $d''(q) \geq 0$, for every $q > 0$.

The good is then produced. For a level of production q, M incurs the cost αq, and is paid w yielding an utility $w - \alpha q$. SH enjoys benefit $B(q)$ from q units produced with $B(0) = 0$, $B' > 0$ and $B'' < 0$ [1]. Its utility is $B(q) - w - I$. The total private surplus generated by production is then $\pi(q, \alpha) - I = B(q) - w - I$. It is maximised at the (ex-post) private efficient level q_α^*.

The shareholders ST care about the environmental damage $d(q)$.

Notice that the technology h might be interpreted like a non-environmental friendly technology in the broad sense that might be replaced by the more environmental friendly technology l. It requires investing in R&D and technological change. This investment might fail for many reasons so we might end up choosing how much to produce with the original "bad" technology. So involving shareholders in decision increase the benefit of a l technology but reduces the profit in case of a h technology. This increases the incentive to invest in technological change but might increase or reduce the firm's expected profit.

4. ACKNOWLEDGMENT

The author thanks Dr. Stefan Ambec for helpful comments.

5. BIBLIOGRAPHY

Ambec S. & Barla P. 2002. A Theoretical Foundation of the Porter Hypothesis. *Economic Letters*, 75(3): 355-360.

Beaudry, P. & Poitevin, M. 1995. Contract renegociation: A simple framework and implications for organization theory. *Canadian Journal of Economics*, 28(2): 302-335.

Boatright, J. 1994. What's so special about shareholders? *Business Ethics Quarterly*, 4: 393-408.

Brenner, S. N. & Cochran, P. 1991. *The stakeholder theory of the firm: Implications for business and society theory and research*. Paper presented at the annual meeting of the International Association for Business and Society, Sundance, UT.

Brenner, S. N. & Molander, E. A. 1977. Is the ethics of business changing? *Harvard Business Review*, 58(1): 54-65.

Cespa, G. and G. Cestone (2002) "Stakeholder Activism, Managerial Entrenchment, and the Congruence of Interests between Shareholders and Stakeholders", manuscript, Universitat Pompeu Fabra.

Clarke, T. & Clegg, 1998. *Changing Paradigms: The Transformation of Management Knowledge for the 21st Century*. London, Harper Collins.

---

[1] $B(q)$ could be interpreted as revenues from marketing the product or as the benefit derived from producing internally an intermediate input.

Clarkson, M. B. 1991. Defining, evaluating, and managing corporate social performance: A stakeholder management model. In J.E. Post (Ed.), *Research in corporate social performance and policy*: 331-358. Greenwich, CT: JAI Press.

Clarkson, M. B. 1995. A stakeholder framework for analyzing and evaluating corporate social performance. *Academy of Management Review*, 20: 92-117.

Donaldson, T. & Preston, L. E. 1995. The Stakeholder Theory of the Firm: Concepts, Evidence and Implications. *Academy of Management Review*, 20 (1): 65-91.

Evan, W. & Freeman, R. E. 1993. A stakeholder theory of the modern firm: Kantian capitalism. In Beauchamp T., Bowie N. (Eds.), *Ethical theory and business*, 75-93. Englewood Cliffs, NJ, Prentice-Hall.

Freeman, R. E. 1984. *Strategic Management: A stakeholder approach*, Boston, Pitman.

Frooman, J. 1999. Stakeholder influence strategies, *Academy of Management Review*, 24.

Goodpaster, K. E. 1991. Business ethics and stakeholder analysis. *Business Ethics Quaterly*, 1(1): 53-73.

Halal, W. E. 1990. The new management: Business and social institutions in the information age. *Business in the contemporary world*, 2(2): 41-54.

Hill, C. W. & Jones, T. M. 1992. Stakeholder-agency theory. *Journal of Management studies*, 29: 131-154.

Jones, T. M. 1995. Instrumental stakeholder theory: A synthesis of ethics and economics. *Academy of Management Review*, 20: 404-437.

Jonker, J. & Foster, D. 2002. Stakeholder Excellence?, Framing the evolution and complexity of a stakeholder perspective of the firm. *Corporate Social Responsibility and Environmental Management*, 9: 187–195.

Kreiner, P. & Bambri, A. 1991. Influence and information in organization-stakeholder relationships. In J. E. Post (Ed.), *Research in corporate social performance and policy*, 12: 3-36. Greenwich, CT: JAI Press.

Mitchell, R. K. Agle, B. R. & Wood, D. J. 1997. Toward a theory of stakeholder identification and salience: Defining the principle of who and what really counts. *Academy of Management Review*, 22: 853-886.

Porter, M.E. 1995. America's green strategy. *Scientific America*, 264:168.

Porter, M.E. & Van der Linde, C. 1995. Toward a new conception of the environment competitiveness relationship. *Journal of Economic Perspectives*, 9(4):97-118.

Preston, L.E. & Sapienza, H.J. 1990. Stakeholder Management and Corporate Performance. *Journal of Behavioral Economics*, 19:361-375.

Preston, L.E. Sapienza, H.J. & Miller, R.D. 1991. Stakeholders, Shareholders, managers: Who Gains What from Corporate Performance?, in A. Etzioni & P. R. Lawrence (Eds), *Socio-Economics: Toward a New Synthesis*, M.E. Sharp, Armonk, New York, 149-165.

Rowley, T. J. 1997. Moving beyond dyadic ties: A network theory of stakeholder influences. *Academy of Management Review*, 22: 897-910.

Sappington, D. 1993. Limited liability contracts between principal and agents, *Journal of Economic Theory*, 29: 1-21.

Tirole, J. (2001) "On Corporate Governance" *Econometrica*, 69, 1-35

Wang, J. & Dewhirst, H. D. 1992. Boards of directors and stakeholder orientation. *Journal of Business Ethics*, 11: 115-123.

In: Business Ethics in Focus
Editor: Laura A. Parrish, pp. 27-47

ISBN: 978-1-60021-684-8
© 2007 Nova Science Publishers, Inc.

Chapter 1

CONSUMER ETHICS RESEARCH REVIEW

Karen S. Callen-Marchione
Bowling Green State University, Bowling Green, OH, USA
Shiretta F. Ownbey
Oklahoma State University, Stillwater, OK, USA

ABSTRACT

Frequently, consumers are portrayed as being victims of marketers rather than consumers exhibiting unethical consumer behavior. This stereotypical portrayal of marketers may have contributed to the extensive research that has been conducted investigating marketers' ethical decision making. Marketers have been found to behave unethically, but consumers have also been found to be accepting of unethical consumption activities. Unethical behavior by either the marketer or the consumer will lead to unproductive exchanges. Shoplifting has been the focus of much of the research that has been conducted investigating consumer ethics. Most people would probably agree that shoplifting is wrong; however, determining the rightness or wrongness of other non-normative consumer behavior may be cause for debate. Non-normative consumer behavior is consumer misconduct in the acquisition, usage, or disposition of goods and services. For example, some consumers may consider fraudulent returns inappropriate while others may approve of it under certain circumstances such as the need to purchase interview clothing when no money has been budgeted for new clothing. Further research is needed investigating non-normative consumer behavior that may be found inappropriate by some and appropriate by others depending on the circumstances.

INTRODUCTION

In order to have a civilized society obeying laws is vital but also behaving in an ethical manner is important. "Ethics refers to the quality of one's inner character or to one's moral philosophy of what is right and wrong behavior. Conversely, unethical means lacking scruples or principles or to ruthlessly seek a personal advantage" (McGregor, 2006, p. 164). Ethics rises above what is legal activity and requires morally correct behavior. Ethics is problematic for two reasons: 1) ethical behavior may not maximize profits in the short term, and 2) there is no universal agreement of what exactly characterizes the "right" behavior (Fisher, Woodbine, & Fullerton, 2002). For example, child labor is considered unethical in Western societies, however, in other cultures it may be considered acceptable and even necessary for the well-being of individuals living in the household (McGregor, 2006).

Individuals may often experience ethical dilemmas where the individual would need to choose between right and wrong behavior. Kohlberg (1969) has suggested an individual's solution to an ethical dilemma is based on the individual's stage of moral reasoning and has developed a model of moral reasoning that is comprised of three levels and each level contains two stages. The pre-conventional level occurs usually between the ages of one and nine and contains the first two stages. In stage one, an individual would choose the right behavior in order to obey rules and authority and to avoid punishment. In stage two, the intent of the individual's ethical decision would be to benefit the individual's own needs. The conventional level occurs usually between the ages of nine and twenty and contains the next two stages. In stage three, the individual would choose the right behavior in order to remain loyal to the group with which the individual most identifies and to gain approval from the people in that group. During stage four, the intent of the individual's ethical decision is based on what the individual thinks is best for the welfare of society by following laws and obeying authority figures. The post-conventional level usually occurs in individuals over the age of twenty and contains the last two stages. In stage five, the individual will create solutions to ethical dilemmas based on the values and basic rights of the society even if the moral and legal viewpoints diverge. During stage six, universal ethical principles are followed to devise solutions to ethical dilemmas and other people are viewed as ends, not means. According to Kohlberg's (1969) model people progress to a higher level of moral development as they age, however, all individuals may not reach the final stages of moral reasoning where the individual would be concerned with how their own actions impact other individuals' lives.

Ethical dilemmas could occur within any facet of an individual's life. Individuals have many different roles that they play, such as, an individual could be an employer or an employee, and likewise, an individual could be a business owner or a customer. A substantial amount of research has been conducted investigating the ethical decision making of marketers (Abdolmohammadi, Gabhart, & Reeves, 1997; Barnett & Valentine, 2004; Ferrell, 2004; Ferrell & Gresham, 1985; Ferrell, Gresham, & Fraedrich, 1989; Ferrell & Weaver, 1978; Glenn & Van Loo, 1993; Hunt & Vitell, 1986; Loe, Ferrell, & Mansfield, 2000; Murphy & Laczniak, 1992; Rao & Al-Wugayan, 2005; Sele, 2006; Vitell & Festervand, 1987; Wahn, 1993; Yoo & Donthu, 2002). Frequently, consumers are portrayed as the victims of marketers rather than consumers exhibiting unethical consumer behavior. Marketers and students aspiring to be marketers have been found to choose unethical options ("Corporate criminals," 2006; Ferrell & Weaver, 1978; Loe, Ferrell, & Mansfield, 2000; Millage, 2005; Vitell & Festervand, 1987; Yoo & Donthu, 2002), but consumers have also been found to be accepting of unethical consumption activities (Cole 1989; Cox, Cox, & Moschis, 1990; Fukukawa, 2002; Fullerton & Punj, 2004; Fullerton, Kerch, & Dodge, 1996; Kallis, Krentler, & Vanier, 1986; Klemke, 1982; Shen & Dickson, 2001; Van Kenhove, De Wulf, & Steenhaut, 2003; Vitell, 2003; Vitell & Muncy, 1992).

Researchers (Bernstein, 1985; Vitell, 1997) have stated that consumers are not any more ethical than marketers. Belk, Devinney, and Eckhardt (2005) found that consumers may justify their own unethical behavior by citing examples of corporate ethical scandals suggesting "that consumers are waiting to follow the ethical example of businesses before they alter their own behavior" (p. 283). Researchers (Fukukawa, 2003; Morgan & Hunt, 1994) have suggested that for profitable relationships to occur between marketers and consumers, both must behave in an ethical manner. Marketers have experienced huge losses due to unethical consumer behavior. Those losses are often passed on to other consumers in the form of higher prices and strict return policies (Al-Wugayan & Rao, 2004).

Models have been proposed to describe ethical decision making in marketing (Brass, Butterfield, & Skaggs, 1998; Ferrell & Gresham, 1985; Hunt & Vitell, 1986; Loe, Ferrell, & Mansfield, 2000; Trevino, 1986). However, there is a lack of theoretical frameworks in the literature that address the multiple variables related to how consumers make ethically related decisions. Muncy and Vitell (1992) stated that "after an extensive search of the literature, fewer than twenty studies could be found which studied ethical issues in the marketplace from the consumer's perspective and most of these studies focused on very specific and limited situations having ethical content (such as shoplifting)" (p. 585). Fukukawa (2003) gave a brief overview of ethical decision making in marketing models and suggested that these business ethics models could be applied to consumer ethics research in order to develop a consumer ethical decision making model.

Vitell (2003) reviewed and synthesized consumer ethical decision making studies that have occurred since 1990. Many of these 31 studies applied a business ethics model [primarily the Hunt and Vitell (1986) theoretical model] in order to investigate consumer ethical decision making. Fukukawa (2003) stated that "if consumer ethics is to further develop theoretically, not only is it important that more, and more varied research be conducted, but equally that more attention is placed upon theoretical debates themselves" (p. 398).

The purpose of this chapter is to summarize research that has investigated consumer ethics and to document the need for future consumer ethics research. The focus of the chapter is to identify research trends within consumer ethics research. While not every research study of unethical consumer behavior is addressed, an overview of the types of studies conducted within consumer ethics research is the focus. Studies investigating shoplifting, as well as other non-normative consumer behavior are discussed. The relationship of numerous variables to consumer ethical decision-making has been investigated. Variables addressed in this chapter are ethical ideologies, Machiavellianism, neutralization techniques, relationship commitment, religiosity, age, gender, and various cultures.

Consumer ethics is defined as "the moral principles and standards that guide behavior of individuals or groups as they obtain, use, and dispose of goods and services" (Muncy & Vitell, 1992, p. 298). Consumer ethics involves many different issues, such as consumers choosing environmentally friendly products, consumers purchasing counterfeit goods, consumers boycotting businesses they find offensive, and consumers benefiting from ethically questionable behavior (consumer honesty). Research has been conducted in these different areas of consumer ethics (Belk, Devinney, & Eckhardt, 2005; Brinkman, 2004; Carrigan & Attalla, 2001; Cleveland, Kalamas, & Laroche, 2005; Klein, Smith, & John, 2004). The focus of this chapter is consumer ethics pertaining to consumers benefiting from ethically questionable behavior.

SHOPLIFTING

Much of the research (Babin & Babin, 1996; Babin & Griffin, 1995; Babin, Robin, & Pike, 1994; Cole, 1989; Cox, Cox, & Moschis, 1990; Kallis, Krentler, & Vanier, 1986; Klemke, 1982; Lin, Hastings, & Martin, 1994; Moschis, 1985; Phillips, Alexander, & Shaw, 2005; "Stealing is bad," 1993; Tonglet, 2002) that has investigated consumer ethics pertaining to consumer honesty focused on shoplifting. Shoplifting has been defined as "the taking, using or consumption of an item or product from a store without paying for it, including the eating of food in supermarkets and the changing of prices" (Kallis, Krentler, & Vanier, 1986, p. 32). Shoplifting not only costs the offender penalties and ultimately costs consumers through an increase in prices and a shopping environment that may be inconvenient, but also the costs for retailers are substantial.

A record number of retailers go in and out of business. The retail businesses that remain in business are not as profitable as they could be due to inventory shrinkage. Inventory shrinkage costs retailers billions of dollars each year. From 1990 to 1995 retailers estimated shrinkage losses ranged from $22.7 billion to $27.0 billion (Hayes, 1996). Shrinkage losses seem to increase each year. Studies (Atkinson, 2005; "Theft cost retailers", 2002) have revealed that approximately $33 billion a year is lost by U.S. retailers to inventory shrinkage. Shrinkage results from shoplifting, employee theft, vendor fraud, and administrative error. Employee theft is believed to cause the largest percentage of inventory shrinkage in terms of dollars lost ("Ernst & Young's", 1992), however, about $10 billion of the $33 billion is attributed to shoplifting (Atkinson, 2005).

According to a National Retail Security Survey about one-third of shoplifters apprehended are 13 to 17 years of age, March and December are the most active months for shoplifting, and Saturday is the most active day for shoplifting (Atkinson, 2005). Shoplifting has been found to increase when unemployment rises, when inflation occurs, when consumers perceive corporations as corrupt, and when the focus of loss prevention turns to dishonest employees ("Using the '3 P's'," 2004; "Lessons to learn," 2002).

Although all shoplifters do not fit one profile, a high percentage of admitted shoplifters have been found to be male, non-white, single, lower income, young, and likely to have been arrested in the past (Kallis, Krentler, & Vanier, 1986). Researchers (Cox, Cox, & Moschis, 1990; Klemke, 1982) found that male adolescents shoplift more than female adolescents shoplift. Lin, Hastings, and Martin (1994) found that females shoplift more from clothing retailers than males. High school students' previous shoplifting activities have been investigated (Klemke, 1982). Of the 1,189 high school students investigated, 63% reported having shoplifted sometime during their lifetime. The students reported the shoplifting activities declined with age. Cox, Cox, and Moschis (1990) found that 40% of apprehended shoplifters are adolescents. Middle adolescent (9th and 10th grade) subjects were found to have a higher incidence of shoplifting than early (7th and 8th grade) or late adolescent subjects (11th and 12th grade).

Researchers (Cox, Cox, & Moschis, 1990) have suggested that the increase in the number of adolescents shoplifting may be due to the increase in the number of adolescents "hanging out" in malls and due to the fact that large impersonal stores with self-service strategies are replacing the small family owned stores. The retailers' tempting advertising practices may also contribute to increases in the number of adolescents shoplifting (Cox, Cox, & Moschis, 1990).

Subjects who reported shoplifting activity tend to have a more positive perception of people who shoplift than those who report no involvement in shoplifting." (Kallis, Krentler, & Vanier, 1986). Possibly shrinkage could be decreased by developing a multiple media promotion aimed at creating a negative perception of shoplifters (Hayes, 1996). Babin and Babin (1996) suggested that posting the number of apprehended shoplifters in local malls may deter shoplifting behavior. In addition to portraying the shoplifter as a wrongdoer, researchers (Strutton, Pelton, & Ferrell, 1997; Strutton, Vitell, & Pelton, 1994) have recommended that companies should create a positive company image and develop a closer bond with consumers in order to reduce unethical consumer behavior. For example, companies could use advertisements and in-store displays to create an image that the company cares about the consumer and is a fair player.

Retailers have used various strategies to decrease the inventory shrinkage problem, such as high-tech electronic devices, pre-employment screening, and offering competitive wages to attract high quality employees ("Theft's multibillion dollar," 1997). Store cameras, security tags, store guards, alert employees, and prosecution of apprehended shoplifters have been cited as possible shoplifting deterrents ("Lessons to learn," 2002).

The '3 P's' (partnerships, practical solutions, and people) have been recommended as a way to combat shoplifting ("Using the '3 P's'," 2004). In many corporations the relationship between the corporate loss prevention department and store management is somewhat adversarial so partnerships between loss prevention and store managers need to be formed to contend with shoplifting. The second 'P', practical solutions, includes using product displays that contain security features. For example, a retailer might use a fixture that clicks when a small item, such as razor blades, is being removed from the display. The third 'P', people, involves training and educating employees to be aware of fraudulent activity and to be knowledgeable about the company's loss prevention policies in order to improve the company's security ("Using the '3 P's'," 2004).

OTHER NON-NORMATIVE CONSUMER BEHAVIOR

Most people would probably agree that consumer behavior such as shoplifting is dishonest and unethical. However, solutions to ethical dilemmas containing other types of non-normative consumer behavior may not appear to be so clear. Non-normative consumer behavior has been defined as "consumer misconduct in the acquisition, usage or disposition of goods and services" (Grove, Vitell, & Strutton, 1989, p. 135). The phrase "consumer misbehavior" has been used when discussing various types of non-normative consumer behavior such as fraudulent returns, vandalism, and physical/verbal abuse of marketer employees (Fullerton & Punj, 2004). Fullerton and Punj (2004) created a typology of non-normative consumer behavior with the main premise of the study being that negative consumer behavior is an inadvertent outcome of the marketing campaigns of companies which seek to endorse their products so consumers will purchase more.

A phrase often used by marketers in order to appeal to consumers is "the customer is always right" but this may not be accurate. Consumers may complain about something that they have no valid reason to complain about or may simply lie. For example, a woman might go to a store and purchase a suit, wear it to a job interview and then return it a week later stating that the suit did not fit well. A consumer may think that purchasing an item with the intent to return it for a full refund after use is acceptable under certain circumstances, such as the need to purchase interview clothing when no money has been budgeted for new clothing. Regardless of whether or not people consider purchasing an item with the intent to return it for a full refund after use as unethical as shoplifting, the result for the retailer is the same, lost profits. A model illustrating ethical decision making of consumers is vital to marketers, as well as consumers, so that mutually beneficial relationships between the two groups can be analyzed and understood. Ethical decision making models for marketers (Ferrell & Gresham, 1985; Hunt & Vitell, 1986; Wotruba, 1991) have been applied to consumer ethical decision making.

DEONTOLOGICAL/TELEOLOGICAL PHILOSOPHIES

Hunt and Vitell (1986) suggest that two methods are used in order to formulate appropriate solutions to ethical issues: 1) a solution could be determined either by consistently following one set of rules or 2) it could be determined by weighing the consequences of the behavior in order to promote the greatest good. The first method of devising an appropriate solution to an ethical issue is referred to as a deontological approach and the latter method is referred to as a teleological approach (Ferrell & Gresham, 1985; Ferrell, Gresham, & Fraedrich, 1989; Hunt & Vitell, 1986). When an individual uses the deontological approach the same set of rules would be followed for every ethical issue to devise an appropriate solution regardless of the impact the solution may have on the individual or on others. An individual using the teleological approach would attempt to devise solutions to ethical issues in order to promote the greatest good for the greatest number of people (utilitarian) or to promote the greatest good for the individual, himself/herself (egoism).

Hunt and Vitell (1986) developed a model suggesting that individuals use both deontological and teleological philosophies when making a decision regarding an ethical dilemma. In order for this model to apply, the individual must perceive the situation as having ethical content. Cultural, industrial, and organizational environments, along with personal experiences, impact the decision making process. Possible alternative solutions to ethical dilemmas are formulated and consequences of the solutions are envisioned. The inherent rightness or wrongness (deontological) of the solutions, and the probabilities and desirability of the consequences (teleological) are evaluated. A solution to the ethical issue is chosen, consequences occur, and then the consequences are considered when devising solutions to future ethical dilemmas.

MUNCY AND VITELL CONSUMER ETHICS SCALE

Using applications from the Hunt and Vitell (1986) model a consumer ethics scale containing 27 items has been developed (Muncy & Vitell, 1992; Vitell & Muncy, 1992) to investigate subject's beliefs about a variety of marketplace practices. U.S. heads of households (n=569) responded to the questionnaire and items were categorized into four factors: 1) actively benefiting from illegal activities (ILLEGAL), 2) passively benefiting (PASSIVE), 3) actively benefiting from deceptive practices (ACTIVE), and 4) no harm/indirect harm (NO HARM). The subjects assessed ILLEGAL practices such as "switching price tags", to be most wrong. The subjects rated the PASSIVE items, such as "getting too much change and not saying anything", as more wrong than the ACTIVE items. The subjects rated the ACTIVE items, such as "breaking a bottle in a store and not paying for it", to be more wrong than NO HARM items, such as "taping a television movie." Many of the NO HARM items were not perceived by the subjects as unethical (Vitell & Muncy, 1992). The consumer ethics scale has been widely used in different cultures and has been validated. For a recent overview, see Van Kenhove, Vermeir, and Verniers (2001) and Vitell (2003).

Using the Muncy and Vitell (1992) Consumer Ethics Scale, Fukukawa (2002) investigated the influence explanatory factors have on U.K. consumers' ethical decision making. Results indicated that subjects were more accepting of NO HARM items than ILLEGAL items. Subjects' consumer ethical decision-making was found to be influenced by the perceived consequences to others, perceived benefits to the individual, amount of perceived social approval, and perceived unfairness with business.

Swaidan, Vitell, Rose, and Gilbert (2006) investigated the role of acculturation in U.S. immigrant populations using the Muncy and Vitell (1992) Consumer Ethics Scale. The populations (Middle Eastern and Asian immigrants) were chosen for the study because their cultures are the direct opposite of the U.S. in three of four of Hofstede's (2001) classifications. Middle Eastern and Asian cultures are considered collectivistic, exhibit power distance, and display uncertainty avoidance, while masculinity is prevalent within the cultures. Results indicated that the immigrant subjects who wanted to keep their original culture were found to be less accepting of unethical consumer behavior than subjects who wanted to adopt U.S. culture (Swaidan, Vitell, Rose, & Gilbert, 2006).

Vitell and Muncy (2005) modified the Consumer Ethics Scale by rewording items and adding items pertaining to downloading/buying counterfeit goods, recycling/environmental awareness, and doing the right thing/doing good. The modified scale was used in a study comparing non-student and student subjects' acceptance of unethical consumer behavior. Student subjects were found to be more accepting of unethical consumer behavior than non-student subjects in all dimensions except the "recycling" and the "doing good" dimensions where no difference was found.

ETHICAL IDEOLOGIES

Much consumer ethics research has investigated the relationship of the acceptance of unethical consumer behavior to ethical ideologies (Cho, Yoo, & Johnson, 2005). Forsyth (1980) developed a taxonomy of four ethical ideologies (situationists, subjectivists, absolutists, and exceptionists) based on the levels of relativism and idealism. Relativism has been associated with the teleological moral philosophy and is defined as "the extent to which individuals reject universal moral rules" (Forsyth, 1980, p. 175). Idealism has been associated with the deontological moral philosophy and describes "the extremes, some individuals idealistically assume that desirable consequences can, with the 'right' action, always be obtained" (p. 176). The Ethical Position Questionnaire (Forsyth, 1980) contains a relativism scale and an idealism scale. Each scale includes 10 items in which subjects indicate their degree of agreement on a 9-point Likert scale ranging from "completely disagree" to "completely agree."

According to Forsyth (1980) relativism and idealism are not mutually exclusive. An individual ranking high in both relativism and idealism is considered a "situationist," who will reject absolute moral rules and examine each situation on a case by case basis. A "subjectivist" ranks high in relativism and low in idealism and will use personal values rather than absolute universal moral rules to evaluate ethical dilemmas. An "absolutist" ranks low in relativism and high in idealism and advocate using absolute universal moral principles to evaluate ethical dilemmas. An "exceptionist" ranks low in both relativism and idealism and uses moral principles as a guide but will make exceptions to these rules if it will be more beneficial to a greater number of people (Forsyth, 1980).

Using the Forsyth (1980) Ethical Position Questionnaire, Rao and Al-Wugayan (2005) found that overall Kuwaiti business student subjects had higher idealism and relativism scores and were less accepting of unethical consumer behavior than the U.S. business student subjects. Cho, Yoo, and Johnson (2005) found that ethical ideologies were significantly associated with U.S. university student subjects' acceptance of unethical consumer shopping behaviors. Of the four ethical ideology groups "subjectivists" (ranking high on relativism and low on idealism) were found to give the most negative rating of the unethical consumer shopping behaviors. The majority of the subjects were apparel merchandising majors with retail experience so their views may have been influenced by company policies that they have been trained to implement (Cho, Yoo, & Johnson, 2005).

The Muncy and Vitell (1992) Consumer Ethics Scale has been used in conjunction with the Forsyth (1980) Ethical Position Questionnaire in studies (Steenhaut & Van Kenhove, 2006; Swaidan, Rawwas, & Al-Khatib, 2004; Swaidan, Vitell, & Rawwas, 2003; Vitell & Paolillo, 2003). Steenhaut and Van Kenhove (2006) investigated the associations of ethical ideologies, acceptance of unethical consumer behavior, and values. Results indicated that subjects who value security, conformity, and tradition (conservation) were found to be more idealistic and less accepting of unethical consumer behavior than subjects who value self-direction, stimulation, and hedonism (openness to change). Also, subjects who value universalism and benevolence (self-transcendence) were found to be more idealistic and less accepting of unethical consumer behavior than subjects who value achievement and power (self-enhancement).

The relationship of African American university students' acceptance of unethical consumer behavior and ethical ideologies was investigated (Swaidan, Rawwas, & Al-Khatib, 2004). Subjects scoring higher on the idealism scale and lower on the relativism scale were less accepting of unethical consumer behavior in all dimensions except for the NO HARM dimension than other subjects. The majority (66.5%) of the sample were found to be "situationists" (high in both relativism and idealism) (Swaidan, Rawwas, & Al-Khatib, 2004).

The relationship of African American professionals' acceptance of unethical consumer behavior and ethical ideologies was investigated (Swaidan, Vitell, & Rawwas, 2003). Subjects with higher idealism scores were less accepting of unethical consumer behavior in three dimensions (ILLEGAL, ACTIVE, and PASSIVE) but more accepting of NO HARM activities than subjects with lower idealism scores. Subjects with higher relativism scores were less accepting of NO HARM activities than subjects with lower relativism scores.

Vitell and Paolillo (2003) found that U.S. adult subjects with higher idealism scores were less accepting of unethical consumer behavior in all four dimensions than subjects with lower idealism scores. Subjects with higher relativism scores were found to be more accepting of unethical consumer behavior in all four dimensions than subjects with lower relativism scores.

MACHIAVELLIANISM

The relationship between an individual's personality characteristics and acceptance of unethical consumer behavior has been investigated. A particular personality characteristic, Machiavellianism, has received much attention from researchers (Shen & Dickson, 2001). High Machiavellians focus on their own individual goals and do whatever they believe is necessary in order to achieve those goals. They are not concerned about the feelings and interests of others and do not care if their behaviors impact others negatively (Shen & Dickson, 2001). Individuals exhibiting Machiavellianism tend to "manipulate more, win more, are persuaded less, and otherwise differ significantly from" individuals exhibiting low Machiavellianism (Christie & Geis, 1970, 312). High Machiavellians are not emotionally attached to others and use manipulation to achieve their goals (Robinson & Shaver, 1973).

Christie and Geis (1970) developed the MACH IV Scale, consisting of 20 items used to evaluate a subject's level of Machiavellianism. Using the MACH IV Scale (Christie & Geis, 1970), Shen and Dickson (2001) investigated the relationship of Machiavellianism and acceptance of unethical consumer behavior of a sample of U.S. and Chinese students at a university in the U.S. Results indicated that subjects with higher Machiavellian scores were more accepting of unethical consumer behavior than subjects with lower Machiavellian scores. Also, subjects identifying with U.S. culture were more accepting of unethical consumer behavior than subjects identifying with Chinese culture.

Studies (Al-Khatib, Robertson, & Lascu, 2004; Al-Khatib, Vitell, Rexeisen, & Rawwas, 2005; Rawwas, Swaiden, & Oyman, 2005) investigating the associations of consumer ethical decision making, ethical ideologies, and Machiavellianism have used the Muncy and Vitell (1992) Consumer Ethics Scale, the Forsyth (1980) Ethical Position Questionnaire, and the Christie and Geis (1970) MACH IV Scale. Al-Khatib, Robertson, and Lascu (2004) found that a sample of Romanian consumers who rated higher on idealism, lower on relativism, and lower on Machiavellianism were found to be less accepting of unethical consumer behavior in the PASSIVE dimension than subjects rating lower on idealism, higher on relativism, and higher on Machiavellianism. Romanian subjects rating lower on Machiavellianism were found to be less accepting of unethical consumer behavior in the NO HARM dimension than subjects rating higher on Machiavellianism.

Al-Khatib, Vitell, Rexeisen, and Rawwas (2005) found that urban consumers' (Saudi, Omani, Kuwaiti, and Egyptian) acceptance of unethical consumer behavior, ethical ideologies, and Machiavellian tendencies vary across the Arab region. Rawwas, Swaiden, and Oyman (2005) found that a sample of Turkish consumers were less accepting of unethical consumer behavior than a sample of U.S. consumers. The Turkish subjects scored higher on the idealism scale and lower on the Machiavellian scale than the U.S. subjects scored.

Relationship Commitment

Researchers (Strutton, Vitell, & Pelton, 1994; Vitell, Singhapakdi, & Thomas, 2001) have suggested if marketers develop a committed relationship with consumers, customer loyalty may increase, which ultimately may lead to ethical consumer behavior. Al-Wugayan and Rao (2004) developed four scenarios depicting differing levels of customer-retailer relationships with differing levels of customer payoffs. Results indicated that non-student Kuwaiti subjects were less accepting of unethical consumer behavior when substantial payoffs accrued to the customer who has a strong customer-retailer relationship than when no substantial payoffs accrued to the customer who has a weak customer-retailer relationship. Results indicated that subjects rating high on negative perceptions of business practices were found to be more accepting of unethical consumer behavior than subjects rating low on negative perceptions of business practices. Also, subjects differing in ethical ideologies differed in the level of acceptance of unethical consumer behavior.

Van Kenhove, De Wulf, and Steenhaut (2003) investigated associations among relationship commitment, behavioral loyalty, acceptance of unethical consumer behavior, and actual ethical behavior of Belgian consumers. Subjects were asked to keep a diary; recording clothing purchases over a 10 month period. Subjects also completed three different mail surveys containing relationship commitment items, behavioral loyalty items, the consumer ethics scale, and ethical behavior items. Results indicated that subjects with high relationship commitment scores reported less unethical behavior towards the store than subjects with low relationship commitment scores.

In order to measure actual unethical consumer behavior, Steenhaut and Van Kenhove (2005) conducted a field experiment investigating associations among relationship commitment, amount of excess change, and one type of unethical consumer behavior (receiving too much change at the checkout). Results indicated that subjects with a low commitment to the retailer were less likely to report a large excess of change than a small excess of change. Subjects with a high commitment to the retailer were more likely to report excess change than subjects with a low commitment, especially when the amount was large. Because the participants in the field experiment were not aware that they were participating in a study, business undergraduate students were asked to complete a questionnaire containing excess change scenarios in order to explore motives for not reporting excess change (Steenhaut & Van Kenhove, 2005). Results indicated that subjects with a low commitment to the retailer were found to be driven by opportunism while subjects with a high commitment to the retailer were found to be driven by guilt-related feelings.

Religion and Religiosity

Ethical behavior may be influenced by religion depending upon if the person ascribes to a religion and if so, how devoted the person is to their religious teachings. Religiosity intensity varies from one person to another (Rao & Al-Wugayan, 2005). Rao and Al-Wugayan (2005) found that overall Kuwaiti business student subjects had higher religiosity scores and were less accepting of unethical consumer behavior than the U.S. business student subjects had. Pronounced differences between U.S. subjects and Kuwaiti subjects were attributed to cultural differences such as Kuwait being collectivistic while U.S. citizens are more individualistic (Rao & Al-Wugayan, 2005).

Vitell, Paolillo, and Singh (2005) investigated associations between intrinsic/extrinsic religiousness and unethical consumer behavior of university undergraduate students. Intrinsic religiousness pertains to spirituality and developing a relationship with God, while extrinsic religiousness pertains to using religion for comfort and social support. Subjects with higher intrinsic religiousness were less accepting of unethical consumer behavior than subjects with lower intrinsic religiousness in all dimensions except NO HARM. No associations were found between extrinsic religiousness and unethical consumer behavior. Likewise, in a later study (Vitell, Paolillo, & Singh, 2006), U.S. consumers who had higher intrinsic religiousness were found to be less accepting of unethical consumer behavior than subjects with lower intrinsic religiousness in all dimensions except for the NO HARM dimension. Extrinsic religiousness was not investigated in this later study.

Cornwell, Cui, Mitchell, Schlegelmilch, Dzulkiflee, and Chan (2005) used a modified version of the Forsyth (1980) Ethics Position Questionnaire to investigate associations between three different major religions and consumers' ethical ideologies. Results indicated subjects following Islam, Buddhism, and Christianity (U.S. and Britain subjects) rated higher on both idealism and relativism, while subjects following Christianity (Austrian subjects) rated lower on both idealism and relativism.

Callen and Ownbey (2003) investigated associations between consistency in practice of faith orientation and acceptance of unethical consumer behavior. Consistency in practice of faith orientation is the respondent's perception of how frequently he/she follows the teachings of his/her primary faith orientation. Three scenarios involving non-normative consumer behavior (not reporting receipt of excess change, not paying for accidental damage to apparel, and purchasing a garment with intent to return it for a full refund after use) were developed. The development of the scenarios was influenced by information from previous studies (Strutton, Pelton, & Ferrell, 1997; Fullerton, Kerch, & Dodge, 1996; Muncy & Vitell, 1992; Wilkes, 1978). Consistency in practice of faith was found to be significantly associated with subjects' ethical response scores for all three scenarios and the total of the three scenarios. Subjects who reported consistently following the teachings of their primary faith had significantly higher ethical response scores than subjects who reported that they do not very consistently follow the teachings of their primary faith.

AGE

Researchers (Fullerton, Kerch, & Dodge, 1996; Muncy & Vitell, 1992) have indicated that older consumers are less accepting of unethical consumer behavior than younger consumers. This lends support to Kohlberg (1969) who proposed that people progress to a higher level of moral development as they grow older. Dubinsky, Nataraajan, and Huang (2005) investigated relationships between age and ethical ideologies, and found age to be the most effective predictor of both relativism and idealism. Older U.S. subjects rated higher on the idealism scale and lower on the relativism scale than younger U.S. subjects rated.

A study (Swaidan, Vitell, & Rawwas, 2003) using a sample of African American professionals has indicated that older, more educated, and married subjects were less accepting of unethical consumer behavior than younger, less educated, and single subjects. Using the diary method, Van Kenhove, De Wulf, and Steenhaut (2003) found that older Belgian subjects reported less actual unethical consumer behavior than younger subjects reported. Vitell and Paolillo (2003) found older U.S. subjects to be less accepting of unethical consumer behavior than younger subjects in the ILLEGAL and PASSIVE dimensions of consumer ethics. No relationship was found between age and unethical consumer decision-making in a study investigating Middle Eastern and Asian immigrants within the U.S. (Swaidan, Vitell, Rose, & Gilbert, 2006).

GENDER

The results of studies investigating the relationship of gender and consumer ethical decision making has been conflicting. Rao and Al-Wugayan (2005) investigated the relationship of gender and ethical ideologies of U.S. and Kuwaiti business students. Results indicated that U.S. female subjects had significantly higher idealism scores than U.S. male subjects had. Kuwaiti male subjects had significantly higher idealism and relativism scores, and more positive attitudes toward marketers than Kuwaiti female subjects had. Kuwaiti male subjects were less accepting of unethical consumer behavior for one scenario (strong customer-retailer interaction and tangible gains for the customer) than Kuwaiti female subjects were (Rao & Al-Wugayan, 2005).

In a study by Callen and Ownbey (2003) female university student subjects were found to be less accepting of unethical consumer behavior than male subjects. Belgian female subjects reported less actual unethical consumer behavior than male subjects reported in the PASSIVE and ACTIVE dimensions (Van Kenhove, De Wulf, & Steenhaut, 2003). Swaidan, Rawwas, and Al-Khatib (2004) found that African American student female subjects were less accepting of unethical consumer behavior in the ILLEGAL dimension but more accepting in the NO HARM dimension than African American male student subjects were. Swaidan, Vitell, and Rawwas (2003) also found female subjects to be more accepting in the NO HARM dimension than male subjects were when investigating African American professionals' consumer ethical decision making. Fisher, Woodbine, and Fullerton (2002) did not find gender differences when investigating Australian and Canadian university students' consumer ethical decision making. Likewise, no relationship was found between gender and unethical consumer decision-making in a study investigating Middle Eastern and Asian immigrants within the U.S. (Swaidan, Vitell, Rose, & Gilbert, 2006).

NEUTRALIZATION TECHNIQUES

Most people who exhibit unethical consumer behavior may view the behavior as wrong, so in order to lessen feelings of guilt, people may rationalize the behavior under certain circumstances. Rationalizing was found to be one of the factors contributing to shoplifting among adolescents (Cox, Cox, & Moschis, 1990). A sample of college students were found to commonly use two rationalizations ("the large impersonal retailers do not notice a loss from stealing" and "the prices the retailers charge are too high") for shoplifting (Hayes, 1996). Sykes and Matza (1957) referred to rationalizations as neutralization techniques and identified five types: denial of responsibility, denial of injury, denial of the victim, condemnation of the condemners, and appeal to higher loyalties.

Sykes and Matza's (1957) techniques of neutralization framework has been applied to consumer behavior (Grove, Vitell, & Strutton, 1989). The "denial of responsibility" technique might be used if a consumer shoplifts during the holidays and justifies the behavior by thinking, "it is not my fault; I don't have enough money to pay for this item." A consumer might use the "denial of injury" technique when shopping in a large impersonal department store by thinking, "this store is so big; no one will ever notice that this shirt is missing." The "denial of the victim" technique is used when the consumer believes the retailer deserves to be treated in a negative manner, such as when a shoplifter thinks, "It is the store's fault for not having more sales associates on the floor to watch the customers." The "condemnation of the condemners" technique is used when the attention from the consumer's own unethical behavior is deflected onto the retailer's possible unethical behavior. For example, a consumer may return a worn garment and justify the behavior by thinking, "the store will do anything to make a profit with no concern for the consumer." The consumer using the "appeal to higher loyalties" technique will sacrifice the norms of society to benefit his/her smaller social circle, such as when an adolescent shoplifts to impress friends.

To test consumers' use of neutralization techniques and consumers' evaluation of unethical behavior in retail environments, Strutton, Vitell, and Pelton (1994) used acquisition and disposition scenarios. Results indicated that consumers are more likely to use neutralization techniques in unethical disposition activities, such as fraudulent returns than unethical acquisition activities, such as switching price tags. Condemning the condemners, denial of victim, and denial of injury were the techniques most frequently used by subjects (Strutton, Vitell, & Pelton, 1994).

Rosenbaum and Kuntze (2003) investigated associations of neutralization techniques, cynicism, materialism, and consumer ethical decision making of U.S. consumers. Subjects rating high in cynicism were more accepting of unethical consumer behavior than subjects rating low in cynicism. Subjects with higher cynicism scores were found to be more likely to use neutralization techniques to justify unethical consumer behavior than subjects with lower cynicism scores. Also, subjects with higher cynicism scores had higher materialism scores than subjects with lower cynicism scores. Cynical subjects were found to view success by the number and quality of possessions accumulated.

"PERCEPTIONS OF" VS. "ACTUAL" UNETHICAL CONSUMER BEHAVIOR

The majority of consumer ethics research has investigated subjects' *perceptions* of unethical consumer behavior but not *actual* unethical consumer behavior (Shen & Dickson, 2001). Most consumer ethics research is conducted by using scenarios or brief statements to ascertain the subjects' agreement or disagreement with the behavior depicted. According to Hunt and Vitell (1986), "the use of scenario techniques is well established in ethics research and would be a suitable vehicle for early research efforts" (p. 11). Measurement accuracy can be enhanced when measuring ethics by using the scenario technique. When subjects evaluate other people's ethics the subjects must refer to his/her own ethics (Strutton, Vitell, & Pelton, 1994). This technique evaluates beliefs about unethical behavior but does not measure actual unethical behavior. A subject who accepts unethical consumer behavior may or may not behave unethically in a consumer situation.

Researchers (Steenhaut & Van Kenhove, 2005; Van Kenhove, De Wulf, & Steenhaut, 2003) have conducted research in order to investigate actual unethical consumer behavior. Van Kenhove, De Wulf, and Steenhaut (2003) used the diary method where subjects were asked to record clothing purchases over a 10 month period. Subjects were also asked to complete three different surveys that contained unethical behavior items. A limitation of the study was that the results were based on the subjects' reporting of their unethical consumer behavior and the subjects may or may not have given truthful responses.

In order to measure actual unethical consumer behavior Steenhaut and Van Kenhove (2005) conducted a field experiment investigating associations among relationship commitment, amount of excess change, and one type of unethical consumer behavior (receiving too much change at the checkout). Employees of a large company within two different divisions were informed that someone was coming to sell baked goods. In one of the divisions of the company the employees were told that the fund raiser was for a small unknown university (low relationship commitment). In the other division the employees were told that the fund raiser was for the organizing committee for the company in which the employees worked for (high relationship commitment). When purchasing the baked goods subjects had to pay immediately, and if they paid too much they were given too much change. A limitation of the study was that because the participants in the field experiment were not aware that they were participating in a study, business undergraduate students were asked to complete a questionnaire containing excess change scenarios in order to explore motives for not reporting excess change (Steenhaut & Van Kenhove, 2005). So again researchers resorted to using scenarios to obtain information on consumer ethical decision making.

IMPLICATIONS

Researchers (Al-Khatib, Robertson, & Lascu, 2004; Al-Khatib, Vitell, Rexeisen, & Rawwas, 2005; Al-Wugayan & Rao, 2004; Fisher, Woodbine, & Fullerton, 2002; Rawwas, Swaiden, & Oyman, 2005; Rosenbaum & Kuntze, 2003; Shen & Dickson, 2001; Steenhaut & Van Kenhove, 2005; Steenhaut & Van Kenhove, 2006) have suggested various strategies in order to persuade consumers to behave ethically. Fisher, Woodbine, and Fullerton (2002) suggested that marketers should behave ethically and foster an environment that focuses on customer service. Marketers should design a store layout and other situational factors that will lessen the opportunity of consumers to behave unethically (Shen & Dickson, 2001).

Marketers should invest in resources to maintain relationships with consumers, such as communication, personalization, pleasant shopping atmosphere, friendly store personnel, and products that meet consumers' needs in order to lessen unethical consumer behavior

(Steenhaut & Van Kenhove, 2005). Marketers should use in-store communications in order to appeal to consumers' personal values such as conservation and self-transcendence (Steenhaut & Van Kenhove, 2006). Al-Wugayan and Rao (2004) recommended creating lenient retail policies to improve customer satisfaction and customer-retailer relationships in order to improve consumer behavior.

Researchers (Al-Khatib, Robertson, & Lascu, 2004; Al-Wugayan & Rao, 2004; Rosenbaum & Kuntze, 2003) have suggested investing in consumer education programs and public awareness campaigns in order to educate consumers about the costs (increased prices and more restrictive retail policies) of unethical consumer behavior. Al-Khatib, Vitell, Rexeisen, and Rawwas (2005) suggested investing in customer loyalty programs and train employees to be aware of tactics consumers use to take advantage of retailers.

Many businesses operate in a global environment so the culture of the target market needs to be considered when developing marketing strategies. For example, Rawwas, Swaiden, and Oyman (2005) recommended that because of Turkish subjects high idealism scores marketers should consider practicing cause-marketing in Turkey, which may lead to a positive brand image and ultimately to customer loyalty.

FUTURE RESEARCH SUGGESTIONS

Studies need to be conducted investigating the relationship of perceptions of unethical consumer behavior with actual unethical consumer behavior (Shen & Dickson, 2001). More research could be conducted using field experiments so that actual unethical consumer behavior can be measured which would lead to a greater understanding of consumer ethical decision making. For example, studies could be conducted similar to the Steenhaut and Van Kenhove (2005) study. Instead of receiving excess change at check out, an extra product could be placed in the consumer's shopping bag. Observations could then be made about the consumers who do and do not report receiving the extra product. This experiment could be conducted at different types of retail establishments, located in different income level areas, such as at a high end specialty shop, at a discounter and at a department store. Comparisons could be made about the types of consumers who shop in these stores and the percentage of consumers at each type of store who does and does not report receiving the extra garment. The results of this type of study could be used to assist marketers when developing store policies and marketing strategies.

Future research could be conducted investigating consumers' perceptions of unethical consumer behavior because the use of scenarios in consumer ethics research is considered acceptable and is well established (Hunt & Vitell, 1986; Strutton, Vitell, & Pelton, 1994). The questionnaires that have been used in consumer ethics research may need to be updated and possibly new questionnaires may need to be developed in order to gain a better understanding of consumer ethical decision making. More research should be conducted using the modified Consumer Ethics Scale (Vitell & Muncy, 2005) in order to establish validity and reliability of the scale. The modified scale contains additional items pertaining to downloading/buying counterfeit goods, recycling/environmental awareness, and doing the right thing/doing good, which are important, timely issues that consumers encounter.

Cui, Mitchell, Schlegelmilch, and Cornwell (2005) suggested that the Forsyth (1980) Ethics Position Questionnaire is not appropriate in its original form for use in multi-culture/multi-country contexts. The questionnaire may need to be modified in order to contain the basic doctrine of all the major religions of the world, such as honesty and justice (Cornwell, Cui, Mitchell, Schlegelmilch, Dzulkiflee, & Chan, 2005). Modifications were suggested and the modified instrument was completed by cross-cultural consumers (Cui, Mitchell, Schlegelmilch, & Cornwell, 2005). Suggestions were made to either conduct further research using the modified scale with a different sample or develop a completely revised instrument (Cui, Mitchell, Schlegelmilch, & Cornwell, 2005).

In order to measure the impact of a university ethics course, Callen and Ownbey (2003) suggested to incorporate scenarios into the course to discuss the impact unethical consumer behavior has on retailer profits. For example, one project might direct the students to visit a retailer, gather prices for a list of products, and estimate potential losses for the retailer resulting from inventory shrinkage. Students' acceptance of unethical behavior could be measured at the beginning of the course and also at the end of the course in order to evaluate the impact the ethics course had on students' acceptance of unethical consumer behavior.

Future research should further investigate demographic characteristics, such as age gender, and religiosity, as well as educational level, and income to determine associations with acceptance of unethical consumer behavior (Vitell, Paolillo, & Singh, 2006). Longitudinal studies need to be conducted to determine if subjects' acceptance of unethical consumer behavior changes as subjects' grow older. In general, older subjects have been found to be less accepting of unethical consumer behavior than younger subjects. Studies were not longitudinal so it is unclear whether the finding is due to differences in generations or if it is due to a growth in moral development. Results of these types of studies could be used by marketers to segment their prospective target markets and to assist in developing marketing strategies.

CONCLUSION

The concept of consumer ethics involves many different issues. The issue this chapter focused on was consumer ethics pertaining to consumers benefiting from ethically questionable behavior. This chapter does not give a comprehensive discussion of every study that has investigated consumer ethics but discusses recent research trends in consumer ethical decision making. Ethical decision making models for marketers have been applied to ethical decision making of consumers in order to initiate the development of a consumer ethics model. Consumers' ethical beliefs have been found to differ by ethical ideology, Machiavellianism, relationship commitment, religiosity, age, and gender, as well as, by culture. Subjects have been found to justify unethical consumer behavior by using neutralization techniques. The majority of consumer ethics research investigates perceptions of unethical consumer behavior rather than actual unethical consumer behavior. Consumer perceptions provide insight into consumer ethical decision making so that it can be analyzed. Implications and suggestions for future research were discussed. More consumer ethics research is needed in order to develop a model illustrating ethical decision making of consumers.

REFERENCES

Abdolmohammadi, M.J., Gabhart, D.R.L., & Reeves, M.R. (1997). Ethical cognition of business students individually and in groups. *Journal of Business Ethics, 16,* 1717-1725.

Al-Khatib, J.A., Robertson, C.J., & Lascu, D.N. (2004). Post-Communist consumer ethics: The case of Romania. *Journal of Business Ethics, 54*(1), 81-95.

Al-Khatib, J.A., Vitell, S.J., Rexeisen, R., & Rawwas, M. (2005). Inter-country differences of consumer ethics in Arab countries. *International Business Review, 14,* 495-516.

Al-Wugayan, A.A., & Rao, C.P. (2004). An empirical investigation of consumer ethics in a collectivist Arab culture: Customer-retailer relationship (CRR) approach. *Journal of International Consumer Marketing, 16*(3), 25-54.

Atkinson, W. (2005). Loss prevention master basics before going high-tech. *Apparel Magazine, 46*(8), 28-32.

Babin, B.J., & Babin, L.A. (1996). Effects of moral cognitions and consumer emotions on shoplifting intentions. *Psychology & Marketing, 13*(8), 785-802.

Babin, B.J., & Griffin, M. (1995). A closer look at the influence of age on consumer ethics. *Advances in Consumer Research, 22,* 668-673.

Babin, B.J., Robin, D.P., & Pike, K. (1994). To steal, or not to steal? Consumer ethics and shoplifting. *AMA Winter Educators' Conference: Proceedings, 5,* 200-206.

Barnett, T., & Valentine, S. (2004). Issue contingencies and marketers' recognition of ethical issues, ethical judgments and behavioral intentions. *Journal of Business Research, 57*(4), 338-346.

Belk, R.W., Devinney, T., & Eckhardt, G. (2005). Consumer ethics across cultures. *Consumption, Markets and Culture, 8*(3), 275-289.

Bernstein, P. (1985). Cheating: The new national pastime? *Business,* 24-33.

Brass, D.J., Butterfield, K.D., & Skaggs, B.C. (1998). Relationships and unethical behavior: A social network perspective. *Academy of Management Review, 23*(1), 14-31.

Brinkman, J. (2004). Looking at consumer behavior in a moral perspective. *Journal of Business Ethics, 51,* 129-141.

Callen, K.S., & Ownbey, S.F. (2003) Associations between demographics and perceptions of unethical consumer behaviour. *International Journal of Consumer Studies, 27*(2), 99-110.

Carrigan, M., & Attalla, A. (2001). The myth of the ethical consumer – Do ethics matter in purchase behavior? *Journal of Consumer Marketing, 18*(7), 560-577.

Cho, H., Yoo, J., & Johnson, K.K.P. (2005). Ethical ideologies: Do they affect shopping behaviors and perceptions of morality? *Journal of Family & Consumer Sciences, 97*(3), 48-55.

Christie, R., & Geis, F.L. (1970). *Studies in Machiavellianism.* New York: Academic Press.

Cleveland, M., Kalamas, M., & Laroche, M. (2005). Shades of green: Linking environmental locus of control and pro-environmental behaviors. *Journal of Consumer Marketing, 22*(4), 198-212.

Cole, C. (1989). Deterrence and consumer fraud. *Journal of Retailing, 65,* 107-120.

Cornwell, B., Cui, C.C., Mitchell, V., Schlegelmilch, B., Dzulkiflee, A., & Chan, J. (2005). A cross-cultural study of the role of religion in consumers' ethical positions. *International Marketing Review, 22*(5), 531-546.

Corporate criminals strike out in 2005. (2006). *Information Management Journal, 40*(2), 10.

Cox, D., Cox A.D., & Moschis, G.P. (1990). When consumer behavior goes bad: An investigation of adolescent shoplifting. *Journal of Consumer Research, 17*, 149-159.

Cui, C.C., Mitchell, V., Schlegelmilch, B.B., & Cornwell, B. (2005). Measuring consumers' ethical position in Austria, Britain, Brunei, Hong Kong, and USA. *Journal of Business Ethics, 62*, 57-71.

Dubinsky, A.J., Nataraajan, R., Huang, W.Y. (2005). Consumers' moral philosophies: Identifying the idealist and the relativist. *Journal of Business Research, 58*, 1690-1701.

Ernst & Young's survey of retail loss prevention trends. (1992). *Chain Store Age Executive, 68*(1), 16-21.

Ferrell, O.C. (2004). Business ethics and customer stakeholders. *Academy of Management Executive, 18*(2), 126-129.

Ferrell, O.C., & Gresham, L.G. (1985). A contingency framework for understanding ethical decision making in marketing. *Journal of Marketing, 49*, 87-96.

Ferrell, O.C., Gresham, L.G., & Fraedrich, J. (1989). A synthesis of ethical decision models for marketing. *Journal of Macromarketing, 9*, 55-64.

Ferrell, O.C., & Weaver, K.M. (1978). Ethical beliefs of marketing managers. *Journal of Marketing, 42*, 69-73.

Fisher, J., Woodbine, G., & Fullerton, S. (2002). A cross-cultural assessment of attitudes regarding perceived breaches of ethical conduct by both parties in the business consumer dyad. *Journal of Consumer Behaviour, 2*(4), 333-353.

Forsyth, D.R. (1980). A taxonomy of ethical ideologies. *Journal of Personality and Social Psychology, 39*(1), 175-184.

Fukukawa, K. (2002). Developing a framework for ethically questionable behavior in consumption. *Journal of Business Ethics, 41*, 99-119.

Fukukawa, K. (2003). A theoretical review of business and consumer ethics research: Normative and descriptive approaches. *The Marketing Review, 3*, 381-401.

Fullerton, R.A., & Punj, G. (2004). Repercussions of promoting an ideology of consumption: Consumer misbehavior. *Journal of Business Research, 57*, 1239-1249.

Fullerton, S., Kerch, K.B., & Dodge, H.R. (1996). Consumer ethics: An assessment of individual behavior in the market place. *Journal of Business Ethics, 15*, 805-814.

Glenn, J.R., Jr., & Van Loo, M.F. (1993). Business students' and practitioners' ethical decisions over time. *Journal of Business Ethics, 12*, 835-847.

Grove, S.J., Vitell, S.J., & Strutton, D. (1989). Non-normative consumer behavior and the techniques of neutralization. In R. Bagozzi & J.P. Peter (Eds.), *Proceedings of the 1989 AMA Winter Educators' Conference* (pp. 131-135). Chicago: American Marketing Association.

Hayes, R.R., Jr. (1996). Selling the concept of loss prevention. *Security Management, 40*(12), 53-57.

Hofstede, G. (2001). *Cultures consequences: Comparing values, behaviors, institutions, and organizations across nations.* Thousand Oaks, CA: Sage Publications.

Hunt, S.D., & Vitell, S. (1986). A general theory of marketing ethics. *Journal of Macromarketing, 6*, 5-16.

Kallis, M.J., Krentler, K.A., & Vanier, D.J. (1986). The value of user image in quelling aberrant consumer behavior. *Journal of the Academy of Marketing Science, 14*, 29-35.

Klemke, L.W. (1982). Exploring juvenile shoplifting. *Sociology and Social Research, 67*(1), 59-75.

Klein, J.G., Smith, N.C., & John, A. (2004). Why we boycott: Consumer motivations for boycott participation. *Journal of Marketing, 68*(3), 92-109.

Kohlberg, L. (1969). Stage and sequence: The cognitive developmental approach to socialization. In D.A. Goslin, (Ed.), *Handbook of socialization theory and research* (pp. 347-480). Chicago: Rand McNally.

Lessons to learn about shoplifting...from shoplifters. (2002). *Security Director's Report, 2*(12), 6-7 & 10.

Lin, B., Hastings, D.A., & Martin, C. (1994). Shoplifting in retail clothing outlets: An exploratory research. *International Journal of Retail & Distribution Management, 22*(7), 24-29.

Loe, T. W., Ferrell, L., & Mansfield, P. (2000). A review of empirical studies assessing ethical decision making in business. *Journal of Business Ethics, 25*(3), 185-204.

McGregor, S.L.T. (2006). Understanding consumers' moral consciousness. *International Journal of Consumer Studies, 30*(2), 164-178.

Millage, A. (2005). Ethical misconduct prevalent in workplace. *Internal Auditor, 62*(6), 13-15.

Morgan, R.M., & Hunt, S.D. (1994). The commitment-trust theory of relationship marketing. *Journal of Marketing, 58*, 20-38.

Moschis, G. (1985). The juvenile shoplifter. *Retail Control, 53*, 36-39.

Muncy, J.A., & Vitell, S.J. (1992). Consumer ethics: An investigation of the ethical beliefs of the final consumer. *Journal of Business Research, 24*, 297-311.

Murphy, P.E., & Laczniak, G.R. (1992). Emerging ethical issues facing marketing researchers. *Marketing Research, 4*(2), 6-11.

Phillips, S., Alexander, A., & Shaw, A. (2005). Consumer misbehavior: The rise of self-service grocery retailing and shoplifting in the United Kingdom c. 1950-1970. *Journal of Macromarketing, 25*(1), 66-75.

Rao, C.P., & Al-Wugayan, A.A. (2005). Gender and cultural differences in consumer ethics in a consumer-retailer interaction context. *Journal of International Consumer Marketing 18*(1/2), 45-71.

Rawwas, M.Y.A., Swaiden, Z., & Oyman, M. (2005). Consumer Ethics: A cross-cultural study of the ethical beliefs of Turkish and American consumers. *Journal of Business Ethics, 57*, 183-195.

Robinson, J.P., & Shaver, P.R. (1973). *Measures of social psychological attitudes*. Ann Arbor, MI: Institute for Social Research.

Rosenbaum, M., & Kuntze, R. (2003). The relationship between anomie and unethical retail disposition. *Psychology and Marketing, 20*(12), 1067-1093.

Sele, K (2006). Marketing ethics in emerging markets – coping with ethical dilemmas. *IIMB Management Review, 18*(1), 95-104.

Shen, D., & Dickson, M. (2001). Consumers' acceptance of unethical clothing consumption activities: Influence of cultural identification, ethnicity, and Machiavellianism. *Clothing and Textiles Research Journal, 19*(2), 76-87.

Stealing is bad unless it's from folks we dislike. (1993). *Agri Marketing, 31*(8), 8.

Steenhaut, S., & Van Kenhove, P. (2005). Relationship commitment and ethical consumer behavior in a retail setting: The case of receiving too much change at the checkout. *Journal of Business Ethics, 56*, 335-353.

Steenhaut, S., & Van Kenhove, P. (2006). An empirical investigation of the relationships among a consumer's personal values, ethical ideology and ethical beliefs. *Journal of Business Ethics, 64*, 137-155.

Strutton, D., Pelton, L.E., & Ferrell, O.C. (1997). Ethical behavior in retail settings: Is there a generation gap? *Journal of Business Ethics, 16*, 87-105.

Strutton, D., Vitell, S.J., & Pelton, L.E. (1994). How consumers may justify inappropriate behavior in market settings: An application on the techniques of neutralization. *Journal of Business Research, 30*, 253-260.

Swaidan, Z., Rawwas, M.Y.A., & Al-Khatib, J.A. (2004). Consumer ethics: Moral ideologies and ethical beliefs of a micro-culture in the US. *International Business Review, 13*(6), 749-761.

Swaidan, Z., Vitell, S.J., & Rawwas, M. (2003). Consumer ethics: Determinants of ethical beliefs of African Americans. *Journal of Business Ethics, 46*, 175-186.

Swaidan, Z., Vitell, S.J., Rose, G.M., & Gilbert, F.W. (2006). Consumer ethics: The role of acculturation in U.S. immigrant populations. *Journal of Business Ethics, 64*, 1-16.

Sykes, G.M., & Matza, D. (1957). Techniques of neutralization: A theory of delinquency. *American Sociological Review, 22*, 664-670.

Theft cost retailers $31.3 billion yearly. (2002). *Westchester County Business Journal, 41*(29), 15.

Theft's multibillion dollar impact on retailers. (1997). *Chain Store Age, 73*(1) 175-178.

Tonglet, M. (2002). Consumer misbehaviour: An exploratory study of shoplifting. *Journal of Consumer Behaviour, 1*(4), 336-354.

Trevino, L.K. (1986). Ethical decision making in organizations: A person-situation interactionist model. *Academy of Management Review, 11*(3), 601-617.

Using the '3 P's' can help control retail shoplifting. (2004). *Safety Director's Report, 4*(7), 4-6.

Van Kenhove, P., De Wulf, K., & Steenhaut, S. (2003). The relationship between consumers' unethical behavior and customer loyalty in a retail environment. *Journal of Business Ethics, 44*, 261-278.

Van Kenhove, P., Vermeir, I., & Verniers, S. (2001). An empirical investigation of the relationships between ethical beliefs, ethical ideology, political preference and need for closure of Dutch-speaking consumers in Belgium. *Journal of Business Ethics, 32*(4), 347-361.

Vitell, S.J. (1997). Consumers no more ethical than business people. *Mississippi Business Journal, 19*(11), 5.

Vitell, S.J. (2003). Consumer ethics research: Review, synthesis and suggestions for the future. *Journal of Business Ethics, 43*, 33-47.

Vitell, S.J., & Festervand, T. (1987). Business conflicts: Conflicts, practices and beliefs of industrial executives. *Journal of Business Ethics, 6*, 111-122.

Vitell, S.J., & Muncy, J. (1992). Consumer ethics: An empirical investigation of factors influencing ethical judgments of the final consumer. *Journal of Business Ethics, 11*, 585-597.

Vitell, S.J., & Muncy, J. (2005). The Muncy-Vitell consumer ethics scale: A modification and application. *Journal of Business Ethics, 62*, 267-275.

Vitell, S.J., & Paolillo, J. (2003). Consumer ethics: The role of religiosity. *Journal of Business Ethics, 46*, 151-162.

Vitell, S.J., Paolillo, J.G.P., & Singh, J.J. (2005). Religiosity and consumer ethics. *Journal of Business Ethics*, *57*, 175-181.

Vitell, S.J., Paolillo, J.G.P., & Singh, J.J. (2006). The role of money and religiosity in determining consumers' ethical beliefs. *Journal of Business Ethics*, *64*, 117-124.

Vitell, S.J., Singhapakdi, A., & Thomas, J. (2001). Consumer ethics: An application and empirical testing of the Hunt-Vitell theory of ethics. *Journal of Consumer Marketing*, *18*(2), 153-178.

Wahn, J. (1993). Organizational dependence and the likelihood of complying with organizational pressures to behave unethically. *Journal of Business Ethics*, *12*, 245-251.

Wilkes, R.E. (1978). Fraudulent behavior by consumers. *Journal of Marketing*, *42*, 67-75.

Wotruba, T.R. (1991). A comprehensive framework of the analysis of ethical behavior, with a focus on sales organizations. In J.W. Bol, C.J. Crespy, J.M. Stearns, & J.R. Walton (Eds.), *Readings in Marketing Ethics* (pp. 277-298). MA: Ginn Press.

Yoo, B., & Donthu, N. (2002). The effects of marketing education and individual cultural values on marketing ethics of students. *Journal of Marketing Education,* 24(2), 92-103.

In: Business Ethics in Focus
Editor: Laura A. Parrish, pp. 49-68

ISBN: 978-1-60021-684-8
© 2007 Nova Science Publishers, Inc.

Chapter 2

ETHICAL ISSUES IN TRAINING FOR DISASTER PREPAREDNESS TO SERVE FRAIL OLDER PEOPLE: AN INNOVATIVE APPROACH TO GRADUATE HEALTH MANAGEMENT EDUCATION

Sarah B. Laditka[*], *James N. Laditka*[†], *Margaret M. Houck*[‡], *Carol B. Cornman*[§] *and Courtney B. Davis*[#]

University of South Carolina, Columbia, SC, USA

ABSTRACT

The aftermaths of September 11, 2001, and Hurricane Katrina underscore the urgent need to enhance education in emergency preparedness for students of health administration. Our purpose is to describe an interactive assignment for teaching ethics to doctoral students of health administration. The assignment, Student-Developed Educational Modules in Preparedness, was designed as a train-the-trainer process: our goal was to teach doctoral students to serve as preparedness educators for masters students. Our experiential assignment required doctoral students to develop a class module for master's students of health administration, on disaster preparedness for

---

[*] *Corresponding author:* Sarah B. Laditka, Ph.D., is Associate Professor and Master of Health Administration Program Director, Department of Health Services Policy and Management, Arnold School of Public Health, University of South Carolina, Columbia, SC 29208; phone: 803-777-1496; fax: 803-777-1836; E-mail: sladitka@gwm.sc.edu.
[†] James N. Laditka, D.A., Ph.D., is Research Associate Professor and Graduate Director of Epidemiology, and Director of Research of the Office for the Study of Aging, Department of Epidemiology and Biostatistics, Arnold School of Public Health, University of South Carolina, 800 Sumter Street, Columbia, SC, 29208; phone: 803 777-6852; fax: 803 777-2524; E-mail: jladitka@gwm.sc.edu.
[‡] Margaret M. Houck, Ph.D., Instructor of Philosophy, Department of Philosophy, College of Liberal Arts, University of South Carolina, Columbia, South Carolina, 29208, U.S.A.; phone: 803 777-4166; email: houckm@gwm.sc.edu.
[§] Carol B. Cornman, R.N., P.A., B.S., is Director of the Office for the Study of Aging, University of South Carolina, 2221 Devine Street, Columbia, SC, 29201; phone: 803 777-5337; fax: 803 777-0246; E-mail: ccornman@sc.edu.
[#] Courtney B. Davis, M.H.A., is Research Associate, Office for the Study of Aging, University of South Carolina, 2221 Devine Street, Columbia, SC, 29201; phone: 803 777-5336; fax: 803 777-0246; E-mail: daviscb@sc.edu.

disabled older people in the community, with an emphasis on ethical considerations. We piloted this training in a doctoral seminar in the fall of 2006 (n=14 students) at the University of South Carolina. The training consisted of three 90 minute weekly classes. Students completed a pre-assignment survey before the first class and a post-assignment survey immediately after the third class. In session one, we provided an overview of disaster preparedness for older populations, and some of the ethical considerations. In class two, students worked in four small groups of 3 or 4 students, to develop teaching materials. In class three, students presented their teaching materials. The results of eight paired Likert scale questions on the pre- and post-assignment surveys showed significant and meaningful improvement in students' perceptions of their learning in disaster preparedness for vulnerable groups, preparedness for frail older people living in the community, and in their confidence in their ability to develop and teach disaster preparedness to students of health administration (all $p<.05$). The students developed several educational approaches to promote a consideration of the ethical dimension of preparedness. From the perspective of teaching about ethics, in their responses to open-ended questions, a number of students wrote that the assignment highlighted the importance of disaster preparedness for frail older people and the ethical implications of disaster planning, and the importance of teaching master's students of health administration about this topic. The Student-Developed Educational Modules in Preparedness approach appears to be an effective way to engage doctoral students in discussing, considering, and teaching about ethical dimensions of managing complex disasters.

INTRODUCTION

The aftermaths of September 11, 2001, and of Hurricane Katrina, underscore the urgent need to enhance education for students of health and business administration in preparedness for complex disasters, including natural disasters, acts of terrorism, accidents in the industrial and transportation sectors, and other threats. Management of complex disasters raises many ethical challenges. Teaching students to recognize and address these ethical challenges can be difficult. Some observers outside academic settings suggest that ethics cannot be taught (Forbes, 1987). Others emphasize the usefulness of specific instructional methods to promote effective learning (Sims, 2002). Some researchers suggest that the key to teaching ethical concepts successfully is to use instructional methods that make the material relevant to students (Laditka & Houck, 2006; McDonald & Donleavy, 1995). Using an experiential assignment is recognized as one approach to make ethics more relevant (Brinkmann & Sims, 2001; Laditka & Houck, 2006; Saynal, 2000; Sims, 2002). Previous research has demonstrated the use and value of experiential learning activities in teaching (Laditka & Houck, 2006; Sanyal, 2000; Sims & Sims, 1991; Van Enyde & Spencer, 1988). Students report that they find experiential assignments action-oriented and enjoyable (Calloway-Graham, 2004; Hemmasi & Graf, 1992; Laditka & Houck, 2006; Sanyal, 2000; Sims, 2002; Sims & Sims, 1991). Further, there is evidence that students retain information longer when instructors use experiential assignments (Calloway-Graham, 2004; Hemmasi & Graf, 1992; Sanyal, 2000).

Our purpose in this chapter is to describe an interactive assignment for teaching ethics to doctoral students of health administration. We refer to our assignment as: Student-Developed Educational Modules in Preparedness. A large proportion of doctoral students obtain academic positions. Doctoral students are our future faculty in colleges and universities, those who will educate managers in health care and in many other business sectors. Individuals with doctoral degrees also often assume high level positions in the private and public sectors. Thus, it is essential that doctoral students have the skills to use teaching approaches that stimulate students and employees to consider the ethical dimensions of management decision-making. We are not aware of any previous studies that have addressed this area using the experiential approach we developed and implemented. Our experiential assignment requires doctoral students to develop a class module for master's students of health administration, on disaster preparedness for disabled older people in the community, with an emphasis on ethical considerations.

Increasingly, accrediting organizations for business administration and health management programs stress the need to integrate ethics into the curricula. Standards of the Association to Advance Collegiate Schools of Business (AACSB International) emphasize the need to promote a greater understanding of the importance of ethics, and to enhance students' ethical reasoning (AACSB International, 2005). For example, the AACSB "Assurance of Learning" standards require graduate programs to include "learning experiences" in ethical reasoning, and in ethical responsibilities of society and organizations (AACSB International, 2005). Further, the AACSB "Participants – Students and Faculty" standards require programs to demonstrate that instructors use active learning techniques to effectively engage students in learning. The Commission on Accreditation of Healthcare Management Education (CAHME), an accrediting body for master's programs in health care management, requires the curriculum to include ethical analysis applied to evaluate clinical and business decision making (Criterion III, Teaching and Curriculum – Self Study Guide for Graduate Programs in Healthcare Management Education, CAHME, 2004). Our approach uses active learning to enhance students' ethical reasoning. It can be adapted for use by other faculty, allowing faculty to incorporate a "stand alone" assignment on ethical considerations of preparedness into courses that focus on other areas in business administration or health care management. The Student-Developed Educational Modules in Preparedness address requirements of accrediting bodies such as AACSB and CAHME to include instruction in ethics, and may help business and health administration programs to meet accreditation standards. Further, preparedness is an emerging area for programs in business and health administration. Graduate students now readily recognize that preparedness training may be useful to their management careers. In addition, for schools of administration and management, developing faculty experience with preparedness issues may motivate sponsored research activity in this area that continues to be a national priority.

STUDENT-DEVELOPED EDUCATIONAL MODULES IN PREPAREDNESS

Overview

The authors comprise a multi-disciplinary research team. All of the authors are affiliated with the University of South Carolina; four are affiliated with the Arnold School of Public Health (SBL, JNL, CBC, CBD); one is affiliated with the School of Liberal Arts and Sciences (MMH). One author (SBL) is a gerontologist and professor of health administration with extensive teaching experience in graduate and undergraduate health management and business and education. One (JNL) is a gerontologist and professor of epidemiology and biostatistics who also has over twenty years of experience teaching humanities, including ethics. One author (MMH) is an instructor of philosophy, with extensive experience teaching undergraduates and medical students in ethics, including biomedical ethics. Another (CBC) is the Director of the Office for the Study of Aging, a center within the Arnold School of Public Health that conducts research and provides education, program planning, and evaluation services to state agencies and other organizations whose work focuses on older populations. One author (CBD) is a research associate at the Office for the Study of Aging, with substantial experience in nursing home care and long-term care services provided in the community. Four of the authors (SBL, JNL, CBC, CBD) have collaborated together for two years on three long-term care preparedness projects: two of these studies focused on disaster preparedness for nursing homes (Laditka et al., 2006, 2007, In Press); a third focuses on disaster preparedness for frail, disabled older people residing in the community.

This assignment, developed by the authors, was piloted in a doctoral-level seminar in health policy and management (n=14 students) at the University of South Carolina in the fall of 2006. The assignment, Student-Developed Educational Modules in Preparedness, requires doctoral students to develop a class module for master's students of health administration (hereafter, MHA students) on disaster preparedness for frail older people in the community, highlighting ethical considerations. The assignment consisted of three classes of 90 minutes each. These classes spanned three weeks in October of 2006. This study was approved by the Institutional Review Board at the University of South Carolina.

Educational Module Assignment and Approach

The Assignment

The assignment was designed as a train-the-trainer process (Stanford Faculty Development Center, 2004): our goal was to teach doctoral students to serve as preparedness educators for MHA students. Doctoral students were asked to work in small groups of three to four, to develop materials for a class for MHA students focusing on disaster preparedness for home care and home health agencies serving disabled, frail older people living in the community. Students were required to include a component that promoted ethical considerations as a foundation for caring for frail older people before, during and after a disaster. In a brief discussion with students in the first of three classes for this assignment, we emphasized that preparing for emergencies or disasters, responding to them, or mitigating their effects, requires trade-offs of time, personnel, supplies, and of resources generally. Responding to disasters with regard to vulnerable populations also involves weighing judgments. Questions we asked students to consider include: Is it better to evacuate an individual or a group of individuals in the target group? Or is it better to ride out a disaster? We pointed out that choices often involve complex judgments for older people, because their frailty predisposes them to emotional and physical stress. For older people, evacuation can promote physical and/or cognitive decline, and possibly death. Remaining in the disaster area, or potential disaster area, when the disaster may or may not strike nearby, as in the case of a hurricane, may be a viable option in some instances; however, this option also involves risks.

We stressed that health care managers who prepare for and respond to disasters inevitably make ethical value judgments.

Students were also asked to use teaching approaches that would actively engage MHA students, such as role play or another type of interactive exercise. To provide feedback to doctoral students before their presentations in the third class, we required them to submit their teaching plan to the instructor at least one day before their presentation. An overview of the assignment is shown in Appendix A.

Class One

Students were asked to complete a pre-assignment survey at the beginning of the class (please refer to Appendix B). The instructor (SBL) provided an overview of disaster preparedness for disabled, frail older people as well as some of the ethical considerations described in "The Assignment" section, above. The instructor also led an interactive discussion about the benefits of using various teaching methods, including, lecture, discussion, and interactive assignments, to accommodate different learning styles of students. The instructor distributed the instructions shown in Appendix A, a manuscript on nursing home preparedness, a case study of home health and home care disaster preparedness in South Carolina, and an interactive role play assignment in long-term care preparedness designed for master's students in public health. The instructor addressed student questions about the assignment. Students were asked to review all distributed materials prior to class two.

Class Two

This class was facilitated by the instructor and two of the authors (JNL, CBC) (hereafter facilitators). The instructor and facilitators met with the students in a 10 minute plenary session to review the assignment. Next, the student teams were given 70 minutes to meet in groups to develop teaching materials. There were four student teams. The instructor and facilitators circulated among the teams, serving as observers and addressing questions. All of the students were highly engaged in the process. All of the teams began to develop various educational materials, such as PowerPoint presentations, presentation outlines, and descriptions of role play exercises. The class concluded with a brief plenary discussion of 10 minutes in which the instructor and facilitators addressed student questions about the assignment.

Class Three

Students presented their teaching materials. The student presentations were video-taped. The instructor and one of the other authors (JNL) served as facilitators and participated in the student-developed interactive exercises. Each student team had 20 minutes to present its module. There was a brief discussion period of 5 to 10 minutes following each presentation. Finally, students completed a post-assignment survey (please refer to Appendix C).

Students' Reactions and Learning Experiences

Overview

Several methods were used to evaluate the effectiveness of the Student-Developed Educational Modules in Preparedness for student learning. We evaluated the content of the student-developed modules by reviewing the video-tape of student presentations. We described student class participation. We analyzed quantitative and qualitative student responses to the assignment using the pre- and post-assignment surveys.

Classroom Responses – Summary of Student-Developed Educational Modules

In all instances, students were highly engaged in the assignment and stayed on task. Also in all instances, students worked on their projects between the classes. Each student team used a different instructional approach. Student-developed teaching materials included video clips, brief lectures, PowerPoint presentations, and experiential assignments. We describe the approach used by each team below, focusing on the ethical issues highlighted by the students.

Team 1 described a scenario of a home health agency facing a disaster in a rural area with a rapidly growing Hispanic population. Students organized their presentation as a mini-lecture, followed by an interactive role play exercise, which they piloted in the class. The first presenter emphasized that agencies in rural areas face barriers due to limited access to health care resources, lack of public transportation, and geographic isolation. She stressed the translation needs for older Hispanics as an emerging challenge for disaster preparedness. The second presenter reviewed key ethical concepts with the class, pointing out that although many of these principals seem self evident, addressing them in practice can require the manager to weigh contradictory values and actions, and the advantages and disadvantages of each. The ethical concepts reviewed were: non-malfeasance (or, "first, do no harm"); autonomy and the need to respect rational people making informed decisions; beneficence; and social justice or fairness, giving each person her due. The student emphasized that MHA students must state how their plans would address these ethical concepts. A third presenter reviewed the interactive exercise in which one team of master's students would create a disaster preparedness tool for home health agencies to use to assess the needs of their clients during a disaster. A second student team would create a strategic plan for the home health agency, addressing staffing, transportation, and communication. The presenter divided the doctoral students into two teams, to role play how master's students might address this assignment; each team had 2-3 minutes to discuss their approach.

Team Two began their presentation with a three to four minute video clip they would show at the beginning of the class for MHA students. The presenting student described the importance of using an attention-getting device (an icebreaker) as an effective way to engage students in a topic. The video clip showed an older female driver and a younger male driver driving on a highway that had been cleared of all other traffic by emergency responders, to make it available as a runway for an emergency landing of a jumbo jet passenger plane. Both drivers had made it through the road blocks. The younger driver became frantic when he spotted the approaching plane. The older female driver was oblivious to the impending disaster. The clip was designed to be dramatic, an "attention-getter," yet humorous, and highlight stereo-types of older people (e.g., slow to react, hard of hearing, impaired vision). She asked each doctoral student to pair with another student, and to take "five seconds" to identify differences between the young man and older woman. Students responded that the young man was frantic, whereas the older woman was calm. Next the presenter asked each student pair to identify a feature of the older woman that predisposed her to injury. Students identified a number of sensory deficits of the older driver: slow, impaired hearing, poor vision, and poor awareness. The presenter said this approach could be used to develop a picture of some of the problems faced by vulnerable populations. Next, students were asked to identify strengths exhibited by the older driver. Students described her strengths as "attitude," "spunk," and "resilience." The presenter emphasized that vulnerable populations have both strengths and weaknesses, which need to be addressed in disaster planning. Finally, students were asked to identify the ethical dilemma illustrated by the video. Students described the decision to sacrifice the lives of the younger male and older female to save hundreds of lives on the plane as the ethical dilemma. The presenter emphasized that ethical dilemmas are inherent in most disasters and potential disaster situations, where life and death decisions need to be made quickly.

In the second part of the presentation, another student described the disaster scenario they would present to the MHA students, using a PowerPoint presentation. The scenario is a home health agency faced with a major ice storm, such as the ice storm that occurred in upstate South Carolina in January of 2004. The student stated that MHA students would be split into three teams: one team of administrators, a second team of nurses, and a third team of family members. The student teams would be asked to identify problems associated with reaching and providing home health services to a disabled 72 year old woman, isolated in her home during the ice storm, in the immediate aftermath of the storm. The MHA students would be asked to consider how the agency should weigh risks associated with asking their staff to travel to clients' homes during and immediately after the ice storm. The master's student teams would also be asked to identify the problems that would occur as time passed, because the older woman was without heat or food. The student emphasized, "as we learned after Katrina, as days go by after a major disaster, things get worse." The MHA student teams would be asked to describe the ethical, social, and technical problems with providing care to disabled older people in the community following the disaster. Due to time constraints, Team 2 did not pilot their interactive exercise with doctoral students.

Team 3 kicked off their presentation with an overview of home health and home care agencies and disaster preparedness. One student presented photos taken in the immediate aftermath of Hurricane Katrina and the evacuation of residents of New Orleans, embedded in a PowerPoint presentation. Their educational module included plans to show a video-clip of an actual disaster, focusing on problems faced by disabled older people in an evacuation. Next, another student presented an interactive assignment in which MHA students would be divided into three teams: one team would focus on the pre-disaster phase, a second on the disaster phase, and the third on the post-disaster phase. The students asked each group to consider the "ethical implications related to disaster preparedness and older people." Students in Team 3 piloted their interactive assignment in the class, again with the doctoral students taking the roles of master's students in the class for which the module was designed. Focusing on the ethics-related discussion, the students in the first group emphasized the importance of pre-disaster planning and identifying clients who would prefer to shelter-in-place, and those that would want to evacuate.

Team Four described a disaster scenario of a major hurricane in Charleston, South Carolina—an event that has actually occurred in recent memory, when Hurricane Hugo, which struck the coast of South Carolina in 1989 as a category 4 hurricane. The presenting student distributed a paper outline of the scenario and role play, and did not rely on other audio-visual aids. In this scenario, a home health agency in the Charleston area served 400 to 500 older clients. The interactive exercise for MHA students was to describe how the home health agency would plan for and manage several key functions, including transportation, and coordination with other agencies before, during, and after the hurricane. The presenter stressed the importance of pre-disaster planning. He emphasized the need to have realistic disaster drills every six to twelve months to keep the staff in readiness, and because of relatively rapid turnover of staff and changes in the client base. The presenter also asked students to consider who would pay for the extra costs of caring for clients during and after a disaster. He also described the need to ask each client, "if there is a major disaster, is it your preference to stay or to leave?" The student stressed that we cannot force people to leave their homes. The student remarked that in the case of Hurricane Katrina, some of the houses in New Orleans that people refused to leave were prominently marked, to facilitate periodic checks—and, when required, evacuation.

Next, the presenter described an interactive exercise for MHA students; as with the two other teams, this exercise was piloted with the doctoral students playing the roles of master's students. Students were divided into three groups. The first group was asked to focus on the communication process. The second was asked to focus on transportation. Students in the third group were tasked with addressing two ethical questions. First, should the home health agency distinguish between clients' ability to pay when providing services following a disaster? Second, what should the employees of the home health agency do on the day of the disaster if they are presented with older people who are not clients of their agency, who have care needs that are unaddressed because of the disaster? We focus on the responses of the third student group. Responding to the first ethical question, the students said they would, "just get them out," without concerns about their ability to pay. The presenter followed this response with another question: "If your decision to help older people without reimbursement were to put your agency out of business, would this change your decision?" The students said their decision would not change. In response to the second ethical question, students said they would provide services to older people who were not clients of the agency. In the discussion following this presentation, several students asked if the government provides reimbursement to home health agencies for developing disaster preparedness, or for extra care provided during and following a disaster.

Students Reactions in a Pre- and Post-Assignment Survey

Fourteen students completed a pre-assignment survey. The average age of students was 32.8 years (standard deviation 8.7, range 25 to 55 years); 9 students were female (69.2%). Only two students (15.4%) reported work experience in long-term care. Six students (46.2%) reported having participated in formal disaster preparedness training. One female student was not available to participate in the third class session, or to complete a post-assignment survey.

The remainder of the students completed a post-assignment survey. As most of the survey questions were designed for paired analysis, we report the results based on 13 students who completed both surveys.

In both the pre- and post- assignment surveys, students responded to the same set of ten questions using a 5-point Likert scale: strongly agree, agree, neutral, disagree, and strongly disagree (questions are shown Table 1), where strongly agree was equal to 5 and strongly disagree equal to 1. To test for differences between the scores in the pre-and post-surveys, we used the Wilcoxon signed rank sum test. The results are reported in Table 1, which shows the mean values of the pre-assignment survey, the mean values of the post-assignment survey, and the p-value for the difference scores. Responses to eight of the 10 questions showed statistically significant improvement in students' perceptions of their confidence in preparedness for disabled, frail, older people in long-term care settings and in the community, and in their teaching skills; most of the differences were notable in magnitude. Students reported improvement in their perceptions of being able to write clearly about the importance of studying emergency response plans of health care organizations ($p=0.006$). Also reported were improvements in perceptions in being able to: (1) identify and clearly state some of the major problems facing vulnerable populations during and after a disaster ($p=0.001$); (2) identify and clearly state the major problems faced by home care and home health agencies in disaster preparedness ($p=0.002$); (3) describe the limits of their knowledge about identifying key resources that might be needed by a health care facility during and after an emergency ($p=0.044$); (4) identify and clearly state the importance of having a personal and family disaster plan for older people living in the community ($p=0.044$); (5) develop and discuss several approaches that could be successfully used to assist vulnerable populations during and after a disaster ($p=0.004$); (6) develop and apply creative strategies to teach students in health administration about the importance of disaster preparedness in long term care ($p=0.001$); and (7) develop and pilot an experiential teaching experience for health administration students in disaster preparedness for health care organizations serving vulnerable populations ($p<0.0001$).

In the post-assignment survey, we asked students to respond to two additional questions using a 5-point Likert scale: strongly agree, agree, neutral, disagree, and strongly disagree (questions shown in Appendix C). We combined responses for strongly agree (equal to 5) and agree (equal to 4) (hereafter referred to as agree). Results are reported in Table 2. In response to the question, "Completing this experiential project helped me to understand the importance of training health administration students in disaster preparedness, about 70% of students said the project helped them to understand the importance of training students. Responding to the question, "Completing this experiential project will help prepare me to incorporate disaster preparedness learning materials into my teaching," about 70% of students reported that the project helped them prepare.

In both the pre- and post-assignment surveys, we asked students to respond to the same statement: "Describe how you would go about teaching health administration students the importance of disaster preparedness in long term care." Two of the authors used thematic analysis to identify the recurring themes (Luborsky, 1994). We first worked independently. Next we reviewed the recurring themes together, and were in agreement in almost all instances. The few instances of disagreement were resolved through discussion. The results are reported in Table 2. Responses fell into three areas. We provide one to four representative quotations in each area to illustrate the responses. We review the results for the pre-assignment survey first, and then the post-assignment survey.

Table 1. Responses to Paired Pre- and Post- Assignment Survey Questions, Changes in Students' Perceptions about Confidence in Preparedness and Teaching Disaster Preparedness (N=13)

Question	Pre-test	Post-test	P-value
1. I am able to describe the role of health administrators in responding to a range of emergencies that might arise.	3.615	4.384	0.054
2. I am able to write clearly about the importance of studying the emergency response plans of health care organizations	3.923	4.692	0.006
3. I am able to identify and clearly state some of the major problems facing vulnerable populations during and after a disaster.	4.076	4.461	0.096
4. I am able to identify and discuss the major problems faced by nursing homes in disaster preparedness	2.923	4.538	0.001
5. I am able to identify and clearly state the major problems faced by home care and home health agencies in disaster preparedness	2.923	4.384	0.002
6. I can tell someone clearly what the limits are of my own knowledge about identifying key resources that might be needed by a health care facility during and after an emergency	3.923	4.615	0.044
7. I am able to identify and clearly state the importance of having a personal and family disaster plan for older people living in the community.	3.769	4.461	0.044
8. I am able to develop and discuss several approaches that could be successfully used to assist vulnerable populations during and after a disaster.	3.083	4.384	0.004
9. I am able to develop and apply creative strategies to teach students in health administration about the importance of disaster preparedness in long term care.	3.307	4.615	0.001
10. I am able to develop and pilot an experiential teaching experience for health administration students in disaster preparedness for health care organizations serving vulnerable populations	2.923	4.615	<0.001

Students used a 1-5 Likert scale where 1=strongly disagree, 5=strongly agree.

Table 2. Student-Developed Educational Modules of Preparedness, Student Responses to Selected Questions in the Pre- and Post-Assignment Surveys (N=13)[a]

Likert scale questions[b]	Percentage (n)
Completing this experiential project helped me to understand the importance of training health administration students in disaster preparedness	69.2 (9)
Completing this experiential projected will help prepare me to incorporate disaster preparedness learning materials into my teaching	69.2 (9)
Open-ended questions	
Pre-Assignment Survey: Methods to teach importance of long term care preparedness	
Primarily interactive	15.4 (2)
Mixture of lecture and interactive	53.8 (7)
Primarily lecture	30.8 (4)
Post-Assignment Survey: Methods to teach importance of long term care preparedness	
Primarily interactive	15.4 (3)
Mixture of lecture and interactive	69.2 (9)
Primarily lecture	0.8 (1)
Primary advantage of incorporating disaster preparedness training in health administration curriculum	
Improved awareness of important public health issue	23.1 (3)
Better understanding of the connection between preparedness training and health administration	53.8 (7)
Improved awareness of the connection between preparedness training, health administration, and vulnerable populations	15.4 (2)
Primary advantage of incorporating ethical perspective in disaster preparedness training for future health administrators	
Promote awareness / critical thinking about ethical issues	61.5 (8)
Raise awareness about need to protect vulnerable populations	38.5 (5)

[a] Surveys shown in Appendices B and C.
[b] Percentage (number) of students responding agree or strongly agree.

In the pre-assignment survey, two students replied they would use primarily interactive teaching methods. One wrote, "I would structure the class in a hands on type of way. I would include partnering with a long term health care facility to examine what procedures are in place and test the effectiveness." Seven students responded that they would use a mixture of teaching methods, lecture and interactive assignments. One commented, "I think that past experiences and learning from those past experiences serve as real examples. I would present students with scenarios such as response to 9/11 attacks or natural disaster responses or plans for people that utilize long term care facilities. Students would design disaster response plans given their scenarios." Another student wrote, "My experience(s) have been geared toward follow up health survey & assessment following disasters (namely, Graniteville). Therefore, I would go about teaching preparedness principles using real-example of disasters, incorporating tabletop exercises and facility overview (i.e. which facilities would serve as shelters), etc." ("Graniteville" in the preceding passage refers to a train wreck and subsequent chlorine spill that affected a community in South Carolina in 2005; ten people died, and at least 250 people were treated for chlorine exposure.) A third student wrote, "I would start by discuss[ing] disasters that have recently taken place in the US. During this discuss[ion] I would clearly define disaster preparedness and health care. In reviewing recent disasters I will look at and discuss the pros and cons of the actions of the health care administrator. In addition to this discuss[ion] I would allow the student to develop a plan showing what they would do different." Four students replied they would rely primarily on lecture methods. One student commented:

> I would want them to become familiar with the facilities & the residents of facilities so that they would have a better understanding of the population they are dealing with, as well as LTC [long-term care] agencies that serve this population; (2) develop curriculum on psychosocial/medical/physical aspects of aging, so that the health administration students know more about aging; (3) arrange for guest speakers from community/state agencies who have developed disaster preparedness plans & learn how they include LTC facilities in their plans.

In the post-assignment survey, three students responded that they would rely on primarily interactive teaching methods. One wrote, "I am a proponent of exercises (functional, tabletop, etc.) so I would have students participate in and design an exercise modeling a disaster." Nine students replied they would use a mixture of teaching methods, lecture and interactive assignments. One student commented, "I would incorporate several different teaching methods. I would assign groups to spend some time with real facilities to see what they have in place and to critique them (field project)." Another wrote, "I would bring in support staff from the community (e.g. transportation officials, nursing home administrator safety/law enforcement, communication systems administrators, public health officials, etc.) to talk about their roles in disaster preparedness for different possible disasters. Then I would have the students form small groups of 3 and have each one take on the roles of team members in a particular long term setting (e.g. ALF [assisted living facility], home health agency, home care agency) and develop their own strategy for disaster preparedness for a specific natural disaster. They would then present this." A fourth student wrote, "I would make sure to incorporate more active learning techniques/instruction rather than simply passive lecture. This would help to make the concepts more applied, rather than merely themes." Only one student said they would rely on primarily lecture methods. This student wrote, "1. Define key concepts [and] term[s]. 2. Apply thematic responses to previous disasters."

The post-assignment survey also asked students to respond to two additional statements: (1) "The primary advantage of incorporating disaster preparedness training material into a graduate health administration program is …" and (2) "The primary advantage of incorporating an ethical perspective in disaster preparedness training material for future health care managers is …" We used a recurring theme approach to analyze students' responses. Results are reported in Table 2. We identified three themes regarding the question about the importance of incorporating disaster preparedness training into health administration curricula. Each theme is summarized below, followed by one to two representative quotations to illustrate the theme. In the first theme, three students commented that the material engaged students in an important public health issue. One wrote, "Allows students to address an important component of addressing public health issues." Another commented, "Receiving basic information about an emerging public health issue." In the second theme, seven students emphasized that incorporating disaster preparedness material would help health administration students understand the connection between preparedness training and the field of health management. One student commented, "To get them thinking about disaster preparedness training and its relation to health administration." Another student wrote, "It's an emerging field, and in light of recent events a very necessary topic of discussion for future administrators." In the third theme, two students highlighted the importance of an improved awareness of the connection between preparedness training, health administration, and vulnerable populations. One student wrote, "Graduates of an MHA program will have a tangible sense of the importance of disaster planning regarding vulnerable populations."

Two themes were identified regarding the question about the primary advantage of incorporating an ethical perspective into preparedness training for future health administrators. We provide three representative quotations to illustrate these themes. Eight students commented that this would promote greater awareness and/or stimulate critical thinking about ethical issues. One student wrote, "Another viewpoint at working through ethical dilemmas involving ethics." Another student commented, "To get the students thinking about the ethical perspective and its effect on all aspects of our lives and the lives of others." A third wrote, "That managers do not violate ethical principles, and are considerate of them during planning – not after the fact." In the second theme, five students commented that incorporating this material would improve awareness about the need to protect vulnerable populations. One student wrote, "Explore some of the dilemmas that can arise from disasters. I also think that it is…important to consider ethical issues because they may change the outlook of the plan/procedure." Another student commented, "Provides [an] opportunity to think about/plan for disasters/concern that may not previously been considered." A third wrote, "To make them aware of the critical decisions that need to be made to protect a vulnerable population that relies on others for all their basic needs (shelter, food, medication management, etc.)."

CONCLUSION

We presented an interactive, train-the-trainer instructional approach: Student-Developed Educational Modules in Preparedness. Our assignment required doctoral students to develop a class module for students of health administration on disaster preparedness for disabled older people in the community, highlighting ethical considerations. The total class time allocated to this assignment was relatively modest (4.5 hours). In addition, the guidelines for the assignment were purposely broad, to promote creative problem-solving among the students. Despite these constraints, our results suggest that our instructional approach was effective. The results of eight paired Likert scale questions on the pre- and post-assignment surveys showed significant and meaningful improvement in students' perceptions of their learning in disaster preparedness for vulnerable groups, preparedness for frail older people living in the community, and in their confidence in their ability to develop and teach disaster preparedness to students of health administration. The students developed several educational approaches to promote a consideration of the ethical dimension of preparedness, including: (1) a review of underlying ethical principals and an interactive assignment that would require students to apply these principals; (2) use of a dramatic video to promote discussion about challenges facing vulnerable populations and some of the ethical dilemmas posed by disasters; and (3) use of interactive role play that required students to address two practical ethical issues. From the perspective of teaching about ethics, in their responses to open-ended questions, a number of students wrote that the assignment highlighted the importance of disaster preparedness for frail older people and the ethical implications of disaster planning, and the importance of teaching MHA students about this topic. Teaching about the importance of a topic is teaching about the value of the topic, which is central to the teaching of ethics. The high level of engagement of all of the students suggests that they recognized the topic of the assignment as important; we acknowledge that this recognition may have been sparked by the aftermaths of September 11, 2001, and the more recent developments following Hurricane Katrina, including the deaths of nursing homes residents (King, 2006; U.S. Office of Inspector General, 2006). Collectively, the Student-Developed Educational Modules in Preparedness approach appears to be an effective way to engage doctoral students in discussing, considering, and teaching about ethical dimensions of managing complex disasters.

Moreover, we suggest there is an urgent need to develop effective approaches to highlight ethical issues in preparedness beyond academic settings. In the fall of 2006, for example, the World Health Organization (WHO) convened three panels of experts to address ethical issues in planning for a pandemic influenza outbreak (WHO, 2006). One of these panels evaluated the roles and obligations of health care workers in the event of an outbreak (Upshur, 2006). The panel emphasized the importance of considering the ethical implications of the duty to care (Clark, 2005; Reid, 2005). That is, physicians and health care workers have a greater obligation to provide care during a pandemic outbreak of disease, because they have chosen a profession devoted to caring for people who are ill (Clark, 2005), and in many instances have consumed societal resources in the course of their educations. Further, medical ethicists argue that the medical profession has a social contract, which obligates them to be available during an emergency (Clark, 2005). Yet, a recent survey of public health workers in Maryland found that nearly half of employees said they would not report to work during a pandemic (Balicer, 2006). Other biomedical ethicists have argued that disaster planners should ensure working conditions that are as safe as possible for health care professionals and other workers during a pandemic or other disasters (Sepkowitz, 1996a, 1996b). The instructional approach we developed could be adapted to train leaders in the private and public sectors, as well as health care professionals, to train health care and public health workers and volunteers to plan for disasters and respond to them, with consideration of the ethical dimensions of these activities.

APPENDIX A.
STUDENT-DEVELOPED EDUCATIONAL MODULES IN PREPAREDNESS ASSIGNMENT GUIDELINES

Your task in this project is to work in a team of 3 to 4 students to develop an experiential exercise for students in the Master of Health Administration program in disaster preparedness for health care organizations serving vulnerable older people living in the community.

Your experiential exercise should incorporate a component that will lead students to consider the ethics of preparedness for organizations serving vulnerable older people living in the community. Inevitably preparing for emergencies or disasters, or responding to them, or mitigating their effects, require trade-offs of time, personnel, supplies, and of resources generally.

This may be particularly an issue for disasters, which occur infrequently in given areas. Preparing for disasters involves opportunity costs, so health care managers need to weigh the known and anticipated direct costs, and opportunity costs, against the risks and benefits of no preparation, or less preparation. Responding to disasters with regard to the population that is the target of this exercise also involves weighing judgments. As a simple example, is it better to evacuate an individual or a group of individuals in the target group? Or is it better to ride out a disaster? The choice often involves complex judgments for those responsible for the target group, because their frailty predisposes them to emotional and physical stress. Evacuation itself can promote a cascade of decline, and possibly death. Remaining in the disaster area--or potential disaster area, when the disaster may or may not strike nearby, as in the case of a hurricane--may be an option in some instances, as well; but this option also involves risks.

As for responding to disasters, analogous ethical challenges arise. Health care managers who prepare for and respond to disasters inevitably make ethical value judgments. Your experiential exercise should include a component that requires students to weigh ethical issues such as these, with specific regard to the target population designated for this experiential learning exercise.

Your team needs to submit written instructions that clearly describe the exercise and the steps involved to the instructor prior to the final session.

APPENDIX B.
• STUDENT-DEVELOPED EDUCATIONAL MODULES IN PREPAREDNESS
• STUDENT-DEVELOPED CASE STUDIES OF ETHICAL SITUATIONS IN THE WORKPLACE
• STUDENT PRE-TEST

Your responses to this brief survey will help us to improve training and education in emergency preparedness.

Please indicate the extent to which you feel confident about the following areas by circling your response:

	Strongly Disagree	Moderately Disagree	Neutral	Moderately Agree	Strongly Agree
1. I am able to describe the role of health administrators in responding to a range of emergencies that might arise	1	2	3	4	5
2. I am able to write clearly about the importance of studying the emergency response plans of health care organizations	1	2	3	4	5
3. I am able to identify and clearly state some of the major problems facing vulnerable populations during and after a disaster.	1	2	3	4	5
4. I am able to identify and discuss the major problems faced by nursing homes in disaster preparedness	1	2	3	4	5
5. I am able to identify and clearly state the major problems faced by home care and home health agencies in disaster preparedness	1	2	3	4	5
6. I can tell someone clearly what the limits are of my own knowledge about identifying key resources that might be needed by a health care facility during and after an emergency	1	2	3	4	5
7. I am able to identify and clearly state the importance of having a personal and family disaster plan for older people living in the community.	1	2	3	4	5
8. I am able to develop and discuss several approaches that could be successfully used to assist vulnerable populations during and after a disaster.	1	2	3	4	5
9. I am able to develop and apply creative strategies to teach students in health administration about the importance of disaster preparedness in long term care.	1	2	3	4	5
10. I am able to develop and pilot an experiential teaching experience for health administration students in disaster preparedness for health care organizations serving vulnerable populations	1	2	3	4	5

Describe how you would go about teaching health administration students the importance of disaster preparedness in long term care.

Have you worked/currently working in the long-term care field? ____ Yes ____ No

Have you participated in formal disaster preparedness training? ____ Yes ____ No

Please indicate your age: _____

Please indicate your gender: _____

APPENDIX C.
STUDENT-DEVELOPED EDUCATIONAL MODULES IN PREPAREDNESS STUDENT POST-TEST

Your responses to this brief survey will help us to improve training and education in emergency preparedness.

Please indicate the extent to which you feel confident about the following areas by circling your response:

	Strongly Disagree	Moderately Disagree	Neutral	Moderately Agree	Strongly Agree
1. I am able to describe the role of health administrators in responding to a range of emergencies that might arise	1	2	3	4	5
2. I am able to write clearly about the importance of studying the emergency response plans of health care organizations	1	2	3	4	5
3. I am able to identify and clearly state some of the major problems facing vulnerable populations during and after a disaster.	1	2	3	4	5
4. I am able to identify and discuss the major problems faced by nursing homes in disaster preparedness	1	2	3	4	5
5. I am able to identify and clearly state the major problems faced by home care and home health agencies in disaster preparedness	1	2	3	4	5
6. I can tell someone clearly what the limits are of my own knowledge about identifying key resources that might be needed by a health care facility during and after an emergency	1	2	3	4	5
7. I am able to identify and clearly state the importance of having a personal and family disaster plan for older people living in the community.	1	2	3	4	5
8. I can tell someone clearly what the limits are of my own knowledge about identifying key resources that might be needed by a health care facility during and after an emergency	1	2	3	4	5
9. I am able to identify and clearly state the importance of having a personal and family disaster plan for older people living in the community.	1	2	3	4	5
10. I am able to develop and discuss several approaches that could be successfully used to assist vulnerable populations during and after a disaster.	1	2	3	4	5

APPENDIX C. (CONTINUED)

11. I am able to develop and apply creative strategies to teach students in health administration about the importance of disaster preparedness in long term care.	1	2	3	4	5
12. I am able to develop and pilot an experiential teaching experience for health administration students in disaster preparedness for health care organizations serving vulnerable populations	1	2	3	4	5

Describe how you would go about teaching health administration students the importance of disaster preparedness in long term care.

Completing this experiential project helped me to understand the importance of training health administration students in disaster preparedness (please circle one).

Strongly Agree   *Neutral*   *Strongly Disagree*
1   *2*   *3*   *4*   *5*

Completing this experiential projected will help prepare me to incorporate disaster preparedness learning materials into my teaching (please circle one).

Strongly Agree   *Neutral*   *Strongly Disagree*
1   *2*   *3*   *4*   *5*

Please complete the following statements:

The primary advantage of incorporating disaster preparedness training material into a graduate health administration program is:

The primary advantage of incorporating an ethical perspective in disaster preparedness training material for future health care managers is:

ACKNOWLEDGEMENTS

We thank the following doctoral students at the University of South Carolina for their outstanding contributions to this project: Jessica Bellinger, MPH, Greg Carlson, MPH, Abdoulaye Diedhiou, MS, Minnjuan Flournoy, MPH, Drew Gerald, MPH, Susan Kelsey, MS, Asole TaQuesa McClain, MA, Selina Hunt McKinney, MSN, Chinelo Ogbuanu, MPH, Tracey Powell, MSW, Wendy Smalls, MA, Lekhena Sros, MPH, Larrell Wilkinson, MSPH, and Brandi Wright, MPH.

We are grateful to Dale Morris for her excellent research assistance. This study was supported by the Centers for Disease Control and Prevention in conjunction with the Association of Schools of Public Health, through the University of South Carolina Center for Public Health Preparedness.

REFERENCES

Association to Advance Collegiate Schools of Business (AACSB International): 2005. Eligibility Procedures and Accreditation Standards for Business Accreditation. Adopted 25 April, 2003; revised 1 January 2005. Available at: http://www.aacsb.edu/accreditation/standards.asp. Accessed 22 January 2005.

Balicer, R.B., Omer, S.B., Barnett, D.J., & Everly, GS, Jr. (2006). Local public health workers' perceptions toward responding to an influenza pandemic. *BMC Public Health, 6,* 99.

Brinkmann, J., & Sims, R.R. (2001). Stakeholder-sensitive business ethics teaching. *Teaching Business Ethics, 5,* 171-193.

Calloway-Graham, D. (2004). The art of teaching and learning. [Presidential Address]. *Social Science Journal, 41,* 689-694.

Clark C.C. (2005). In harm's way: AMA physicians and the duty to treat. *Journal of Medical Philosophy, 30,* 65-87.

Commission on Accreditation of Healthcare Management Education: 2007. Accreditation Criteria, adopted fall 2004. Available at: http://www.cahme.org/. Accessed 6 January 2007.

Forbes, M.S. (1987). Fact and Comment. *Forbes, 140(4),* 17-19.

Hemmasi, M. & Graf, L.A. (1992). Managerial skills acquisition: A case for using business policy simulations. *Simulation & Gaming 23(3),* 298-310.

King R. (2006). Flood-ravaged hospitals are diagnosing their needs for this hurricane season. *New Orleans Times-Picayune,* 27 May 2006.

Laditka, S.B., & Houck, M.M. (2006). Student-developed case studies: An experiential approach for teaching ethics in management. *Journal of Business Ethics, 64,* 157-167.

Laditka, S.B., Laditka, J.N., Cornman, C.B., Davis, C.B., Richter, J.V.E., & Xirasgar, S. (2006). Disaster preparedness in nursing homes: Lessons learned from Hurricane Katrina. Presented at 59th Annual Scientific Meetings of the Gerontological Society of America. Dallas, TX, November 16-20, 2006.

Laditka, S.B., Laditka, J.N., Xirasagar, S., Cornman, C.B., Davis, C.B., & Richter, J.V.E. (2007). Protecting nursing home residents during disasters: an exploratory study from South Carolina. *Prehospital and Disaster Medicine, 22(1),* 46-52.

Laditka, S.B., Laditka, J.N., Xirasagar, S., Cornman, C.B., Davis, C.B., & Richter, J.V.E. (In Press). Providing shelter to nursing home evacuees in disasters: Lessons from Hurricane Katrina. *American Journal of Public Health.*

Luborsky, M. R. (1994). The identification and analysis of themes and patterns. In J. F. Gubrium & A. Sankar (eds.), (pp. 189-210). *Qualitative methods in aging research.* Sage Publications: Thousand Oaks, CA.

McDonald, G.M., & Donleavy, G.D. (1995). Objectives to the Teaching of Business Ethics. *Journal of Business Ethics, 10(1),* 829-835.

Reid, L. (2005). Diminishing returns? Risk and the duty to care in the SARS epidemic. *Bioethics, 19,* 348-361.

Sanyal, R.N. (2000). An experiential approach to teaching ethics in international business. *Teaching Business Ethics, 4,* 137-149.

Sepkowitz, K. (1996a). Occupationally acquired infections in health care workers. Part 1. *Annals of Internal Medicine, 125,* 826-834.

Sepkowitz, K. (1996b). Occupationally acquired infections in health care workers. Part 2. *Annals of Internal Medicine, 125,* 917-928.

Sims, R.R. (2002). Business ethics teaching for effective learning. *Teaching Business Ethics, 6,* 393-410.

Sims, R.R., & Sims, S.J. (1991). Increasing applied business ethics courses in business school curricula. *Journal of Business Ethics, 10,* 211-219.

Stanford Faculty Development Center. Stanford University. Available at: www.standford.edu/group/SFDP/. Accessed July 17, 2004.

U.S. Office of Inspector General. (2006). Nursing home emergency preparedness and response during recent hurricanes. Department of Health and Human Services, OEI-06000020. Available at: http://oig.hhs.gov. Accessed August 18 2006.

Upshur, R. (2006). The role and obligations of health-care workers during an outbreak of pandemic influenza. Project on addressing ethical issues in pandemic influenza planning. Draft paper for working group three (14 September 2006). Available at: http://www.who.int/ethics/influenza_project/en/index.html. Accessed January 19, 2007.

Van Enyde, D.F., & Spencer, R.W. (1988). Lecture versus experiential learning: Their differential effects on long-term memory. *Organizational Behavior, Teaching Review 12,* 52-58.

World Health Organization. (2006). Addressing Ethical Issues in Pandemic Influenza Planning. Available at: http://www.who.int/ethics/influenza_project/en/index.html. Accessed January 19, 2007.

Chapter 3

FACILITATING HARM

Gregory Mellema
Department of Philosophy, Calvin College, Grand Rapids, MI, USA

ABSTRACT

Discussions of moral issues typically concentrate upon situations that are the result of what individuals have done. Much less typical are discussions that focus upon moral agents assisting others in producing wrongdoing. As a result, situations where some agents make it possible or likely for others to cause harm are not as well understood as those standardly treated in the literature. But as the dynamics of decision making in institutions such as corporations become more complex, those producing harm are frequently aided in various ways by what others have done. Codes of criminal conduct specify what qualifies as aiding or abetting in crime, but in the moral realm there remains much uncertainty and confusion about the moral status of one who helps make possible the wrongdoing of another.

In this paper I concentrate upon the notion of facilitating harm. Roughly speaking, one facilitates harm when one makes it more likely that another is able to produce harm. Elsewhere I have analyzed the stronger notion of enabling harm. One enables harm, according to my analysis, just in case one makes it possible for the actions of another to produce harm, and one is aware that one is doing so. And just as facilitating harm is a weaker notion than enabling harm, it is a stronger notion that condoning harm. One who merely condones harm is aware of the relevant actions of another but does not do anything to make the harm produced by the other more likely to occur (or, for that matter, anything to make the harm less likely to occur). Thus, facilitating harm is less serious, morally speaking, than enabling harm, but more serious than condoning harm (where all of these are varieties of complicity in wrongdoing).

Discussions of moral issues typically concentrate upon situations that are the result of what individuals have done. Much less typical are discussions that focus upon moral agents assisting others in producing wrongdoing. As a result, situations where some agents make it possible or likely for others to cause harm are not as well understood as those standardly treated in the literature. But as the dynamics of decision making in institutions such as corporations become more complex, those producing harm are frequently aided in various ways by what others have done. Codes of criminal conduct specify what qualifies as aiding or abetting in crime, but in the moral realm there remains much uncertainty and confusion about the moral status of one who helps make possible the wrongdoing of another.

In this paper I concentrate upon the notion of facilitating harm. Roughly speaking, one facilitates harm when one makes it more likely that another is able to produce harm. Elsewhere I have analyzed the stronger notion of enabling harm. One enables harm, according to my analysis, just in case one makes it possible for the actions of another to produce harm, and one is aware that one is doing so.[1] And just as facilitating harm is a weaker notion than enabling harm, it is a stronger notion that condoning harm. One who merely condones harm is aware of the relevant actions of another but does not do anything to make the harm produced by the other more likely to occur (or, for that matter, anything to make the harm less likely to occur). Thus, facilitating harm is less serious, morally speaking, than enabling harm, but more serious than condoning harm (where all of these are varieties of complicity in wrongdoing).

The key characteristic of facilitating harm is that of making it more likely that another moral agent produces harm. For the sake of simplicity assume that the agent producing harm H is doing so intentionally and has decided to perform a particular action A as a means of bringing about H. Another agent facilitates H, then, by increasing the antecedent likelihood that either A is successfully performed by the agent or that H is brought about by the performance of A, and doing so in a manner that is morally blameworthy. To take a simple example of increasing the likelihood that another's action is successfully performed, a manager in a large financial corporation learns that a co-worker has been dispensing insider information to selected clients and plans to do so again. Other shareholders are harmed by this type of activity, and they will be further harmed if this activity is repeated in the future. The manager could alert federal authorities, or he could alert senior managers in the organization, but he decides to do neither. His decision therefore makes it more likely that further harm will take place because he increases the likelihood that his co-worker once again is able to dispense insider information.

An example in which facilitating harm takes place by way of increasing the likelihood that action A produces harm H involves a sales representative who is making dishonest claims about a product to a customer. A second sales representative overhears the sales pitch, and when the skeptical customer turns to the second sales representative with a look of disbelief regarding these dishonest claims, the customer receives nods of approval from him. On the basis of seeing the second representative expressing tacit agreement with the first she comes to believe that the claims are true, and she purchases the product. In this example the nods of approval make it more likely that the dishonest claims bring about the intended outcome.

The degree of likelihood necessary for qualifying as facilitating harm need only be a value greater than zero. As long as the likelihood of A's being produced by the agent in question is increased by a value greater than zero, or the likelihood that H is brought about by the performance of A is increased by a value greater than zero, the harm has been facilitated.

---

[1] The precise definition of enabling harm is as follows. Suppose that moral agent A intentionally acts in such a way as to cause or produce harmful outcome O. Then moral agent B can be said to enable the production of O just in case A's acts would not produce O were it not for B's action, and B is aware that this action may contribute to O's occurrence. See my article, 'Enabling Harm', *Journal of Social Philosophy*, 32 (2006), pp. 214-220.

Increasing the antecedent likelihood that A is produced or that H is brought about by the performance of A does not require that facilitating harm is causally efficacious. Suppose that in the example of the co-worker dispensing insider information the manager who learns of this activity decides to offer words of encouragement to the co-worker regarding his future activities. He sends the co-worker an e-mail saying that he knows what the co-worker intends to do and that the selected clients in question deserve special treatment. As it happens, the co-worker does not read his e-mail with regularity and does not actually read the e-mail until he has once again dispensed insider information. It might be argued that the e-mail fails to increase the likelihood that A be performed since it was not read until after A's performance. But all that is required of the definition of facilitating harm is that the antecedent likelihood is increased. And this condition is met by the e-mail since the manager knows that the e-mail might be read by the co-worker prior to the performance of A. Prior to the performance of A, it is possible relative to what the manager knows that the e-mail is read by the co-worker and that it influences the co-worker. What happens afterward does nothing to change this fact.

The definition of facilitating harm requires that the harm actually take place. In other words, it is impossible to facilitate harm if no harm actually occurs. Of course, one may set out to facilitate harm and fail to do so. In the example of the deceptive sales representative the customer may end up believing neither sales representative. In this way the one who nods approval with the intent of influencing the customer's beliefs ends up facilitating no harm involving the customer. In such a case he is guilty of no more than attempted facilitation. He has not succeeded in facilitating the customer's being deceived for the simple reason that this does not occur.

It is possible to facilitate a harm H in a manner other than what one intends. Suppose that one believes that a co-worker is planning to perform action B in an effort to bring about H. In an effort to increase the likelihood that B actually takes place, the facilitator performs action C. Unbeknownst to the facilitator, the co-worker is actually planning to perform action A in order to bring about H. Thus, the facilitator's performance of C is based on a misguided notion of the co-worker's intentions. Fortunately, one of the side-effects of performing C is increasing the likelihood of A's performance. Thus, the facilitator is successful after all in increasing the likelihood of A's performance. Intending to increase the likelihood of B's performance, the facilitator succeeds in increasing the likelihood of A's performance.

An example of this phenomenon is as follows. A co-worker wishes to have a copy of a highly classified company document in his home files, a serious breach of company policy. His strategy is to fax the document to a machine located in his home. The facilitator is a friend who knows that the co-worker wishes to have a copy in his home files but mistakenly believes that the co-worker is planning to photocopy the document and take the copy home in his briefcase. Acting toward that end, the facilitator finds the original document in the company files and attempts to photocopy it for the convenience of his friend. Unfortunately, he mistakes the fax machine for the photocopy machine. The co-worker finds him fumbling at the controls of the fax machine and is amazed to find that his own plan to fax the document to his house has just been made so convenient. In addition the co-worker realizes that he might have forgotten to fax it to his house were it not for the actions of the other.

In this example the facilitator sets out to make it more likely that the document will be photocopied, but he ends up making it more likely that the document is faxed to the house of the co-worker. Thus, he still succeeds in facilitating harm, because the co-worker's strategy is to bring about the harm by means of faxing the document to his house. Facilitating harm does not presuppose that one has a perfect grasp of the intentions and purposes of the person producing the harm.

A person who facilitates harm normally does so with the intention that the harm actually takes place. But this is not always the case. In some instances the person facilitating harm might be indifferent as to whether the harm takes place, and in other instances the person might actually prefer that the harm not occur. An example where the person facilitating harm is indifferent to the harm's taking place might be one in which the person's motive is to please another person who is attempting to produce harm. Thus, in the example of the two sales representatives, the one who nods approval might be indifferent as to whether or not the customer believes the claims of the other. The one nodding approval might do so only to curry favor or demonstrate solidarity with the other.

An example where the person facilitating harm might actually wish that the harm not occur might be a situation in which the occurrence of the harm may prevent the occurrence of a greater harm. Imagine a situation where a manager wishes to open a locked file cabinet. He knows two administrative assistants possess keys that will open the locked cabinet, and they keep the keys in their purses. Right now they are both on lunch break and the manager knows that their purses are in locked drawers of their desks. He has keys to open these locked drawers, and he expresses the intention to obtain one of the keys that will open the locked file cabinet. A co-worker tells the manager that it is wrong to look through someone's purse without that person's permission, but the manager will not be dissuaded. He believes that time is of the essence, and he cannot wait for them to return. The co-worker happens to know that one of the administrative assistants has illegal drugs in the locked drawer of her desk, and it would be devastating for the manager to learn that they are there. Consequently, the co-worker suggests to the manager that he open the drawer of the other administrative assistant's desk, and the manager follows his advice.

Here the co-worker facilitates harm because he suggests to the manager that he open the drawer and search the purse of an administrative assistant, where such a search is a clear violation of the employee's privacy. His suggestion increases the likelihood that the manager searches the purse of this employee. At the same time, the co-worker does not desire that this harm take place. On the contrary, the co-worker is upset that an employee's privacy is violated. Therefore, in this scenario the co-worker facilitates harm, but the co-worker nevertheless desires that the harm not occur.

The definition of facilitating harm does not specify that the person facilitating harm does so intentionally or purposefully. It is possible, therefore, that one increase the likelihood that harm will take place (because of the efforts of another) without intending to do so. Suppose that a worker in a lumber yard is loading tools into the trunk of his automobile, tools that belong to the lumber company. Another worker sees what he is doing but thinks nothing of it, because he assumes that the vehicle is a company car and cannot imagine someone employed by the company stealing tools. When the first worker asks him not to say anything to a supervisor, he readily agrees and is initially puzzled as to why he would be asked such a question. Subsequently he comes to believe that the reason he is being asked not to say anything is that the first worker is supposed to be somewhere else at the time.

Without realizing it, the second worker is facilitating harm. By agreeing not to say anything to a supervisor, he is making it more likely that the first worker is successful in stealing tools from the lumber yard. Nevertheless, he is anything but aware that this is what he is doing. He is totally ignorant of the fact that tools are being stolen from company premises, and he is totally ignorant that he is doing anything to facilitate this state of affairs. He is facilitating harm, but is clueless about this fact.

What this shows is that facilitating harm does not always render one morally responsible for the harm one facilitates (the second worker is nevertheless blameworthy for something else, agreeing not to say anything when he believes the first worker is at fault for being in the wrong place). One who facilitates harm in ignorance may be entirely innocent of any moral wrongdoing. At the same time, it is relevant to ask whether the ignorance in question is culpable ignorance. There are situations in which one facilitates harm in ignorance, but one should have been in a position to know that one was facilitating harm. Suppose that the worker stealing tools develops a guilty conscience and decides to tell a fellow worker that he has stolen tools and plans to do so again in the near future. When he begins by announcing that he has done something highly unethical, the fellow worker announces that he doesn't want to hear about it or know anything about it. Subsequently, when this worker sees the other worker loading tools he doesn't know anything wrong is taking place.

Here it is plausible to argue that the ignorance of the second worker is a culpable ignorance, for he was acting irresponsibly in refusing to hear the confessions of his co-worker (see Aristotle, *Nicomachean Ethics,* 1111a 22ff.). Hence, when he subsequently facilitates harm in ignorance, it is not at all clear that he is entirely innocent in his role as facilitator. It is quite reasonable to judge that he bears some degree of responsibility for facilitating harm, even though he does so in ignorance, because his ignorance was itself intentional. What this example shows is that even when one facilitates harm in ignorance, one might still incur moral responsibility.

It is worth noting that moral responsibility is a concept capable of coming in degrees. Other things being equal, one is less responsible for facilitating harm when one does so in ignorance than when one does so knowingly or intentionally. And two moral agents can bear moral responsibility for the same state of affairs but to differing degrees. The agent producing harm, except perhaps in exceptional cases, is more responsible for the occurrence of the harm than another agent who facilitates the harm.

All of the examples presented so far have been cases in which a moral agent facilitates harm by performing an action that makes it more likely that harm will occur as the result of another's action (or that the other's action is successfully performed). I shall now argue that it is possible for a moral agent to facilitate harm through inaction. It is possible, in other words, for a moral agent to facilitate harm through an omission to act (in one of the previous examples someone makes a decision not to take action, but that is not the same thing as plain and simple inaction).

In a large manufacturing company two people are assigned the task of buying materials for the components that are assembled in its several plants. They are expected to purchase materials that are up to code, and they are expected to check up on each other to make sure that this is done. One of the buyers conscientiously and consistently purchases materials that are up to code, but he resents the expectation that he must check up on the other buyer. Consequently, he simply does not do so. It is not that he has made a decision not to do so; he just never checks up on the other purchases initiated by the other buyer. One day the other buyer orders inferior materials that are not up to code, and since the first buyer does not bother to review the order, these materials are in fact ordered. The result is that the products containing these materials are themselves inferior.

What this example shows is that facilitating harm can take place when the facilitator performs no actions that serve to facilitate the harm. All that is required in certain cases is that the facilitator omits to perform an action in order to facilitate harm. When one buyer orders materials that are not up to code, the other buyer's failure to review the order makes it more likely that the products made from these inferior materials are themselves inferior. In this way the other buyer's inaction qualifies as facilitating harm.

Sometimes a moral agent facilitates the facilitating of harm. It is possible, in other words, for Andrew to facilitate Bill's facilitating the harm produced by Charles. Suppose that Charles is a financial officer in a large corporation, and he has recently returned from an out of town business trip. While out of town Charles was able to stay at the home of his friend Andrew for the three nights he was away. Bill, who is another friend of Andrew, works in a large hotel in that city and agrees (as a favor to Andrew, who requested it) to prepare a dummied up hotel receipt showing that Charles stayed at the hotel for those three nights and that he incurred charges of nearly $500. Charles submits the receipt to his company upon returning, and several days later he receives reimbursement for his expenses. The reimbursement includes the amount he allegedly spent at the hotel where Bill is employed.

In this example the company is reimbursing Charles for nearly $500 that he never actually spent. This state of affairs is facilitated by Bill, whose actions make it more likely that Charles is wrongly reimbursed. And what Bill does is in turn facilitated by Andrew, whose actions make it more likely that Bill cooperate in the manner that he does. In this way Andrew facilitates Bill's facilitating the harm produced by Charles.

The discussion up to now has dealt with individuals facilitating harm produced by other individuals. Sometimes harms are produced by two or more agents, and here too it makes sense to speak of someone facilitating harm. In other words, someone can facilitate harm where the same harm is produced by two or more agents. Suppose that two employees are considering playing a very mean practical joke on a co-worker, one that will cause the co-worker to miss a day of work with no pay. Their supervisor learns of this plan, thinks it is a delightful idea, and encourages the two employees to carry it out. Subsequently they do so, and as a result the co-worker misses a day of work. In this example the supervisor makes it more likely that the harm will take place, a harm that is produced by two moral agents, and hence the supervisor facilitates the harm.

Just as one agent can facilitate the harm produced by two or more agents, so more than one agent can facilitate the harm produced by a single agent. A senior level manager in a large corporation wishes to make changes in the company's policy regarding pensions. If it is implemented, the change will make it harder for employees not born in the United States to qualify for the company's plan. The manager decides to take a straw vote among the managers who report to him to determine whether the plan has support. All seven managers indicate that they support the plan. Following this, the manager feels more confident than ever that implementing the plan is a good idea.

Here it is reasonable to hold that the seven managers facilitate the harm that will be experienced by employees (both present and future) not born in the United States. By indicating that they support the plan proposed by the senior level manager, each one makes it more likely that he will decide to implement the plan. No doubt this is the result that was hoped for by the manager, since making the change was what he wished for from the outset. In this manner a group of two or more moral agents can facilitate the harm produced by one person. In addition, it is plausible to judge that they bear at least some measure of moral responsibility for the harm.

The people who belong to a group facilitating the same harm might be under the impression that the responsibility or blame for the harm is diluted as more facilitators are added to the group. They might be tempted to hold that the responsibility for the harm is spread more thinly as additional participants are added. A great many professional people, I believe, are attracted to the spirit of ethical dilutionism, as we might call it. They may be reluctant to make decisions alone, for fear of bearing a greater share of the responsibility for what results from the decisions. Involving other people in decision making feels safer and more comfortable, and an ethical dilutionist perspective seems to play at least part of the role in such a feeling.

In another article I have defended an anti-dilutionist perspective regarding moral responsibility.[2] According to the anti-dilutionist position, as the number of people who are morally responsible for the same state of affairs gets larger, it does not follow that the degree of each person's responsibility gets smaller or is diluted. Moral responsibility cannot be compared to a pie whereby the portions are diminished in size as the number of people sharing the pie gets larger. Someone cannot assume with justification that increasing the number of fellow facilitators will serve to diminish the degree to which he or she bears responsibility for the harm in question.

The anti-dilutionist perspective regarding the degree of a participant P's moral responsibility can be further explained by imagining a possible world very similar to the actual world. In this possible world every facilitator is replaced by an elaborate android or robot performing the actions of the other participants and P is the only moral agent facilitating the outcome. In this world there is no possibility of P's moral responsibility being diluted, because the other facilitators are not moral agents. P is responsible for exactly what he does and what his actions bring about, no more and no less. My suggestion is that P's moral responsibility in the actual world be regarded in the same way. Now if P is coerced or in any manner under the influence of another participant, this fact should be included in a complete description of what P does. But the degree of P's responsibility should not vary according to the sheer number of others who happen to facilitate the same outcome.

At the outset of the paper I contrasted the notion of facilitating harm with the notion of condoning harm. I remarked that when one condones harm one is aware of the relevant actions of another that may produce harm but does not do anything to make the harm more likely to occur. We have seen that facilitating harm can take the form of omitting to act. From this it follows that some overlap exists between facilitating harm and condoning harm. When one facilitates harm by way of inaction, one is strictly speaking not doing anything to make the harm more likely to occur; it is only one's inaction that makes harm more likely to occur.

These thoughts can be expressed in another way. When one condones harm, one does not do anything to make harm more likely to occur. However, it is possible that one's inaction makes the harm more likely to occur, and hence one who condones harm may end up making the harm more likely to occur. In other words, one who condones harm might also facilitate the same harm. Nevertheless, if one who facilitates harm makes a decision not to take action and the ensuing inaction makes the harm more likely to occur, then it is not an instance of

---

[2] 'Shared Responsibility and Ethical Dilutionism', *Australasian Journal of Philosophy*, 63 (1985), pp. 177-187.

condoning harm. In this instance one is doing something that makes the harm more likely to occur.

In addition, one who condones harm does not always facilitate harm through inaction. Recall the example in which one buyer fails to take action when a second buyer orders sub-standard materials. The first buyer facilitates harm because he would make the harm less likely to occur by reporting it to management. Suppose that a custodian happens to be in the room when the second buyer places a telephone call in which he is ordering the materials, and suppose the custodian realizes that sub-standard materials are being ordered. The custodian's failure to report this matter to management counts as facilitating harm only if there is some likelihood that the harm would thereby be subverted by the failure to report it. If, on the other hand, management (or anyone else in a position to prevent the harm from occurring) would dismiss the report of a custodian as a mere annoyance, the inaction counts only as condoning harm. What this shows is that, although there is some overlap between condoning harm and facilitating harm through inaction, the category of condoning harm is certainly not completely swallowed up by the category of facilitating harm through inaction. Sometimes it is not in one's power to affect the likelihood of preventing harm brought about by another, and when this happens one's inaction counts as condoning harm, not facilitating harm.

In my treatment of facilitating harm through inaction, someone might suppose that it has been my tacit assumption that one makes it more likely for harm to occur if one fails to do something that makes it less likely for the same harm to occur. But this assumption is open to question in part because there are many ways to fail to do something that makes it less likely for harm to occur. Some of these ways involve the failure to perform a routine action such as reporting something to a supervisor, and others involve failing to perform actions that necessitate a great deal of time and effort, such as traveling to an African nation and trying to convince authorities that a political prisoner is being held unjustly (where there is a slight likelihood that one's pleading will actually result in the prisoner's being freed). According to the account so far presented, the failure to travel to Africa and undertake to have the political prisoner freed might appear to count as facilitating harm. But that seems counter-intuitive, and for this reason it is prudent to call into question the principle that one makes it more likely for harm to occur if one fails to do something that makes it less likely for the same harm to occur.

When one fails to do something that makes an outcome less likely to occur, I believe that it does not follow that one's failure makes the outcome more likely to occur. Examples such as that of the two buyers might tempt one to suppose that the inference is valid, because in this example the failure to make it less likely for the outcome to occur serves to make the outcome more likely to occur. If one buyer reported to management that the other buyer was ordering sub-standard materials, then management would step in and prevent the order from being placed (or, if it were already placed, to contact the vendor and have the order cancelled). The truth of this counter-factual supports the truth of the proposition that the harm is more likely to occur if the buyer does not report that the other buyer is ordering sub-standard materials.

If the custodian, on the other hand, reported to management that sub-standard materials were being ordered, management may well not elect to step in and prevent the order from being place. If this is true, then (supposing there are no alternative channels by which the custodian could prevent the harm) the inaction of the custodian does not cause the outcome to be more likely to occur. The inaction of the custodian has no affect upon the likelihood of the harm's taking place.

Robert Stalnaker has proposed truth conditions for counter-factual propositions as follows: A counter-factual proposition is true if and only if it is true in the closest possible world (the world most closely resembling) to the actual world.[3] That is to say, a counter-factual proposition of the form, if P were true, then Q would be true, is itself true if and only if Q is true in the closest possible world in which P is true.

Suppose that in the closest possible world to the actual world in which the custodian reports the sub-standard materials to management, management does nothing to prevent the harm (in fact, in this world there is not even any likelihood that management prevents harm). Then the following counter-factual proposition is false: If the custodian were to report to management that sub-standard materials were being ordered, then management would prevent the harm from occurring. Consequently, the custodian condones harm through inaction but does not facilitate harm through inaction. The closest possible world in which one buyer reports that the other buyer is ordering sub-standard materials, on the other hand, will also be a world in which management steps in to prevent the harm. Thus, a buyer facilitates harm through inaction because the following counter-factual proposition is true: If a buyer were to report that the other buyer is ordering sub-standard materials, management would step in to prevent the harm. In fact, facilitating harm in this example requires an even weaker counter-factual: If a buyer were to report that the other buyer is ordering sub-standard materials, it is likely that management would step in to prevent harm.

In this paper I have concentrated upon the notion of facilitating harm, a concept that is weaker than that of enabling harm but stronger than that of condoning harm (although there is a bit of overlap between facilitating harm and condoning harm). I have characterized facilitating harm as increasing the likelihood that the harm takes place through the actions of another. More specifically, if an action of another brings about harm, then one facilitates the harm either by making more likely that the action is performed or by making it more likely that the action produce the harm. The dynamics of decision making in modern organizations are increasingly complex, and members of these organizations frequently seem confused or uncertain about the moral status of their involvement in a course of action that a co-worker is initiating. My suggestion is that if one clarifies the notions of enabling harm, facilitating harm, and condoning harm, one will be in a better position to gauge the seriousness of one's involvement when someone else is the primary actor. In this essay I hope to have offered a clear account of what it means to facilitate harm, and I hope to have indicated the contrast between enabling harm and facilitating harm, on the one hand, and the contrast between facilitating harm and condoning harm on the other.

---

[3] Robert Stalnaker, 'A Theory of Conditionals', in *Studies in Logical Theory*, ed., Nicholas Rescher, Blackwell, 1968.

In: Business Ethics in Focus
Editor: Laura A. Parrish, pp. 79-91

ISBN: 978-1-60021-684-8
© 2007 Nova Science Publishers, Inc.

Chapter 4

MACRO VERSUS MICRO ETHICAL DILEMMAS: UNDERSTANDING ETHICS ON A SMALLER SCALE

Susan Fredricks[*]
Penn State University Delaware County,
25 Yearsley Mill Road, Media, PA 19063, USA

Andrea Hornett[†]
Penn State University Great Valley, School of Graduate and Professional Studies
30 East Swedesford Road, Malvern, PA 19355-1443, USA

ABSTRACT

Learning ethics can be assisted by a focus on everyday mundane matters. Experience with students and prior research suggests that students readily engage in ethical discernment when they can comprehend a connection between the situation and themselves or their families. This chapter presents research with both graduate and undergraduate business and communications students who change their responses to ethical dilemmas when the scenarios are repeated with the addition of a relationship or connection.

Respondents change their proposed course of action when family is present. Consistent with Gilligan (1982), females perceive relationship and take action more readily. However, males will chose an ethical approach to a situation when family relationships are specifically introduced. The conclusion is that with a perceived relationship, ethical choices are made.

The use of 'micro' ethical scenarios, everyday dilemmas, may offer the basis for a more effective ethical pedagogy than reliance on the 'macro' scenarios or less immediate and more abstract situations from the news or from traditional ethical pedagogy. In addition, more research is needed on ethical reasoning and the non-cognitive motivators of ethical discernment.

---

[*] Tel: 610-892-1373; smf17@psu.edu
[†] 610-648-3241; axh45@psu.edu

INTRODUCTION

We have seen enormous ethical challenges in recent years. Everything from the collapse of many telecoms and Enron to the jailing of Martha Stewart has become fodder for case study material on ethics. Organizations, business schools, and educators (Cagle & Baucus, 2006; Hudson & Miller, 2005; Kienzler & David, 2003) are embracing these 'macro' examples of ethical dilemmas to prove points and to drive home to employees and students that ethical behaviors are a requirement.

Do these macro examples of unethical behavior really teach others, especially those seemingly untouched by most scandals, to behave ethically? Can the collapse of a company based in Texas, impact those not in Texas? Perhaps the answer to solid ethical pedagogy lies not in teaching from these 'macro' examples but in assisting students with the 'micro' dilemmas that can affect anyone on a daily basis and lead to a slippery slope.

'Micro' ethical dilemmas are those daily situations to which we respond with denial or little white lies in the interest of harmony. Pedagogically, they can provide a buy-in, an opportunity for students to cognitively discern behavior, or an opportunity to apply moral codes. Our teaching experiences suggest that once students learn from a micro ethical dilemma, they may become better able to apply ethics to the macro level.

The purpose of this chapter is to consider nascent research regarding when and how ethical discernment and ethical action in mundane pedestrian situations (micro) may be something other than an aspect of cognitive maturation (Kohlberg et al., 1983). Then, we consider some implications of those findings for those of us teaching and learning ethics.

ETHICS PEDAGOGY

We agree that "ethics courses ... can be unwieldy" (Fort & Zollers, 1999), because the theory base of such courses is fraught with choices, polarities or paradoxes (Table 1).

As Table 1 suggests, instructors are divided between emphasizing the classics (Aristotle) and challenging students with idealistic ethical views, or allowing a pragmatic view that relies on Friedman's (1961) exhortation for maximizing shareholder value. Should students be given issues they can address through maximization of self-interest or should there be attempts to acculturate a sense of communitarianism? Should they learn to make 'right' decisions or should they learn to make optimal decisions (Sims & Felton, 2006)? Should instructors assume that students' discernment processes are rational and developmental or should they accept that students' judgments will reflect what is normative for society, particularly their age group? Perhaps some students will operate out of an orientation toward caring (Gilligan, 1982) and relationship.

How experiential should ethics classes be (Bean & Aquila, 2003; Sims, 2002; Sims & Felton, 2006; Solberg et al., 1995)? Should they focus on ethical thinking (the discernment process) or should they simulate ethical choice (taking action)?

In addition to these polarizing questions illustrated in Table 1, the roots of ethical pedagogy are found in several disciplines; for example, economics (Kulshreshtha, 2005) with models and heuristics to maximize value, or social construction (Berger & Luckman, 1966) approaches that view businesses as co-creations of members expressing their values, or the liberal arts (Kennedy & Lawton, 1992). Somewhere, perhaps in the middle (Gibbs, 2003; Kanjirathinkal, 1990; Power et al., 1989; Reimer et al., 1983; Schrader, 1990), is the split in psychology between Kohlberg (Kohlberg et al., 1983) and his research identifying the developmental stages of ethical reasoning and Gilligan (1982) with her non-cognitive aspect of moral reasoning based on relationship.

Finally, there are the dilemmas about delivery: should the pedagogical approach be learner-centered (Fornari, 2006), simulated (Schumann et al., 1997; White & Dooley, 1993), industry-specific and derived from structuration theory (Yuthas & Dillard, 1999), or built from an interdisciplinary 'canon' of ethics literature (George, 1988) and geared toward today's world (Quinn, 2004)?

Regardless of which choices an instructor makes after sorting through this garden of confusion (Adams et al., 1998), the published offerings are essentially based on one of two approaches: (1) moral philosophy predicated on what suits character development and the stability of the state, or (2) research designed by experts where subjects choose between or respond to previously constructed dilemmas or questions. We explored a different path.

Table 1. Conflicts and Polarities in Ethical Pedagogy

Ontology / Epistemology:	*On the one hand:*	*On the other hand:*
Theoretical Roots:	Economic Rationality	Social Construction
Social Orientation:	Self Interest	Community Interest
Discernment Process:	Rational / Cognitive/ Rule-based Normative	Social Contract / Caring / Group-based Normative
Philosophy:	Realistic Utilitarian	Idealistic Aristotelian

LESSONS FROM THE FIELD

Our research with undergraduate students (Hornett & Fredricks, 2005) led us to abandon the abstractions presented by macro cases in order to assess the value in micro situations for creating ethical action. In accordance with recommended practices for interpretive research (Babbie, 1998; Lincoln & Guba, 1985; Yin, 1994), we identified some aspects of ethical reasoning that were emergent from papers and presentations by undergraduates at two separate schools over a period of years (Hornett & Fredricks, 2005). The students refrained from condemning as unethical someone who has positive homey qualities that they valued. For example, they considered John Rigas of Adelphia a good father and Jack Welch of G.E. a real business leader, despite the excesses of his retirement. They admired Dennis Kozlowski of Tyco for staying on good terms with his ex-wife. They disconnected the deed from the doer and did not condemn even those who are already convicted (e.g. WorldCom and Enron executives). A 'one-universe' sensitivity, where people view everything as being connected, is attractive but it is not evident in our research. Our research participants report that the ethical discernment process privileges 'me and mine.' They take action to redress ethical issues when family may be involved. Otherwise, they remain relatively passive.

In accordance with theory (Kohlberg et al., 1983) we assumed that they lacked cognitive development and higher levels of reasoning but then we took another look at what the students were telling us. When analyzing a macro case (e.g. Boeing) students readily discerned the ethical issues because they had family or neighbors employed there, a micro view. Apparently, they did possess the cognitive ability to engage in ethical discernment; however, this ability was only activated when they had a relationship to the case at the micro level. In addition, when given ethical issues of a micro nature to consider in class, they readily discerned the problem and selected a course of action. We decided to explore what the students were telling us by examining kinship connections and micro issues in further research.

Research at the 'Micro' Level

Initially, we decided to try an experiment using the values the students were communicating to us in their class papers and presentations, and through videotaped discussions. We proposed to use their own values to try to change their thinking from non-involvement to ethical action. In other words, we developed an experiment to test whether students would or could move from passive observers to active ethical leadership.

The Experiment

As we looked for some way to develop ethical discernment in our students, we decided to base our pedagogy on the primary value that they were communicating to us: family matters. They expressed admiration for John Rigas of Adelphia for employing his children (Moules & Larsen, 2002). They admired Sam Waksal of Imclone for crying because his actions involved his father and his daughter in his scandal. They saw "family" as a more important value than "ethics." Accordingly, we hypothesized that students will make definitive judgments in ethical scenarios that include a family relationship or connection to themselves. Therefore, we began by using a sample questionnaire conducted through web-based technology to engage students in ethical decision-making in an interactive way. This sample involved twenty-five students that tested two ethical dilemmas. We further refined our sample questionnaire to the scenarios employed in this research.

The current scenarios posed an ethical dilemma from a real situation that both we and some of our students had experienced. Then, we altered the scenario to make an explicit relationship between the student's family and the situation. We hypothesized that where students could select their course of action we would have created an action learning (Marquardt, 1999) environment and possibly a basis for improved leadership pedagogy.

Scenarios 1 and 2

The scenarios what were developed are as follows:

Scenario 1:
You are shopping at the local supermarket and are second in line at the checkout. The man in front of you has emptied his cart on the conveyor belt. You start to empty your cart and notice that he has a package of chicken hidden. The cashier does not notice. What do you do?

- Nothing
- Speak to the man
- Speak to the cashier
- Other

Scenario 2:
You are shopping at the local supermarket and are second in line at the check out. The man in front of you has emptied his cart on the conveyor belt. You start to empty your cart and notice that he has a package of chicken hidden. The cashier does not notice. Your closest relative is the manager of the meat department in this store and personally pays for inventory shortages. What do you do?

- Nothing
- Speak to the man
- Speak to the cashier
- Other

The differences between the two scenarios, the addition of a personal attachment and financial loss from the first scenario to the second scenario, provides an opportunity for students to pose different reactions to the each scenario.

Conducting the Questionnaire

We created paper copies of the scenarios (Appendix 1) and distributed them to both graduate and undergraduate students in either business or communication classes at two northeastern university campuses. The questionnaires were conducted through three semesters, Fall, Summer, and Spring sessions. Students were told that they could fill out the questionnaire only if they felt inclined; there were no extra credit points awarded for responding. All questionnaires would be anonymous in nature, but not confidential because we would share our findings. Students were allowed to complete the survey only once to ensure there would be no repeat responders. The following findings illustrate how the students reacted to each scenario.

Table 2. Frequency Distribution for Scenario I

Choice	*Frequency*	*Valid Percent*	*Cumulative Percent*
Nothing	48	41.7	41.7
Speak to the man	44	38.3	80.0
Speak to the cashier	6	5.2	85.2
Other	17	14.8	100.0
Total	115	100.0	

Table 3. Frequency Distribution for Scenario II

Choice	*Frequency*	*Valid Percent*	*Cumulative Percent*
Nothing	7	6.3	6.3
Speak to the man	67	60.4	66.7
Speak to the cashier	17	15.3	82.0
Other	20	18.0	100.00
Missing	4		
Total	115	100.0	

FINDINGS

The survey was administered to graduate and undergraduate classes in business or communications. A total of 115 students responded to the first scenario, 111 students responded to the second scenario with four students providing incomplete information. Table 2 illustrates the basic frequencies for the respondents' choices for Scenario I.

As the frequencies indicate, most respondents chose to do nothing (41.7%) when faced with this ethical dilemma. The second most frequent choice was to speak to the man (38.3%). The final two options of speak to the cashier was the last one chosen (5.2%) while the doing something other was the third choice (14.8%). The 'other' category ranged from saying something out loud but not in a confrontational style to saying something at the customer service desk.

Table 3 shows that Scenario II yielded the following frequencies for the four choices. In these frequencies, the respondents overwhelming chose to take action, either speak to the man (60.4%) or speak to the cashier (15.3%). When a family relationship is introduced, 'Doing nothing' changes to the least preferred option, decreasing from 41.7% in the first scenario to 6.3% in the second.

Based upon the research of Kohlberg and Gilligan, we decided to test the demographics of our sample to see if gender or age/status in school would yield better insight into the choices made. Demographic information including gender and year in school is provided in the Appendix in tables 4, 5, 6, and 7 for Scenarios I and II.

Overall, more males (n=62) than females (n=53) responded to the scenarios consistent with the demographics of the classes. The findings for gender show that most of the males (48.4%) chose to do nothing in Scenario I while most of the females (39.6%) chose to speak to the man. The second preference for the males was to speak to the man (37.1%) while the women chose the inaction step of doing nothing (34.0%). Two males and two females are missing responses to Scenario II. This was due to misinformation or incorrect responses. Scenario II yielded different results for males, more so than females. Most males decided to speak to the man (63.3%) over any other choice. Females still chose to speak to the man (56.9%) over any other choice, with eight more female respondents making this selection than did in response to Scenario I. In response to Scenario II, both genders selected doing nothing the least amount (males - 6.7% and females - 5.9%).

Most of the respondents were graduate students (n=48) followed by undergraduate seniors (n=30). Undergraduate juniors represented the third largest (n=23) and first year (n=8) and sophomore (n=6) followed. For Scenario I, at four of the five levels, the respondents chose to do nothing; 37.5% graduates, 46.7% seniors, 43.5% juniors, and 83.3% sophomores. Only the first-year class chose to speak to the man (62.5%) the first time over other choices and they stayed with this choice when the scenario changed. The other levels changed in Scenario II to the choice 'speak to the man' (graduate - 59.1%; senior - 73.3%; junior - 47.8%; sophomore - 50.0%; first-year - 62.5%).

Limitations to the Survey

As with all surveys, the one tested in this study is weak on validity but strong on reliability. The artificiality of scenarios (as opposed to real dilemmas) and the attempt to have the respondents change decisions affects the validity. Simply having respondents read about ethical dilemmas may make them more responsive than in real situations. In addition, this idea of measuring ethical decisions may not be amicable to study through questionnaires. To help alleviate this limitation in validity, the scenarios were developed through a variety of pilot tests before putting them forward as a survey to respondents.

However, by presenting a standardized survey to the 115 respondents, we were able to increase the reliability over observation techniques. In addition, we focused on careful wording of the survey (Babbie, 1998) to increase the reliability of this methodology.

INTERPRETATION OF FINDINGS

Our methodology differs from Gilligan and from Kohlberg because we did not construct an ethical dilemma for participants to consider. We utilized an ethical issue from the students' and our own direct experience. However, our results are consistent with Gilligan because our findings suggest that ethical discernment is not a purely cognitive process, as Kohlberg found, but one that is triggered by relationship, specifically in this case by a kinship relationship. Without a relationship, participants (with the exception of Freshmen) tended to avoid ethical action. When a relationship is introduced into the same scenario, participants chose ethical action. Accordingly, this research suggests that students will practice ethical actions when they apprehend that possible injustice and monetary penalty will occur to someone in a relationship with them. When they do not perceive a relationship, they do not choose to pursue a course of action that could be labeled ethical.

In our previous research (Hornett & Fredricks, 2005), the various corporate scandals (e.g. Enron, WorldCom, etc.) involved business leaders who did not see a direct connection between their practices and potential injustice to others. Indeed, the telecoms engaged in a group behavior that for a short period seemed to benefit them all before it imploded. It may be that at the executive level the motivations for action found at the micro level cannot pertain. More research is needed.

CONCLUSIONS

People identify ethical actions when they are motivated to do so by a relationship to those who may suffer an injustice. Women may perceive a relationship more readily than men but without a perceived relationship, ethical action may not occur. Therefore, ethical discernment appears to be primarily motivated by relationship and may be as much a function of evolutionary psychology as developmental psychology.

In the earlier days of capitalism and industrialization, localization provided opportunities for caretaking, albeit imperfectly and leading to the rise of unionization and governmental regulation. In today's knowledge society with its global dispersion of workers and work, where is the connection between self and society? Work and home are separated despite the anomalies of home-based businesses and telecommuting. When business leaders advise: "It's not personal, it's just business" can we agree? Can we accept an absence of relationship when we have preliminary findings that relationship may motivate ethical conduct?

Much more research is needed: why are some CEOs oriented towards caretaking and other not? Why do some employees prefer the ethic of non-involvement? What other values are in play that are preferred over ethical conduct and why? Is individual survival the only moral imperative of the knowledge worker society? Can more emphasis and experience with micro ethical issues build stronger ethical practices and extend to discernment and action with regard to macro issues? In the meantime, ethical pedagogy may benefit by starting where the students are.

APPENDIX I: PENN STATE SCENARIO SURVEY

Please check the box that best answers the question.

1. Are you currently a full-time or part-time student? (Check one)
   ☐ Full-time student
   ☐ Part-time student

2. What is your current status? (Check one)
   ☐ First-Year Student
   ☐ Sophomore
   ☐ Junior
   ☐ Senior
   ☐ Graduate Student

3. Please indicate your major or area of study. _____

4. Gender:	☐ Male	☐ Female

The following scenarios ask for your choice on how you would handle a particular situation. Please read each scenario and then check the box that best fits your answer. After certain scenarios there will be open-ended questions for you to answer. Please do your best in providing as much information as possible. Thank you for your time.

Scenario I

You are shopping at the local supermarket and are second in line at the check out. The person in front of you has emptied their cart on the conveyor belt. You start to empty your cart and notice that they have a package of chicken hidden. The cashier does not notice.

5. What do you do?
   ☐ Nothing
   ☐ Speak to the person
   ☐ Speak to the cashier
   ☐ Other, please explain: _____

Scenario II

You are shopping at the local supermarket and are second in line at the check out. The person in front of you has emptied their cart on the conveyor belt.

You start to empty your cart and notice that they have a package of chicken hidden. The cashier does not notice.

Your closest relative is the manager of the meat department in this store and personally pays for inventory shortages.

6. What do you do?
   ☐ Nothing
   ☐ Speak to the person
   ☐ Speak to the cashier
   ☐ Other, please explain: _____

---

7. Have you changed your answer from Scenario I to Scenario II?
   ☐ Yes (Go to #8)
   ☐ No (Go to #9)

8. If Yes, Why? (Please explain with as much detail as possible): _____

9. If No, Why not? (Please explain with as much detail as possible): _____

APPENDIX II

Table 4. Frequency Distributions of Scenario I by Gender

Gender	Scenario I Nothing	Speak to the man	Speak to the cashier	Other	Total
Male Count	30	23	2	7	62
% within Gender	48.4	37.1	3.2	11.3	100.0
% within Scenario	62.5	52.3	33.3	41.2	53.9
% of Total	26.1	20.0	1.7	6.1	53.9
Female Count	18	21	4	10	53
% within Gender	34.0	39.6	7.5	18.9	100.0
% within Scenario	37.5	47.7	66.7	58.8	46.1
% of Total	15.7	18.3	3.5	8.7	46.1
Total Count	48	44	6	17	115
% within Gender	41.7	38.3	5.2	14.8	100.0
% within Scenario	100.0	100.0	100.0	100.0	100.0
% of Total	41.7	38.3	5.2	14.8	100.0

Table 5. Frequency Distribution of Scenario II by Gender

Gender	Scenario II Nothing	Speak to the man	Speak to the cashier	Other	Total
Male Count	4	38	9	9	60
% within Gender	6.7	63.3	15.0	15.0	100.0
% within Scenario	57.1	56.7	52.9	45.0	54.1
% of Total	3.6	34.2	8.1	8.1	54.1
Female Count	3	29	8	11	51
% within Gender	5.9	56.9	15.7	21.6	100.0
% within Scenario	42.9	43.3	47.1	55.0	45.9
% of Total	2.7	26.1	7.2	9.9	45.9
Total Count	7	67	17	20	111
% within Gender	6.3	60.4	15.3	18.0	100.0
% within Scenario	100.0	100.0	100.0	100.0	100.0
% of Total	6.3	60.4	15.3	18.0	100.0

Table 6. Frequency Distribution of Scenario I by Status

Status	Scenario I Nothing	Speak to the man	Speak to the cashier	Other	Total
First Year Count	1	5	0	2	8
% within Status	12.5	62.5	0	25.0	100.0
% within Scenario	2.1	11.4	0	11.8	7.0
% of total	.9	4.3	0	1.7	7.0

Sophomore Count	5	1	0	0	6
% within Status	83.3	16.7	0	0	100.0
% within Scenario	10.4	2.3	0	0	5.2
% of total	4.3	.9	0	0	5.2
Junior Count	10	6	2	5	23
% within Status	43.5	26.1	8.7	21.7	100.0
% within Scenario	20.8	13.6	33.3	29.4	20.0
% of total	8.7	5.2	1.7	4.3	20.0
Senior Count	14	12	0	4	30
% within Status	46.7	40.0	0	13.3	100.0
% within Scenario	29.2	27.3	0	23.5	26.1
% of total	12.2	10.4	0	3.5	26.1
Graduate Count	18	20	4	6	48
% within Status	37.5	41.7	8.3	12.5	100.0
% within Scenario	37.5	45.5	66.7	35.3	41.7
% of total	15.7	17.4	3.5	5.2	41.7
Total Count	48	44	6	17	115
% within Status	41.7	38.3	5.2	14.8	100.0
% within Scenario	100.0	100.0	100.0	100.0	100.0
% of total	41.7	38.3	5.2	14.8	100.0

Table 7. Frequency Distribution of Scenario II by Status

Status	Scenario II Nothing	Speak to the man	Speak to the cashier	Other	Total
First Year Count	0	5	0	3	8
% within Status	0	62.5	0	37.5	100.0
% within Scenario	0	7.5	0	15.0	7.0
% of total	0	4.5	0	2.7	7.0
Sophomore Count	1	3	1	1	6
% within Status	16.7	50.0	16.7	16.7	100.0
% within Scenario	14.3	4.5	5.9	5.0	5.4
% of total	.9	2.7	.9	.9	5.4
Junior Count	1	11	4	7	23
% within Status	4.3	47.8	17.4	30.4	100.0
% within Scenario	14.3	16.4	23.5	35.0	20.7
% of total	.9	9.9	3.6	6.3	20.7
Senior Count	1	22	2	5	30
% within Status	3.3	73.3	6.7	16.7	100.0
% within Scenario	14.3	32.8	11.8	25.0	27.0
% of total	.9	19.8	1.8	4.5	27.0
Graduate Count	4	26	10	4	44
% within Status	9.1	59.1	22.7	9.1	100.0
% within Scenario	57.1	38.8	58.8	20.0	39.6
% of total	3.6	23.4	9.0	3.6	39.6
Total Count	7	67	17	20	111
% within Status	6.3	60.4	15.3	18.0	100.0
% within Scenario	100.0	100.0	100.0	100.0	100.0
% of total	6.3	60.4	15.3	18.0	100.0

REFERENCES

Adams, J.S., Harris, C. & Carley, S.S. (1998). Challenges in teaching business ethics: Using role set analysis of early career dilemmas. *Journal of Business Ethics, 17*, 12: 1325-1335.

Babbie, E. (1998). *The Practice of Social Research.* New York: Wadsworth Publishing.

Bean, D.F. & D'Aquila, J.M. (2003). Accounting students as surrogates for accounting professionals when studying ethical dilemmas: A cautionary note. *Teaching Business Ethics, 7*, 3: 187-204.

Berger, P.L., & Luckman, T. (1966). *The social construction of reality: a treatise in the sociology of knowledge.* Garden City, NY: Doubleday.

Cagle, J.A.B. & Baucus, M.S. (2006). Case studies of ethics scandals: Effects on ethical perceptions of Finance students. *Journal of Business Ethics, 64*: 213-229.

Fornari, A. (2006). Developing an ethics curriculum using learner-centered pedagogy. *The Internet Journal of Allied Health Sciences and Practice*, 4, 2: 1-6.

Fort, T.L. & Zollers, F.E. (1999). Teaching business ethics: Theory and practice. *Teaching Business Ethics, 2*: 273-290.

Friedman, M. (1961). *Capitalism and freedom.* Chicago: University of Chicago Press.

George, R.J. (1988). The challenge of preparing ethically responsible managers: Closing the rhetoric-reality gap. *Journal of Business Ethics, 7*, 9: 715-720.

Gibbs, J.C. (2003). *Moral development & reality: Beyond the theories of Kohlberg and Hoffman.* Thousand Oaks: Sage.

Gilligan, C. (1982; 1993). *In a different voice: Psychological theory and women's development.* Cambridge, MA: Harvard University Press.

Hackman, M.Z. & Johnson, C. E. (2000, 3rd Ed.). *Leadership: A communication perspective.* Prospect Heights, Illinois: Waveland Press, Inc.

Hornett, A. & Fredricks, S. (2005). An empirical and theoretical exploration of disconnections between leadership and ethics. *Journal of Business Ethics, 59*: 233-246.

Hudson, S. & Miller, G. (2005). Ethical orientation and awareness of tourism students. *Journal of Business Ethics, 62*: 383-396.

Kanjirathinkal, M.J. (1990). *A sociological critique of theories of cognitive development: The limitations of Piaget and Kohlberg.* Lewiston, N.Y.: The Edwin Mellen Press.

Kennedy, E.J. & Lawton, L. (1992). Business ethics in fiction. *Journal of Business Ethics, 11*, 3: 187-195.

Kienzler, D. & David, C. (2003). After Enron: Integrating ethics into the professional communications curriculum. *Journal of Business and Technical Communication, 17*, 4: 474-489.

Kohlberg, L., Levine, C. & Hewer, A. (1983). *Moral stages: A current formulation and a response to critics.* New York: Karger.

Kulshreshtha, P. (2005). Business ethics versus economic incentives: Contemporary issues and dilemmas. *Journal of Business Ethics, 60*: 393-410.

Lincoln, Y.S., & Guba, E.G. (1985). *Naturalistic inquiry.* Beverly Hills, CA: Sage Publications.

Marquardt, M. (1999). *Action learning in action.* Palo Alto, CA: Davies-Black.

Moules, J. & Larsen, T. (2002). Rigas' allegations: Adelphia boss charged with orchestrating one of the most extensive frauds at a public U.S. company. *Financial Times (London), July 25*: 2.

Power, F.C., Higgins, A. & Kohlberg, L. (1989). *Lawrence Kohlberg's approach to moral education*. New York: Columbia University Press.

Quinn, M.J. (2004). *Ethics for the information age*. Boston: Pearson Addison/Wesley

Reimer, J., Paolitto, D.P. & Hersh, R.H. (1983, 2nd Ed.). *Promoting moral growth: From Piaget to Kohlberg*. Illinois: Waveland Press.

Schrader, D. (Ed.) (1990). The legacy of Lawrence Kohlberg. San Francisco: Jossey-Bass.

Schumann, P.L., Anderson, P.H. & Scott, T.W. (1997). Using computer-based simulation exercises to teach business ethics. *Teaching Business Ethics, 1*: 163-181.

Sims, R.R. (2002). Business ethics for effective learning. *Teaching Business Ethics, 6*, 4: 393-410.

Sims, R.R. & Felton, E.L. Jr. (2006). Designing and delivering business ethics teaching and learning. *Journal of Business Ethics, 63*: 297-312.

Solberg, J. Stong, K.C. & McGuire, C. (1995). Living (not learning) ethics. *Journal of Business Ethics, 14*, 1:71-82.

White, C.S. & Dooley, R.S. (1993). Ethical or practical: An empirical study of students' choices in simulated business scenarios. *Journal of Business Ethics, 12*, 8: 643-651.

Yin, R.K. (1994, 2nd Ed.). Case study research: Design and Methods. Thousand Oaks: Sage. Applied Social Research Methods Series, Vol. 5.

Yuthas, K. & Dillard, J. (1999). Teaching ethical decision making: Adding a structuration dimension. *Teaching Business Ethics, 3*, 4: 339-361.

Chapter 5

CONTEXT AND WHISTLE-BLOWING

Janne Chung[1*]*, Gary S. Monroe*[2†] *and Linda Thorne*[1‡]

[1]Schulich School of Business, York University, 4700 Keele St.,
Toronto M3J 1P3, Canada
[2]School of Business and Information Management,
Australian National University, Canberra, ACT 0200, Australia

ABSTRACT

Our study uses an experiment to investigate three important contextual factors associated with individuals' tendency to whistle-blow: internal versus external whistle-blowing, rule-based or principle-based climate, and power of the wrongdoer. As predicted, individuals are more likely to whistle-blow internally than externally and they are more likely to whistle-blow in a principle-based organizational climate compared to a rule-based organizational climate. Furthermore, individuals are more likely to whistle-blow on a less powerful wrongdoer compared to a more powerful wrongdoer, but only if the complaint recipient is within the organization. The paper concludes with a discussion on the implications of these findings for theory and practice.

Keywords: principle-based, rule-based, organizational climate, power of the wrongdoer, internal control weakness, complaint recipient

INTRODUCTION

Alleged wrongdoings by corporate executives abound after the recent Enron and Worldcom scandals. In both instances, corporate executives internal to the corporation blew the whistle on their superiors - Sherron Watkins of Enron and Cynthia Cooper of WorldCom. However, unlike the whistle-blowing behavior displayed by these two courageous women,

---

[*] Data for correspondence: Tel: 1-416 736 2100 ext 77930; Fax: 1-416 736 5687; Email: jchung@schulich.yorku.ca
[†] Tel: 61-2-6125 5906; Fax: 61-2-6125 5005; Email: gary.monroe@anu.edu.au
[‡] Tel: 1-416 736 2100 ext 30223; Fax: 1-416 736 5687; Email: lthorne@schulich.yorku.ca

other executives did not. In fact, the known behavior of Andersen's (Enron's and WorldCom's auditor) employees appears to be the opposite. Not only did Andersen's employees not whistle-blow, instead, they assisted in covering up wrongdoing by Enron's executives and failed to identify the seriousness of the transgressions. During Andersen's trial for obstruction of justice, evidence produced by the prosecution showed that on the instructions of the partner-in-charge, certain Andersen audit managers encouraged other employees to dispose of evidence concerning Enron (Toffler and Reingold, 2003). Court evidence also showed that some employees made light of the destruction of documents and joked about the lack of shredding bags (see for example, Forbes, March 2002). This raises the question what factors contributed to individuals' propensity to blow the whistle on these infamous transgressions.

Whistle-blowing is "the disclosure by organization members (former or current) of illegal, immoral, or illegitimate practices under the control of their employers, to persons or organizations that may be able to effect action" (Miceli and Near, 1992, 4). Although some researchers have identified individual characteristics that influence individuals' propensity to whistle-blow (Arnold and Ponemon, 1991; Hooks et al., 1994; Finn, 1995; Jones et al., 2003), much remains to be learned about what contextual factors influence individuals' propensity to whistle-blow.

In light of this gap, our study considers the effects of three contextual factors, which appear to be salient in light of recent infamous corporate transgressions, on individuals' propensity to whistle-blow: 1) internal versus external whistle-blowing, 2) rule-based versus principle-based organizational climates and 3) power of the wrongdoer. First, we consider individuals' tendency to whistle-blow internally compared to their tendency to whistle-blow externally. Organizations prefer to see whistle-blowing about valid allegations pass through internal channels so that wrong doings can be corrected and prevented in the future, and so that the organization's "dirty linen" is not aired in public (Near and Miceli, 1985). As a result, there may be more pressure to internally whistle-blow than to externally whistle-blow. Accordingly, we consider the relative likelihood of individuals to whistle-blow internally compared to externally.

Second, rule-based organizational climates are those that reinforce the necessity to comply with detailed rules and the law while principle-based organizational climates are those that reinforce the need to apply overall principles in ethical decisions. The literature suggests that the emphasis an organization places on rules or principles has an effect on ethical decision-making (Dillard and Yuthas, 2002; Jones et al., 2003; Victor and Cullen, 1998), and to date there is little research on the effect of these organizational climates on individuals' propensity to whistle-blow. Our paper adds to the limited literature by examining the propensity of organization members to whistle-blow in rule-based relative to principle-based organizational climates.

Finally, we also consider the importance of the relative power of the wrongdoer to individuals' tendency to whistle-blow. Near and Miceli (1995) argue that while less powerful employees are sometimes involved in wrongdoing, overwhelmingly, it is the senior, and consequently the more powerful, employees who can commit acts of greatest harm to their organization and to society. For example, extremely powerful individuals at Enron approved the publication of misleading financial information, and apart from Sherron Watkins, the employees did not blow the whistle on them. Accordingly, our study examines whether the likelihood of reporting wrongdoing is influenced by the power of the wrongdoer involved in the transgression.

We find that, consistent with our hypotheses, there is an association between individuals' propensity to whistle-blow and the three contextual factors. Firstly, individuals are more likely to whistle-blow internally than externally. Secondly, individuals are more likely to whistle-blow in a "principle-based" organizational climate compared to a "rule-based" organizational climate. Thirdly, individuals are more likely to whistle-blow on a less powerful wrongdoer compared a more powerful wrongdoer, but only if the complaint recipient is within the organization.

This paper is organized as follows. First, we develop three hypotheses to predict the association for each of the factors and individuals' propensity to whistle-blow. Second, we present our experimental design. Third, we report the results and, finally, we discuss the implications of our findings, and future research opportunities.

HYPOTHESIS DEVELOPMENT

The importance of context for whistle-blowing has been made salient by the now infamous Enron accounting scandal, which was uncovered by an internal whistle-blower. Accordingly, we test three contextual factors that have been made salient in this recent scandal, which are grounded in Near and Miceli's (1995) work on whistle-blowing.

Near and Miceli's (1995) model of whistle-blowing identifies several contextual factors associated with individuals' tendency to whistle-blow. These factors are supported by change theories (organization change and resistance to change) and power theories (external control of the organizations, value congruence with managers, power relationships among groups and individuals, and power bases of the whistle-blower). Near and Miceli (1995) consider whistle-blowing to be the end result of a decision making process, and subject to contextual influences as perceived by the potential whistle-blower. People who observe wrongdoing are more likely to whistle-blow if they believe their whistle-blowing will be effective. Near and Miceli argue that an individual whistle-blower attempts to exert power to change the behaviour of some member(s) of the organization in such a way as to terminate the wrongdoing.

Although many different contextual factors are encompassed under Near and Miceli's (1995) model, sample size and experimental resources limit our investigation to three that we believe to be pertinent to whistle-blowing in today's workplace: (1) internal versus external whistle-blowing, which considers whether whistle-blowers report the transgression internally - to their organization, or externally - outside their organization; (2) characteristics of the organization (e.g., climate supportive of whistle-blowing); (3) characteristics of the wrongdoer such as credibility and power. Each is considered in turn.

Internal versus External Whistle-blowing

Whistle-blowing in the business context may be classified as internal or external (Near and Miceli, 1995). Internal whistle-blowing is the reporting of wrongdoing to sources within the organization that can bring about change. Internal whistle-blowing occurs when the transgression is reported to parties outside the chain of command, but inside the organization. This may include the board of directors, a senior officer such as the chief executive officer or designated complaint recipient within the organization (Finn, 1995). Reporting to coworkers (peer-reporting) is not classified as whistle-blowing (King, 1999). External whistle-blowing occurs when the complaint recipient is outside of the organization, for example, law enforcement agencies and regulators, professional bodies, external "watch dog" organizations and interest groups, and the media (c.f., Near and Miceli, 1995).

While some researchers (e.g., Miceli and Near, 1992; King, 1999) argue that internal and external whistle-blowing are conceptually similar, others (Barnett, 1992; Somers and Casal, 1994) argue that they are different. Those who propose that they are similar argue that the starting point of both is when an employee perceives wrongdoing (King, 1999). Both internal and external whistle-blowing require the whistle-blower to take an active part in reporting the wrongdoing instead of a more insidious act like sabotage, or worse, violence (Miceli and Near, 1992).

In Near and Miceli's (1995) model, the characteristics of the wrongdoing and the characteristics of the organization interact to affect the whistle-blower's use of external channels. When the whistle-blower goes external to the organization, the external complaint recipient is usually not known personally by the whistle-blower while the internal complaint recipient is usually known personally by the whistle-blower (Miceli et al., 1991). While internal reporting may include both illegal acts and wrongdoings that are not illegal, external reporting appears to be confined to only illegal acts. This is because society has put in place various agencies as recipients of complaints of illegal acts (Miceli et al., 1991). Regardless of the location of the complaint recipient, the whistle-blower is exposed to potential retaliation for his/her action (Miceli and Near, 1992). The form and type of retaliation may differ for internal and external whistle-blowing. This may be because unlike external whistle-blowing, internal whistle-blowing allows the organization the opportunity to address and correct problems before they become worse, and subsequently, prevent potential scandals that may embarrass and negatively impact the organization (Barnett, 1992). Thus, internal whistle-blowing may be considered to be a demonstration of loyalty and commitment to the organization (Somers and Casal, 1994). This discussion gives rise to our first hypothesis:

H1 Individuals have a higher propensity to whistle-blow internally than externally.

Rule-based versus Principle-based Climate

Another variable identified by Miceli and Near (1992) is the prevailing climate within an organization. Climate has the ability to affect organizational members' ethical decision-making process (c.f. Dillard and Yuthas, 2002). For example, at Enron, there was a strong corporate culture of towing the line and adhering to the way things were done (Toffler and Reingold, 2003). An application and integration of these theoretical perspectives suggests that critical to their propensity to whistle-blow is the nature of the organizational climate under which they operate. The literature identifies two organizational climates – "rule-based" and "principle-based" (Dillard and Yuthas, 2002). A "rule-based" climate emphasizes conformity to the rules and the law, whereas a "principle-based" climate has broadly formulated rules that permit interpretation by and communication between organizational members (Dillard and Yuthas, 2002). Principle-based climates convey to members the necessity of following general principles in the formulation of professional judgment (Dillard and Yuthas, 2002).

The authority structure of a rule-based organization is likely to be more bureaucratic than a principle-based organization (Dillard and Yuthas, 2002) and the greater the bureaucracy, the less effective the whistle-blowing (Miceli and Near, 1992; Weinstein, 1979). Bureaucratic organizations are less responsive to changes than other organizations are (e.g., Daft, 1978). For example, Perry (1992) found that allegations of wrongdoing requiring greater organizational change were less likely to be resolved than issues requiring less change. Consequently, Weinstein (1979) argues that bureaucracies respond more negatively to whistle-blowing than other organizations, because whistle-blowing represents a challenge to the authority structure, which is the basis of the bureaucracy. Therefore, rule-based organizational climates are more likely to be undermined by whistle-blowing than principle-based organizational climates.

We argue that the extent to which an organization reinforces rules versus principles is a key influence on individuals' ethical behavior of which whistle-blowing is a subset (c.f., Finn, 1995; Near and Miceli, 1995). On the one hand, in a "rule-based" organizational climate, individuals take less responsibility for ethical decision-making; therefore, their propensity to whistle-blow would be lower than in a "principle-based" climate. On the other hand, in a "principle-based" climate, individuals' retain responsibility for the definition and exercise of their own ethical behavior. Therefore, individuals are more likely to blow the whistle in a "principle based" than in a "rule-based" climate because "principle-based" organizations are more receptive to the whistle-blowers compared to "rule-based" organizations.[1] Based on the above arguments, we hypothesize the following:

H2 Individuals in a "rule-based" climate are less likely to whistle-blow relative to individuals in a "principle-based" climate.

Power of the Wrongdoer

In the recent debacles involving Andersen, allegations have been made that individuals at the highest level of the organization had been involved in the cover up of Enron's transgressions. Shredding and wholesale destruction of Enron work papers by Andersen staff was undertaken in Andersen's Houston office:

> "Tonnes of paper relating to the Enron audit were promptly shredded as part of the orchestrated document destruction. The shredder at the Andersen office at the Enron building was used virtually constantly. To handle the overload, dozens of large trunks filled with Enron

---

[1] An alternative view is that bureaucracy would be positively related to the effectiveness of whistle-blowing if there are formal channels for resolving complaints and stated guarantees of protection for the potential whistle-blower. However, unless these conditions are met in a bureaucratic organization, less bureaucratic organizations are expected to be less resistant to change and, therefore, more likely to experience effective whistle-blowing (Near and Miceli, 1995).

documents were sent to Andersen's Houston office to be shredded." ('Back time' may catch Andersen", *Toronto Star*, March 21, 2002, D11)

These transgressions were sanctioned by the organization. For example, on October 10, 2001, Chicago-based Andersen lawyer Nancy Temple e-mailed Michael Odom (at Andersen's Houston office): "it might be useful to consider reminding the (Enron audit) team that it would be helpful to make sure that we have complied with the policy, ...which calls for destruction of extraneous and redundant material" (*Toronto Star*, 2002, D12).

The popular press (see for example, *Forbes*, March 2002 issue) has argued that the high level of involvement of Andersen personnel inhibited their staff from whistle-blowing. This has been reinforced by academic research including Near and Miceli (1995) who identify the importance of power of the wrongdoer to individuals' propensity to whistle-blow. Power is defined as the ability of an individual to overcome resistance in bringing about his/her desired objective or result without the use of coercion, physical force, or other negative connotations that is implied by the word (Near and Miceli, 1995). Power is normally associated with high status individuals because low status individuals can be easily replaced (Near and Miceli, 1986). High status individuals are powerful because of certain desirable attributes that they bring to the organization. For example, high status individuals may have technical or management skills, they may be in control of valuable resources, or they may have influence over the careers of other organizational members (Near and Miceli, 1995).

Powerful status is not only reflected in hierarchical position but also in the degree to which individuals are considered to be central and critical to the organization (Perry, 1993). Power has a direct effect on whether the organization will protect them or sanction them (Near and Miceli, 1995). That is, wrongdoing is less likely to be terminated if the organization is dependent upon the wrongdoer for its resources. In such situations, the wrongdoer would be able to dominate and sanction the whistle-blower. Ryan and Oestreich (1991) argue that individuals are less likely to whistle-blow on powerful individuals because they fear retaliation and powerful individuals have greater opportunity and resources to retaliate against whistle-blowers. For example, the literature reports that internal auditors are reluctant to report high-level wrongdoing such as release of questionable financial information because of the seriousness of the consequences that would be incurred (Miceli et al., 1991). Historical evidence shows that when an internal audit partner warned other Andersen partners in 1999 that Enron's accounting practices were too aggressive; the in-charge partner of Enron's audit together with Enron executives had him removed from Enron's audit (Manor and Yates, 2002). Consequently, we hypothesize as follows:

H3 Individuals are more likely to whistle-blow on a less powerful wrongdoer compared to a more powerful wrongdoer.

METHOD

The Enron and WorldCom scandals raised many questions regarding auditor responsibility, culpability, and ethical behavior. Consequently, our study examines the whistle-blowing propensity of a group of auditors using case materials that were based on an actual but disguised audit case.

Table 1. Demographic data

	Average/n (sd)
Gender (n): Males	38
Females	57
Average (sd) age in years	24.1 (3.0)
Average (sd) general work experience in months	48.1 (43.9)
Average (sd) domain work experience in months	31.1 (17.8)
Average (sd) tenure at current job in months	23.2 (12.4)
First language: (n)	
English	79
Others	16
Percentage of time spent on audit work:	
Average	75.1%
Range	10% to 100%

Participants

The participants were 96 professional staff attending a national accounting training program. This allowed us to isolate variation that may have otherwise been otherwise attributable to differences in employers and/or type of employment than the factors under investigation. All participants had audit experience and worked for an audit firm. There was one incomplete response, and this resulted in 95 (38 males and 57 females) useable responses. The average (SD) age of respondents was 24.1 (3.0) years. Descriptive data are shown in Table 1.

Experimental Design

The experiment is a 2 ("rule-based" and "principle-based" organizational climate) by 2 (power of the wrongdoer – less powerful and more powerful) between-subjects full factorial design, with a within-subject comparison for internal versus external whistle-blowing. The experimental materials included a general description of the purpose of the experiment (which was to study decision-making by auditors) and provided an assurance of confidentiality. The participants were randomly assigned to one of the four treatment groups.

The experimental task comprised an audit vignette that was divided into two parts. In the first part, auditor participants were asked to read the "organizational climate condition" description and initial the document after reading it (see below). In the second part, all participants were presented with a case containing information about a recent audit assignment. Participants were required to take the role of an auditor (the inferior) who had been assigned to the audit of a client.

The case involves a wrongdoing by the partner-in-charge (the superior) of the audit.[2] The auditor brought to his superior's attention the existence of a serious weakness in the client's internal control system[3] that would allow fraud[4] to be committed by the client. The superior refuses to bring the weakness to the attention of the client's board of directors because of a personal association with a member of the client staff.[5] The superior warns the inferior not to follow up on the matter. An excerpt from the case materials is shown below.

> Because of your experience in auditing organizations of a similar nature, you are assigned to audit the museum's acquisition section. Acquisitions form the major part of the museum's annual budget. From your review of LMMA's procedures, you find that the acquisition manager has the responsibility of finding, negotiating, and finalizing the purchase of paintings, sculptures, and other objects of art from the artists directly or from other collectors or art dealers after authentication by experts. When the acquisition price is agreed upon, Don McDonald, the acquisition manager, will complete an authorization form that contains the vendor's details, a detailed description of the object to be acquired as well as the agreed price. This form authorizes the accounting department to release the funds to the vendor.
>
> Upon learning this, you are immediately concerned for the lack of independent verification of the acquisition price, the lack of internal controls, and the lack of reporting of internal control weaknesses to the LMMA board. Auditing standards stipulate that material weaknesses in internal controls must be reported to the client's board of directors. You immediately raise this issue with Chris, the audit partner, and in your discussion you question the adequacy of internal controls that gives rise to the possibility of collusion between McDonald and the vendors to defraud the museum. Chris replies that he is aware of the internal control weakness but does not believe that it warrants reporting to the board because a material fraud is unlikely. Besides, McDonald is a good and trusted friend who would never do anything to harm Chris's career. His parting words to you are: "Leave it alone, I'm warning you!"

After reading the case materials, the participants were asked to respond to three questions: (1) Will you report your concerns to the managing partner of the firm (your superior's superior)? (2) Will your peers, in an identical situation, report their concerns to the managing partner of their firm? and (3) Will you report your concerns to LMMA's [the client company being audited] board of directors? For all questions, the participants responded on a seven-point scale that was anchored by "Definitely will" (1) and "Definitely will not" (7). To facilitate ease of reading, in the data analyses, all three scales were reversed. Question 1 was used to measure internal whistle-blowing. Question 2 was included to test for social desirability. Question 3 was used to measure external whistle-blowing.

After completing these tasks, the participants responded to manipulation checks and control and demographic questions and were paid $20 for completing the instrument and dismissed.

---

[2] These requirements are reflected in Australian, International, Canadian and American auditing standards.
[3] The internal control system refers to the system of checks and balances that are put in place by management to assist them in running the organization more effectively. The corporations' law of many countries makes management responsible for putting in place an adequate system of internal controls.
[4] Fraud refers to intentional misstatements whereas unintentional misstatements are referred to as errors.
[5] Australian, Canadian, American, and International auditing standards require the auditor to communicate weaknesses in the client's internal control system to an appropriate level of authority.

Rule-based versus Principle-based Organizational Climate Manipulation

We used a between-subjects' manipulation of rule-based versus principle-based organizational climate. This was manipulated by putting participants in a situation where their audit firm had a new managing partner who had introduced a new code of conduct. Participants were required to read the new Code of Conduct and sign it as evidence of having read it. One-half of our participants received the "rule-based" manipulation and the other half received the "principle-based" manipulation. The "rule-based" version emphasized the need to comply with the various rules of the organization whereas the "principle-based" version encouraged individual values and independent thought. Both versions are shown in the appendix (Appendix A and B).

Power of the Wrongdoer Manipulation

Near and Miceli (1995) propose that the power of the wrongdoer may be based on his/her position in the hierarchy, professional status, tenure, support from superiors, and membership of a majority group. In public accounting firms, in particular, high status individuals bring and are associated with large and high profile clients. To manipulate power, but to assure ourselves that power was not confounded by level in the firm, we held position level constant (partner-in-charge) and describe the partner-in-charge (their superior) as either less powerful or more powerful using the following descriptors:

- *Less powerful:* The audit partner you are working for is Chris Budd. Chris has developed good friendships with the senior managers of LMMA. He is especially friendly with Don McDonald, the acquisitions manager of LMMA. However, Chris has very limited power and influence at your firm. He is the newest partner and he is not well known among the partner ranks. Because of his lack of power and influence, he is seldom consulted on human resource matters such as promotions and pay rises.
- *More powerful:* The audit partner you are working for is Chris Budd. Chris has developed good friendships with the senior managers of LMMA. He is especially friendly with Don McDonald, the acquisitions manager of LMMA. Moreover, Chris possesses a great deal of power and influence at your firm. He is well liked and respected by all other partners. Because of his power and influence, he often has the final say on human resource matters such as promotions and pay increases.

Control Variables

Because whistle-blowing is a form of ethical decision making (Finn, 1995), we control for the effect of social desirability bias and gender as done in previous ethics research. Social desirability was measured by the difference between the participants' likelihood of reporting the wrongdoing to the managing partner and their perception of the likelihood that their peers would act in a similar manner (c.f., Schoderbek and Deshpande, 1996). This difference is referred to as the social desirability bias score in our statistical analysis. Gender was measured by a self-report on the questionnaire.

RESULTS

Correlation Analyses

Before presenting the results of hypotheses testing, we consider the findings of the correlation analysis and manipulation checks for our experiment. Correlation analyses between the dependent variables and the control and demographic variables were carried out and these are reported in Table 2.

As shown on Table 2, the social desirability bias score and age were significantly correlated to the likelihood of reporting wrongdoing to the managing partner and were included in the ANCOVA model as covariates. As the social desirability bias score was calculated by taking the difference between the participants' own likelihood of reporting the wrongdoing to the managing partner and their perception of their peers' intentions, the larger negative score indicates the larger social desirability bias and the larger positive score indicates the smaller social desirability bias. There is a significant relation between the social desirability bias score and the likelihood of reporting the matter to the managing partner (F = 15.669, p = .000), i.e., those who were more likely to report wrongdoing to the managing partner had the higher social desirability bias score. Age was significantly related to the likelihood of reporting the wrongdoing to the managing partner (F = 4.580, p = .035). Correlation analysis shows that younger participants were more likely than older participants to report wrongdoing to an internal complaint recipient. Future research is needed to substantiate the importance of these individual factors to whistle-blowing.

Manipulation Checks

To test the success of the organizational climate (rules/principles) manipulation, four items were measured on seven-point scales – strongly disagree (1) and strongly agree (7). These were: (1) The firm likes employees "just the way they are"; (2) The firm expects employees to adopt its set of values;[6] (3) The firm expects employees to share a single professional identity; and (4) The firm values individuality. The scores of these four items were totaled to form the rule/principle score (theoretical range is 4 to 28). A *t*-test indicated a significant difference between the two treatment groups (t = 9.18, p = .000).[7] The mean (SD) for participants in the "rule-based" treatment was 9.13 (3.9) and the mean (SD) for participants in the "principle-based" treatment was 16.84 (4.56).

---

[6] This and the following item were reverse scored.
[7] All tests of significance in this paper are two-tailed.

Table 2. Correlations

	Likelihood of reporting to managing partner	Likelihood of reporting to board of directors	Gender	Age	General work experience	Domain work experience	Tenure at current job	Firm type	First language	Percentage of time spent in auditing
Gender	.146	.027								
Age	-.207*	-.159	-.053							
General work experience	-.167	-.101	-.100	.786**						
Domain work experience	-.099	-.037	.009	.431**	.436**					
Tenure at current job	-.074	-.030	.014	.105	.144	.533**				
Firm type	.108	.111	.000	.044	.071	.127	.057			
First language	-.152	.160	.204*	.074	-.072	.081	.152	-.028		
Percentage of time spent in auditing	-.021	-.047	-.062	.014	-.062	-.116	-.043	-.175	.086	
SD bias score	-.329*	.133	-.137	.041	.044	.035	-.027	.076	.010	-.114

- Correlation is significant at the 0.05 level (2-tailed). ** Correlation is significant at the 0.01 level (2-tailed).

Similar procedures were carried out to test the success of the power of the wrongdoer manipulation. The four items that measured this were: (1) Chris Budd is a senior partner; (2) Chris Budd has influence over your career; (3) Chris Budd has the support of the other partners; and (4) Chris Budd is not a powerful partner.[1] The ends of these scales were anchored by "strongly disagree" (1) and "strongly agree" (7) (theoretical range is 4 to 28). The mean (SD) for the less powerful wrongdoer was 12.02 (4.00) and for the more powerful wrongdoer, it was 22.14 (3.93), and these were significantly different (t = 12.45, p = .000). This and the previous result show that both manipulations were successful.

Hypothesis 1

H1 proposes that individuals have a higher propensity to whistle-blow internally than externally. To test H1, we used within-subjects' ANCOVA for the two dependent variables: (1) likelihood of reporting the wrongdoing to the managing partner; and (2) likelihood to reporting to the board of directors, Questions 1 and Question 3 of the instrument respectively. The overall mean (SD) likelihood of reporting the wrongdoing to the managing partner was 4.98 (1.36) while that of reporting to the clients' board of directors was 3.84 (1.61). While these scores were highly correlated (r = .641, p = .000), they were also highly significantly different (t = 8.679, p = .000). These results provide support for H1.

Hypothesis 2

Recall that H2 proposes that individuals in "rule-based" climates are less likely to whistle-blow compared to individuals in "principle-based" climates. To test this hypothesis we used a 2 (organizational climate - "rule-based" and "principle-based") x 2 (power of the wrongdoer – less powerful and more powerful) ANCOVA on the two dependent variables: Likelihood of reporting to the managing partner, and likelihood of reporting to the board. We included age and social desirability as covariates in our analysis when significant correlations were found with the respective dependent variable, as shown on Table 2 (Tabachnick and Fidell, 1996). A significant main effect for the organizational climate variable is required to provide support for H2.

Results for the first dependent variable, likelihood of reporting to the managing partner, are reported in Table 3. Panel A, Table 3 shows a significant main effect for the organizational climate variable (F = 6.922, p = .010). The means (SD) are shown in panel B, Table 3. Participants in the "principle-based" treatment (mean [SD] = 5.33 [1.20]) were more likely to report wrongdoing to the managing partner compared to participants in the "rule-based" treatment (mean [SD] = 4.61 [1.44]). These results provide support for H2.

The second dependent variable, the likelihood of reporting wrongdoing to the client's board of directors, was tested using a 2 (organizational climate – "rule-based" and "principle-based") x 2 (power of the wrongdoer – less powerful and more powerful) ANCOVA with age and social desirability as covariates. Results for the second dependent variable: Likelihood of reporting to the board of directors, are reported in Table 4. Table 4, panel B, shows a

---

[1] This item was reverse scored.

significant main effect for organizational climate (4.714, p = .033). Consistent with the previous result, the "principle-based" respondents (mean [SD] = 4.20 [1.47]) were more likely to report wrongdoing to an outside party such as the client's board of directors compared to the "rule-based" respondents (mean [SD] = 3.46 [1.67]) (panel B, Table 4). These results also provide support for H2; therefore, H2 is supported for both dependent variables.

Table 3. Dependent Variable: likelihood of reporting to managing partner*

Panel A: Tests of Between-Subjects Effects

Source	Type III Sum of Squares	df	Mean Square	F	Sig.
Covariates:					
Age	6.373	1	6.373	4.685	.033
Social desirability bias	20.534	1	20.534	15.097	.000
Main effects:					
Organizational bias	9.415	1	9.415	6.922	.010
Power of the wrongdoer	14.596	1	14.596	10.731	.001
Error	122.415	90	1.360		
Corrected Total	173.958	94			

R Squared = .296 (Adjusted R Squared = .265)

Panel B: Means (SDs)

	Organizational climate	
	"Rule-based"	"Principle-based"
Likelihood of reporting to managing partner	4.61(1.44) (n = 46)	5.33 (1.20) (n = 49)
	Power of the wrongdoer	
	Less powerful	More powerful
Likelihood of reporting to managing partner	5.37 (1.29) (n = 46)	4.61 (1.34) (n =49)

* Will you report your concerns to the managing partner of your firm? (Definitely will not - 1; Definitely will – 7).

Table 4. Dependent Variable: likelihood of reporting to the client's Board of Directors*

Panel A: Tests of Between-Subjects Effects

Source	Type III Sum of Squares	df	Mean Square	F	Sig.
Covariates:					
Age	4.970	1	4.970	2.081	.153
Social desirability bias	4.670	1	4.670	1.955	.165
Main effects:					
Organizational climate	11.258	1	11.258	4.714	.033
Power of the wrongdoer	5.317	1	5.317	2.226	.139
Error	214.960	90	2.388		
Corrected Total	242.632	94			

R Squared = .114 (Adjusted R Squared = .075)

Table 4. (Continued)

Panel B: Means (SDs)

	Organizational climate	
	"Rule-based"	"Principle-based"
Likelihood of reporting to the client's board of directors	3.46 (1.67)	4.20 (1.47)

	Power of the wrongdoer	
	Less powerful	More powerful
Likelihood of reporting to the client's board of directors	4.09 (1.79)	3.61 (1.40)

* Will you report your concerns to LMMA's [the client company being audited] board of directors? (Definitely will not – 1; Definitely will– 7).

Hypothesis 3

H3 predicts that the likelihood of reporting wrongdoing is affected by the power of the wrongdoer. We tested this hypothesis using the same statistical analysis as that used to test H2, which is a 2 (organizational climate - "rule-based" and "principle-based") x 2 (power of the wrongdoer – less powerful and more powerful) ANCOVA on two different dependent variables. Support for H3 is found in a significant main effect for the power of the wrongdoer variable.

Table 3 reports the results for the dependent variable: Reporting to the managing partner. There is a significant power of the wrongdoer main effect for reporting to the managing partner ($F = 10.731$, $p = .001$) (panel A, Table 3), and the likelihood of the wrongdoing being reported was higher when the wrongdoer was less powerful (mean [SD] = 5.37 [1.29]) and lower when the wrongdoer was more powerful (mean [SD] = 4.61 [1.34]) (panel B, Table 3). There was, however, no significant main effect when the reporting was to the client's board of directors ($F = 2.226$, $p = .139$) (panel A, Table 4). The mean (SD) of the likelihood of reporting a less powerful wrongdoer was 4.09 (1.79) and the mean (SD) of the likelihood of reporting a more powerful wrongdoer was 3.61 (1.40). Thus, H3 is supported but only when the dependent variable is internal whistle-blowing that was operationalized as reporting to the managing partner.

DISCUSSION AND CONCLUSION

Organizations face many choices in the way they organize their work environment to respond to wrongdoing by members, which include ensuring the organizational context is one that encourages whistle-blowing. This article examines three factors associated with individuals' tendency to whistle-blow: internal versus external whistle-blowing, rule-based versus principle-based organizational climates and power of the wrongdoer.

Our results show that individuals are more likely to whistle-blow internally than externally. This is not surprising as internal (compared to external) whistle-blowing may have less negative consequences for the whistle-blower, the wrongdoer, and the organization.

Internal whistle-blowing provides organizations with the opportunity to correct the wrongdoing before the consequences escalate that may include public, media and professional sanctions, loss of reputation, loss of client base, and general public embarrassment. Furthermore, internal whistle-blowing may be considered a necessary step to be taken by an individual before s/he resorts to external whistle-blowing. While further work is required to investigate the differences between internal and external whistle-blowing, our initial results indicate that organizations may avoid the negative repercussions associated with external whistle-blowing by developing organizational climates, procedures and policies that encourage internal whistle-blowing.

Our results also show that a "rule-based" organizational climate is less conducive to whistle-blowing relative to a "principle-based" climate. They suggest that if organizations increase their emphasis on principles, whistle-blowing may increase in their organizations.[2] Individuals in "principle-based" climates may feel that the organization gives them permission or even expects them to whistle-blow. As a principle-based climate encourages organizational members to think for themselves and to follow general guidelines more than rules; it follows that focusing on principles and encouraging independent thought may result in an increase in whistle-blowing (Near and Miceli, 1995).

Our findings also show that individuals were more likely to whistle-blow on a less powerful wrongdoer compared a more powerful wrongdoer, but only if the complaint recipient is within the organization. More powerful wrongdoers have control over organizational resources, they have technical and management skills, and they are more central and critical to the organization; therefore, powerful wrongdoers are likely to have the ability to retaliate against the whistle-blower. Ryan and Oestreich (1991) suggest the main reason people do not speak up is because of fear. Whistle-blowers fear being ignored, ridiculed, and sidelined; but most of all, they fear retaliation by the wrongdoer. Therefore, without a safe environment for whistle-blowing, individuals may be forced to report the wrongdoing externally rather than internally especially when the wrongdoer is powerful. To avoid such an eventuality, it is incumbent upon organizations to create a climate that emphasizes positive norms, and leading by example is one such step. As demonstrated in the cases involving the audit firm of Andersen, not speaking up and not reporting wrongdoing has severe organizational consequences and may have contributed to the demise of the firm.[3]

Finn, Hunt and Chonko (1988) have long emphasized the importance of senior management attitude or "The tone at the top" in creating an environment that nurtures speaking up and reporting wrongdoing. The tone at the top requires management "to walk the talk", as well. This may be communicated through procedures that facilitate internal whistle-blowing, lack of sanctions for whistle-blowers, and appropriate sanctions for senior management responsible for the transgression (Near and Miceli, 1986; Miceli, Near and Schwenk, 1991; Near and Miceli, 1985). Employees learn by observation; if they observe the fair treatment of whistle-blowers even when the wrongdoer is powerful, they would be more likely to report any wrongdoing they observe.

---

[2] The Sarbanes-Oxley Act 2002 that was introduced after the Enron scandal extends employees of issuers of financial statements and public accounting firms "whistleblower protection" that would prohibit the employer from taking certain actions against employees who lawfully disclose private employer information to, among others, parties in a judicial proceeding involving a fraud claim. Whistle blowers are also granted a remedy of special damages and attorney's fees.

[3] Andersen's practicing license was cancelled by the State of Texas on August 16, 2002.

The generalizability of our results is limited by two factors. First, in our manipulation of the power of the wrongdoer, we made use of a male wrongdoer. As women are just as likely to be involved in wrongdoing and as their numbers in the senior ranks of business organizations increases, what effect this will have on the participants' responses remains unclear. Second, all our participants were auditors. Whether the behaviors observed in this study are generalizable to the other areas of the business environment are untested. These, however, represent interesting extensions that future research could undertake.

APPENDIX A :
"RULE-BASED" ORGANIZATIONAL CLIMATE CODE OF CONDUCT

This Code of Conduct replaces the Code dated September 1, 1995 and comes into effect immediately.

Introduction

At this firm, our values support our strategy and help us achieve our ambition - to be the leading global professional services organization, solving complex business problems for top tier clients in global, national and local markets, and the best in our industry. To achieve this strategy, we believe that we must act as a single body that always speaks with one voice. Consequently, if your attitudes and values are different from what are acceptable to the firm, you will be required to change them.

Fair and Ethical Conduct

A staff member shall carry out his/her responsibility with all due attention to the establishment of fair and ethical dealings with clients, colleagues, and the firm. Employees must always act in accordance with the law and must always follow the rules and procedures as outline in the firm's Human Resource (HR) manual.

Respect for Colleagues

Employees must refrain from discriminatory behaviour as identified by legal statutes and the firm's HR manual.

Continuing Education

Employees must undertake at least one continuing education course per year; recognized courses are listed in the firm's HR manual.

Dress Code

Casual dress, as defined by the firm's HR manual, may be won on days that employees are not meeting with clients. When employees are meeting with clients, formal business attire must be worn.

APPENDIX B :
"PRINCIPLE-BASED" ORGANIZATIONAL CLIMATE CODE OF CONDUCT

This Code of Conduct replaces the Code dated September 1, 1995 and comes into effect immediately.

Introduction

In this firm, our values support our strategy and help us achieve our ambition - to be the leading global professional services organization, solving complex business problems for top-tier clients in global, national and local markets, and the best in our industry. At this firm, we believe in integrity, respect and always speaking our minds. We do not want to change who our employees are nor expect them to conform to a particular mould. Consequently, our employees are guided by their own personal conscience.

Fair and Ethical Conduct

A staff member shall carry out his/her responsibility with all due attention to the establishment of fair and ethical dealing with clients, colleagues, and the firm; the pattern of these duties may vary from individual to individual consistent with the employee's specialties and qualifications.

Respect for Colleagues

In the performance of their duties, employees should respect their colleagues and avoid discrimination.

Continuing Education

We believe in maintaining a passion for excellence in people, service and innovation, and we demonstrate this commitment to personal growth through our on-going support of continuing education courses that employees choose.

Dress Code

Under this code, staff can choose to wear either traditional business attire or adopt a more contemporary dress style depending on what is most appropriate to their specific working environment, daily schedule, and client interaction.

ACKNOWLEDGEMENT

Funding for this study was received from the School of Business and Information Management at the Australian National University, Deloitte & Touche/Canadian Academic Accounting Association Research Grant, and the Schulich School of Business at York University. We thank Shirley Gregor and the seminar participants at the University of Melbourne for their helpful comments and suggestions.

REFERENCES

Arnold, D. F., and L. A. Ponemon: 1991, 'Internal auditors' perceptions of whistle-blowing and the influence of moral reasoning: An experiment', *Auditing: A Journal of Practice & Theory* 10 (Fall), 1-15.

Barnett, T.: 1992, 'A preliminary investigation of the relationship between selected organizational characteristics and external whistle-blowing by employees', *Journal of Business Ethics* 11, 949-959.

Daft, R. L.: 1978, 'A dual-core model of organizational innovation', *Academy of Management Journal* 21, 193-210.

Dillard, J. F., and K. Yuthas: 2002, 'Ethical audit decisions: A structuration perspective', *Journal of Business Ethics* 36 (1/2), 49-64.

Finn, D. W.: 1995, 'Ethical Decision Making In Organizations: An Employee-Organization Whistle-blowing Model', Research *On Accounting Ethics* 1, 293-315.

Finn, D. W., S. Hunt, and L. Chonko: 1988, 'Ethical Problems In Public Accounting: The View From The Top' *Journal of Business Ethics* 7, 1988, pp. 605-615, Reprinted in *Professional Ethics For Accountants* (New York: West Publishing Company, 1995: 284-295).

King, G. III.: 1999, 'The implications of an organization's structure on whistle-blowing', *Journal of Business Ethics* 20, 315-326.

Jones, J., D. Massey and L. Thorne, 2003. "Auditors' Ethical Reasoning: Insights from Past Research and Implications for the Future" *Journal of Accounting Literature.* 21: 45-103.

Manor, R., and J. Yates: 2002, 'Faceless Andersen partner in spotlight's glare: David Duncan vital to federal probe after plea', *Chicago Tribute* April 14, C-1.

Miceli, M. P., and J. P. Near: 1992, *Blowing the Whistle: The Organizational and Legal Implications for Companies and Employees*. New York: Lexington Books.

Miceli, M. P., J. P. Near, and C. R. Schwenk: 1991, 'Who blows the whistle and why?' *Industrial and Labor Relations Review* 45 (1), 113-130.

Near, J. P., and M. P. Miceli: 1985, 'Characteristics of organizational climate and perceived wrongdoing associated with whistle-blowing decisions', *Personnel Psychology* 38, 525-544.

Near, J. P., and M. P. Miceli: 1986, 'Retaliation against whistle-blowers: Predictors and effects', *Journal of Applied Psychology* 71, 137-145.

Near, J. P., and M. P. Miceli: 1995, 'Effective whistle-blowing', *Academy of Management Review* 20 (3), 679-709.

Perry, J. L.: 1992, 'The consequences of speaking out: Processes of hostility and issue resolution involving federal whistleblowers', *Academy of Management Best Paper Proceedings* 52.

Ryan, K. D., and D. K. Oestreich: 1991, *Driving Fear Out of the Workplace: How to Overcome the Invisible Barriers to Quality, Productivity, and Innovation*. San Francisco, CA: Jossey-Bass Publishers.

Schoderbek, P. P. and S. P. Deshpande: 1996, 'Impression management, overclaiming, and perceived unethical conduct: The role of male and female manager', *Journal of Business Ethics* 15 (4), 409-414.

Somers, M. J. and J. C. Casal: 1994, 'Organizational commitment and whistle-blowing: A test of the reformer and the organization man hypothesis', *Group & Organization Management* 19 (3), 270-84.

Tabachnick, B., and L. Fidell: 1996, *Using Multivariate Statistics*. New York, NY: Harper Collins College Publishers.

Toffler, B., and J. Reingold, 2003. *Final Accounting: Ambition, Greed, and the Fall of Arthur Andersen*, Random House.

Toronto Star: 2002, 'Back time' may catch Andersen', March 21, D11.

Victor, B., and J. B. Cullen.: 1988. 'The organizational bases of ethical work climates', *Administrative Science Quarterly* 33 (1), 101-125.

Weinstein, D.: 1979, *Bureaucratic opposition*. New York: Pergamon Press.

In: Business Ethics in Focus
Editor: Laura A. Parrish, pp. 113-134

ISBN: 978-1-60021-684-8
© 2007 Nova Science Publishers, Inc.

Chapter 6

ETHICAL VIEWS OF JAPANESE MANAGERS: INSIGHTS FROM THE RATIONALITY OF ENDS/MARKET ORIENTATION-GRID

Sigmund Wagner-Tsukamoto[*]
University of Leicester, School of Management, Ken Edwards Building
Leicester LE1 7RH, UK

ABSTRACT

The paper positions empirical views of Japanese managers in the groceries / retail sector with the novel theoretical tool called the 'rationality of ends/market orientation-grid.' The grid distinguishes different managerial predispositions, ranging from self-interested opportunism and self-interested egoism to self-interested altruism and authentic altruism. These rationality features are related to a continuum of market features which range from perfect competition to imperfect competition. Based on the theoretical application of the rationality of ends/market orientation-grid, the researcher found that most observed business ethics behavior in the Japanese groceries / retail sector did not step outside charitable altruism and the compliance with legal regulation that reflected organizational slack. Ethical innovation or ethical stakeholder management showed up only in minor degrees. This leaves room for future business ethics programs. Based on the theoretical analysis and the empirical findings made, the paper makes certain business ethics recommendations for managers in this respect.

Keywords: managerial rationality; market features; ethics and organizational slack; ethics and law; stakeholder management; altruism

---

[*] Tel. ++44 – (0)116 252 5327; E-mail: saw14@le.ac.uk

I. INTRODUCTION

The 'rationality of ends/market orientation-grid' provides a simple tool for classifying a firm's orientation towards business ethics. It is a theoretical tool that allows for conclusions regarding the nature and type of moral agency a firm is involved in. (Wagner-Tsukamoto, forthcoming). It specifies different motivational predispositions of managers, on the one hand, and different market features, on the other hand. By interrelating motivational predispositions and market features, the grid spells out four different conceptual, programmatic scenarios for business ethics, which also have practical implications for advising on different action programs for business ethics. The present study conducted research into Japanese business ethics in the groceries / retail sector by applying the 'rationality of ends/market orientation-grid.'

As Erffmeyer, Keillor and LeClair (1999, pp. 35-36), Lewin, Sakano, Stephens and Victor (1995, pp. 85-86) or Nakano (1999, p. 337) noted, there is little empirical evidence on the specific features a managerial concern with business ethics takes in Japan, especially regarding external stakeholders and how dealings with external stakeholders are institutionalized by the Japanese firm. Erffmeyer et al. (1999, p. 38) even found that '... almost no empirical evidence dealing with Japanese consumers is currently available in the international marketing literature.' The present study closes such a gap regarding consumer ethics and its effects on Japanese firms. It specifies and raises in this regard questions such as whether Japanese business ethics is conducted primarily for philanthropic reasons that have little association with instrumental stakeholder management but are more an issue of organizational slack; or whether Japanese business ethics is conducted for reasons of profitability that are compatible with instrumental stakeholder management and which are less a matter of spending organizational slack on charitable causes. Regarding its specific research focus, the paper examines one particular stakeholder group – customers and consumers. They were identified by Lewin et al. (1995, p. 87) as an important stakeholder group of Japanese firms, although Lewin et al.'s mail-based questionnaire survey said little about the specific nature of the ethical relationship of Japanese firms with customers and consumers. Due to the open, qualitative research approach of the present study, such research questions could be addressed in detail.

As a result, the paper makes suggestions on how to more effectively institutionalize business ethics in Japanese firms, as called for by Nakano (1999, p. 337). Such suggestions focus on the internal institutionalization of business ethics in Japanese firms, which was found to be the dominant frame for ethical decision-making in Japanese firms (in contrast to 'outside' pressure by government or activist groups; see Nakano, 1999, pp. 335, 337).

In the following, section II briefly outlines the 'rationality of ends/market orientation-grid'. Section III provides a literature survey on previous empirical research on Japanese business ethics that is of relevance to the present study. Section IV presents the research method. Section V presents and interprets findings by applying the 'rationality of ends/market orientation grid.' Section VI concludes the paper.

II. THEORETICAL ISSUES RELATING TO THE 'RATIONALITY OF ENDS/MARKET ORIENTATION-GRID'

Wagner-Tsukamoto (forthcoming) provides the conceptual framework for the empirical research of the present project. At this conceptual stage, he contrasted different approaches to business ethics and addressed the question how far and what type of business ethics is feasible in different scenarios. Rather than presenting economic, legal, ethical and discretionary issues in a hierarchical manner, as done by some of the older models of corporate social performance, he interrelated these issues. Conclusions were spelled out regarding the empirical observance of business ethics and the programmatic, 'theoretical' positions that are behind empirical observations. This yielded practical implications for the fostering of business ethics.

The Rationality of Ends/Market Orientation-Grid

The rationality of ends/market orientation-grid depicts along the horizontal axis the market orientation-dimension and along the vertical axis the rationality of ends-dimension (See Figure 1). The market orientation-dimension reflects a continuum which distinguishes two extreme states: on the one hand, perfect competition, no information problems in the market place and perfectly dispersed power in a market. On the other hand, the market orientation continuum depicts an extreme state of imperfect competition, with high information problems and concentrated power in the market place. The former reflects conditions conventionally associated with classical and neo-classical economics; the latter reflects conditions associated with more recent developments in economics such as institutional economics (See also Wagner-Tsukamoto, 2003, 2005, 2007a, 2007b).

The rationality of ends-dimension of the grid distinguishes four states of motivational predispositions of managers when they interact with internal and external stakeholders: opportunism, self-interested egoism, self-interested altruism, and authentic altruism. Opportunism refers to 'self-seeking with guile' (Williamson, 1985, p. 65); self-interested egoism refers to 'honest' egoism, as it is commonly associated with classical and neo-classical economics; an example of self-interested altruism is offspring-related altruism; and authentic altruism refers to 'true' altruism where there is no external payoff rationale for giving behavior.

By interrelating the market orientation-dimension and the rationality of ends-dimension, four different scenarios for business ethics can be set out. They reflect different policy means that are available to the firm to enact business ethics. In the following, these four scenarios are discussed in turn.

Scenario One: Uncontrolled Capitalism and the Argument of Slack

When opportunism is not legally or economically effectively controlled, it can be expected that over time ethical behavior will be eliminated from social interactions. Especially in highly competitive markets where there are no information problems and where power concentration is low, those who act ethically – assuming the costliness of ethical behavior – will be at a competitive disadvantage. Hence at this end of the market orientation-dimension (see Figure 2), competitive pressures eliminate business ethics. On the other hand, if a market is comparatively uncompetitive, if information problems and power concentration in a market are high, then business ethics is enabled because of available organizational slack. An underlying assumption of scenario one is that business ethics and profitability are not compatible, that business ethics costs more than it pays back, and that stakeholders of the firm, such as customers, are not prepared to pay the costs of business ethics.

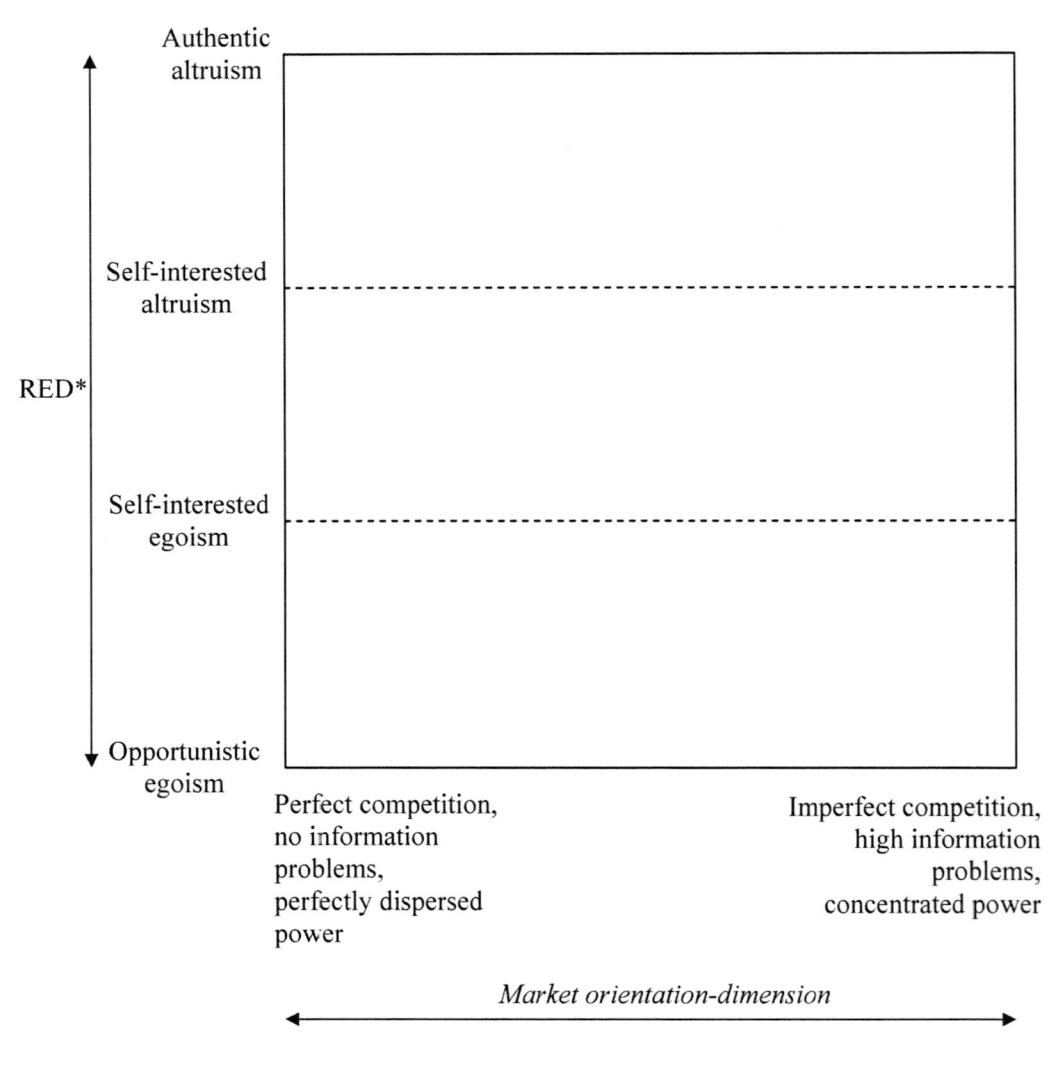

RED*

Authentic altruism

Self-interested altruism

Self-interested egoism

Opportunistic egoism

Perfect competition, no information problems, perfectly dispersed power

Imperfect competition, high information problems, concentrated power

Market orientation-dimension

* RED : Rationality of ends-dimension

Figure 1. Rationality of Ends/Market Orientation-Grid.

[Figure: diagram showing a triangular shaded region labeled "Policy means of the firm" with vertical axis "RED*" ranging from "Opportunistic egoism" at bottom through "Self-interested egoism", "Self-interested altruism", to "Authentic altruism" at top; diagonal line labeled "Efficiency barrier"; horizontal axis "Market orientation-dimension" from "Perfect competition, no information problems, perfectly dispersed power" (with left-side label "Complete elimination of ethics from market interactions") to "Imperfect competition, high information problems, concentrated power"]

* RED: Rationality of ends-dimension

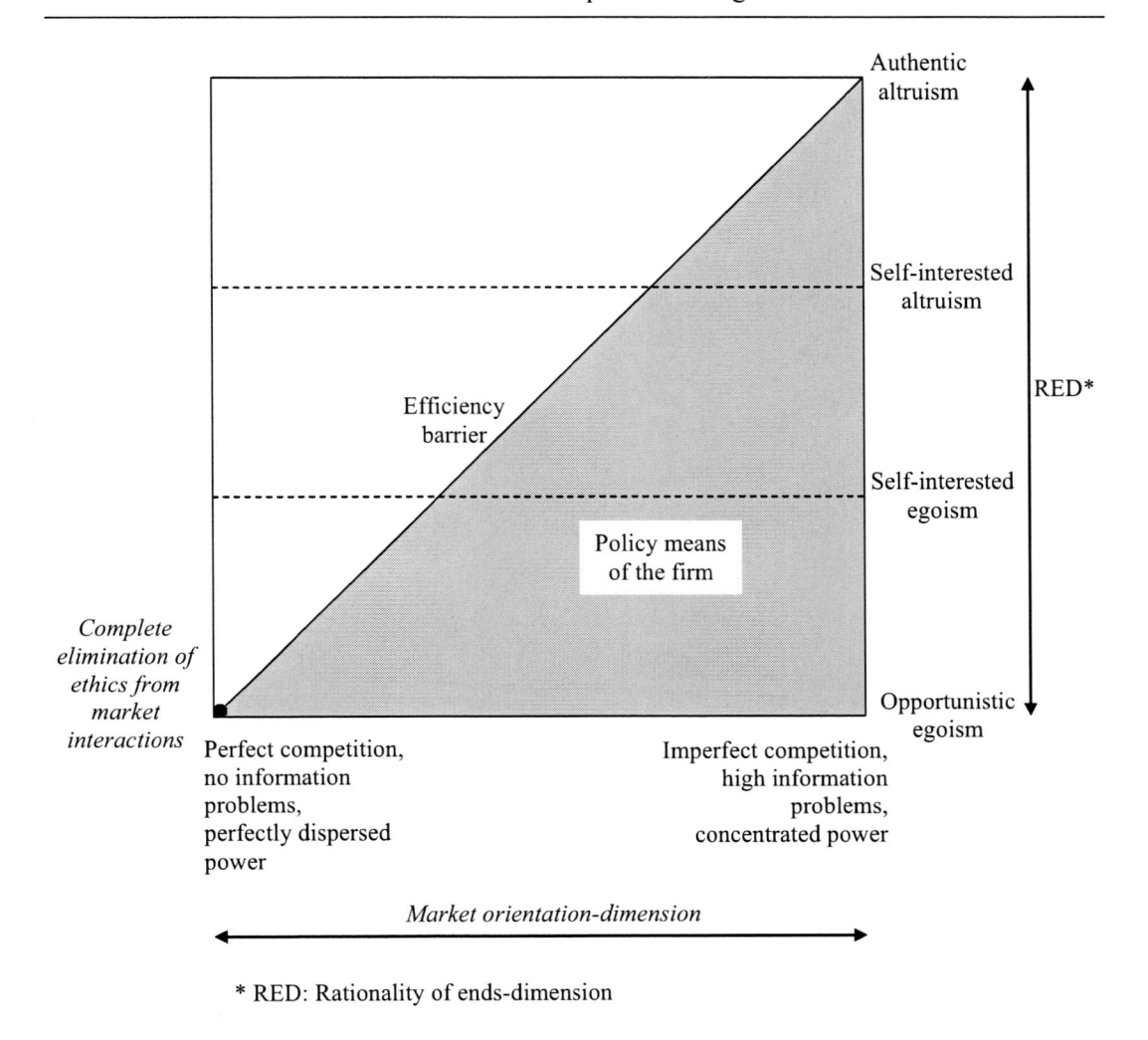

Figure 2. Scenario one – Uncontrolled capitalism and the argument of slack

Scenario Two: Legally Controlled Capitalism (Partly Effective Laws) and the Argument of Slack

Scenario two introduces laws as a moral regulative for corporative behavior. Laws codify certain moral precepts and thus restrain self-interest. Figure 3 depicts this by introducing a moral-legal barrier at the level of self-interested egoism. This also implies that costs are imposed for the moral conduct of firms. In a highly competitive environment where no information problems and no power concentration in a market are encountered, laws present the upper and lower bounds for business ethics. This assumes that laws have been effectively sanctioned in economic terms, that means gains expected from breaking a law must be lower than expected sanctions. However, if one moves along the market orientation-dimension towards imperfect competition / high information problems / power concentration in a market, then the scope for business ethics widens from outright opportunism to authentic altruism. Opportunism becomes feasible because of a likely, partial ineffectiveness of laws when high information problems in a market are encountered. Grey areas then exist.

Nevertheless, at this end of the market orientation-dimension, altruism is enabled, too, mainly because of organizational slack that can be spent on good causes. Scenario two is still based on the assumption that business ethics and profitability are not compatible and that stakeholders of the firm are not willing to pay for business ethics.

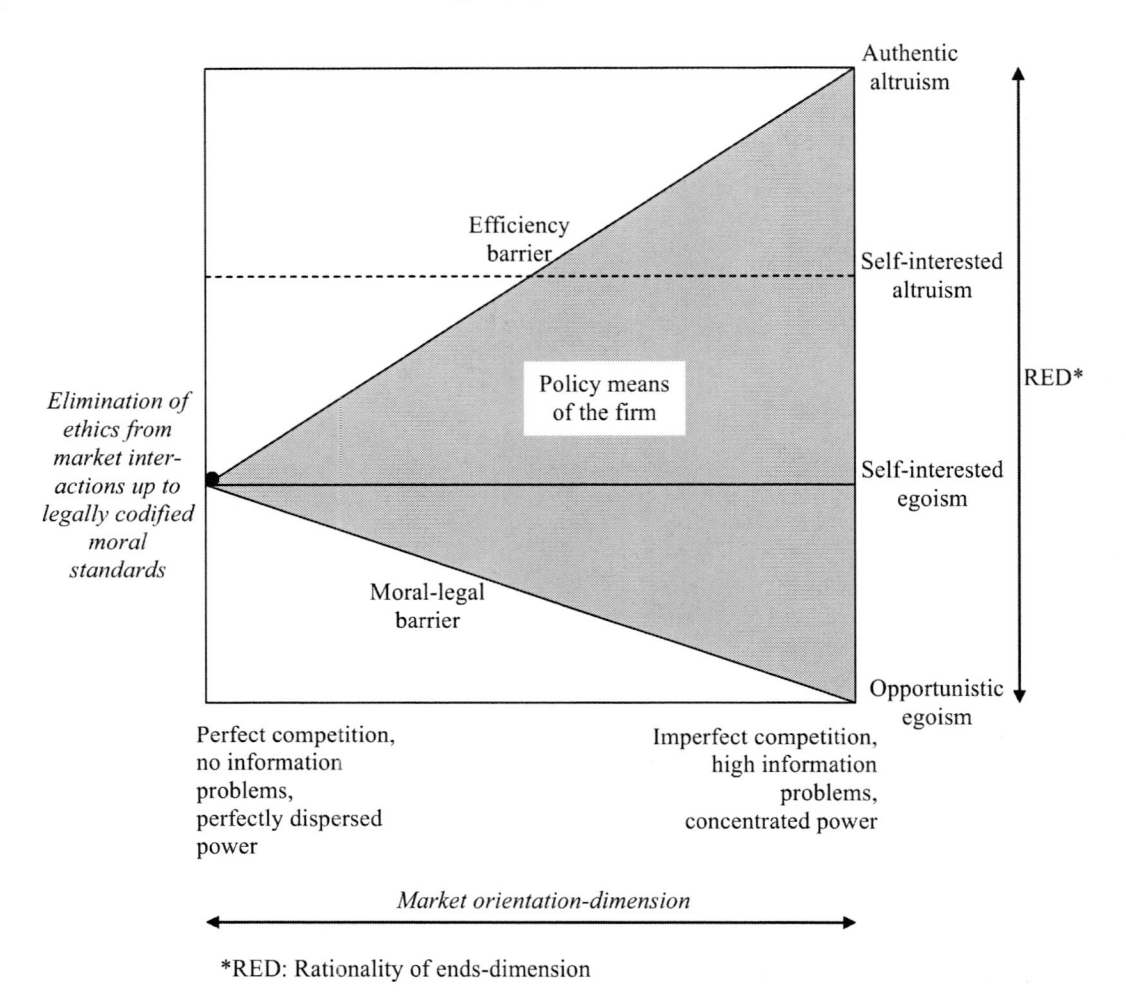

Figure 3. Scenario two – Legally controlled capitalism (partly ineffective laws) and the argument of slack

Scenario Three: Legally Controlled Capitalism (Partly Effective Laws), the Argument of Market Compatibility, and the Argument of Slack

Scenario three gives up the idea that business ethics and profitability are incompatible. It conceptualizes the case that certain ethical policy means of the firm are less costly than policy means that are driven by a mere concern for self-interest or even opportunism. A good example is an environmentally friendly production technology which is less costly than conventional alternatives. A historic example of such ethical innovation is provided by Sena (2005, p. 68). He analyzed the Japanese firm Sumitomo which in 1913 invented, after complaints from the local community, a production technology that no longer emitted sulphur dioxide but converted this substance into a fertilizer which could be sold to local farmers. In the case of ethical innovation, the moralization of corporate behavior is market driven. This is more true, the closer a state of perfect competition with no information problems and no power concentration is met along the market orientation-dimension. Regarding rationality of ends predispositions, one can speak in this respect of self-interested altruism. On the other hand, if one moves along the market orientation-dimension towards imperfect competition and a state of high information problems and power concentration in a market, then the scope for policy means opens up from authentic altruism, due to organizational slack, to opportunism that exploits grey areas of legal regulation. Figure 4 depicts this scenario.

*RED: Rationality of ends-dimension

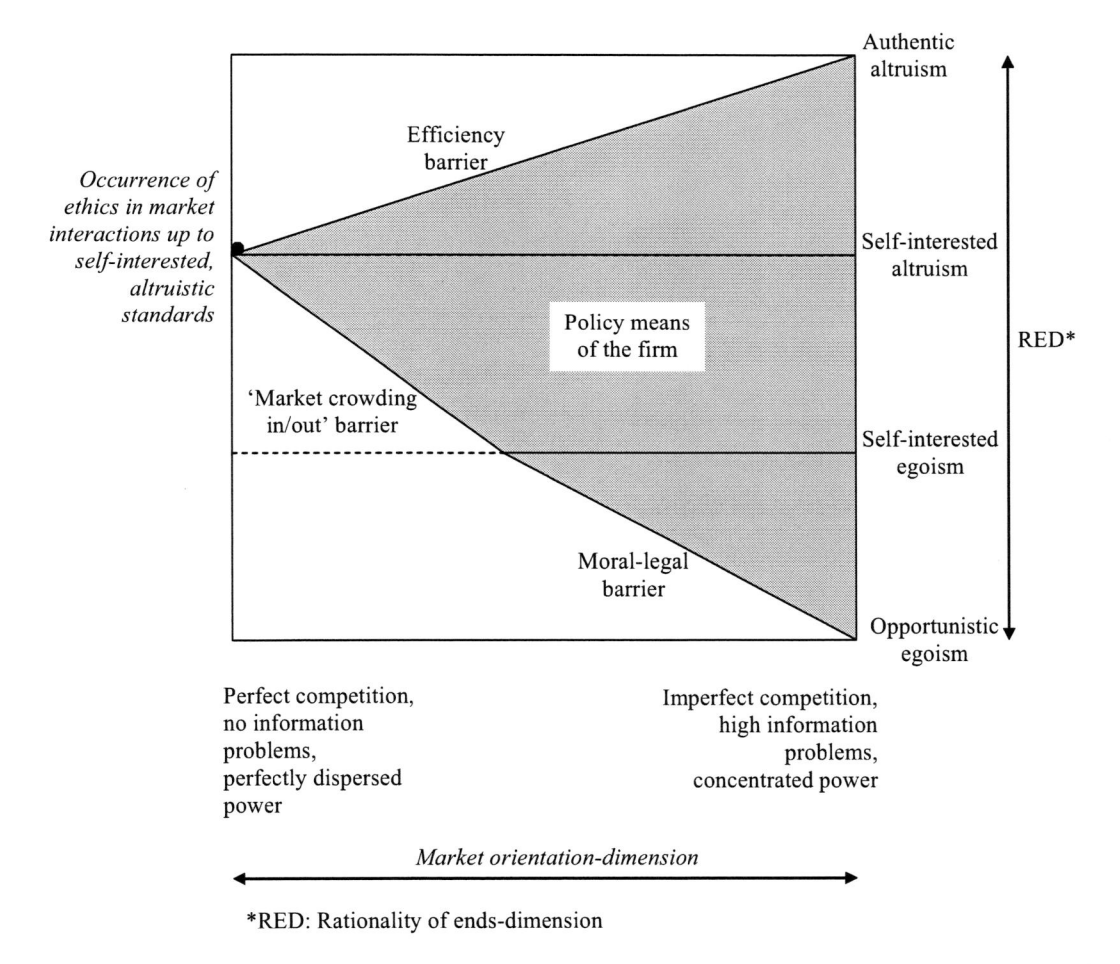

Figure 4. Scenario three – Legally controlled capitalism (partly ineffective laws), the argument of compatibility ('market crowding in/out') and slack

Scenario Four: Legally Controlled Capitalism (Partly Effective Laws) and the Argument of Stakeholder Compatibility

Scenario four radically differs from the previous scenarios. It models the case that business ethics is costly but still can be observed in high degrees in market interactions. This is due to altruistic standards of ethically committed stakeholders who enact their ethical beliefs on the firm. Competition is driven by moral agents who are willing and capable of paying for their moral precepts in the market place: A process of 'stakeholder crowding in' can be observed (see Figure 5). A good example are environmentally committed, green consumers who are willing to pay a price premium for environmentally friendly products. The influence of such stakeholder behavior on the firm can be twofold. It can be actively fostered by the managers of the firm, who, for instance, carve out a niche market in environmentally friendly products, or stakeholders themselves can initiate an interaction process with a firm in which they express their ethical preferences for certain products.

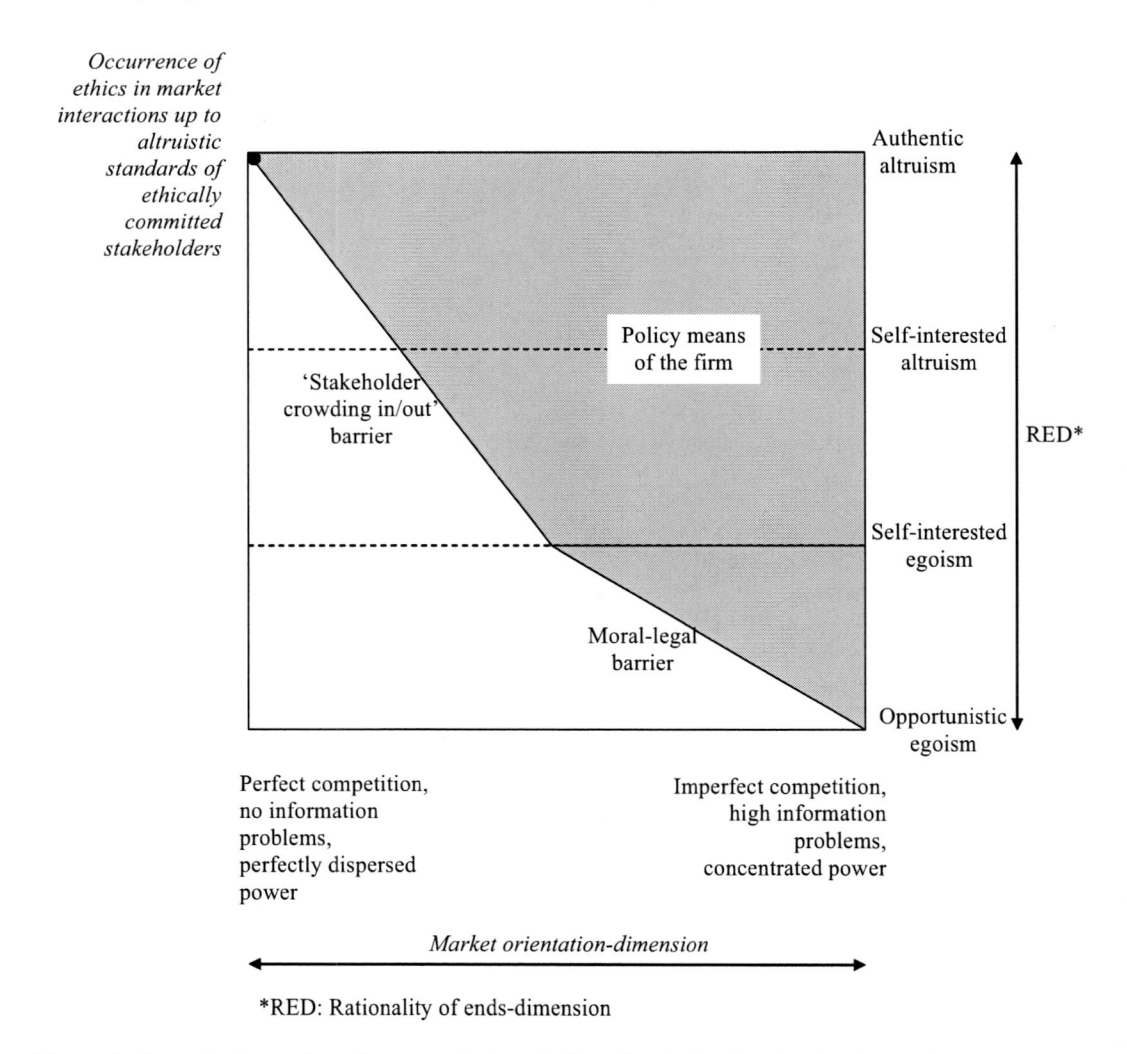

Figure 5. Scenario four – Legally controlled capitalism (partly ineffective laws) and the argument of compatibility ('stakeholder crowding in/out')

If one moves along the market orientation-dimension towards a state of imperfect competition and high information problems and high power concentration in a market place, other policies than business ethics that is driven by altruistic stakeholders can be observed. Less efficient policy means and more egoistic and even opportunistic ones become feasible. The argument of slack applies here in the reverse, being used for 'bad' causes, such as inefficiencies or the opportunistic exploitation of legal grey areas.

Discussion of the Four Scenarios

Each of the four scenarios reflects a specific programmatic, 'theoretical' position, which, however, is significantly blurred when looking at the real world of messy markets where imperfect competition, high information problems and power concentration in a market are encountered. The grid moves ahead of a discussion of unrelated levels of corporate social performance, such as economic, legal, ethical and discretionary ones, as they were hierarchically spelt out by some of the older models of corporate social performance (e.g. Carroll, 1979; Wartick and Cochran, 1985). The grid examines economic issues in terms of efficiency issues that cut across the entire scale of the rationality of ends-dimension; legal issues are discussed with regard to the moral-legal barrier, which can become ineffective because of grey areas in markets in which high information problems are experienced; ethical behavior is discussed with regard to altruism but it is also implied with regard to wider ethical goals that drive the market economy, such as the idea of the wealth of nations; discretionary behavior is discussed with respect to slack-based approaches to business ethics, which could cut across the entire scale of the rationality of ends-dimension.

Regarding the concept of altruism, the grid moves ahead of the idea of optional or voluntary altruism or philanthropy as it has already been discussed by some models on corporate social performance (e.g. Carroll, 1979; Fry et al., 1982; Tuzzolino and Armandi, 1981; Wood, 1991). Besides philanthropy and optional altruism, which the grid covers in relation to the idea of organizational slack that can be spent on good causes, a different concept of altruism is spelt out. The grid details that ethically minded, altruistic stakeholders can economically enable corporate moral agency. This reflects a broader economic concept of altruism than the one implied by optional altruism and philanthropy.

An important conclusion has emerged from the grid regarding empirical research. For each of the four scenarios the scope of policy means of the firm ranged, at the extreme end of the market orientation-dimension where imperfect market, high information problems and power concentration were encountered, from opportunism to authentic altruism. That means from the mere observance of a certain type of rationality of ends, little or no conclusions can be drawn regarding the specific nature of a business ethics program a firm is involved in. Rather, one has to look carefully at the programmatic positions 'behind' empirical observances. Empirical observations have to be grounded in theory. This is typical for qualitative research (Glaser and Strauss, 1967; Strauss and Corbin, 1990). Each of the four models reflected a particular theoretical position regarding a slack-based approach to business ethics and different types of compatibility of business ethics with profitability. In scenarios one, two and three, the occurrence of authentic altruism was largely due to market imperfections and organizational slack while in scenario four it reflected a high compatibility of business ethics with profitability. This has implications for the fostering of business ethics. In scenarios one, two and three, authentic altruism is enabled because of the availability of organizational slack that can be spent on good causes, but this relies on the existence of ineffective markets.

Scenarios three and four outlined additional routes to altruism. Scenario three discussed self-interested altruism as the case that a business ethics program is profitable and less costly than conventional programs. A good example is an environmentally friendly production technology that is less costly than a conventional one. Scenario four discussed the case that business ethics is enabled by ethically minded stakeholders of the firms. This calls on managers to educate stakeholders regarding the ethical services a firm can offer in its interactions with stakeholders.

The grid functions as a diagnostic and consultancy tool in so far as it allows for conclusions regarding where a firm locates on the grid. For example, if ethical dilemmas are observed between profitability and ethical predispositions of managers, it is safe to conclude that this firm does not locate in scenarios three or four and that it does not locate at the right-hand side of the market orientation-dimension of scenario 1 and 2 where authentic altruism is feasible because of organizational slack.

For the Japanese case study of the groceries / retail sector the paper researched where the views of Japanese managers could be positioned on the grid. Specifically:

1. Is firm X involved in moral agency in its market segment? If so, what specific examples of moral agency can be given?
2. If firm X perceives itself involved in moral agency, what role do self-interested and altruistic motivations play? Is moral agency driven by self-interested concerns or by altruistic concerns?
3. Is moral agency viewed as compatible with profitability or not? If moral agency is costly, how is it enabled? By organizational slack or by resourceful, ethically high-minded stakeholders?
4. Is moral agency sustainable under tough competitive conditions or does it reflect a 'luxury' in a comparatively, uncompetitive environment? Are dilemmas perceived regarding corporate moral agency?
5. How constraining and effective is the moral-legal barrier perceived to be? Are there grey areas in legal regulation which cause certain problems to behave ethically?
6. Overall, what programmatic business ethics position, as depicted by scenarios one to four, best characterizes the policy means of a firm? What practical implications emerge from here regarding the fostering of business ethics?

III. LITERATURE SURVEY ON PREVIOUS EMPIRICAL RESEARCH

There are few studies available which directly contribute theoretical or empirical knowledge on the issues raised above in section II. A couple of studies provide some indirect insights. For example, Nakano (1997, p. 1740) reported that about 30 percent of Japanese managers experienced ethical conflicts between company interests and personal ethics. However, Nakano could say little about the specific nature of these conflicts since he did a quantitative survey. With regard to the categories and scenarios of the present study, as specified above, it can be examined whether and how dilemmas did relate to scenario one and two and how far consumer issues played a role. Another finding of Nakano (1997, pp. 1740-1741) was that conflicts with the fair treatment of consumers provided the second most important issue when it came to ethical conflicts in a firm. This indicates that scenarios three and four were not reached, especially the productive and cooperative stakeholder relations that characterize scenario four.

Taka (1994, pp. 59-60) outlined that Japanese ethics is generally characterized by a high affinity towards family ethics. The typical example of such ethical behavior is enlightened altruism shown by parents for their off-spring; for instance benevolence by a mother to accept nearly all behaviors of her children (See also Wokutch and Shephard, 1999, p. 533). In terms of the rationality of ends-dimension of the grid introduced in section II, such an ethical predisposition is classified as self-interested altruism. Whether and how such a predisposition in Japanese society feeds through to business relationships between firm and consumers, as captured by scenario three, has to be examined by the present study.

A key idea of scenario three is more directly addressed by Tanimoto (2004, p. 160); namely that the provision of ethical services to the market place can provide for profitable business opportunities to a firm. He writes '… by taking an innovative approach to … social and environmental problems, … these may provide opportunities to break through and reconstruct an obstructed social economic system.' (Tanimoto, 2004, p. 160).

Regarding the observance of stakeholder management and ethical capital in Japan, Petrick (2003, p. 592) makes the theoretical point that eastern moral philosophy, such as Confucianism, is conceptually close to stakeholder approaches to business ethics. Similarly, the Japanese concept of 'moralogy' implies 'omni-directional fairness and benevolence' for every stakeholder (Taka and Dunfee, 1997, pp. 508-510, 514). It moves into a different conceptual direction than the instrumental approach to stakeholder management outlined above in section II. Moralogy is '… most dissimilar to the instrumental [stakeholder] approach' (Taka and Dunfee, 1997, p. 514), although it does not imply extreme altruism per se, as Taka and Dunfee (1997, p. 513) stress. The very presence of these conceptual ideas may hint that there is a heightened awareness not only among Japanese academicians but also among Japanese managers regarding ethical stakeholder behavior and management. In a more empirical tradition, Taka (1997, p. 1501) noted that already from the mid-1960s onwards consumer groups had begun to affect Japanese firms, although he said little regarding the specific nature and extent of such effects. But basically this hints at effects that come under scenario four (See also Loewenstein, 2002, p. 1684). Here, Tanimoto (2004, pp. 155, 167) is more precise. He found that some 85 percent of Japanese consumers were prepared to buy environmentally friendly products and accept price differentials of up to 20 percent for such products. Also, Lewin et al. (1995, pp. 84-86) noted that it is especially international stakeholder pressure which makes Japanese firms adopt business ethics programs. They also found that consumer issues and customer relationship issues present very significant topics of Japanese corporate citizenship (Lewin et al., 1995, pp. 88-89, 94). Here, the present study sheds light on the specifics of such relationships between ethically motivated consumerism (stakeholder behavior) and the firm. Loewenstein (2002, p. 1690) or Lewin et al. (1995, p. 85) stressed the need for new empirical research on these issues.

Organizational slack that can be spent on good causes provides a significant topic of debate in Japan. A portion of profits is returned to the community. For instance, Tanimoto (2004, p. 162) identified philanthropy as an important element of corporate social responsibility in Japan. Nakano (1999, p. 341) gave an example of a corporate donation to good causes, and the '1 percent club' of Keidanren (the Federation of Economic Organizations) also reflects such an approach to business ethics (See, for example, Lewin et al., 1995, p. 85). But as discussed above in section II, the empirical observance of philanthropy allows for little conclusions regarding programmatic positions behind a business ethics program followed by a firm. Rather, one has to look carefully at the specific determinants of a firm's involvement in corporate social responsibility to find out which scenario marks its approach to business ethics.

IV. RESEARCH METHOD

The paper adopted a qualitative, explorative research methodology. The choice of this method was determined by the lack of current knowledge on economic issues and stakeholder management in the Japanese market. Discovery of new knowledge and insights was the key goal (Mohr, Webb and Harris, 2001; Strauss and Corbin, 1990). This is the more necessary since quantitative surveys on Japanese consumer ethics, such as Nakano (1997, p. 1740), complained about the limitations of quantitative research when generating new meaning about ethical issues and corporate decision-making.

Qualitative research in the form of semi-structured interviews was conducted. Technically and methodically, although not regarding contents, the project replicated the research method of Wagner (1997) and Wagner-Tsukamoto and Tadajewski (2006). Semi-structured interviews have the advantage of allowing the interviewee to discuss freely the phenomenon under investigation while at the same time the interviewer can probe for certain issues and impose some structure on the interview process (Bernard, 1988; Mohr et al., 2001). Managers from the groceries / retail sector were interviewed. The above discussion in section III, e.g. of Tanimoto's (2004) study, hinted that environmental issues here may play a significant role in the Japanese consumption environment, which makes the groceries / retail sector an interesting industry to study. Also, previous studies of Japanese business ethics, such as Lee and Yoshihara (1997, p. 8), only partly focused on the groceries / retail sector and they did so by probing about ethical dilemma scenarios. This reflects a very different approach as compared with the open, qualitative approach taken by the present study.

The researcher conducted 20 interviews, each lasting about 45 – 50 minutes. Purposive sampling was undertaken as it typically characterizes qualitative research (Strauss and Corbin, 1990; Wagner, 1997). The aim of purposive sampling is to collect interviewees who have an interesting story to tell about the phenomenon under investigation. The members' list of the Tokyo-based Business Ethics Research Center (BERC) was used to make contact with managers. The managers interviewed were mostly middle and senior managers from CSR (corporate social responsibility) departments and environmental management departments. The sample included a few directors and chief executives, too. Interviewees were typically 40-60 years of age.

An interview guide was prepared which worked from the general to the specific. This reflects a standard approach in qualitative research (Bernard, 1988; Chikudate, 2000; Mohr et al., 2001; Wagner, 1997). The initial interview guide was refined after a series of discussions with Japanese academic experts in the field of business ethics.

Various quality measures were taken up, as they are recommended for qualitative research (Yin, 1994; Wagner, 1997). The goal is to ensure high reliability and constructive validity. Reliability refers to the feature of a study that enable it to be replicated by another researcher with the same results. This was achieved for the present study by carefully documenting the data collection process through transcribing the interview data word-by-word and by outlining in detail how data interpretation proceeded through various stages of coding and summarizing the interviews. Constructive validity refers to the correctness of the operational issues studied. It was improved through two types of triangulation, as are recommended for this type of research (Cheung and King, 2004, p. 249; Dentchev, 2004, p. 403). Firstly, a variety of information sources was tapped into regarding a selected interviewee (the transcribed interview but also data sources such as memos, internal documents, corporate publications, etc.). Secondly, triangulation was achieved by interviewing not only business managers but also 'experts' on the topics of the chosen research design. Such experts were academicians in the field of business ethics. They were recruited from JABES and BERC. Constructive validity also benefited by sampling interviews up to the point of 'variance saturation' or 'theoretical saturation'. Chikudate (2000), Dentchev (2004), Heugens (2001) and Sandberg (2000) observed such saturation in the range of 12-18 interviewees (See also Mohr et al., 2001). In the present study 20 managerial interviews were conducted. Repetitive answers and hence saturation were found from the 14th interview onwards.

Regarding another quality measure of empirical research, i.e. external validity, that is the generalizability of findings to a larger population, qualitative research is comparatively weak (Dentchev, 2004; Wagner, 1997). In this respect, the explorative insights generated by qualitative research need to be further scrutinized by quantitative research, such as a questionnaire survey. But in general, the validity of qualitative research should not be assessed on the basis of quantitative research criteria (and vice versa) (Chikudate, 2000; Wagner, 1997).

Value-laden research topics, such as business ethics, are often associated with a social desirability bias (Dentchev, 2004; Randall and Fernandes, 1991). Various attempts were made to control such a bias. The triangulation of empirical research through conducting expert discussions in addition to managerial interviews is one such way (Dentchev, 2004, p. 401). Another measure to keep a social desirability bias to a minimum is to guarantee anonymity to interviewees (Mohr et al., 2001, p. 53; Randall and Fernandes, 1991, pp. 808, 813). Furthermore, Chung and Monroe (2003, pp. 296-298) reported that a social desirability bias is less an issue for studies that enquire about ethical behavior (as opposed to unethical behavior). This was the case for the present study since it researched the effects of positive ethical behavior, such as environmentally responsible stakeholder behavior or corporate philanthropy.

Variables were selected and coded in relation to the interview data and the theoretical issues under investigation. As suggested by Glaser and Strauss's (1967) approach to grounded theory, an iterative process of reading and coding the interview data was followed. The development of grounded theory rests on two ideas: On the one hand, a priori, theoretical categories are drawn upon from existing theoretical frameworks (as outlined for this study in section II above). On the other hand, ideas and themes are to emerge from the data. 'Patterns in meaning' are to be sought, as suggested by Spiggle (1994, p. 499). In this respect, the interview data was read repeatedly and recurring ideas were looked for across different interviews.

V. INTERPRETATION OF FINDINGS

Sections II and III have introduced and critiqued a theoretical framework and previous empirical research on issues that related to the rationality of ends/market orientation-grid. In the following, the research questions are answered by relating data to scenarios 1 to 4 of the rationality of ends/market orientation-grid. Interpretation guidelines for qualitative research are followed (for a review of such guidelines, see Wagner, 1997)

Observations on Scenario 1: The Absence of Uncontrolled Capitalism and Opportunistic Business Behavior

Opportunistic business practices were hardly observed in the interviews conducted. This can be ascribed to the comprehensive legal regulation of the Japanese business environment. One interviewee (M14) produced a catalogue of some 80 laws which had to be abided by in the daily practice of management in the groceries and retailing industry. Only in two instances was outright criminal behavior reported which had occurred in the past. Such behavior had been in conflict with legal regulation and it reflected rather opportunistic business practices. But once uncovered, legal proceedings took place against the firm's top management and a management shake-up happened. This indicates that firms face a comparatively effective moral-legal barrier as is depicted by scenario 2. Regarding the observance of business ethics behavior it can be concluded that Japanese firms locate 'at least' in scenario 2.

Observations on Scenario 2: The Dominance of Legally Controlled Capitalism (Partly Effective Laws) and the Argument of Slack

The interviews revealed that the moral-legal barrier presented an effective minimum for enacting moral standards in the Japanese groceries and retailing industry. This became apparent from the comments made by managers on legal issues. A small group viewed legal compliance as unproblematic (6 interviewees) but a larger group mentioned that grey areas had to be faced regarding legal regulation (13 interviewees). Such grey areas also reflect information problems in the market environment and indicate that a firm does not locate at the very left-hand extreme of the market orientation-dimension. Interestingly, those who reported grey areas mostly dealt with them in a proactive manner. In order to avoid problems of legal interpretation related to grey areas, many of the firms interviewed had imposed internal standards which considerably exceeded what was apparently required by law. For example, ISO standards on quality management and environmental management had been implemented: 'We are considerably above legal standards. We also have a quality management system related to ISO. We adopted these standards, they are very high and above the law.' Such 'safe playing' in the face of uncertain legal regulation can be related to certain economic gains expected from playing safe; for instance, firms try to avoid possible, future punishments by law courts in case they are taken to court regarding a certain issue, e.g. environmental pollution. Such proactive business ethics behavior has the potential to be classified into scenarios 3 or 4 and thus imply different action programs for business ethics. It could be classified into scenario 3 if the introduced self-imposed standard and the organizational procedures that accompanied it yielded a cost advantage to the firm. For environmental management such as the implementation of ISO standards, this is frequently not the case since ISO programs tends to come with higher costs than conventional management approaches. Self-imposed standards could also link to scenario 4 if they were successfully marketed to ethically high-minded stakeholders of the firm. Again, this was predominantly not the case. Self-imposed standards were introduced for internal purposes only, not in order to create a market advantage. In this respect, unexploited opportunities exist for ethical marketing. Some of the interviewed business ethics managers (from a CSR department or environmental management department) were in this respect highly critical of a missing link between their department and the marketing department of the firm (e.g. M3). Hence, it is fair to suggest that those who reported self-imposed standards which exceeded legal ones could still be classified into scenario 2 but above legal requirements.

Regarding competition levels, most of the managers interviewed reported a medium to high level of competition (13 interviewees). Some reported very intensive competition and comparatively little market concentration (7 interviewees). This implies they could be located towards the left-hand side of the market orientation-dimension in scenario 2. Such a suggestion is supported by the findings made on corporate donations for good causes. Those who reported very intensive competition linked the absence or low levels of donations to tight profitability. For example, M15: 'We are not involved in philanthropy at present because we just became a profitable company again and we do not have sufficient financial reserves.' Or M10: 'We have almost no profits to think of donations.' On the other hand, those who reported slightly less competition, acknowledged somewhat higher levels of donations for good causes. But again, expressed as a proportion of profits or turnover, donations were largely of a marginal nature. Only two firms reported membership in the '1 percent club' of Keidanren, who regularly donate 1 percent of their profits to good causes. But as for self-imposed internal legal standards, corporate donations were not marketed. The view widely expressed in this respect by the interviewed managers was that donations were a matter of charitable give-aways rather than a potential economic asset that could be communicated to ethically interested stakeholders, such as green consumers.

Hence, donations can largely be classified as authentic altruism in scenario 2, reflecting the availability of organizational slack. Unexploited marketing opportunities exist in this respect, as they did for self-imposed internal standards.

Observations on Scenario 3: The Sporadic Presence of Ethical Innovation (Driven by Cost Advantages of Business Ethics)

Ethical innovation, as it relates to self-interested altruism along the rationality of ends-dimension, could hardly be observed. Few firms had pioneered ethical management practices that led to cost advantages for their firms. Tanimoto's (2004, p. 160) optimism that many Japanese firms would show an innovative approach to business ethics that provided for profitable market opportunities could not be confirmed by the present study. Exceptions found by the present study were issues relating to the amount of packaging. They were reported by M5, M6, M9 and M18. These managers pointed out that reduction in the amount of packaging helped to save costs. M6 related this to life-cycle assessments of the product. However, these firms did not further exploit such an achievement by communicating it to ethically aware consumers and other stakeholders (which would have linked this achievement to scenario 4 and the generation of ethical capital). Another example of ethical innovation which helped to save costs is 'universal product design'. This again relates to packaging design issues, namely easy-to-use packaging for the elderly and disabled adults and children. The aim is packaging simplification, which tends to come with cost savings for the firm. M1, M2, M4 and M15 reported such a design approach for some products. But again, universal product design was not linked to the marketing communications approach of the firm. This prevented these firms from entering scenario 4 and the further economic exploitation of these ethical business practices.

Observations on Scenario 4: The Sporadic Presence of Ethical Stakeholder Management that was Compatible with Profitability

The earlier speculation of this paper that Japanese managers would show a heightened awareness regarding stakeholder management because of a conceptual affinity between stakeholder management and Japanese ethics, such as Confucianism or moralogy (Petrick, 2003, p. 592; Taka and Dunfee, 1997, pp. 508-510), could not be substantiated by the present research project. Only a few firms engaged in instrumental stakeholder management that economically exploited the ethical business practices of a firm. M14, M17 and M19 stated that, besides conventional product lines, also an organic line of products had been introduced and this was actively and successfully marketed. 'Being organic' is a unique product proposition that differentiates a product to the extent that special niche markets are created. In niche markets for organic products competition levels are reported as very low. On average, price premiums of up to 30 percent as compared to conventional products are earned. Most other managers typically commented that environmental or other ethical product features would not be appreciated by the Japanese consumer; for example, M15: 'Our industry is not so much influenced by ethical consumer interests. The consumer is very much interested in product safety but not environment or animal rights; they are very much concerned about safety.' Green consumerism, for example, is not as widely addressed by Japanese firms as some studies seem to imply (Lewin et al., 1995; Loewenstein, 2002). Possibly in this respect certain managers could be accused of being short-sighted. As indicated, a few firms in the groceries and food retailing industry had demonstrated that ethical product propositions can be successfully created. Also, there exist further examples of ethical stakeholder management that targeted ethically aware consumers outside the groceries and food retailing industry in Japan. For instance, for cars and electronics, environmental features have been very successfully used to organize ethical stakeholder management and create ethical capital. To assume that consumers behave differently when it comes to choosing durable products as compared to non-durable ones reflects the view of a split personality of the Japanese consumer. Whether such a view is tenable can be critically questioned.

A few firms ran active donations-collection programs through their shops (M17, M19). The purpose of collecting donations through shops is to increase a sense of community in the neighborhood of the shop and foster customer loyalty to the shop. For instance, M17:

'In order to be successful, we need a very close contact with people, we need to develop very close relationships with the people of our neighborhoods and philanthropic activities and donation activities here play a key role. ... We are very active about donations and philanthropy. We replant forests all over Japan. We also collect donations for disasters and typhoons. In the case of typhoon 14 we collected 20 million Yen from consumers.'

These firms stimulate the giving behavior of their customers through the promise to match customers' donations. Such an economic approach to running a donations program along the lines of cause-related marketing has not been reported in the earlier literature on giving behavior of Japanese firms (e.g. Lewin et al., 1995; Nakano 1999; Tanimoto 2004).

M8 reported a different approach by his firm to the marketing of donations. A price premium was added to a product and the additional earnings made through the price premium were then donated to social causes, mainly support of elderly people. This approach was actively communicated to consumers and in this respect the market share generated and the profit premium earned by this product reflected ethical stakeholder management and the building of ethical capital.

Thus, these firms' donation programs are strongly linked to relationship marketing and cause-related marketing. They actively market products (organic ones) to ethically aware consumers and keep consumers informed about corporate donations. In this respect, these firms create ethical capital: They occupy a special niche market in which their products and donations are marketed. In scenario 4, these products are located at the level of authentically altruistic dispositions of stakeholders that were catered for by firms. In this way a firm had succeeded to avoid head-on competition. It had differentiated its products from competitors which gave it a niche market advantage but also left it with an 'additional' communication task, namely to get an ethical message credibly across to consumers. Along the market orientation-dimension these products locate towards the right-hand side where low levels of competition, of information problems and of market concentration are experienced.

Although these examples look quite impressive from 20 interviews, it has to be kept in mind that the main bulk of the discussion led by the managers who gave these examples focused on conventional products for which no ethical concerns were marketed. Most of the other interviewees were outright critical of ethical stakeholder management. They stated that markets for ethical products, such as organic ones, are very limited in Japan, much below the 1 percent level expressed in market share. Equally, the internal activities of most firms regarding environmental management, universal product design, the auditing of corporate social responsibility, or corporate donations were not communicated to the market. Unexploited potential for ethical stakeholder management exists in this respect. A reason why such potential has remained unexploited was, at times, actively contemplated by interviewees. M3 complained the department in charge of environmental management and the auditing of corporate social responsibility (CSR) lacked formal and informal links with the firm's marketing department. In particular, a marketing communication problem became apparent when M3 commented about the way his firm communicated an ethical message to interested audiences: 'I announce our environmental activity through the CSR report but the general consumer probably does not read this, only professionals and researchers read this report. In Japan many consumers do not know about our environmental activities.' It can be speculated that the absence of formal and informal links between CSR departments and marketing departments is due to the comparatively young history of CSR departments in Japan, with most such departments having been established by firms only after the year 2000 (See also Demise, 2005, pp. 213-215).

VI. CONCLUSION

The paper positioned managerial views of Japanese managers in the groceries / retail sector with the tool called the 'rationality of ends/market orientation-grid.' It examined whether business ethics was driven by self-interested or altruistic motivations and whether corporate moral agency, if costly, was thought to be enabled by organizational slack in a comparatively uncompetitive environment or by resourceful, ethically minded stakeholders. Such classifications are of interest for giving advice on how to differently and more effectively organize business ethics programs by a firm. The study found that most of the observed business behavior could be classified into scenario 2, which relates to self-interest and legal regulation. Ethical behavior observed for scenario 2 largely reflected charitable altruism that implied organizational slack. Ethical innovation (as depicted by scenario 3) or ethical stakeholder management (as depicted by scenario 4) showed up only in minor degrees. This leaves room for future business ethics programs. On a positive note, opportunistic business behavior (as depicted by scenario 1) could not be observed.

The most commonly observed business ethics practice in Japan related to scenario 2 of the rationality of ends/market orientation-grid. Firms paid attention at least to the moral minimum standards set by laws. In the cases when legal grey areas and hence certain information problems were encountered, many firms had set up internal standards that considerably exceeded what was apparently required by law. In economic terms, the setting of high internal standards can be linked to the avoidance of potential penalties by law courts for entering and transgressing legal grey areas. High internal standards can also be economically explained in relation to additional product quality advantages that arise by following, for example, stricter production standards. With regard to the rationality of ends-dimension, scenario 2 and the behaviors observed largely reflect self-interested behavior. The dominance of scenario 2 implied the absence of opportunistic business practices but it also implied that most firms did not achieve altruistically motivated business practices as reflected by scenarios 3 and 4.

Altruistically motivated business practices could only be observed in minor degrees. A couple of examples of cost saving business ethics programs were found, mostly relating to product packaging issues. This reflected business ethics programs in scenario 3. Ethically motivated stakeholder management and the authentic altruism it implies on behalf of stakeholders could be observed in even fewer instances. Business ethics programs, as characterized by scenario 4, were exceptional. This is the more regrettable since business ethics programs in scenario 4 offer highly attractive, economic opportunities for generating market share and income. Ethical stakeholder management in scenario 4 reflects economically attractive niche markets in which ethical capital is generated. Unexploited marketing opportunities exist in this respect regarding instrumental stakeholder management (See also Wagner-Tsukamoto 2005, 2007b). For instance, high internal standards that are achieved through an ISO scheme on environmental management can be marketed to ethically aware consumers. A business ethics program then shifts from scenario 2, where it faces 'mainstream' competition, to scenario 4, where it can avoid conventional competition and occupy a special niche market for ethical business practice. The same observance can be made for scenario 3. As far as firms were involved in business practices that reflected scenario 3, namely ethically motivated cost savings programs, this could have been further economically exploited by communicating the specific ethical issues (that had led to cost savings, such as universal product design), to ethically aware stakeholders. Then additional economic benefits (in addition to costs savings) could have been realized, namely the generation of ethical capital in protected niche markets where ethical stakeholder behavior is present. In these respects, the present study could not confirm Lee, & Yoshihara's (1997: 20) finding that Japanese firms were well on the way to implementing business ethics programs that contributed to the long-term profitability of a firm.

As far as donation behavior could be observed, it largely reflected charitable give-aways that were based on organizational slack. Hence, donations implied authentic altruism in scenario 2. For example, M4: 'We donate not for commercial reasons but for charity.' Or M10: 'Basically we donated for charitable reasons, not for image related reasons but we could go one step further and link the two. Maybe this will be the next step.' In general, only very few firms had realized that ethical stakeholder management could be fostered through a donations program that actively targeted stakeholders such as consumers (See below when scenario 4 is discussed) . Unexploited marketing opportunities exist in this respect for shifting a firm's donations program from scenario 2 to scenario 4. The purpose of such a shift would be to integrate a firm's donations program into its general approach to stakeholder management and marketing management.

A key reason why many firms had not realized shifts from scenarios 2 and 3 to scenario 4 was a missing link between CSR departments, environmental management departments or production departments and a firm's marketing department. CSR departments, environmental management departments or production departments are in charge of issues like internal standards setting behavior, donation programs or universal product design. In this respect, many Japanese firms have now institutionalized business ethics in their own departments, which was not the case some ten years ago (See Nakano, 1997: 1750). Some managers of CSR or environmental management departments were outspokenly critical of a lack of links between their departments and marketing, especially in the areas of marketing communication and development of ethical stakeholder management. Informal and formal hierarchical links need in this respect to be strengthened and developed between a firm's marketing department and its CSR department, environmental management department and production department.

Regarding the market orientation-dimension, most firms, who were located in scenario 2, could be found around the center of the dimension and towards the left-hand extreme where very intense competition was encountered. Apparently the groceries and food retailing industry in Japan is a highly competitive industry. This was stressed time and again by the managers interviewed. One way to escape head-on price competition is through differentiation, and one type of differentiation discussed and analyzed in detail in this paper is ethical stakeholder management. Once this is achieved a firm can occupy a special niche market where comparatively attractive earnings and stable market shares can be enjoyed. A firm then is close to the right-hand extreme of the market orientation-dimension, where competition levels are low, markets are concentrated and information problems exist, for example regarding the credible communication of an ethically motivated product message.

The study identified various areas for future research. Issues concerning each of the four scenarios can be deepened by targeting separately a scenario and the research questions it implies. For example, the question of ethical stakeholder management (relating to scenario 4) can be addressed by conducting a study on green consumerism in Japan. Or issues surrounding scenario 3 can be further examined by exclusively focusing on cost-saving programs of ethical innovation that have been introduced by a firm. Regarding sampling, findings of the present study can be checked by researching firms who are not members of BERC. It can be speculated that such firms, because of the absence of ethics education through BERC, are even more strongly concentrated in scenarios 1 and 2 than the sample of the present study.

ACKNOWLEDGEMENTS

The research project was made possible by a research fellowship from the Japan Foundation and by research leave granted by the University of Leicester, UK. The researcher greatly acknowledges the support given by BERC (Business Ethics Research Center) and JABES (Japan Society for Business Ethics Study), Tokyo, especially its chairman Professor Masakazu Mizutani, Research Fellow Toshio Sena as well as Chief Researcher Kuniaki Matsumoto. Very special thanks also to Professor Shunji Kobayashi of Waseda University where a preliminary version of this paper was presented at a business ethics seminar on November 24, 2005.

REFERENCES

Bernard, R. (1988). *Research Method in Cultural Anthropology.* Newbury Park, CA: Sage.
Cheung, T. S. and King, A. Y. (2004). 'Righteousness and profitableness: The moral choices of contemporary Confucian entrepreneurs.' *Journal of Business Ethics,* 54, 245-260.
Chikudate, N. (2000). 'A phenomenological approach to inquiring into an ethically bankrupted organization: A case study of a Japanese company.' *Journal of Business Ethics,* 28, 59-72.
Chung, J. and Monroe, G. S. (2003). 'Exploring social desirability bias.' *Journal of Business Ethics,* 44, 291-302.
Demise, N. (2005). 'Business Ethics and corporate governance in Japan.' *Business & Society,* 44, 211-217.
Dentchev, N. A. (2004). 'Corporate social performance as a business strategy.' *Journal of Business Ethics,* 55, 397-412,
Erffmeyer, R. C., Keillor, B. D. and LeClair, D. T. (1999). 'An empirical investigation of Japanese consumer ethics.' *Journal of Business Ethics,* 18, 35-50.
Glaser, B. G. and Strauss, A. L. (1967). *The Discovery of Grounded Theory: Strategies for Qualitative Research.* Hawthorne, NY: Aldine Publishing.
Heugens, P. (2001). *Strategic Issues Management: Implications for Corporate Performance.* Unpublished Doctoral Dissertation. Erasmus Universiteit, Rotterdam.

Lee, C.-Y. and Yoshihara, H. (1997). 'Business ethics of Korean and Japanese managers.' *Journal of Business Ethics*, 16, 7-21.

Lewin, A. Y., Sakano, T., Stephens, C. U. and Victor, B. (1995). 'Corporate citizenship in Japan: Survey results from Japanese firms.' *Journal of Business Ethics*, 14, 83-101.

Loewenstein, M. J. (2002). 'Stakeholder protection in Germany and Japan.' *Tulane Law Review*, 76, 1673-1690.

Mohr, L. A., Webb, D. J. and Harris, K. E. (2001). 'Do consumers expect companies to be socially responsible? The impact of corporate social responsibility on buying behavior.' *The Journal of Consumer Affairs*, 35, 1, 45-72.

Nakano, C. (1997). 'A survey study on Japanese managers' views of business ethics.' *Journal of Business Ethics*, 16, 1737-1751.

Nakano, C. (1999). 'Attempting to institutionalize ethics: Case studies from Japan.' *Journal of Business Ethics*, 18, 335-343.

Petrick, J. A. (2003). 'Chinese and Japanese ethics and the promise of global ethics in business.' *Business Ethics Quarterly*, 13, 591-593.

Randall, D. M. (1991). 'The social desirability response bias in ethics research.' *Journal of Business Ethics*, 10, 805-817.

Sandberg, J. (2000). 'Understanding human competence at work: An interpretative approach.' *Academy of Management Journal*, 43, 9-25.

Sena, T. (2005). 'CSR is the way to the "long-life corporation."' *[Korean] Journal of Business Ethics* [ISSN 1229-2788], 10, August, 49-76.

Spiggle, S. (1994). 'Analysis and interpretation of qualitative data in consumer research.' *Journal of Consumer Research*, 21, 491-503.

Strauss, A. L. and Corbin, J. (1990). *Basics of Qualitative Research: Grounded Theory Procedures and Techniques.* Newbury Park, CA: Sage.

Taka I. (1994). 'Business ethics: A Japanese view.' *Business Ethics Quarterly*, 4, 53-78.

Taka, I. (1997). 'Business ethics in Japan.' *Journal of Business Ethics*, 16, 1499-1508.

Taka, I. and Dunfee, T. W. (1997). 'Japanese moralogy as business ethics.' *Journal of Business Ethics*, 16, 507-519.

Wagner, S. A. (1997). *Understanding Green Consumer Behaviour.* London: Routledge.

Wagner-Tsukamoto, S.A. (2003). *Human Nature and Organization Theory.* Cheltenham, UK & New York: Edward Elgar.

Wagner-Tsukamoto, S.A. (2005). 'An economic approach to business ethics: Moral agency of the firm and the enabling and constraining effects of economic institutions and interactions in a market economy.' *Journal of Business Ethics*, 60, 75-89.

Wagner-Tsukamoto, S.A. (2007a). 'An institutional economic reconstruction of Scientific Management: On the lost theoretical logic of Taylorism.' *Academy of Management Review*, 32 (1), 105-117.

Wagner-Tsukamoto, S.A. (2007b), 'Moral Agency, Profits and the Firm: Economic Revisions to the Friedman Theorem,' *Journal of Business Ethics* 70 (2), 209-220.

Wagner-Tsukamoto, S.A. (forthcoming). 'The rationality of ends/market orientation-grid: Positioning and contrasting different approaches to business ethics.' *Business Ethics. A European Review.*

Wagner-Tsukamoto, S. A. and Tadajewski, M. (2006). 'Bricolage and the green consumer: The contextual nature of intelligent problem framing behaviour of green consumers.' *Journal of Consumer Behaviour.*

Williamson, O. E. (1985). *The Economic Institutions of Capitalism*. New York: The Free Press.
Wokutch, R. E. and Shepard, J. M. (1999). 'The maturing of the Japanese economy: Corporate social responsibility implications.' *Business Ethics Quarterly*, 9, 527-540.
Yin, R. K. (1994). *Case Study Research: Design and Methods*. London: Sage.

In: Business Ethics in Focus
Editor: Laura A. Parrish, pp. 135-148

ISBN: 978-1-60021-684-8
© 2007 Nova Science Publishers, Inc.

Chapter 7

MONEY PROFILE AND UNETHICAL BEHAVIOR: A STUDY OF FULL-TIME EMPLOYEES AND UNIVERSITY STUDENTS IN CHINA

Du Linzhi[*1], *Thomas Li-Ping Tang*[†2] *and Yang Dongtao*[‡3]

[1]Department of Social Psychology, School of Zhou En'lai Government Management, Nankai University, Tianjin, 300071, People's Republic of China
[2]Department of Management and Marketing, Jennings A. Jones College of Business Middle Tennessee State University, Murfreesboro, TN 37132, U.S.A
[3]Business School of Nanjing University, Nanjing 210093, People's Republic of China

ABSTRACT

With two questionnaires named Money Ethics Scale (MES) and Propensity to Engage in Unethical Behavior Scale (PEUBS), which are designed by ourselves, this study investigates randomly 204 managerial staffs and 395 university students, to analyze their money profiles, and the relation between money profiles and unethical activity. The results show that Achieving Money Worshiper and Careless Money Admirer have more possibility to involve unethical activity than Apathetic Money Handler and Money Repeller when they are faced with work stress, but Apathetic Money Handler and Money Repeller have more possibility to involve unethical activity than Achieving Money Worshiper when they are faced with unethical organizational context; University students have more possibility to involve unethical activity than Managerial staffs when they are faced with work stress, conformity and organizational context.

Keywords: managerial staffs and university students, money profiles, unethical activity

---

[*] E-mail:lzd6613_nj@163.com
[†] E-mail:ttang@mtsu.edu
[‡] E-mail: yangdt@nju.edu.cn

INTRODUCTION

There are more and more fake, inferior, non-genuine, and bastard products in China today than ever before. Business ethics is a major concern due to the lack of ethical culture at the organizational and individual level in the society. Most unethical behaviors performed by various organizations and employees are related to the desire to make more money. In this paper, we examine unethical behaviors among full-time employees and university students in China from people's money attitude perspective. More specifically, we apply cluster analysis and develop four money profiles based on people's endorsement of the Money Ethic Scales (Luna-Arocas and Tang, 2004) and then examine the differences in the propensity to engage in unethical behavior across these four money profiles.

THEORY AND HYPOTHESES

We trace the inspiration to study the love of money construct to the oldest references in the literature: "Poverty consists, not in the decrease of one's possessions, but in the increase of one's greed" (Plato, 427-347 BC). "People who want to get rich fall into temptation and a trap and into many foolish and harmful desires that plunge men into ruin and destruction. For the love of money is a root of all kinds of evil" (http://www.biblegateway.com, 1 Timothy, 6: 9-10, New International Version). These quotes suggest that "wanting to be rich" or "being rich" may be related to "the love of money" and that the love of money may be related to "evil".

There is a dearth of empirical research concerning *the love of money* and *evil*. Many researchers and lay people may consider this issue as a *taboo*, a religious/controversial issue, not a scientific/academic issue, and to be excessively value-laden, thereby, may have shown great *reluctance* to study this taboo (e.g., Vardi and Weitz, 2004; Vardi and Wiener, 1996). While sociologist, psychologists, criminologists, and anthropologists have studied it for many years, many management scholars, however, have largely "ignored misbehavior in organizations" (Ivancevich et al., 2005, p. 247). Thereby, the construct of unethical behavior is an under-represented area of research in the management field and deserves further attention.

Money has been used *universally* around the world. *The meaning of money*, however, is "in the eye of the beholder" (Tang, 1992). There are many measures of money attitudes in the literature (e.g., see Furnham and Argyle, 1998). Tang and his associates have developed several versions of the multidimensional Money Ethic Scale or MES (Tang, 1992; Tang et al., 2000) and the Love of Money Scale or LOMS that is a subset of the MES (Du and Tang, 2005; Tang and Chiu, 2003). Mitchell and Mickel (1999) considered "the Money Ethic Scale" (Tang, 1992) as one of the most "well-developed" and systematically used measures of money attitude (p. 571). MES and LOMS have been cited and published in Chinese, English, French, Italian, Spanish, Romanian, Russian, and many other languages (see Luna-Arocas & Tang, 2004).

People have different attitudes toward money (i.e., positive, indifferent, and negative). Due to individual differences in money attitudes, researchers have classified people into money profiles using cluster analysis based on their scores on the Money Ethic Scale (e.g.,

Tang, 1992, 1995; Tang & Tang, 2002; Tang, Luna-Arocas, & Whiteside, 2003). People in different money profiles may have different demographic variables, income, and other work-related attitudes and behaviors (e.g., Du & Tang, 2003; Du, Xu, & Tang, 2004; Luna-Arocas & Tang, 2004; Tang, Tillery, Lazarevski, & Luna-Arocas, 2004). We will briefly summarize relevant studies below.

Luna-Arocas and Tang (2004) identified four money profiles among university professors in the US and Spain. They used cluster analysis and Factors Budget, Evil, Equity, Success, and Motivator of the 15-item Money Ethic Scale and identified (1) Achieving Money Worshipers (37.6% of the sample), (2) Careless Money Admirers (19.9%), (3) Apathetic Money Managers (16.1%), and (4) Money Repellent Individuals (26.4%). We will briefly present these four money profiles below.

Achieving Money Worshipers have the most positive attitudes toward money. They worship money as their Success and Budget money carefully. Money Repellent Individuals have the most negative attitudes toward money. They consider that money is Evil and is not Success. The other two clusters of people fall between these two. Careless Money Admirers value Success but do not Budget money carefully. Apathetic Money Managers have somewhat indifferent attitudes toward money. They think that money is neither Evil nor a Motivator and tend to have high intrinsic job satisfaction and life satisfaction. American Business professors have the highest income among all different colleges. Further, most of Business professors (75%) are in the Achieving Money Worshiper cluster. Thus, high-income professors have the most positive attitudes toward money and the highest satisfaction with pay and pay administration. They also tend to have the highest work ethic and the longest work experiences. Money Repellent Individuals have the most negative attitudes toward money, the lowest income, the lowest work ethic, and the lowest satisfaction with pay administration.

Later, Tang, Tillery, Lazarevski, and Luna-Arocas (2004) investigated university students and small business owners in Macedonia. The same four money profiles were also identified in the Macedonian sample using the same 15-item Money Ethic Scale (Luna-Arocas & Tang, 2004): Achieving Money Worshipers (33.7%), Careless Money Admirers (21.3%), Apathetic Money Managers (15.7%), and Money Repellent Individuals (29.2%). The largest cluster for business owners is Achieving Money Worshiper (45.0%) and the smallest one is Apathetic Money Manager (6.7%). For students, the largest money profile is Money Repellent Individual (53.6%). Those who have money tend to have the most positive attitudes toward money and are Achieving Money Worshipers. Four money profiles can be consistently identified in different populations and cultures using the 15-item Money Ethic Scale.

More recently, Tang, Tang, and Luna-Arocas (2005) selected the original 30-item-6-factor Money Ethic Scale (Tang, 1992) and revealed four money profiles in a sample of 564 university students in the US: Achieving Money Worshipers (23.22%), Careless Money Admirers (30.16%), Apathetic Money Managers (31.08%), and Money Repellent Individuals (15.54%). It can be concluded that similar clusters can be identified using several versions of the Money Ethic Scale among different samples in several countries. The major attributes of the four clusters are similar across these studies and the percentage of people in each of these four clusters does vary from one sample to the next.

The main purpose of the present study is to investigate the money profiles using a different Money Ethic Scale and apply that to a sample of full-time employees and a sample of university students in People's Republic of China. Our focus is on people's propensity to engage in unethical behavior.

Hypotheses 1: Achieving Money Worshiper and Careless Money Admirer have a high propensity to engage in unethical behavior.

Achieving Money Worshipers tend to have the most positive money attitude. They worship money as their Success and Budget their money carefully. They have the highest competitive and winning attitude, high tendency to take actions and relatively high external locus of control. Although they are not the slave of money, they are still highly motivated by money. They, too, are very vulnerable to external pressures and opportunities. Careless Money Admirers also value Success, they exert effort trying to succeed and want to be millionaire, but they do not budget their money carefully, so they always feel lack of money. Otherwise, they tend to have high Work Ethic endorsement, the highest external locus of control, the highest tendency to take actions and be involved as a leader, but low intrinsic job satisfaction, pay satisfaction, and life satisfaction and the lowest fear of success (Tang, T. L. P., Luna-Arocas, R.and Sutarso, T. ,2005). So it is reasonable to expect that those people, whose are either Achieving Money Worshipers or Careless Money Admirers, will have a higher propensity to perform unethical behavior.

Hypotheses 2: Apathetic Money Handler and Money Repeller have a low propensity to engage in unethical behavior.

Money Repeller tend to have the most negative attitudes toward money, they negate all positive character of money (e.g. good, success, rich, respect, etc). To them money is not a power of motivation, (Lawler, 1971), but a kind of health protection (Herzberg et al., 1959), they have a low level of protestant work ethic endorsement, the highest fear of success, high internal locus of control, and low in winning attitude and involved as a leader. Apathetic Money Handlers think that money is not Evil and is not a Motivator and tend to have the highest intrinsic job satisfaction and life satisfaction. They would not work hard to make money and budget their money carefully, they have the highest internal locus of control, and the lowest degree of work devotion. So the power of money to attract, keep and promote them is quite weak, money is only a tool for them to sustain their lives. So it is reasonable to expect that Apathetic Money Handlers and Money Repeller may have a low propensity to engage in unethical behavior.

METHOD

Participants

Data were collected from 204 full-time employees in different locations (Nanjing, Shanghai, and Xining) and 395 university students at Hohai University in China. The mean age of employees was 31.57, and the mean age of university students was 20.9.

Table 1. Results of exploratory factor analysis (EFA) for the 42-Item Money Ethic[2] Scale

	\multicolumn{10}{c}{Component}
	1	2	3	4	5	6	7	8	9	10
1	**.785**	3.245E-02	.260	-.034	.103	-.077	9.848E-02	-.024	5.503E-02	3.249E-02
2	**.759**	.068E-02	.233	-.002	.100	-.082	5.879E-02	.279E-02	.136	.113
3	**.712**	-.007	.286	-.026	.841E-02	-.108	.119	2.237E-02	5.518E-02	.144
4	**.689**	.118	.164	-.077	.208	3.192E-02	.133	-.040	5.711E-02	.117
5	**.608**	3.926E-02	.217	-.064	.293	.117	9.898E-02	-.047	5.113E-02	5.769E-02
6	.961E-02	**.804**	3.983E-02	-.036	-.037	-.026	5.992E-02	.884E-02	-.267E-02	5.937E-02
7	.372E-02	**.794**	5.536E-03	-.009	-.002	-.084	-.035	5.368E-02	-.032	2.001E-02
8	.905E-02	**.782**	5.859E-02	-.009	-.071	-.028	7.666E-02	5.338E-03	-.025	9.662E-02
9	-.164	**.675**	5.232E-02	.790E-02	.128	.103	.153	.808E-02	9.231E-02	.457E-02
10	.897E-02	**.596**	5.064E-02	-.083	5.342E-02	.147	2.675E-02	.130	.133	-.052
11	.158	**.543**	-.040	-.009	-.014	-.017	.119	5.209E-02	5.518E-02	-.063
12	.198	5.917E-02	**.779**	-.628E-02	5.832E-02	.513E-02	.101	5.772E-02	-.010	.122
13	.173	.498E-03	**.752**	-.059	.106	-.100	5.623E-02	-.034	9.949E-02	5.397E-02
14	.175	-.021	**.723**	-.045	5.374E-02	-.046	.652E-02	-.057	.180	5.755E-02
15	.156	7.047E-02	**.701**	.102	5.035E-02	5.421E-03	7.128E-02	5.925E-02	-.041	2.888E-02
16	.254	7.234E-02	**.637**	-.120E-03	.212	.116	-.623E-02	-.028	2.676E-02	.608E-03
17	.074E-02	-.100	-.018	**.784**	-.100	.790E-02	5.298E-02	-.020	5.562E-03	5.331E-02
18	-.106	5.807E-02	5.504E-02	**.736**	-.007	2.019E-02	2.136E-02	.246E-02	2.470E-02	-.063
19	-.152	-.042	5.358E-03	**.734**	-.158	-.013	-.004	-.063	7.875E-02	.133
20	.206E-02	-.046	-.030	**.727**	5.879E-02	-.057	.197	.139	-.162	-.041
21	.821E-02	9.967E-04	5.656E-02	**.718**	5.293E-02	.555E-02	.185	.214	-.111	-.150
22	.161	2.324E-02	.179	-.037	**.828**	-.001	-.283E-02	-.034	.162	.259
23	.190	2.264E-02	.120	-.022	**.815**	-.012	7.023E-02	5.166E-02	.109	.219
24	.246	-.032	.180	-.086	**.765**	2.708E-02	-.009	-.098	.150	.190
25	.045E-02	.299E-02	5.451E-03	-.064	-.009	**.817**	.620E-03	-.024	9.468E-02	5.030E-02
26	.163E-02	2.888E-02	5.863E-03	5.869E-02	5.952E-02	**.815**	-.023	-.439E-02	5.574E-02	.128
27	-.138	-.114	.113	5.866E-02	5.464E-02	**.700**	5.692E-03	2.524E-02	9.597E-02	.809E-03
28	.047E-02	.135	-.176	-.025	-.052	**.583**	-.124	.109	7.359E-04	-.036
29	.130	7.923E-02	2.315E-02	.168	-.027	2.621E-03	**.801**	.149	5.421E-02	-.015
30	.237	.519E-02	.107	.133	5.154E-02	-.054	**.780**	9.859E-02	9.049E-02	5.146E-02
31	.234	.129	.202	9.203E-02	-.041	-.072	**.611**	2.072E-02	5.002E-02	.126
32	-.077	.186	5.361E-03	2.296E-02	.121	-.025	**.604**	5.054E-02	5.848E-03	-.003
33	-.139	9.848E-02	-.024	5.323E-02	-.026	2.148E-02	5.586E-02	**.830**	5.780E-02	5.845E-03
34	-.173	5.439E-02	2.128E-02	-.043	-.119	5.942E-03	2.931E-02	**.711**	-.012	.133
35	.116	5.597E-02	-.023	.153	5.878E-02	5.769E-02	.136	**.706**	.146	-.074
36	.256	9.281E-02	2.766E-02	.183	5.477E-02	.154	.125	**.560**	5.488E-02	-.176
37	.822E-02	.103	5.595E-02	-.073	.105	.148	5.042E-02	5.773E-02	**.814**	5.354E-02
38	.179	.130	5.593E-02	5.950E-02	2.915E-02	5.354E-02	2.129E-03	.103	**.791**	.125
39	.332E-02	2.698E-02	9.326E-02	-.097	.224	-.022	.114	5.976E-02	**.701**	-.003
40	.248	5.977E-02	.130	-.010	.203	-.018	5.205E-02	-.170E-03	9.606E-02	**.814**
41	.254	5.386E-02	.110	-.025	.236	-.017	5.534E-03	-.063	5.831E-02	**.788**
42	.180E-02	-.044	5.312E-02	-.012	.231	.290	5.822E-02	.209E-02	5.487E-02	**.594**

Extraction Method: Principal Component Analysis.
Rotation Method: Varimax with Kaiser Normalization.
a. Rotation converged in 7 iterations.

Table 2. Results of Exploratory Factor Analysis for the 15-Item Unethical Behavior Unethical Behavior Context Questionnaire[a]

	Component 1	Component 2	Component 3	Component 4	Component 5
1	**.745**	-.092	.226	.150	7.714E-02
2	**.713**	-.105	.351	2.010E-02	3.562E-02
3	**.669**	.240	7.688E-03	.136	-.027
4	**.663**	-.067	.138	.295	.104
5	**.656**	.269	7.137E-02	.244	-.040
6	**.644**	.126	8.028E-02	.142	-.020
7	**.621**	.341	2.407E-02	-.043	-.132
8	5.775E-02	**.828**	8.167E-02	7.136E-02	7.266E-02
9	.205	**.803**	5.227E-02	8.212E-02	.150
10	.147	.106	**.856**	.121	-.020
11	.246	4.483E-02	**.852**	1.426E-02	1.779E-02
12	.164	9.089E-02	.121	**.848**	-.032
13	.309	6.859E-02	4.931E-03	**.817**	1.536E-02
14	-.012	-.044	9.569E-02	-.006	**.855**
15	9.393E-03	.339	-.124	-.009	**.773**

Extraction Method: Principal Component Analysis.
Rotation Method: Varimax with Kaiser Normalization.
a. Rotation converged in 6 iterations.

Measure

The Money Ethic Scale (MES)

In the present study, we employed the Money Ethic Scale with (1) *disagree strongly*, (3) *neutral*, and (5) *agree strongly* as anchors (e.g., Tang and Tang, 2002; Tang and Chiu, 2003; Luna-Arocas and Tang, 2004; Du & Tang, 2005; Tang, Luna-Arocas, and Sutarso, 2005). Results of exploratory factor analysis (EFA) based on the whole sample are reported.

From the Exploratory Factor Analysis, there are ten factors: Rich (from item 1 to 5 in MES), Budget Money (from item 6 to 11 in MES), Good (from item 12 to 16 in MES), Evil (from item 17 to 20 in MES), Success (from item 21 to 23 in MES), Equity (from item 24 to 26 in MES), Charitable Giving (from item 27 to 30 in MES), Respect (from item 31 to 33 in MES), Motivator (from item 34 to 38 in MES), and Make Money (from item 39 to 42 in MES), which explain 62.34% total Variance. The coefficient alphas of Cronbach of them are: Total (0.8442), Good (0.8275), Evil (0.7636), Rich (0.8564), Success (0.8825), Equity 0.7391), Motivator (0.8084), Respect (0.7465), Budget Money (0.8048), Make Money (0.7426), Charitable Giving (0.7302).

Propensity to Engage in Unethical Behavior Scale (PEUBS)

We adopted the 15-item Propensity to Engage in Unethical Behavior Scale (Chen and Tang, in press; Tang and Chiu, 2003; Tang and Chen, 2006). Results of exploratory factor analysis (EFA) based on the whole sample are reported.

From the Exploratory Factor Analysis, there are five factors: Opportunity Context (from item 1 to 7 in PEUBS), Stressful Context (from item 8 to 9 in PEUBS), Non-master Feeling (from item 10 to 11 in PEUBS), Conformity (from item 12 to 13 in PEUBS), Unethical Organizational Context (from item 14 to 15 in PEUBS), which explain 66.16% total variance. The coefficient alphas of Cronbach of them are: Total (0.6372), Opportunity Context (0.8046), Stressful Context (0.7042), Non-master Feeling (0.7462), Conformity (0.6976), Unethical Organizational Context (0.5739).

RESULTS

Money Profiles Using the Money Ethic Scale

Using cluster analysis and discriminant analysis based on factors of the Money Ethic Scale, this study identified four money profiles using the 42-item, 10-factor Money Ethic Scale. The four money profiles are listed as follows: Achieving Money Worshiper (23.88% of participants in that sample), Careless Money Admirer (29.1%), Apathetic Money Handler (28.73%), and Money Repellent Individual (18.28%).

Table 3. Means (and Standard Deviations) of the Money Ethic Scale for the Four Clusters

Variable n=536 %	Cluster 1 Achieving Money Worshipers 128 23.88	Cluster 2 Money Repellent Individuals 98 18.28	Cluster 3 Apathetic Money Managers 154 28.73	Cluster 4 Careless Money Admirers 156 29.1	排序
Rich	4.29(0.55)	3.00(0.70)	3.57(0.61)	3.87(0.57)	1>4>3>2
Budget Money	3.66(0.71)	3.13(0.74)	3.56(0.62)	3.37(0.64)	1>3>4>2
Good	4.46(0.49)	3.54(0.63)	3.89(0.49)	4.09(0.55)	1>4>3>2
Motivator	1.85(0.70)	2.14(0.86)	1.56(0.52)	2.83(0.66)	4>2>1>3
Success	3.87(0.64)	2.21(0.70)	2.26(0.64)	3.16(0.75)	1>4>3>2
Evil	2.75(1.01)	2.87(0.75)	2.80(0.78)	2.55(0.79)	2>3>1>4
Make Money	4.35(0.50)	3.45(0.74)	4.05(0.49)	3.61(0.58)	1>3>4>2
Charitable	3.44(0.64)	3.15(0.72)	3.68(0.56)	3.10(0.54)	3>1>2>4
Giving	3.92(0.76)	2.10(0.66)	3.20(0.68)	3.11(0.76)	1>3>4>2
Equity Respect	3.42(0.80)	2.24(0.70)	2.23(0.64)	2.96(0.67)	1>4>2,3

Note: The data which are out bracket are Mean, and the data which are in bracket are Standard deviation.

Achieving Money Worshipers tend to have the most positive money attitudes (the highest score on Factors Good, Budget, Make Money, Success, Respect, Rich, Equity, and low score on Factor Evil). Careless Money Admirers have the highest score on Factors Motivator, high score on Success, good, Rich and Respect, but the lowest score on Factors Charitable Giving and Evil. Apathetic Money Handlers have the highest score on Factors Charitable Giving, and the lowest score on Factors Motivator. Money Repellent Individuals tend to have the most negative attitudes toward money (the highest score on Factor Evil and the lowest score on Factors Good, Rich, Equity, Budget, Success, and Make Money).

The Differences of Unethical Behavior Among Four Money Profiles

We examine the differences of unethical behavior among four Money Profiles (Achieving Money Worshiper, Careless Money Admirer, Apathetic Money Handler and Money Repellent Individual) and two groups of participants (employees and university students) in a Univariate Analysis of Variance. Results of Univariate and Post Hoc Tests (LSD) suggested that there were significant differences among four money profiles in two unethical contexts such as Stress and Organization, that is: Achieving Money Worshiper and Careless Money Admirer have higher propensity to engage in unethical behavior than Apathetic Money Handler and Money Repellent Individual when they face unethical stressful context, but Apathetic Money Handler and Money Repellent Individual have higher propensity to engage in unethical behavior than Achieving Money Worshiper when they are face with unethical organizational context.

Furthermore, there were significant differences between Employees and University Students in three unethical contexts such as Stressful Context, Conformity and Unethical Organizational Context. University students had higher propensity to engage in unethical behavior than employees.

Table 4. Univariate Analysis of Variance of Stressful Context Among Money Profiles

Source	Type III Sum of Squares	df	Mean Square	F	Sig.	Observed Power
Corrected Model	1.489	4	0.372	11.786	0.000	1.000
Intercept	30.635	1	30.635	970.11	0.000	1.000
Money Type	0.933	3	0.311	9.849	0.000	0.998
id	0.635	1	0.635	20.117	0.000	0.994
Error	16.737	530	0.032			
Total	69.327	535				
Corrected Total	18.225	534				

Table 5. Univariate Analysis of Variance of Conformity Context Among Money Profiles

Source	Type III Sum of Squares	df	Mean Square	F	Sig.	Observed Power
Corrected Model	9.971	4	2.493	3.021	0.018	0.802
Intercept	1440.776	1	1440.776	1746.257	0.000	1.000
Money Type	3.379	3	1.126	1.365	0.253	0.365
id	3.235	1	3.235	3.921	0.048	0.507
Error	433.984	526	0.825			
Total	2636.5	531				
Corrected Total	443.956	530				

Table 6. Univariate Analysis of Variance of Unethical Organization Context Among Money Profiles

Source	Type III Sum of Squares	df	Mean Square	F	Sig.	Observed Power
Corrected Model	87.541	4	21.885	32.884	0.000	1.000
Intercept	1762.546	1	1762.546	2648.371	0.000	1.000
Money Type	12.512	3	4.171	6.267	0.000	0.965
id	53.801	1	53.801	80.841	0.000	1.000
Error	348.733	524	0.666			
Total	3497.25	529				
Corrected Total	436.274	528				

DISCUSSION

Different people have different money profiles. The way of people to deal with unethical context also varies with different attitude they have towards money. To classify people's money profiles can deepen our understanding of their behavior and attitude towards work. Using the Money Ethic Scale which includes ten factors (Good, Evil, Success, Rich, Equity, Respect, Motivator, Budget Money, Make Money, Charitable Giving), this study identified four types of money profiles: Achieving Money Worshipers, Money Repellent Individuals, Apathetic Money Handlers and Careless Money Admirers.

This study examined a sample of managerial staffs and university students generally and found that when faced with the "Stressful Context", Achieving Money Worshipers and Careless Money Admirers have a higher propensity to engage in unethical behavior than Apathetic Money Handlers and Money Repellent Individuals. Hypotheses 1 was fully supported here. From the results we can see that Achieving Money Worshipers think highly about the value of money, they view money as a symbol of success and a means of winning respect and keeping an affluent life. Careless Money Admirers may have negative attitude towards money to some extent, but they usually feel lack of money most strongly. This is because they are relatively weak in the ability to make money and they do not budget their money carefully. So the attraction of money to them would be the strongest. The motivating power of money is also the strongest to them. Therefore, Achieving Money Worshipers and Careless Money Admirers are more likely to conduct unethical behavior to make personal profits when they are faced with Stressful Context. According to Professor Tang T. L. P.'s research, Careless Money Admirers are usually young and they are lack of work experience, have low income and low job and life satisfaction. They worship money, but do not have money. The great contrast between low income and high expectation of money brought them oppressive psychological pressure. There are two behavioral possibilities of such kind of employees: on one hand, they will work hard to make money, sometimes may take on work load beyond their capability; on the other hand, their utmost desire for money and failing to budget money carefully may easily leads them to behave illegally to get money. To managers, Careless Money Admirers are the employees easiest to be motivated by money and the most active ones, but the managers must pay attention to keep them away from engaging in unethical or illegal behavior.

The study also found that Apathetic Money Handlers and Money Repellent Individuals are more likely to engage in unethical behavior than the others when faced with Unethical Organizational Context. This result corresponds with hypotheses 2. Apathetic Money Handlers and Money Repellent Individuals all have negative attitude towards money; they never view money as success or a means of winning respect and never think money is the root of self value. Money is only external things besides the body to them and never be regard as motivator. They will not use unfair methods to gain financial advantages or take risk to do unethical or illegal things. According to Professor Tang T. L. P.'s research, although Apathetic Money Handlers get low incomes and make few job-hopping, they have high job satisfaction and life satisfaction and they can gain intrinsic self satisfaction from their work and life. They can never become slave of money, they are poor but happy. But in the Unethical Organizational Context, each member of the organization is using unfair method to make money, Apathetic Money Handlers and Money Repellent Individuals may also follow them to engage in unethical behavior, while Achieving Money Worshipers are more likely to restrain themselves from doing unethical behavior in such a context. According to Professor Tang T. L. P.'s research, Achieving Money Worshipers are the ones who get high income, plenty experience of work, older age, more diligent spirit and high life satisfaction. In addition, people's money profiles are also influenced by cultural value orientation and this orientation can restrict unethical behavior. The author's another research indicated that Achieving Money Worshipers have more remarkable sense of masculine superiority, self-protection and tendency of independent self-care than Apathetic Money Handlers, Careless Money Admirers and Money Repellent Individuals (Du Linzhi, 2005). This difference may implied that the Achieving Money Worshipers may intentionally restrain themselves from engaging in unethical behavior in order to keep their self image and well protect themselves. However, further and scientific analysis of this conclusion still depends on future studies.

The present study still reveals that university students are more inclined to engage in unethical behavior than managerial staffs when they are faced with Stressful Context, Conformity and Unethical Organizational Context. This result should be thought deeply. University students are the managers in the future; they are the main driven power for the development of society and economy of China in the future. It is uneasy to imagine the future picture of the national economy and society if our university students are all lack of trust and honesty. However, Professor Tang has pointed out that the money profile of individual will vary with the increase of experience and the change of income. But some other research indicated that money profile formed in the early period of childhood. It would go on to adulthood (Kirkcaldy & Furnham, 1993) and varies more or less to the change of experience of development and social and economic environment (Bruner & Goodman, 1947). While university students have more negative attitude towards money, the full-time employees hold more positive attitude towards money, this may implied that the university students will appreciate money when they get into the society, and when they begin to work hard to make money and become self-consumptive. The direct experience of money will change their money profiles. Relative studies show that people get high income tend to view money as not evil (Tang, 1992). The importance of demands of people and satisfaction of life (Tang & West, 1997) and money profiles may change with the increase of income (Furnham & Argyle, 1998). There is a process for the development from the lack of physical demands to the psycho needs. Therefore, as long as we emphasize the money profile education on one hand, and build a healthy business environment of honesty in our society on the other hand, along with strict and standardized system of trust supervision, the national economy and society will keep developing stably, healthily and orderly.

APPENDIX 1

Money Ethics Scale (MES)

1. Having a lot of money (being rich) is good.
2. I want to be rich
3. It would be nice to be rich.
4. Money is a motivator.
5. My life will be more enjoyable, if I am rich and have more money.
6. I use my money very carefully.
7. I spend my money based on a budget.
8. I budget my money very well.
9. I am proud of my ability to save money.
10. I save money for the future.
11. I pay my bills immediately.
12. Money is important.
13. Money is valuable.
14. Money is good.
15. Money is an important factor in the lives of all of us.
16. Money is attractive.
17. Money is a major cause of people's unethical and evil acts.
18. Money motivates people to perform unethically.
19. Money undermines one's ethical norms and standards.
20. The love of money is the root of all evil.
21. Money represents my achievement.

22. Money is power.
23. Money is a symbol of my success.
24. More money should be paid to people with more talent.
25. More money should be paid to people with higher merit (performance).
26. More money should be paid to higher-level jobs with more responsibilities.
27. I give generously to charitable organizations.
28. I believe in charitable giving.
29. I give money to the Church (religious organization(s)).
30. I give money to the Hoping Program.
31. Money helps me gain respect.
32. Money makes people respect me in the community.
33. Money allows me to express myself.
34. Money does NOT enhance the "love" of my job.
35. Money offers less excitement than achievement on my job.
36. Money is less important than recognition and achievement.
37. Money does NOT make my job exciting, interesting, and challenging.
38. Money does not increase my enjoyment of my work.
39. I find smarter and better ways of making money.
40. I am proud of my ability to make money.
41. I look for new and legal ways to make money.
42. I use (invest) my money to make more money.

Propensity to Engage in Unethical Behavior Scale (PEUBS)

1. Take merchandise and/or cash home.
2. Borrow $20 from a register overnight without asking.
3. Reveal company secrets when a person offers several million dollars.
4. Abuse the company expense accounts and falsify accounting records (time cards).
5. Accept money, gift, and kickback from others.
6. Overcharge customers to increase sales and to earn higher bonus.
7. Sabotage the company to get even due to unfair treatment.
8. Manager in my company often engages in behaviors that I consider being unethical.
9. In order to succeed in my company, it is often necessary to compromise one's ethics.
10. Take no action for employees who steal cash/merchandise.
11. Take no action for shoplifting by customers.
12. Use office supplies (paper, pen), Xerox machine, and stamps for personal purpose.
13. Make personal long-distance (mobile phone) calls at work.
14. If a manager in my company is discovered to have engaged in unethical behaviors that result primarily in *corporate gain* (rather than personal gain), he or she will be promptly reprimanded.
15. Top management in my company has let it be known in no uncertain terms that unethical behaviors will not be tolerated.

ABOUT THE AUTHORS

Du Linzhi (Ph.D., Nankai University) is an Associate Professor in the Department of Social Psychology, School of Zhou En'lai Government Management, Nankai University, Tianjin, People's Republic of China. Currently, he is conducting his post-doctoral research at Nanjing University in Nanjing, PRC. His primary research interests are in the areas of organizational behavior, money attitudes, and social psychology. He has published more than 20 journal articles and presented many papers at several international conferences around the world. He received the First Place Award of Research Excellence from the Ministry of Personnel, China (2004).

Thomas Li-Ping Tang (Ph.D., Case Western Reserve University) is a Full Professor of Management in the Department of Management and Marketing, Jennings A. Jones College of Business, Middle Tennessee State University (MTSU) in Murfreesboro, TN USA. He has taught Industrial and Organizational Psychology at National Taiwan University and at MTSU. His primary research interests are in organizational behavior, the love of money, unethical behaviors in the financial domain, work motivation, compensation decisions, satisfaction, turnover, OCB, and cross-cultural issues. He has published more than 93 journal articles (e.g., Journal of Applied Psychology, Personnel Psychology, Human Relations, Journal of Organizational Behavior, Journal of Management, Journal of Business Ethics, etc.), presented more than 160 papers in many countries, and reviewed papers for 24 journals around the world. He has received two Outstanding Research Awards (1991, 1999) and the Distinguished International Service Award (1999) at MTSU and the Best Reviewer Award from the International Management Division of the Academy of Management in Seattle, WA (2003).

Yang Dongtao (Ph.D., Nanjing University) is a Full Professor of Management in the Department of Management, School of Business, Nanjing University in Nanjing, Jiangsu Province, PRC. She has taught human resource management, operate management at Nanjing University. Her primary research interests are in human resource management, operate management and organizational behavior. She has published more than 50 journal articles and presented many papers at several international conferences around the world.

REFERENCES

Bruner, J. S., & Goodman, C. C. (1947).Value and needs as organizing factors in perception. *Journal of Abnormal and Social Psychology,* 42, 33-44.

Chen, Y. J., & Tang, T. L. P. (2006). Attitude toward and propensity to engage in unethical behavior: Measurement invariance across major among university students. *Journal of Business Ethics*, in press.

Du Linzhi (2005, August).A Study about the Relation between Money Profiles and Cultural Tendency of University Students in China. Paper presented at the 2005 Conference of China's Social Psychology Association. Tianyuan, China.

Du, L.Z., & Tang, T. L.P. (2005). Measurement invariance across gender and major: The Love of Money among university students in People's Republic of China. *Journal of Business Ethics*, 59, 281-293

Du, L. Z., Xu, X. S. & Tang, T. L. P. (2004). Endorsement of Money Ethics and Work Stress: the Case of Full-Time Employees in China. *Journal of Hohai University* (Philosophy and Social Sciences), 6(2), 65-69.

Herzberg, F., Mausner, B., & Snyderman, B.(1959). *The motivation to work.* New York: John Wiley & Sons.

Ivancevich, J. M., Konopaske, R., & Matteson, M. T. (2005). *Organizational behavior and management* (7th ed.). Boston: McGraw-Hill Irwin.

Kirkcaldy, B., & Furnham, A. (1993). Predictors of belief about money. *Psychological Report*, 73, 1079-1082.

Lawler, E. E. (1971). *Pay and organizational effectiveness: A psychological view.* New York: McGraw-Hill.

Luna-Arocas, R., & Tang, T. L. P. (2004). The love of money, satisfaction, and the Protestant Work Ethic: Money profiles among university professors in the USA and Spain. *Journal of Business Ethics*, 50 (4), 329-354.

Luna-Arocas, R., & Tang, T. L. P. (2005). The use of cluster analysis to segment clients of a sport cent in Spain. *European Sport Management Quarterly,* 5 (4), 381-413.

Tang, T. L. P. (1992). The meaning of money revisited. *Journal of Organizational Behavior*, 13, 197-202.

Tang, T. L. P.(1995). The Development of a Short Money Ethic Scale: Attitudes Toward Money and Pay Satisfaction revisted. *Personality and Individual Differences*, 19, 809–817.

Tang, T. L. P. & Tang, T. L. N. (2002). The Money Ethic Scale and Money Attitude in the USA. Paper presented at the XXV International Congress of Applied Psychology (Singapore), July, 7–12.

Tang, T. L. P., & Chiu, R. K. (2003). Income, Money Ethic, pay satisfaction, commitment, and unethical behavior: Is the love of money the root of evil for Hong Kong employees? *Journal of Business Ethics*, 46,13-30.

Tang, T. L. P., Tillery, K. R., Lazarevski, B., & Luna-Arocas, R. (2004). The love of money and work-related attitudes: Money profiles in Macedonia. *Journal of Managerial Psychology*, 19 (5), 542-548.

Tang, T. L. P., Tang, D. S. H., & Luna-Arocas, R. (2005). Money profiles: The love of money, attitudes, and needs. *Personnel Review*, 34 (5), 603-618.

In: Business Ethics in Focus
Editor: Laura A. Parrish, pp. 149-226

ISBN: 978-1-60021-684-8
© 2007 Nova Science Publishers, Inc.

Chapter 8

LEVINAS AND CORPORATE RESPONSIBILITY: A NEW PHILOSOPHICAL PERSPECTIVE

Conceição Soares[*]

Faculty of Economics and Management,
Portuguese Catholic University, Rua Diogo Botelho, 1327
4169-005 Porto, Portugal

ABSTRACT

Today in the mature economies and democracies of the West, with the increasing pace of globalisation, businesses as corporations have assumed unprecedented importance both nationally and internationally. Like all agents, they are capable of acting in ways with consequences said to be beneficial as well as harmful to society. Their increasing overwhelming prestige, power and resources have led some critics to argue that such entities should be held responsible for the latter. In other words, we need a notion of corporate responsibility both in the legal and moral domains. However, in such societies, the notion of responsibility is primarily that of individual responsibility which seems to run counter to that of corporate responsibility. As a result, the defenders of the *status quo* have seen fit to maintain that the concept of corporate responsibility is unintelligible and that the difficulties in rendering it intelligible and applicable, both morally and legally, are insurmountable.

This thesis is an attempt to overcome such objections and to construct a plausible defence of the notion of corporate responsibility. To do this, I use the following strategies:

1. I argue that some of the major criticisms of corporate (legal) responsibility can be overcome; in other words, that it makes sense to hold certain people within the structure of a corporate hierarchy to be responsible for manslaughter, and that even the notion of *mens rea*, a fundamental requirement for attributing responsibility in the law of homicide within the framework of individual

---

[*] Assistant Professor of Business Ethics. Ph.D Lancaster University- UK csoares@porto.ucp.pt

responsibility applies. I use the tragedy of the sinking of the Herald of Free Enterprise, to illustrate the points under discussion.

2. (a) However, I also claim that such a defence of corporate legal/moral responsibility may be too limited, too piecemeal and therefore not enough. The deep hostility and resistance to it will weaken only if the cultural ethos within which the theory of individual responsibility itself is embedded weakens, both at the level of theory and practice. In other words, I argue that a shift in moral paradigm is urgently needed.

(b) On the former level, an outline of an alternative perspective on responsibility must first be made available. To this purpose, I rely on some of the key insights of the philosophy of Levinas, especially his fundamental notion of infinite responsibility for the Other, to construct a plausible account in outline of corporate responsibility.

(c) In the context of practice, I set out some evidence to show that, of late, society, for example, in the UK (standing as surrogate for many economically advanced Western countries) – at the level of committed individuals, of NGOs and even of the government appear to be turning away from the theory of individual responsibility and reaching out or groping towards (though, perhaps, not consciously) what may be the central value of Levinasian philosophy, that is, infinite responsibility for the Other.

As a way of focusing this set of themes, I have chosen one case study – (a) the circumstances and events relating to the sinking of the Herald of Free Enterprise to stand as surrogate for problems in the domain of corporate legal and moral responsibility. The chapter attempts to demonstrate the relevance of Levinasian philosophy to these problems. Further Levinasian concepts are invoked to elucidate them.

It concludes in the light of all the arguments presented that the Levinasian philosophy which sees ethics as first philosophy, that the Levinasian concept of infinite responsibility for the Other, which is interpreted and defended in this chapter as an attempt to forge an *aretaic* ethic based on secular saintliness/holiness constitute a genuine new moral paradigm, and that this new paradigm may be relevant to the pre-occupations of the increasingly globalised world in the twenty-first century.

INTRODUCTION

There is a clear tendency in contemporary moral/political/legal thought to limit agency to individual agents, thereby denying the existence and relevance of collective moral agency in general, and corporate moral agency in particular. This tendency is ultimately rooted in the particular forms of individualism – ontological, methodological and fictive (abstract) – which have their source in the Enlightenment. Furthermore, the notion of moral agency which owes a lot to the Kantian tradition of moral philosophy is grounded on abstract reason and personal autonomy, to the detriment of a due recognition of the socio-historical grounds of moral social conduct (in conformity especially with fictive individualism). This tendency is reinforced by another, deriving from the principles of liberalism, which can be traced ultimately to Mill who also advocates that (normal adult) humans are rational/critical and autonomous beings. As a result of these two very powerful strands of philosophical thought in modern Western culture, agency is thought of invariably in individualistic terms, which leads us to think of responsibility in the same terms.[1] For this (and other) reasons individualism, in the forms mentioned, has attracted a great deal of critical debate in the social sciences to which the two nineteenth-century giants in sociology contributed – Weber, writing from the individualist stance, and Durkheim, from the holistic one.[2]

An adequate theory of responsibility is needed, which goes beyond individual responsibility, to include collective and corporate responsibility which is more open to taking into consideration society and its problems. This new theory of responsibility must also rest on a theory of agency, which holds, as Hegel and Arendt contend, that individuals are not isolated fictive, abstract entities, but beings shaped by society; furthermore, it is also the case that while individuals are shaped by society they in turn shape society itself.[3]

This chapter is an attempt to clarify the notion of corporate responsibility, rather than collective responsibility in general, I shall ignore the latter except to raise the following question — how is a corporation to be distinguished from collectivities in general — and then to answer it, here, in the briefest way possible. Collectivities like society, the family, the public, etc are general, amorphous, non-specific and ill-defined, whereas, corporations, *ex hypothesi*, are specific legal entities. Furthermore, corporations are consciously and carefully structured organisations with different levels of management and have clearly defined aims and objectives, a central feature upon which I shall be focusing.

For my purpose the most important issue about corporate responsibility is to know if it makes sense to impute moral and legal responsibilities to a corporation. I would like first to analyse critically the legal and moral theories of corporations and then to look at some theories of corporate criminal culpability. The case study of the sinking of the Herald of Free Enterprise[4] exemplifies that even some of these theories may not ultimately be sufficient to

---

[1] See May (1992).
[2] See Gerwen (2000), 43. For influence of Weberian conceptualisation, see, for example, Donaldson (1982), Jackall (1988). The Durkheimien view underpins French (1984).
[3] This latter point will be raised later in section 3.
[4] For details of this disaster, see Department of Transport, Report of Court No. 8074 (1987). This report, throughout the rest of this chapter, will be referred to, for short, as the Sheen Report.

In brief outline, the salient facts of the case and the findings of the Sheen Report are as follows:

The day 6th March of 1987 was a terrible day for the passengers of the Roll on/Roll off ferry *Herald of Free Enterprise*. The ferry capsized in the approaches to the Belgian port of Zeebrugge en route to Dover in England at 19.05 local time. There was a light easterly breeze and the sea was calm. The ship had a crew of 80 and carried 459 passengers, 81 cars, 3 buses, and 47 trucks. After leaving the harbour, 90 seconds later, she capsized ending on her side half-submerged in shallow water. Only an accidental movement to starboard in her last moments prevented her from sinking totally in deeper water.

After the capsize, a courageous search and rescue operation was raised. At least 150 passengers and 38 members of the crew died from hypothermia, many of them inside the ship or in the frozen water. Many others were injured. The rescuers soon realised that the *Herald of Free Enterprise* had left the Zeebrugge port with her bow doors open.

The design of the Roll on/Roll off ferry boats are essentially pontoons covered by a superstructure, with bow and stern doors which provide the means for vehicles to drive on and off via adjustable ramps at the dock. The speed of a ferry loading and unloading is improved for a Roll on/ Roll off ship, abbreviating the time a ship spends in port.

The Sheen Report identified five faults related to safety as the direct cause of the disaster:
(a) pressure to leave the berth immediately after the loading;
(b) excessive number of passengers;
(c) lack of indicator lights – "there is no indicator on the bridge as to whether the most important watertight doors are closed or not";
(d) failure to ascertain the ship's draught: "The ship's draught is not read before sailing, and the draught entered into the Official Log Book is completely erroneous. It is not standard practice to inform the Master of his passenger figure before sailing. Full speed is maintained in dense fog";

explain the complex structure of culpability, which is shaped as much by shared cultural understanding as by moral/legal theory.

Second, I will concentrate on outlining and defending Levinas's fundamental concept of infinite responsibility. However, this is not, *per se*, a chapter on the philosopher, Emmanuel Levinas, but a much less ambitious and extremely limited project of selectively examining a very few of his key concepts with the aim of borrowing whatever insights could be drawn from them, in order to provide the outline of a much needed new moral paradigm and a new perspective on responsibility in general, and a corporate responsibility in particular. One caveat must be entered immediately. The way this chapter proposes to handle all the concepts of Levinas philosophy which may not win the approval of Levinas himself (posthumously, so to speak) or of those who call themselves Levinasian scholars; furthermore, they would also be examined, in the main, within a mode of philosophising somewhat different from the European tradition to which Levinas belong. However, in spite of the potential charge of misunderstanding, misusing the texts, and indeed, even of abusing them in order to advance my own purpose, I believe this attempt to be intellectually justified – in the sole end of the exercise is simply to borrow insights, wherever they could be found, to help explicate a crucial notion, under-theorised by philosophers working in the so-called analytic, Anglo-Saxon style of philosophising today. As already mentioned, the key Levinasian concept upon which this second part concentrates is that of infinite responsibility for others. However, to make this intelligible, one must give a very brief intellectual biography of Levinas, as well as relating the notion of infinite responsibility to a few other concepts closely related to it in Levinas thought.

Third and finally I will argue for a shift in moral paradigm and suggest that Levinas's conception of ethics as first philosophy and his *aretaic* account of ethics constitute a genuine moral paradigm. I have also defended it against possible criticisms in general and against his fundamental notion of infinite responsibility for the Other together with some of its associated concepts in particular. This is with the aim of giving a radically new orientation to the notion of responsibility itself, which goes beyond the narrow philosophical/moral confines in which the theory of individual responsibility is embedded. If the spirit of the Levinasian account of infinite responsibility for the Other were to filter through to individual and social consciousness, then, perhaps, the powerful cultural resistance to corporate responsibility/culpability would be eroded.[5] Society and its legal system (such as that in

---

(e) inadequate capacity of the ballast pumps. The existing pump took 1.30 minutes to empty the tanks, which meant that the ferry could not get back on to an even keel until it was well out to sea. A new pump would only have cost £25,000, but the Company regarded this as prohibitive.

The Report found that "(f)rom top to bottom the body corporate was infected with the disease of sloppiness". The board of directors ignored the several recommendations about the safety management of their vessels. Yet, as far as culpability was concerned, the Sheen Report found Captain David Lewry and Mr Leslie Sabel (the Chief Officer) to have been "guilty of serious negligence causative of the casuality. Both these officers have suffered the penalty of having their Certificates suspended (The Sheen Report, 74)." In the light of that, the "Court does not wish to impose on them a heavy financial penalty. (ibid)" As for Townsend Car Ferries Limited, the Report merely concluded that it had no way of marking its "heavy responsibility for the disaster" than paying the sum of £350,000 towards the payment of the costs of the Court's investigation into the whole tragedy. Justice Sheen significantly remarked: "That seems to me to meet the justice of the case (The Sheen Report, 74-75)."

[5] Two limitations immediately spring to mind. First, it is true that Levinas himself had no interest in the legal issue of corporate responsibility *per se*. However, as legal responsibility (especially in the law of homicide) overlaps with moral responsibility, there is nothing in principle objectionable to extending his insight regarding moral responsibility to the area of the law, which this thesis is, amongst other things, concerned with. Second, the

England and Wales) as well as its moral outlook would be more ready to accept that corporations could be found guilty of even manslaughter, and be duly punished for it (as in the case of the Herald of Free Enterprise and similar tragedies), or that they could be said to be morally responsible for these deaths/harm caused.

In my opinion, one of Levinas's biggest contribution to the debate could lie in making a case – an affirmation – for saying that saintliness/holiness as a virtue is neither unintelligible, absurd nor impracticable in both interpersonal conduct and in public life.[6] Levinas has also argued against the view – a denial – that morality is grounded solely on autonomy, freedom and reason, and that moral obligation rests essentially on reciprocity. His two-pronged strategy – affirmation on the one hand and denial on the other – opened the way for his central notion of infinite responsibility for the Other which in turn can be defended against the charge of either unintelligibility or absurdity. Instead, I shall, first, attempt to set out some empirical evidence[7] to show that, at long last, society at large (to take the UK as an example) may be groping (not admittedly, self-consciously) towards the central Levinasian insights in its concern and pre-occupation with certain increasingly pressing issues of our time. Next, I shall add to the analytical framework set out in the second part by raising a few more Levinasian concepts, which are particularly germane to the respective discussions of corporate legal responsibility and of corporate moral responsibility (the Herald of Free Enterprise).

But before doing that, I need to show how my arguments in first part about the applicability of *mens rea* to corporate agency can be linked up with my arguments in this one about the relevance of the Levasian account of responsibility to corporate agency itself.

Given this understanding, there should then be no problem, as far as I can ascertain, to extending the personal "I" which is the bearer of Levinasian responsibility to the "I" or perhaps more appropriately, the "we" (as more than one individual in the corporate structure may be said to occupy key positions) of corporate responsibility. If the arguments in first part are plausible, they should provide an appropriate background, in turn, to borrowing some of Levinas's insights to elucidate the concept of corporate responsibility, both in the legal and moral domains.

---

scope of his responsibility is only responsibility for the Other human being. As Llewelyn (1991:114) points out: "(Levinas) is so preoccupied with doing justice to the human being that he fails to do justice to the non-human being, for despite his rare references to our responsibility "for everything"... these go unexplained and stand out as anomalies in writings which say or imply that direct, unmediated responsibility is responsibility to the other human being." But for the purpose of this chapter, the latter objection will just be noted, as acknowledging it is not necessarily so damaging. The main remit of this thesis is to defend the intelligibility of the notion of corporate responsibility, in particular with reference to death/harm caused to human beings by the action of corporate agents.

[6] His own life witnessed some of the most violent events in recent history: the Second World War, the Holocaust, and after that, other countless destructions, including the Gulag. Yet, his faith in holiness remained unshaken: "I want to say that this business of Auschwitz did not interrupt the history of holiness. God did not reply, but he has taught that love of the other person, without reciprocity is a perfection in itself. (Mostley (1991): 21)."

[7] The evidence is necessarily limited, given the remit of this chapter and is confined to those issues raised by the case study selected.

I. CORPORATE RESPONSIBILITY WITHIN INDIVIDUALIST PARAMETERS AND CAUSATION

1. The Meaning of Corporate Moral Responsibility

Is a corporation an entity in relation to which one can apply the ideas of moral responsibility such as agency, rationality, and autonomy? Can we apply responsibility and blame to a corporation? For the upholders of the theory of individual responsibility rooted in methodological individualism and its related metaphysics, one cannot, as we has seen, ascribe moral responsibility to a corporation, only to "flesh-and-blood" individuals who are moral persons.

1.1. A Metaphysical Issue: Nominalist or Realist?

Fisse and Braithwaite (1988) argue that methodological individualism, especially the kind advocated by Hayek, amounts to a dualist ontology. On the one side are individuals; on the other corporations. Individuals are observable, and therefore, real; corporations are abstractions without the possibility of direct observation.[8] If it is so, it is not possible to ascribe moral accountability to a corporation, and ideas such as agency, autonomy and rationality do not apply to a corporation. John Ladd appears to agree with this view, when he says:

> We cannot and must not expect formal organizations, or their representatives acting in their official capacities, to be honest, courageous, considerate, sympathetic, or to have any kind of moral integrity. Such concepts are not in the vocabulary, so to speak, of the organizational language game. ((1970), 499)

In the "game " of corporations moral responsibility is a word without meaning.

The debate around this problematic have two contestants: nominalists and realists. For the former, corporations are collections of individuals, or aggregations of human beings. For the latter, a corporation has an existence and a meaning as well as a moral/legal personality of its own. Both of these views have implications for moral and legal responsibility. If we accept that corporations are merely aggregations of individuals, it is difficult to ascribe moral responsibility to them. In this nominalist view, corporations do not exist apart from their members; any blameworthiness or responsibility can only be attributed to an individual servant or employee. This would leave one with the problem of deciding whether the corporation should be responsible for the behaviour of all of its employees or only for some of them. On the realist view, corporations do represent something beyond individuals, which means that following from this point of view, it may be possible to find a new candidate for attributing responsibility.

1.2. A Question of Rational Agency

Behind the controversy involving these two positions in metaphysics, stands another crucial but related issue, namely, about rational agency. Can we apply to a corporation, ideas such as, agency, rationality, autonomy?

---

[8] However, Lukes ((1973): 111-22) comments that a corporation is eminently observable.

Peter French first sets out the individualist answer as follows:

> (a corporation) is understood to be nothing more than a contractual nexus, a collection of self-interested humans acting either as principals or agents with respect to each other. ... The agents, agency theory assumes, only work for their principals because of what those agents expect personally to gain from the relationship. A corporation is but the financial and contractual "playing field" for a number of individual dealings, and it has no existence independent of those dealings. (1997: 149)[9]

However, French goes on to reject it, and argues that corporations are moral persons in the sense that they are entities and they are intentional actors. He sees corporations as entities with dominant roles to play in our society. Therefore, in this view, corporations are more than mere collections of individuals, which means that they are capable of moral decisions and hence susceptible to moral blame.[10]

Every corporation creates a general set of policies (as well as an image) that are easily accessible to both its agents and those with whom it interacts. When an action performed by someone in the employ of a corporation is an implementation of its corporate policy, then it is proper to describe the act as done for corporate reasons or for corporate purposes to advance corporate plans, and so as an intentional action of the corporation. (French (1995: 27))[11]

French argues that all corporations have internal decision structures (CID) that supply the basis for attributing moral agency to them. He identifies two elements in these structures, the first is related to "an organizational flow chart" and the second involves rules that enable one to go between individual and corporate decisions.[12] The CID structures have two kinds of rules: organisational and policy rules. He compares the former to the descriptive rules of sport events, like the rules of a basketball game. These organisational rules in corporations distinguish between and clarify the role of each member, "delineate stations and managerial levels, and plot the lines of authority, subordination, and dependence among and between such stations and the organization (1984: 41)." The policy rules are what he calls, "recognition" rules, because they provide "affirmative grounds for describing a decision or an act as having been made or performed for corporate reasons in the structured way (1997: 150)."

We can say with Brytting, that "together they form the 'letter' and the 'spirit' of the company (2000: 89)." It is even possible for the CID structure to be so tightly construed that individual responsibility and freedom no longer makes sense. However, French argues that, in practice, it makes sense to talk about actions, which are informed by the corporation's plans, aims and interests beyond those of the individuals who work inside the company. Under those circumstances the corporation is a moral agent in its own right.

---

[9] See also, French (1984) and (1996).

[10] See, Goodpaster and Matthews (1982).

[11] This view is also shared by MacDonald: "Not only does the organization have all the capacities that are taken to ground autonomy – viz., capacities for intelligent agency – but it also has them to a degree no human can. Thus, for example, a large corporation has available and can make use of far more information than one individual can. Moreover, the corporation is, in principle, 'immortal' and so better able to bear responsibility for its deed than humans, whose sin dies with them. (1987: 219-20)." According to this view, a corporation has moral responsibility for all its actions during its life. The IBM faces "a multi-billion dollar lawsuit over the allegations that the Nazis used the company's data processing technology in the mass murder of Jews". See *The Independent*, Monday, 12 February 2001.

[12] French (1997: 149).

Corporate moral agency enables the possibility of describing an event in two ways: First, the intentional action of the individuals, and second, the intentional action of the corporation for which the individuals work. This means that intentionality is not only confined to the level of the individual. Take a sentence like the following which one might read in the daily papers: "Corporation X today signed an agreement with Government Y to lower the price of certain drugs it sells to Y". The corporation in question has certain rational goals in mind — for instance, Government Y has already started legal proceedings against it for over-pricing, that Y has threatened to take its custom to a rival, etc. However, the corporation can only achieve its goals and interests through the actions of certain designated "flesh-and-blood" individuals. In the example cited, its CEO, a certain Mr A would have put his signature to the same document as the Minister for Health of Y, a certain Mr B. Mr A, not in his capacity as CEO of X, but as a mere shareholder of X, might be very unhappy about the corporation's action, as he personally could stand to lose out on his dividends as he has shares in the corporation. The corporation's interests and goals could diverge from those of the individual within the corporation in any one specific context. All this means is that corporations have rational reasons for behaving in certain ways because they have interests in pursuing their established corporate goals despite the temporary, conflicting self-interests of managers and directors.

In this non-mysterious sense, we can say that corporations are intentional actors, capable of being motivated to respond not only to internal challenges but also to external ones. As intentional actors, why then should they not have responsibilities? But responsibilities to whom? Commonly, corporations are said to be responsible to their share-holders; by this is meant that should share-holders be displeased with their annual dividends, they could sell off their shares, or try to get rid of the CEO, etc. These actions appear to cause no difficulty. Nobody seems to find it unintelligible to hold the "fat cat" responsible for the slump in the corporation's fortune; some people find it, however, morally offensive that often "failing fat cats" in our present culture are "rewarded" for their incompetence. But the latter difficulty is only morally bizarre; from the theoretical point of view of holding someone responsible for the down-turn in the corporation's fortune, every one seems to be clear that it is the CEO and/or other top managers, rather than the porter at the front door who could be said to be responsible.

However, difficulties of an insuperable theoretical kind are alleged to arise the moment one claims that corporations ought to be responsible to a wider set of people, other than their share-holders, such as their customers, citizens at large who have to suffer the effects of their actions (like polluting air, water, soil). But if the incompetent "fat cats" could be held responsible for having allowed the corporation to perform miserably on the stock market (through admittedly the morally bizarre act of buying them off handsomely for their incompetence), surely the same incompetent "fat cats" could be held responsible for manslaughter when the policies they formulate and put into practice lead to death (as in the case of the Herald of Free Enterprise).

To labour a point, recall that these individuals are no ordinary intentional actors, so to speak, but owing first and foremost, to their power, their actions have impact upon a large number of people. They have extensive resources enabling them to formulate and articulate certain policies and strategies, for carrying them out, as well as to monitor their outcome.[13]

---

[13] The really large trans-national corporations have assets and turnovers which far exceed the GDP (gross domestic product) of many nation states in the world today.

If the above were admitted, then corporations may even be held to a more stringent level of responsibility than a mere "flesh-and-blood" private citizen, as its field of action is more embracing than that of individual agents. This is the reason why French says:

> Business firms in this century occupy social positions roughly equivalent to the prominent posts held in other eras by the church, the nobility, the army, even the feudal lords. They dominate the lives of all but a few members of the community. They control the financial and economic aspects of society and are possessed of monetary power far greater than the world's governments. ... Corporations today enjoy the prestige associated with creating and maintaining the scale or worth against which the majority of adults in Western societies judge their own value. ... Corporations are far from being social fictions. (1984: ix)[14]

Nonetheless, this view has been subject to critical scrutiny, namely by the individualist side.[15] I cannot discuss in detail all the different points of each critique, but it is important to underline that these positions consider French's view to be flawed, because he compares the corporation's capability of decision-making with that of the human mind, implying that corporate intentionality could be compared to human intentionality. But his critics may have missed the point, namely if corporations can act rationally (and autonomously), it would follow that they can be said to be moral agents.[16]

But how can this view be sustained against the central charge mounted by the individualist critique? Let us begin by setting out in brief an analysis of what the individual theory of responsibility could mean by the notion of human agency. An individual is said to be an effective agent if at least the following conditions obtain:

1. He/she has desires and emotions.
2. He/she has knowledge of some (though necessarily not all) of the causal connections in the world in which he/she operates.
3. He/she can foresee (to some extent) the consequences of his/her action.
4. He/she is capable of formulating intentions and plans based on 1, 2, 3.

The notion of (moral) responsibility may at the same time be attributed only to those human beings who satisfy the above. That is why, as already observed earlier, not all human beings are moral agents[17] — the very young, for instance, do not qualify. Babies have desires, of course, but these are very limited ones; their knowledge of causal connections is again at best absolutely minimal, although not totally absent. In pre-modern times, animals were credited with responsibility but since modernity, they have not been so charged on the

---

[14] In a similar vein, Anita Roddick says: "In terms of power and influence, you can forget the church, forget politics. There is no more powerful institution in society than business – I believe it is now more important than ever before for business to assume a moral leadership. The business of business should not be about money, it should be about responsibility. It should be about public good, not private greed (2000: 3)."

[15] The main critics of French's position are Velasquez (1983), Donaldson (1982), Danley (1999) and Werhane (1985). They deny that corporations are moral agents, as only individuals are moral agents.

[16] See Velasquez (1983); Friedman (1970). See also Werhane (1985: 57) who develops a moderate position on corporate moral agency, based on the notion of "secondary actions." "Because corporate 'actions' are what I have called secondary actions, a corporation is not an independent moral agent. Unlike individual actions, which are presumed to be free choices of autonomous agents, corporate 'action' is an outcome of groups of choices of constituents and agents acting on behalf of the corporate." Such a position implies ontological individualism. For a detailed discussion about all these positions, see Danley (1999).

[17] However, the proposition that "All moral agents are human beings" is true.

grounds that, as they lack language, they are incapable of being aware (in the way a normal human adult is) of the consequences of their behaviour and, therefore, of the harm they could cause to others.

Next, let us apply the criteria listed above to a corporation. Surely, it is unproblematic to admit that a corporation has desires, purposes and goals (the key ones being to maximise profits and growth), it can and must articulate and formulate intentions and plans, short- and long- term (including its so-called "mission statement" and business plan(s), it is capable of apprising itself of causal connections in the domain in which it operates, it can foresee and monitor (even to a greater extent, as we have seen, than any ordinary intentional actor) the consequences of its actions (although it may choose to turn a blind eye to some of these, and that is common enough). After all, a corporation is not like a loose cannon, a somnambulist, a baby, a mentally retarded or a mad person. As we have already seen, it is essentially a clearly defined organisation with stated aims and objectives, with worked out strategies for achieving them, with resources to monitor closely the impact of its strategies on its customers, its competitors, on governments, etc., and to take steps to revise its strategies in the light of new developments, social, political as well as scientific and technological. In the free market, no corporation can be expected to survive unless it adapts itself intelligently to the changing world in which it operates. Could such an organisation not be said to be rational and autonomous (its aims and objectives are, after all, self-chosen and defined)? As to whether *mens rea* can be attributed to such an entity, this matter will be left to the next section to explore.

2. Corporate Legal Responsibility

2.1. The Theoretical Debate

According to Celia Wells, the question of attributing legal responsibility to a corporation depends on the area of the law concerned. There are two main areas involved, corporate and criminal law. Corporate law has two main purposes, one internal and another one external. The former involves and regulates the corporation's membership and relationship with its own members, its need for establishing the procedures for its functioning, the duties of directors, and the role of share-holders. In the last decade a great improvement in this area has been made, particularly in the domain of corporate governance.[18] After a series of business scandals in the United Kingdom, namely the "Maxwell affair",[19] the issue of corporate governance has come under intense scrutiny, and what at that time seemed to be unproblematic became very problematic, namely the roles and responsibilities of boards and directors. [20] The latter aspect of corporate law concerns the legal duties and responsibilities that regulate the relationship of the company with outsiders.[21]

---

[18] A lot has been written on this subject. See Stiles (1997); Kitson and Campbell (1996).

[19] The "Maxwell affair" was the scandal related to the theft of pension funds by Robert Maxwell, which shocked the public. The auditors were also unable to expose the imminent bankruptcy of the Bank of Credit and Commerce International. At the same time, senior business executives were offered undeserved pay rises. The Enron affair in the last year adds to the unease.

[20] The Cadbury Report (1992); Boyd (1996).

[21] For more references to these points, see Third Part, section 2.1.

But it is criminal law and the issues it raises for corporate responsibility that are addressed here rather than matters arising from corporate law *per se*. How can a legal entity such as a corporation be said to be criminally responsible? According to Celia Wells:

> Criminal law is pre-eminently concerned with standards of behaviour enforced, not through compensation, but through a system of state punishment negotiated via standards of fault such as intention, knowledge, and subjective recklessness (1998: 654).

If it is difficult to ascribe civil liability to a corporation it is even more difficult to ascribe criminal responsibility. The most serious offence which corporations can be charged with is manslaughter; others, less serious, are connected with failure to enforce standards pertaining to environment, health and safety, conditions of trade. C. Clarkson distinguishes criminal from civil liability in at least four important aspects.

> First, criminal liability involves stronger procedural protections such as the safeguards under PACE and the requirement for proof beyond reasonable doubt. Secondly, criminal law is enforced by moral more powerful enforcement agencies, whether it be the police or the HSE, with more resources at their disposal than many private plaintiffs. Thirdly, criminal punishment involves stigma and censure, and fourthly and related to the last point, criminal sanctions have a symbolic and "message-sending" role. (1998: 2)

Some theorists, such as G. R. Sullivan argue that there is no such thing as corporate crimes. In a good many cases (such as the example of the Herald of Free Enterprise), there is no one single individual who has caused the harm; what has happened is a conjunction of several actions committed by several individuals producing the harm. As the company structure is so complex, it is difficult to know who ultimately bears the responsibility. Even when we do attribute culpability to a corporation it is always an individual (or individuals) within the company who is (are) held culpable, as crimes "can only be committed by human, moral agents".[22] However, the position Clarkson advocates is totally different:

> The argument in favour of corporate criminal responsibility is that in many cases it is the company itself, through its policies or practices, that has done wrong and prosecution and punishment should be directed at the real wrongdoer. (1982: 4)

---

[22] Sullivan (1995). This, as we have seen, is a red herring. Of course, it is true that if a corporation were to be found guilty, say of manslaughter, it would be a "flesh-and-blood" individual within the company structure which would be sent to prison. But, as already observed, it is not any individual but the particular individual or individuals who make(s) policies and decisions in the name of the corporation, as a result of which, deaths have occurred. (I shall be returning to this matter in what follows.) David Bergman (2001: 18) may have been a little misleading when he writes: "Under current law, a company can be convicted of manslaughter only if a senior manager or director – a "controlling mind" of the company – is found guilty as an individual ... . The government agreed four years ago to reform this archaic law and allow a company to be convicted of homicide without the need to prosecute one of its directors." He has failed to make it clear that while it may make sense to prosecute a corporation and convict it of manslaughter, there is no way in which you could suitably punish the corporation in question by a sentence of imprisonment without sending a "flesh-and-blood" individual or individuals to prison. Ultimately, it must be those "flesh-and-blood" individuals which constitute the controlling mind of the company who are fit candidates "to be" the company for the purpose of incarceration, as they are the ones who, in their roles of executive directors, etc., articulate and formulate the goals and policies and endorse strategies for implementing them.

One of the main purposes of enforcing corporate criminal responsibility is to guarantee that corporations ameliorate their work practices. As Clarkson underlined one of the means to put pressure on the corporations with the aim of improving their practices is prosecution as well as the media attention which prosecution will bring.

Discussions about corporate criminal responsibility reflect concerns about the safety of employees, customers, as well as of the public at large. As Wells puts it:

> Disasters such as rail crashes, ferry capsizes, and chemical plant explosions that can be attributed to corporate enterprise operations have led to calls for those enterprises to be prosecuted for manslaughter. It is the cultural origins in changing perceptions of risk and hazard from various sources as well as the legal acceptance of these demands that are of interest. (1998: 658)

A key source of resistance against the notion of corporate conviction is that, under the dominant theory of individual responsibility, individuals could be blamed for their actions only if *mens rea* obtains. Surely *mens rea* fails to obtain in the case of corporate conduct? In spite of this, Clarkson suggests that corporate conviction could apply:

> (by) humanising companies in the sense of breaking them down, metaphorically, into their underlying human components to see if there was an individual within the company who had committed the *actus reus* of a crime with the appropriate *mens rea*. (1996: 560)

If the individual is a senior member of the company and has a key place, in the corporation's structure of command it is possible to say that he/she represents the corporate brain and his/her acts could be identified with the company itself. If so, corporations could be held directly responsible (in the same terms as the individual).[23]

In English law, for a type of crime involving proof of *mens rea*, the established way of prosecution is via the *identification doctrine* which we have already come across in the last section. This doctrine establishes that this kind of crime is only applicable to (a) senior member(s) who stand(s) for the mind of the corporation and in this case the company can be liable for his/her act and *mens rea*. By this process there is identification between the acts of the individual and of the company, which means that direct accountability could be applied. Such a theory allows for the prosecution of the company via the individual. However, if the individual is not a senior member, the prosecution is only imputed to the individual and not to the company.

Some objections could be applied to this theory. As Field and Jörg (1978) point out, this theory makes a division between "brains" and "hands" within the corporation structure, which leads to a real obstruction in the efficacy of legal control in at least, two ways. First, in large corporations in which the corporate structures are more diffused it is current practice to give power to quasi-autonomous managers; in these cases it is easy to avoid responsibilities. For instance, when a corporation is at risk of prosecution for manslaughter, a similar process of

---

[23] As Lord Denning says: "A company may in many ways be likened to a human body. It has a brain and nerve centre which controls what it does. It also has hands, which hold the tools and act in accordance with the corporate structure as to represent the "brains" of the company as opposed to the mere "hands". The *Bolton (Engineering) Co Ltd v T.J. Graham & Sons Ltd*, 1995, 1 QB 159, 172.

transferring power could occur with the aim of evading responsibilities. Second, this account limits corporate responsibility only to the "brains" of the corporation.

Whilst the first objection may have some force in some contexts, the second seems not to be really valid. I've already argued in the last section that it makes sense to single out the "brains" of the corporation as the embodiment of the corporation as it is at this level of top management that goals are chosen and strategies adopted.

One alternative to the identification doctrine is the *aggregation doctrine*. In order to overcome the problems of the identification doctrine, this theory aggregates all the acts and *mens rea* of several pertinent individuals in the company in order to verify if it is possible to consider it a crime as if those acts have been committed by only one person. But, as Clarkson says:

> The doctrine ignores the reality that the real essence of the wrongdoing might not be what A, B, C and D did but the fact that the company had no organisational structure or policy to prevent A, B, C and D each doing what they did in a way that cumulatively amounts to a crime. (1982: 8)

Again, critics point out that this view does not reflect corporate decision-making in reality. Even when the acts of A, B, C or D might be gathered together to determine a crime, the reality might show that none of these agents need be at fault. The corporation may be structured in such a way that B could and would not know what C was doing or has failed to do.

Another solution to corporate criminal responsibility is the theory of *Reactive Corporate Fault* which advocates that when the *actus reus* of an offence by the corporation is established, a court gives the corporation the power to guide its own investigation, with the aim of finding out who was the responsible employee and after that of applying the adequate measures. No criminal responsibility will be imputed if the corporation takes the necessary measures. Criminal responsibility is only prescribed in case the corporation does not implement in a satisfactory way the court order. According to Wells this theory has at least two advantages. First, traditionally corporate liability needs proof of responsibility for causally relevant acts or omissions at or before the time the wrongdoing is manifest; however, this theory does not presuppose antecedent fault.[24] Second the corporation has the possibility to demonstrate grief and rehabilitative measures.[25]

However, in Clarkson's opinion, this theory also has some distinct disadvantages. What kind of practices or measures could be applied in terms of avoiding criminal responsibility? In the case that the corporation does not take satisfactory steps, what kind of offence is committed? Would admonishing an employee and warning the staff be enough to prevent people from doing certain actions in the future?[26]

In Clarkson's view, the best way to ascribe criminal responsibility to a corporation is to combine the *doctrine of corporate mens rea* with the *corporate compliance programme* (this is a formal programme with the aim of ensuring that every employee in the corporation knows the laws related to the corporation's actions) which tries to guarantee corporate compliance with the law. As Laufer and Clarkson point out, such a programme is an attempt

---

[24] See Fisse and Braithwaite (1993: 47-49).
[25] See Wells (1998: 659).
[26] See Clarkson, (1982: 9).

at recognising all the complexities of the dynamism of a corporation, namely, its structure, culture, aims and positions, which together form the corporation ethos that help or even animate the commission of crimes in certain instances.[27] The first element, the *doctrine of corporate mens rea*, enables us to think of corporations as "culpability-bearing agents who "act" through their officers and employees and whose "mens rea" is to be found in their corporate practices and policies (1982: 11)."

This approach is based on the combination of two main theories of culpability, the *capacity theory* and the *character theory*.[28] The *capacity theory* is largely based on the work of H.L.A. Hart and bears resemblance to my own account set out earlier. This theory advocates that the defendant has both the physical as well as the moral capacity to avoid the wrongdoing. When an agent makes choices it is expected that he/she take reasonable steps to avoid harming others. When extended to the context of the corporation, one must remember that the policies, plans, aims and the set of practices within a corporation are evidence of corporate culture, intention and knowledge that are irreducible to the purposes, intentions and knowledge of individuals in the corporation. These aims and practices of the corporation are authoritative because they have emerged not from the decision of a single individual but by a decision-making process accepted and confirmed as authoritative in the corporation. The capabilities that such an account considers important to moral responsibility, such as understanding, reasoning and control can also be found in the policies and plans of corporations. The advantage of this theory in terms of corporate criminal responsibility is that it includes and explains negligence liability.

The *character theory* holds agents responsible for those actions, which manifest their character. To cause harm intentionally, knowingly, recklessly or negligently expresses a defective character trait, the result in turn of a morally defective character.[29] In the case of the (private) individual defendant, John Smith, John Smith may be said to be morally deficient if he either, knowingly, and, therefore recklessly, or negligently causes death to another through having too much alcohol in his bloodstream while driving. In an analogous way, a corporation upholds a morally deficient culture if it permits or tolerates the dumping of poison into a well or river — it would do this either, knowingly, and therefore recklessly, or negligently, thereby causing harm, even death to those who draw water from the well. But if the corporation could be said to be morally deficient, and therefore responsible for the harm, it could also be held legally responsible. As Clarkson explains:

> Both these ... theories of responsibility can encompass organisations as moral agents capable of being regarded as culpable in their own right, irrespective of the culpability of the human agents behind the façade. Companies today cannot be viewed as a simple conglomeration of individuals. (1996: 567-68)

In other words, a corporation could most certainly be held responsible for manslaughter through recklessness (which requires *mens rea*) or gross negligence (which does not require *mens rea*). Furthermore, a corporation by failing to implement the necessary safety measures may also be said to be guilty of gross negligence as was the case with the Herald of Free Enterprise.

---

[27] See Laufer (1994: 660).
[28] See Horder (1993).
[29] An illustrative account of this theory is made by Bayles (1982).

The great issue concerning all this problematic is about the efficacy of censuring corporations. The types of sanction, presently available, range from corporate inspection, hostile publicity, and community service to fines, but not imprisonment. In Wells's opinion, these measures are all ineffective, and a combination of fines and imprisonment of directors will probably be the most effective punishment. If so then, one must lean on the so-called identification theory, as ultimately, it would be the really top managers who justifiably ought to be "carrying the can", both from the moral and the legal points of view, as far as incarceration is concerned.

2.2. *The Practice*

J. Horder calls our attention to the fact that criminal culpability is not merely a question about theorising the notion itself in the abstract; the debate necessarily reflects the values of our society in which the law is embedded.

> (Criminal) law reflects the cultural significance attributed in our society to a particular relationship between chance, fate, and responsibility, and to the fear of force or coercion over and above other motivations to commit crime. ... Our criminal law shows itself to be the product of the shared history of cultural-moral evolution, assumptions, and conflicts that is the mark of the community principle. (1993: 214-5)

This indicates that the difficulty about applying criminal responsibility to corporations is not only due to the inadequacy of the individual theory of responsibility but also to the values, which inform that theory and the law, which endorses it. As Clarkson expresses it:

> When a doctor, for instance, kills through gross negligence, a prosecution for manslaughter can, and sometimes does, follow. When the companies kill and injure, however, the practice is different. ... When persons are killed or seriously injured at work (even when they are not employees), the typical response is to describe this as an "accident". (1996: 558)

This explains why in general prosecutions of corporations are rare; and even when they occur, the law is applied very softly, which may be due in particular to three interrelated causes. First, only in rare cases is there a police inquiry, although there is always a coroner's inquest. Second, sometimes the establishment of the offence does not take into account the injury caused and ignore the consideration of levels of culpability. Third, very soft sentences are applied with relatively light fines as the preferred mode. As Bergman underlined, "the prosecutions appear criminal in name only (1993: 14)."

In the case of the Herald of Free Enterprise, it was only in November 1987, eight months after the disaster and three months after the publication of the public inquiry report that the police initiated a criminal investigation.[30] However, the investigation was very limited in scope due to the absence of applicable criminal offences. The only crime applicable to the

---

[30] In the *Marchioness/Bowbelle* case, it was eleven years after the disaster that on the 14th February 2000, the Deputy Prime Minister, John Prescott ordered a formal investigation under the Merchant Shipping Act 1995 into the circumstances surrounding the collision. Mr. Prescott announced the appointment of Lord Justice Clarke to act as Wreck Commissioner to the Formal Investigation. A Non-Statutory Inquiry into the identification of victims began on the 30 November 2000; on 24 March 2001, the *Guardian* made available on the internet the access to the Formal Investigation Report. See "Report Spreads Blanket of Blame for Thames Tragedy", *Guardian*, Saturday March 24, 2001.

corporation was reckless manslaughter, but for the applicability of this crime there was the need of proof that a senior officer in the corporation had acted recklessly. As Wells argues, the applicability of recklessness supposes two elements:

(a) she does an act which in fact creates an obvious (and serious) risk of causing physical injury and
(b) has either failed to give any thought to the possibility of there being any such risk or has recognized that there was some risk involved and has none the less gone on to do it. (1993: 69)

However, negligence and recklessness under the identification doctrine could only be considered if a senior officer of the corporation was identified as culpable. This is the drawback previously mentioned about the identification doctrine, the fact that a corporation under this doctrine is not considered a person. However, I have argued in the last section that even if one were to acknowledge the corporation as a moral/legal agent, it remains the case that punishment for manslaughter, either under recklessness or gross negligence, must involve recognising that the suitable agent(s) to incarcerate are those at the top of the management in a corporation.

However, this is not the only difficulty in terms of attributing negligence and recklessness to a corporation. Another difficulty is related to the fact that the application of responsibility to directors concerns, at most, only fiduciary matters, but does not traditionally apply to concern about safety.[31] According to the Sheen Report, in the case of the Herald of Free Enterprise, although it was the case that at least two of the seven litigants "were sufficiently senior to be identified", (Mr. Develin, director and chief superintendent and Mr. Ayers, director, and group technical director), nevertheless, none of them was convicted. (See the Sheen Report.)

The absence of proper definitions concerning roles and individual responsibilities or as mentioned in the words of Mr. Owen (a member of the Council for the National Union of Seamen) "a vacuum at the centre (the Sheen Report: 15)" was one of the causes of the disaster and also the reason why senior officers escaped from conviction.

Under English criminal law (at least in recent years), only one corporation was ever convicted of manslaughter.[32] According to Clarkson there are two main reasons for this. The first is related to the media, the state and even to the large corporations that shape and influence public attitudes. As previously mentioned, when persons are killed or injured at work it is typical to describe this as "accidents". The Health and Safety at Work Act 1974 is

---

[31] The Marchioness/Bowbelle case represents very well the difficulty of attributing criminal res-ponsibilities in matters relating to safety. The dredger (Bowbelle) struck from behind the Marchioness on the night of August 1989 on the river Thames, with the loss of 51 lives. "Lord Clarke's report said: The basic cause of the collision is clear. It was poor lookout on both vessels. Neither vessel saw the other in time to take action to avoid the collision... . The owners of the Bowbelle, East Coast Aggregates, and the managing company for the dredger, South Coast Shipping, must bear their share of responsibility for the collision for failing properly to instruct their masters and crews [on lookout duties] and for failing thereafter to monitor them. ... Lord Clarke criticised the former Department of Transport, which he said had been well aware of the problems posed by the limited visibility from the steering positions." Even when it is not difficult to find the causes of the disaster it is not simple to bring a criminal prosecution against the corporation. See, "Report Spreads Blanket of Blame for Thames Tragedy", *The Guardian*, Saturday March 24, 2001.

[32] See " Boss is Jailed over Canoe Deaths", *The Independent*, Friday 9 December 1994, pp.1 and 6. "Peter Kite 45, former managing director of the owners of the St Albans centre in Lyme Regis, was sentenced to three year of imprisonment." In this case it was not very difficult to find someone to blame due to the size of the company.

an attempt to increase safety and prevent "accidents" at work. This is in sharp contrast to the offences that individuals commit outside their workplaces involving harm. These differences of structures contribute to the general sense that death and injuries at work are not crime. The main purpose of the Health and Safety Executive (HSE) is to enforce legislation with the aim of notifying corporations that particular matters need attention. When injuries or deaths occur in a corporation normally the investigation is conducted by the HSE. However, as Clarkson underlines:

> This marginalisation of corporate crime is reinforced by the procedures adopted at inquests into workplace deaths where a verdict of "accidental death" is virtually automatic. Bereaved families have no right to legal aid inquests and when they are represented, often financed by a trade union, the solicitors are usually more interested in civil compensation. Company managers and directors with responsibility for safety are seldom called as witness. Again, such procedures simply legitimate the current role of the HSE, at the expense of the police, and reinforce public conceptions that these deaths are "accidents". (1996: 560)[33]

Another reason has to do with the fact that the traditional penal mechanism geared to individual wrongdoing does not take into account the structures of large corporations. In the case of the Herald of Free Enterprise, as I have mentioned earlier, it is not certain who within the company was responsible for safety. The individuals who were directly involved in the disaster were Mr. Stanley (the assistant bosun) who failed to close the bow doors; Mr. Sabel (the bosun) who also failed to check and supervise Mr. Stanley; Mr. Lewry (the captain) who started the over-crowded vessel at maximum speed without verifying that the doors had been closed; and finally the corporation Townsend Car Ferries Limited which had been notified of previous open-door incidents without taking any real measures to rectify the matter. In June 1989, after fifteen months of police investigation, Mr. Stanley, Mr. Sabel, Mr.Alcindor, Mr. Ayers, Mr. Develin, Captain Lewry and Captain Kirby were charged with manslaughter and P&O European Ferries[34] was charged with corporate manslaughter. Nonetheless, one year later, on October 19th, after 27 days of a trial expected to last five to six months, the judge dismissed the case by instructing the jury to find the litigants not guilty of manslaughter. The conclusion failed to prove that the litigants should have noticed the possibility of the Herald sailing with its doors open to be "an obvious risk".

At the end of the prosecution, as Clarkson comments, "it is hardly surprising that the trial judge, Turner J, directed acquittals against P&O and the five most senior employees (1996: 561)", because it could not be proved that the risks of open-door sailing were the direct responsibility of one senior officer. As Field and Jörg contend, "collective responsibility becomes lost in the crevices between the responsibilities of individuals (1978: 162)."

However, one must then raise the questions: Why should it be assumed that only one or at best two people be held responsible? Why cannot all be charged in the name of corporate responsibility? Admittedly one would have to have a scale of punishment with the "brains" at the hierarchy of "brains", so to speak, bearing the heaviest. It is worth labouring the point (already made earlier) that if senior "brains" could be held responsible for fiduciary probity, then why cannot they be held responsible also for the health and safety of the operations they run as a business? As Wells noted:

---

[33] See also Bergman (1993); Wells (2001).
[34] P & O European Ferries took over Townsend Car Ferries Limited.

> Someone, if not more than one person, in P&O's (then Townsend Car Ferries Limited) management knew that roll on-off ferries were potentially unstable. One task for criminal lawyers is to question critically how such knowledge within corporations can be related to familiar notions of individual culpability. (1989: 934)

As it was mentioned in the Sheen Report, the management was aware of the instability of the ferry; however, no measures were taken. As it can be read in the Report, it is interesting to note that a similar situation occurred with the vessel PRIDE, before what happened with the Herald. "On the 29th October the assistant bosun of the PRIDE neglected to close both the bow and stern doors (The Sheen Report: 23)." In June, Prides's Captain Blowers sent a memorandum to Mr. Develin (director and chief superintendent) in which he said that an indicator light would enable the "bridge team to monitor the situation". However, no measures were adopted and the Sheen Report concludes:

> If the sensible suggestion that indicator lights be installed had received, in 1985, the serious consideration which it deserved, it is at least possible they would have been fitted in the early months of 1986 and this disaster might well have been prevented. (p. 24)

In spite of all the memoranda written to the higher management by employees in their attempts to improve the safety conditions, the corporation did not feel either morally or legally responsible for having acted so negligently. On the contrary, the corporation put pressure on the crew to turn round the ferry in record time, to transport an excessive number of passengers, and to maintain full speed in bad weather conditions. It also ignored the necessity of another ballast pump. It is clear that it was the corporation, which deserved to be found guilty and punished. As Clarkson mentioned, the families of the Herald's victims did not primarily press the prosecution of the individuals but the prosecution of Townsend Car Ferries Limited, as they intuitively had felt that above all it was the corporation, which was at fault.[35]

We can say that it is, the corporation, Townsend Car Ferries Limited (and then P & O which took it over), which had failed in its duties because the highest management systematically refused to implement and improve the measures for safety, profit being probably its only concern. As the Sheen Report has said, installing another pump would only cost £25,000 but this "was regarded by the company as prohibitive."[36] Mr Sterling, a P&O chairman says, "my first responsibility is to the shareholders of P&O and profit is what it is all about".[37] However, according to critics, corporate responsibility should go beyond profits and in this concrete case, safety should have been one of the priorities of the corporation. However, such moral "sloppiness at the top leads to sloppiness down the line."[38]

According to Field and Jörg, the Dutch law of corporate liability, unlike English Law, "rests on those who have the power to control the *general practices* of the corporation. ... It was not necessary to identify any individual as responsible for the sloppy supervision: it could be seen simply as a collective failure by management (1987: 167)." This reinforces

---

[35] See Clarkson (1996: 563). See *The Independent,* Saturday 14 November 1987 in which Sue Haney, the spokeswoman for the Herald Families' Association says: "We are still fighting for the company to be charged with corporate manslaughter (p.1)."
[36] The Sheen Report, p.24.
[37] Crainer (1993: 17).
[38] Crainer (1993: 47).

French's arguments that corporate intentions and responsibility can be investigated within a system of rules and commands, which are determined by corporate policy. But in English law, at present, there is neither the political nor the legal will to undertake such prosecution, a reluctance one can see yet again in the aftermath of the rail crash in Hatfield on 17 October 2000. Four people have been killed and many others injured. Gerald Corbett, Railtrack's chief executive during the inquiry refused to accept that the rail industry's safety problems were due to management failure. He said, "it's more of a system rather than a management failure....[39] When Robert Owen, QC, counsel for the inquiry asked him who has responsible for the crash he answered: "I think it's me. It's clear in the public's mind that they think it's me (*ibid*)." Three months later it was confirmed that Railtrack was aware of the unsafe conditions of the track but had failed to act to remedy the situation till after the disaster. The report published by the HSE revealed that "the Hatfield track was so bad at the point of the crash that it shattered into 300 pieces, like a sheet of glass, and was therefore the direct cause of the accident."[40]

This case shares some similarities, concerning safety problems with the Herald of Free Enterprise disaster, in terms of causes and of consequences. As Box advocates:

> The essence of corporate crime is not the behaviour of individuals, but the "behaviour" of corporations. ... *In order to be effective, the level of intervention to regulate corporate crime has to be organizational rather than individual.* (1983: 70)

Mr. Gerald Corbett (director of Railtrack at the time of the Hatfield disaster) expressed his view about the government's plan to introduce a new charge of corporate killing: "I think it would encourage a culture of secrecy and blame which is not necessarily an appropriate safety culture."[41] He did not back this up with detailed arguments. It is hard to make out what he could mean. However, his response was a clear indication that corporations would resist the introduction of such a charge with as much vigour as they are politically capable.

3. Causation: Humean and Reciprocal

A final matter, already hinted at in the preceding sections, which has bearing on the current reluctance in certain legal systems, such as the English one, to attribute culpability to corporations in the law of homicide, must now be looked at in greater detail. It is that the dominant theory of individual responsibility is also embedded in a philosophical framework, which accepts the Humean (sometimes also called the linear) analysis of cause. In cases like the sinking of the Herald of Free Enterprise, the Humean account of cause may be found

---

[39] "Tactless Corbett says sorry to crash families", *The Guardian,* Saturday, November 11 2000, p.4.
[40] *The Guardian,* Monday, January 22 2001, p.1. *The Independent* on Sunday called our attention to the fact that Mr. Gilbert Corbett "was due to receive a £400.000 pay-off after resigning as head of the rail group last November a month after the Hatfield derailment. ... But he has given up a quarter of the total in recognition of the fact he has moved straight into another well-paid job, as chairman of Woolworths *The Independent on Sunday,* March 11 2001, p.2." *The Guardian* said ("Railtrack Faces Charge of Manslaughter"): "Railtrack is facing charges of corporate manslaughter over the Hatfield train disaster... . A senior police officer affirmed that there was enough evidence to prosecute and that those managers were senior enough for a corporate manslaughter prosecution (*The Guardian,* 30 July 2001)." But it remains to be seen if this would ever take place.
[41] *The Guardian* (2000): 4.

wanting, as the causal chains involved may be more complicated than recognised by such an analysis. But first, let me set out briefly the Humean causal analysis itself.

To say that A causes B is to say that:

a) Whenever A occurs B occurs.
b) A precedes B in time (or occurs simultaneously with B).
c) A and B are spatially contiguous.

(This is sometimes called the uniformity of sequence analysis of cause.)

Hume had intended to undermine the notion of necessity in nature as advocated by the Rationalists. According to the latter, whatever is the cause has the power necessary to bring about the effect, such that it is not a mere coincidence that the so-called effect occurs in the presence of the cause. Hume, from the standpoint of empiricism, argued that the uniformity of sequence is all that could be given in terms of the five senses; it follows then that there is no necessity in nature; necessity is but the mere projection of our own psychology on to nature – as B always follows A, so whenever we see A occurring, we expect B to follow. A fourth thesis could then be added to the other three mentioned above – there is no necessity in nature; there is only our own expectation that what is effect would follow what is cause.

The Humean analysis implies that the causal arrow goes only in one direction, that is from A to B to C. Take the example of the billiards player. He/she pushes the cue against the first billiard ball, imparting motion to it, and in turn when the first billiard ball hits the second, it imparts motion to the latter, and so on to a third billiard ball. According to this perspective, the third or second billiard ball could not bounce back against the first ball, causing it to move. This is because it ignores all other possible relevant factors, like the parameters or framework within which the billiard balls are moving. Billiard, as we know, is played on a table bounded by raised wooden edges on all sides. When ball B hits ball C, it could conceivably first hit against one of the edges of the billiard table from which it rebounds with such force as to hit ball A, which in turn moves to hit C. The Humean model appears not to allow for this possibility. By contrast, the reciprocal or non-linear model of causation is able to take account of this kind of reaction.

But what is reciprocal or non-linear causation? Take a current controversy, such as the nature (genes) *versus* nurture (environment) debate, to cast initial light on the matter. Both sides seem implicitly to adhere to the Humean linear model of causation when they claim that a particular trait, such as height in a population, is either determined solely by genetic inheritance or solely by environmental factors. Both sides, therefore, assume that the causal arrow is one directional, either from gene to the trait or environment to the trait in question. In reality, the relationship between genetic endowment and the environment is reciprocal or non-linear and it is their complex interaction, which ultimately causes the individual to manifest the characteristic in a certain way.[42] Children brought up on a poor diet would tend to be shorter than similar children brought up on a more nourishing diet. For instance, children in pre-war Japan were much shorter than their counterparts in post-war Japan. The genetic inheritance of the Japanese population has not altered; what has altered is that post-war

---

[42] The scientists, William Dickens and James Flynn, argue that intelligence is an interactive process between genes and environment, nature and nurture which presupposes reciprocal or non-linear causation. See Dickens and Flynn (2001).

Japanese society is on the whole better fed. At each stage of development, starting from the embryonic stage, the genetic endowment interacts with the environment to lay down the possibilities for the next stage of development. The stage of development achieved at any one time itself constitutes part of the environment for the next stage. The genetic endowment, having been favoured (or disfavoured) by such an environment, would in turn interact with it to lay down possibilities for yet another stage of development. This kind of causal relationship in the context of growth and development may also be called epigenetic.

The linear model cannot do justice to the relationship between the individual and the society of which he/she is a part. The methodological individualist account of the relationship presupposes the Humean linear view of causation. Society is the mere accumulation of the unintended consequences of the actions of individuals, which supposes that we are first and foremost mere abstract individuals, who then enter into various agreements with one another, whether voluntary or under considerable duress. Under this logic most of our behaviour is justified and excusable, since one is not responsible for the unintended consequences of one's actions. For example, if a sufficient number of people bought cars and drove them on the streets, then there would be traffic jams and urban pollution, through the accumulation of the unintended consequences of their respective acts of driving. But this view often ignores that individuals do not buy and drive cars in a social vacuum. They buy and drive cars for a variety of reasons. For instance, cars may be a status symbol; though cars are expensive to buy, relatively easy credit terms are available to encourage car ownership. Public transport may be so badly organised or even non-existent, as to make driving a car a necessity in some cases. Motorways are constructed to encourage car usage and in turn ownership.[43]

In other words, the kind of society individuals find themselves in constrains them to engage in certain kinds of actions, which in turn exaggerate or reinforce certain societal tendencies and traits but not others. The linear model of causation sits comfortably with the Hayekian view – which can be traced back to Adam Smith's "invisible hand" of the market – that society is not the product of any deliberately co-operative venture but simply the accumulation of the unintended consequences of individual actions. Following Adam Smith, such a view takes, as its paradigm, acts of economic exchange – each buyer wants to get as low a price as he/she can get and each seller tries to sell for as much as he/she can ask. Out of these numerous acts of buying and selling, a spontaneous order in society appears. This is how the free market in theory is supposed to work. From this, theorists extrapolate to all social phenomena. Hence Hayek is for spontaneity and against planning. Planning is deliberate, intentional activity, involving formulating goals, foresight, taking into account anticipated outcomes, etc. As such, there are agents called planners to whom one can attribute responsibility. But under spontaneous order, there are no such individual agents; it follows that no-one could then be held responsible for the outcome, which no-one has directly intended anyway. On this model, urban pollution and congestion just appear, with no one agent or set of agents who could be said to be responsible. Take the sinking of the Herald of Free Enterprise. Obviously no-body involved in running the boat directly intended the deaths; the loss of lives may be regarded simply as the accumulation of the unintended consequences of several acts on the part of various actors, such as the assistant bosun, the bosun, the

---

[43] The car lobby in general still refuses to acknowledge this factor and keeps to the view that roads and motorways have to be built simply to meet already existing demands. It fails to recognise that building more roads have the effect of increasing car use, which in turn prompts a demand for yet more roads to be built.

captain, the middle managers, the top managers etc., just as the defacement of the lawn is simply the accumulation of the unintended consequences of each individual agent merely trying to do a short cut by crossing the lawn.

I shall now turn to the five characteristics, which Keekok Lee has identified in her account of the non-linear model of causation:

1. cause may include both events and standing conditions;
2. standing conditions are part of the systemic boundaries;
3. a cause produces an effect, but the effect may in turn be a cause which has an effect on the original cause, and so on, such that the causal nexus approximates to the following schema: $A1 \to \to B1 \to \to A2 \to \ldots$ ($\to\to$ is the causal arrow);
4. (1), (2) and (3) above imply that causes and effects are not simply events, which can be considered and understood as happenings isolated from one another, and independent of systemic boundaries.
5. (5) (4) in turn implies that causes and effects are not merely additive or subtractive. The additive view cannot account for (i) threshold or cumulative effects, (ii) synergistic effects, (iii) exponential effects, (iv) changes to systemic boundaries such that a new set may be said to have emerged.[44]

The following example may illustrate nearly all these theses, namely, the case of the straw, which breaks the camel's back. A straw is very light, let us say 1g in weight. The camel in question is a very heavy animal, and let us say that it can normally bear a weight of 50Kgs. In terms of sheer arithmetic, we can work out that the camel can carry a bale of 50,000 straws. The proverbial camel appeared to be fine when the 50,000th straw was piled on to its back; yet it collapsed when one more, the 50,001th straw, was added. On the linear model of causation, the phenomenon cannot be predicted and its occurrence remains difficult to explain. However, on the non-linear model, the phenomenon is both predicted and can be satisfactorily explained.

On the linear model, the causal impact of each straw weighing 1g is considered totally in isolation from the causal impact of the other straws on the camel's back. Each straw in isolation causes no obvious distress or discomfort to the camel. Indeed, up to the piling of the 50,000th straw, the camel was upright, looking fit. Yet why should the next straw, which weighs exactly the same as each of the others preceding it, have the dramatic effect of making the camel collapse? This dramatic effect cannot be accounted for precisely because the linear model implies that causes and effects are merely additive or subtractive; it ignores cumulative causes and effects. This is to say that the causal impact of the 50,000th straw on the camel's back is not the same as the causal impact of the 1st, 2nd, or 40,000th straw notwithstanding the fact that the camel was on its feet and appeared much the same for wear.

At time tn, when the 50,000th straw was loaded, the causal impact on the camel is not simply the sum of the causal impact of each preceding straw taken separately and in isolation of one another. Suppose the causal impact of each straw taken in isolation is m. On the linear model, the total causal impact would be 50,000m. On the non-linear model, the total causal impact could be many times more than that. Indeed, on this model, the camel could collapse even well before the 50,000th straw was loaded on to its back.

---

[44] Lee (1989a: 70).

Furthermore, the linear model understands cause only in terms of events and not also of standing conditions, which are part of the systemic boundaries of the phenomenon one is studying. In the example under discussion, the only thing it considers to be causally relevant is the fact that straws were being piled on to the camel's back. It does not take into account the more specific fact that these straws were being piled on to back of the particular camel with its particular constitution, its age, its particular state of health, etc., which constitute the standing conditions. In other words, there is a limit to the weight that such a camel can bear given its make-up and the physiological conditions it is under at any one moment in time.

As just mentioned, the state of the camel, which forms part of systemic boundaries, is not static but dynamic. At any one time, it depends very much on how much the animal might have eaten, what exactly it has eaten, the fact that it had been carrying heavy loads without rest for a long period beforehand, whether it might be infected by a bug which could affect its breathing, the circulation of its blood, etc. Each of these less than optimal factors on its own would not distress the camel; but together acting synergistically, the distress could be magnified several times over, so that even before the 50,000th straw was piled on to its back, it promptly collapsed.

On the linear model, the straw (the cause) is always distinct from its causal impact on the camel. As already pointed out, the causal impact upon the camel remains constant and unchanging, irrespective of the state of the camel – in other words, the model is ahistorical in character. In contrast, the non-linear model not only sees the state of the camel to be a dynamic matter, but also regards the straw and its causal impact to be part of the standing conditions and systemic boundaries, which in turn can produce causal effects – in other words, it is historical in character. What constitutes the effect at t1 can be part of the cause at t2. We have already seen this at work above: the state of the camel bearing 50,000 straws together with the 50,001th straw causally brought about the collapse of the camel.

Let us now apply the two models to the sinking of the Herald of Free Enterprise to see how much light each can throw on the causal issues involved. The pressure on the crew (cause A) to leave the port not only led to preventing the Master from being on the bridge (effect B) but also caused a series of failures, such as:

1. the impossibility of Captain Lewry to check if all doors were closed;
2. the impossibility of Captain Kirby to coordinate the practices of the crew and to introduce a fail-safe system;
3. the lack of clear orders about the duties of the officers;
4. the absence of a written report at the time of sailing confirming that the ship was ready for sea;
5. Captain Lewry's assumption that the assistant bosun and the chief officer were able to perform their duties; but this assumption was not justified, given the fact that they were thoroughly exhausted, and that the assistant bosun had fallen asleep because of the exhaustion.

According to the non-linear model, one cannot separate the events from the context; they are neither independent from one another, nor from the systemic boundaries. In contrast, the linear cause presupposes what may be called the additive view of cause, as we have seen above. The additive view plus its failure to recognise the constraints laid down by the parameters of a set of phenomena led to other limitations, leading to a failure to recognise the problem of boundaries. In the case of the Herald of Free Enterprise, it is easy to see that the pressure to leave the berth or the lack of indicator lights taken separately perhaps would not be enough to provoke the accident. Nevertheless, on the non-linear view, which takes into account the boundaries within which the set of the phenomena are observed, the accident would not be a surprise. The lack of indicator lights, the excessive number of passengers, the limited capacity of the ballast pumps and the long working hours of the assistant bosun would together readily explain why the boat left its berth with its bow doors opened, leading to its capsize.

The linear model prompted the singling out of the assistant bosun's failure to close the bow doors as the most obvious cause of the sinking. This is in keeping with its requirement that events alone, and not standing conditions, can be causes. But according to the non-linear model both events and conditions may be so regarded. On this perspective, the failure on the part of the assistant bosun to close the doors could only have caused the capsize because certain standing conditions also obtained, that is to say, no indicator lights on the bridge had been installed, more hands had not been available to ensure proper safety steps were taken before the boat left its berth, staff, like the assistant bosun, had to work such punishing hours that he fell asleep when he should have been awake, the time table had been incredibly tight, the design of the ferry was that of the ro-ro kind, etc. If these standing conditions could legitimately be considered as causes, then the assistant bosun's omission to close the bow doors might be seen in its proper causal context. The less than optimal standing conditions from the safety point of view clearly point to the corporation as the major causally responsible agent. From the moral perspective, it does not seem fair that the assistant bosun's failure to act upon the extant suite of standing conditions regarding the Herald of Free Enterprise should bear sole responsibility for the capsize.

The sinking of the Herald of Free Enterprise makes it clear that one cannot take events in a complex causal chain to be isolated from one another and independent from the context or the boundaries in which the phenomenon occurs. But one important component of the context has still to be mentioned in order to understand fully the tragedy involved, and that is, the economic framework within which the ship was designed and run.

The traffic in the English Channel between England and the continent of Europe is one of the most travelled waterways in the world. The number of passengers using this service increases every year, and the most preferred crossing is the shortest one, between Dover and Calais (90m). Since 1982 the traffic has increased specially for two main reasons. First, Britain became a member of the European Union and second, the introduction of roll-on/roll-off (ro-ro) ships. With the introduction of these ships not only was the time spent in port much reduced, but more cars could be loaded than in a more conventionally designed vessel with bulkheads. The ro-ro design made the capsize inevitable once water had entered through the open bow doors.

Competition in the sector was influenced by the British government's July 1984 privatisation of Sealink Uk Ltd., formerly a subsidiary of the government-owned British rail. At that time the industry was dominated by Sealink UK and Townsend Car Ferries Limited, which was one of the major ferry corporations in Europe until 1987. (One year after the disaster of the Herald of Free Enterprise the company was acquired by P&O.)

The very design of the ro-ro boat, the fast turn-around boat, the long working hours of its staff, the refusal to put in indicator lights in order to reduce cost all bear eloquent testimony to the axiom of maximising profit even at the expense of safety. In that sense, one could even say that shareholders too have to bear their share of the (at least, moral) responsibility for the tragedy.

It seems apt to close this section with a quotation from A. Wilden:

> ...ideology and economics all became united around a conception of the individual ... as isolated systems, like billiard balls governed by "forces" ("instincts" in psychology and ethology), all on the same plane of being, all separate from their environments and from the various levels of the general environment. (1978: 106)

4. The Need for a Paradigm Shift

I wish to sum up the points made in this first part and also those so far developed here. I have tried to establish the following:

1. The Humean linear model of causation, which goes comfortably with the individualist philosophical perspective, appears unable to do justice to the complex causal relationships between the individual and the society of which s/he is a part. As it is, by and large, the accepted model, this makes it difficult in general for social/moral theorists to grasp the alternative concept of non-linear causation (or indeed, to downplay, if not ignore, it altogether), which, however, appears more able to do justice to those complex relationships. At the same time, the Humean model seems also readily to go with the theory of individual responsibility; from such a perspective, the notion of collective responsibility in general and corporate responsibility in particular, looks suspicious, indeed, even absurd and unintelligible.
2. However, contrary to the philosophy of individualism, it is possible to make a case that corporations (a particular kind of collectivity) are real and do exist.
3. Corporations do possess a structure and a set of coherent properties which make it possible to say that they are rational and autonomous agents (provided that agency is not understood simplistically to refer only to so-called "flesh-and-blood" individuals as favoured by the philosophy of individualism.
4. Furthermore, in virtue of the structural properties just cited as exhibited by their agency, it makes sense to hold them legally responsible, through certain key personnel in the corporate hierarchy who must, of course, be "flesh and blood" individuals, even to the extent of attributing to them that hall-mark of the theory of individual responsibility, namely, that of possessing *mens rea*.

In the light of the above, one might be tempted to be complacent and maintain that one has made all the case that is needed to establish the intelligibility, coherence and applicability of the notion of corporate responsibility. However, this complacency is not justified and further work remains to be done. For a start, the arguments so far developed are confined at best to only one limited aspect of the notion of corporate responsibility, that is to say, in the domain of legal responsibility, in particular, to establishing the notion of corporate manslaughter in the law of homicide. They have nothing to say about corporate responsibility in the moral domain. In other words, one should be looking for a broader theory of responsibility in general and of corporate responsibility in particular, which can do the job of challenging the theory of individual responsibility in both the legal and moral domains. In the next two parts , I shall try to do precisely that, by turning to Levinas, to explore his account of infinite responsibility for the Other, offering the outline of a radically different model of responsibility, which may cast an altogether new light on the understanding of corporate responsibility, both in the legal and moral domains. In the absence of such a plausible alternative, no matter the limitations of the individual theory of responsibility posed by the problems facing it in today's globalised world, it would continue to dominate at the level of theory, while at best making some concessions at the edges in the way which this part has itself proposed. It would continue to thrive should no competitor come forward to challenge it. The next part will begin the attempt to make good this lack. In other words, one needs to get away from a "thin" moral universe within which the theory of individual responsibility is situated to one which is "thicker", where a different conception of responsibility prevails, one which is summed up by Levinas's notion of infinite responsibility for the Other.[45]

However, more crucially, I urge that what is required – following Kuhn (1970) – is a shift in moral paradigm, and in the following two parts I shall attempt to make a case for saying that Levinas's philosophy counts as a genuine new paradigm and that it is the paradigm which is relevant to the problems facing the globalised today and towards which the twenty-first century is sub-consciously groping.

II. LEVINAS: A NEW PERSPECTIVE ON RESPONSIBILITY

1. Intellectual Biography and Outline of Some Key Concepts

It is important to grasp that Levinas objected to being classified as a Jewish thinker, in his philosophical works, in spite of the fact, as we shall see, that one of their strands is clearly inspired by the Hebrew tradition. Instead, he situated his thought clearly in the mainstream of European philosophy while, admittedly, challenging it. Although he agreed with Heidegger that philosophy is more than a method, rather that it is "a way of becoming aware of where we are in the world (Kierney (1984): 49)", nevertheless, he held that the whole of Western tradition of philosophy, including Heidegger, has gone astray, as it has made ontology or the study of Being, rather than **ethics, as first philosophy** – "Morality is not a branch of philosophy, but first philosophy (*Totality and Infinity* [*TI*], 304)." Levinas does not prescribe an ethic, his philosophy is far from being normative; nevertheless, by his descriptions and analyses, the ethical perspective is the starting point of his philosophy. The awakening for ethics happens when the agent becomes aware of a responsibility, which is beyond his/her control, of a desire for the Other.

Levinas distinguished between ontology and metaphysics. Ontology, unfortunately, reduces "the Other to the same by interposition of a middle and neutral term that ensures the comprehension of being (*TI*, 43)", thereby blurring the distinction between myself on the one hand and what is other than myself on the other. The Other then becomes a mere "object" of my consciousness. It also seeks a **totality** of the whole being in which all apparent differences

---

[45] For my purpose, this term is somewhat unfortunate, as it immediately invites the criticism that it is too demanding, asking too much of people. I shall address myself to this and other possible criticisms in the next part .

are resolved in the system. Totality in Levinas's thought means that the I is at the centre; the I reduces the Other to itself. In this sense, the Other becomes a kind of object, an element of the I incorporated by it, assimilated by it. Western culture is one of egocentrism in its theoretical expression from the early Greeks to the present. Such a "totalising" system necessarily denies the distinction between **the same** (self) [*Le Même*] and **the Other** [*L'Autre*][46], as it reduces everything in the end to the same. Its logic is such that it only appears to move from the same to the other, but in reality it always returns to the same. In contrast, for Levinas, metaphysics implies a logic of thought which moves beyond totality, which incurs the idea of **infinity** (as we shall see) and goes from the idea of the same to the Other but not in order to return to the same. In the preface to *Totalité et Infini*, Levinas expresses one of the central aims of the book:

> It will proceed to distinguish between the idea of totality and the idea of infinity, and affirm the philosophical primacy of the idea of infinity. It will recount how infinity is produced in the relationship of the Same with the Other, and how the particular and the personal, which are unsurpassable, as it were magnetise the very field in which the production of infinity is enacted. [My own translation of the passage on page 11 of the original text.]

Egocentrism with which the idea of totality is linked is only broken by the idea of infinity.[47] Furthermore, infinity, as we shall see, is really another name for responsibility for the Other:

> Responsibility for another is not an accident that happens to a subject, but precedes essence in it, it has not awaited freedom, in which a commitment to another would have been made. ... The word "I" means, "Here I am", answering for everything and for everyone. Responsibility for the others has not been a return to oneself, but the contracting, which the limits of identity cannot retain. (*OB*: 114)

---

[46] These concepts – *Le Même et l'Autre* (the Same and the Other) – have a great importance especially in *TI*. According to Alphonso Lingis, the English translator of some of the Levinasian texts, *autre/l'Autre* is translated by "other" and *autrui/Autrui* by "Other". It is true that Levinas is not always consistent in the use of these terms throughout his works. However, especially in *TI* and *Otherwise than Being* [*OB*], I have maintained the distinction made by Levinas between *autre* and *L'Autre* which, in the extant English translations and in a significant number of studies in English of Levinas, has been suppressed. In other words, Levinas distinguishes between *autre* (other) *l'Autre* (the Other), while also using *autrui/Autrui* which I have similarly translated as the Other. Whereas the Other/*L'Autre* reveals infinity, other/*autre* belongs to the domain of totality. As an example, one can say that I can kill the other/*autre* (namely, another person) but not I can kill the Other/*l'Autre* (although for Levinas it makes sense to say that "(t)he Other is the sole being I can wish to kill ((*TI*): 198).") According to Colin Davis, *Autrui* is the personalised form of *l'Autre* – see Davis (1996): 6 and 34-62.

In *Totalité et Infini*, he says: "The metaphysical Other is other with an alterity that is not formal, is not the simple reverse of identity, and is not formed out of resistance to the Same, but is prior to every initiative, to all imperialism of the Same. It is Other with an alterity that does not limit the Same, for in limiting the Same the Other would not be rigorously Other: by virtue of the common frontier the Other, within system, would yet be the Same. The absolutely Other is the Other. [*L'absolument Autre, c'est Autrui*.]." (This translation is my own of passage on page 28 of the original text.)

[Unless I indicate to the contrary, all passages cited from Levinas's works are from standard translations. Those, which are my own translations, carry their French titles. This division of labour is necessitated sometimes by the fact that I am not totally happy with the standard translations, and sometimes by the unavailability of the work(s) in translation.]

[47] See *TI*: 49.

This latter point is brought out by Levinas's emphasis on ethics as first philosophy, rejecting the dominant view of individual responsibility which is based on a sense of the self as a spontaneous (autonomous/free/rational) being;[48] instead it sees the self (myself) as a being in relation to an other, who *ex hypothesi* is not myself (that is, the same), but whose strangeness and whose irreducibility to the I (my memories, my thoughts, my feelings as well as my material possessions) calls precisely into question my spontaneity and autonomy for free action.

> A calling into question of the Same – which cannot occur within the egoistic spontaneity of the Same – is brought about by the Other (*l'Autre*). We name this calling into question of my spontaneity by the presence of the Other *(Autrui)* ethics. The strangeness of the Other, his irreducibility to the I *(Moi)*, to my thoughts and my possessions, is precisely accomplished as a calling into question of my spontaneity, as ethics. Metaphysics, transcendence, the welcoming of the Other by the Same, of the Other by Me, is concretely produced as the calling into question of the Same by the Other, that is, as the ethics that accomplishes the critical essence of knowledge. (*Totalité et Infini*) [My own translation of passage on page 33 of the original text.]

The face (*le visage*) is irreducible, being primordial; it encapsulates the Other, as well as its strangeness and the awareness of otherness on my part.

> The face is a living presence; it is expression. The life of expression consists in undoing the form in which the existent, exposed as a theme, is thereby dissimulated. The face speaks. (*TI*: 66).

The Other's face resists all characterisation and classification. I could not fix the face in a picture or even in my memory; the face is expression, discourse. The Other's face appears as something new. In this sense, the Other is my teacher; the face teaches me the deep sense of my own identity and responsibility.

It is in the face that the other's **epiphany** is produced (*TI*, 194). Levinas uses the words "revelation" and "epiphany" to characterise infinity. Again, these words are not meant to have any theological connotations; they indicate the wonder that distinguishes individuals from their self-centred forms of life. This wonder is revealed in the "epiphany of the Other". When I encounter another human, another face, I become aware that "economy" is not an appropriate response in this encounter. The Other condemns my self-centredness and imposes an infinite number of demands on me by simply appearing on my scene. The Other's face, the fact he/she looks at me, makes me responsible for the Other's existence, life, and behaviour.

---

[48] The dominant tradition of Western philosophy views freedom as the most valuable source of morals and politics. Levinas is very critical of this extreme confidence in freedom. In *TI*: 82-84, he devotes an entire section to this matter, "Freedom called into Question". For him, it is not freedom, which is constitutive of the human agent and its identity. For him, morality does not have its source in freedom; instead "morality begins when freedom, instead of being justified by itself, feels itself to be arbitrary and violent (*TI*: 84)." This is to recognise a principle not only of autonomy, but also heteronomy as the source of all morality, the presence of the Other. The negative sense of heteronomy in Kantian philosophy acquires a positive value in the philosophy of Levinas. However, the autonomy of the human agent is not denied in the philosophy of Levinas but must be seen in relation to heteronomy when I am confronted with the non-me in my self and outside of myself. For Kant, the source of morality is the autonomy of the will, but for Levinas, it is the relation to the irreducible exteriority of the face, as we shall see in a moment. (On Levinas's relation to Kant, see Peperzak (1997: 198-200) and Hayat (1995: 54-56).

At the level of sensibility when the egoistic self encounters the Other, it cannot enjoy the Other by incorporating the latter as part of itself. The reason for such failure is not rooted in some deficiency of sensibility, but in the Other who resists absorption and does not allow him/herself to be consumed in the egoism of the self.

The face of the other calls me to **justice**[49] and to justification. On it is written, as it were, the commands: "Thou shalt not kill", "Thou shalt love thy neighbour as thyself", "Thou shalt do all that thou canst to help the other", in spite of the defencelessness and powerlessness of the Other. The face, however, should not be understood merely in terms of physical characteristics. But it remains true that physiognomy crucially renders communication possible between the other and myself.

In **speech**[50] (communication) is the Other. The basic structure of language is a relationship between two singularities, "I", and the "Other". In speaking, the Other is solicited, called upon to respond. In speech the I and the Other solicit each other without appropriation. In *TI*, when Levinas introduces the face, he tells us that the face is not revealed in vision, but in speech. Speech transcends vision:

> Speech cuts across vision. In knowledge or vision the object seen can indeed determine an act, but it is an act that in some way appropriates the "seen" to itself, integrates it into a world by endowing it with a signification, and in the last analysis, constitutes it. In discourse the divergence that inevitably opens between the Other as my theme and the Other as my interlocutor, emancipated from the theme that seemed a moment to hold him, forthwith contests the meaning I ascribe to my interlocutor. The formal structure of language thereby announces the ethical inviolability of the Other … . (*TI*: 195)

Far from abolishing the distinction between individual persons, speech affirms their existence and their difference.

> Speech is not instituted in a homogeneous or abstract medium, but in a world where it is necessary to aid and to give. It presupposes an I, an existence separated in its enjoyment, which does not welcome empty-handed the face and its voice coming from another shore. Multiplicity in being, which refuses totalization but takes form as fraternity and discourse, is situated in a "space" essentially asymmetrical (*TI*: 20).

In entering into a dialogue with another, I am necessarily aware that my counterpart is someone who has his own past, his own memories, his own thoughts and his own preferences, all of which might intrude into my own egoistic world. "For the ethical relationship which subtends discourse is not a species of consciousness whose ray emanates from the I; it puts the I in question. This putting in question emanates from the Other (*TI*: 195)".

Encounter with the Other which occurs in face-to-face dealings with other human beings also points beyond itself towards absolute otherness, recognition of which is recognition of genuine transcendence, beyond Being, or **Otherwise than Being**.[51] This absolute other or infinity cannot be comprehended in the way traditional metaphysics has tried to do; it is

---

[49] For now, no further elucidation or comment will be made of this notion, as a more suitable place to elaborate and discuss it is the next chapter, where a few more Levinasian concepts will also be introduced.

[50] In the next part, section 1.2, the related distinction between the Saying and the Said will be discussed.

[51] Note that this is the very title of the second major *oeuvre* of Levinas.

revealed not in intellectual comprehension but in actual discourse – "Better than comprehension, discourse relates with what remains essentially transcendent (*TI*: 195)". Discourse preserves the "I" in its individuality as well as the distinctiveness of the other, the distinction between the same and the Other.

Ethics as "first philosophy" means that one's fundamental ethical relation to the Other when one encounters it as face is constituted by one's responsibility for it.

> Meeting the face is not of the order of pure and simple perception, of the intentionality which goes toward adequation. Positively, we will say that since the Other looks at me, I am responsible for him, without even having taken on responsibilities in his regard; his responsibility is incumbent on me. (*Ethics and Infinity* [*EI*]: 96)

Ethics for Levinas, is not based on reciprocity (I acknowledge the demands of others only in return that they acknowledge my demands upon them), or on the Golden Rule – to do unto others what you would like others to do unto you; nor is it a question of advancing enlightened self-interests. Our obligations to others do not arise through entering into contracts with them to protect our mutual interests or our separate rights. The "mercantile" calculation of a utilitarian kind, or the rational manoeuvrings of a Kantian kind, the Nietzschean will to power, or the Sartrean pursuit of infinite freedom is alien to the Levinasian orientation, as they bear out no more than the logic of ontology and not of metaphysics (as earlier shown). All these perspectives are profoundly individualistic in orientation, which begin with, and end at the egocentric starting point, and therefore smack of egoism and quasi-Hobbesianism where the self simply acts to defend itself from the other while at the same time assaulting the freedom of others in order to aggrandise itself.

The face is not concerned with instrumentality or rationality. From it flows something that is beyond such mundane modalities, something infinite and good. Here is a heteronomy which is beyond that of autonomy – the self (the same) is not for itself but for the Other; the Other holds sway from **a height** even when the Other is the down-trodden, the despised, the rejected. When I speak, I address myself to another person who reveals that my monopoly of the world has come to an end. He robs me of my sovereignty. The first social relationship is characterised by a radical asymmetry. The mere existence of another human – not his decisions or choices – compels me to acknowledge his existence. I look upon another as someone who commands respect and devotion. The Other is characterised by "height" or "highness".

The ethical relation does not create and cannot tolerate the class of the excluded, no more does it tolerate constraints on one's responsibility for others created by contracts or reciprocity. Furthermore, the power of the same to be in the place of the Other (Levinas's concept of **substitution**) grounds all acts of solidarity or **sociality**. The concept of substitution is the most important focal term in Levinas's second major work, *Otherwise than Being*. It can be seen as being closely related to ideas such as being a hostage, expiation for the Other, responsibility for the freedom of the Other, responsibility for the persecutor, and the gratuity of sacrifice, as his culminating expression of radical responsibility. Substitution is the means by which my being responds to the Other before I know that it does. It is a sign of how the Other directs the human being as he/she actually is. In comporting myself towards the Other in substitution, my identity becomes concrete.

Substitution is recognising myself in the place of the Other, not with the force of a conceptual recognition, but, as we have seen, in the sense of finding myself in the place of the Other as a hostage for the Other:

> To be oneself, otherwise than being, to be dis-interested, is to bear the wretchedness and bankruptcy of the other, and even the responsibility that the other can have for me. To be oneself, the state of being a hostage, is always to have one degree of responsibility more, the responsibility for the responsibility of the other. (*OB*: 117)[52]

Levinas distinguishes between sociality (and true society), on the one hand, and society, on the other, a distinction, which enables him to look at the social order in a way different from the usual one.[53] Society, commonly understood in modern social philosophy, amounts to the following:

1. It is a multiplicity of human beings.
2. Particular human beings are individual instances of the genus "human being" who are equal autonomous subjects with equal rights.
3. The main problem in social philosophy is the question of how a multitude of such autonomous and equal individuals can form a more or less harmonious and peaceful society.
4. Such individuals undertake actual or potential roles, functions without, however, any attempt to grasp and place these in their different contexts of social formations.

To understand what Levinas could mean by sociality (and true society), we shall need to say something briefly about his notion of strangeness, which Levinas does not analyse from the standpoint of the identity of the agent (as in psychoanalysis) but from his/her "original sociality". For him, strangeness is tied up primarily with "the other man": "Nothing is more strange and more foreign than the other man and it is in a clarity of an utopia that man shows himself. Beyond every root and also every dwelling (*Noms Propres: 54*)." The Other forms an "unusual out", a dimension of "exteriority".

This approach of the relation to the Other enables Levinas to overcome two relational impasses. The first consists in seeing the Other by ourselves, the second, conducts the I to see him/herself by the Other. When the Other is found as an "unusual out", he/she provokes in the agent an embarrassment and a split which overwhelms the desire of identification and projection. As Levinas says, the Other disturbs us because he/she is "not autochthonous, is uprooted, without a country, not an inhabitant (*OB*: 91)." In this way the Other does not appear in a confident and common world; however, in spite of that, the encounter with the Other "subtends society (*OB*: 193)." The basis of human sociality is in the relation between the Other and the I; the impact that provokes this encounter makes us feel strangers to ourselves.

Sociality, thus defined by Levinas as the (always) possible encounter with the Other in his/her strangeness, is therefore distinct from society as commonly understood. In Levinas, the social relation is not reduced to culture, race or a common affiliation to land. Neither does he subscribe to the various philosophies of the social contract in which freedom is the basis of

---

[52] For further commentary on the notion, see, for example, Ford (1996).
[53] See "Le Moi et la Totalité" in *Entre Nous*.

the social relation, or to those philosophies in which autonomy of the will is the basis. He does not reduce the human being to a mere "member of society (*OB*: 159)." His account of the social relation has its source in the sentiment of the disquieting strangeness of the Other.

Levinas cites Dostoievski's Aloysha Karamov who says: we are all responsible for everyone else – but I am more responsible than all the others. To a culture steeped in individualism and its related key concepts of instrumentality, rationality and autonomy, such a call of infinite responsibility for others is at once challenging and disturbing. Yet without it, we might not be able ever to escape the tight constraints imposed by the notion of individual responsibility to a more generous account of responsibility, which can make some space for collective responsibility of which corporate responsibility is a part.

2. Ethics as Theology

Infinite responsibility to the absolute other is Levinas's way to encounter God: "For every man assuming responsibility for the Other is a way of testifying to the glory of the Infinite and of being inspired .... This responsibility prior to the law is God's revelation. (*EI*: 113) ". In the relation with other human beings, we enter into relation with the Other, and thereby, we encounter God. Traditional theology treats God basically as one kind of object of knowledge. This is in accordance with traditional metaphysics and epistemology, whose primary pre-occupation is with knowledge of Being, which construes the relation with God as an essentially cognitive enterprise. But for Levinas, this is nothing but atheism, as it denies God's intrinsic Otherness and our responsibility towards Him. Levinas, therefore, construes Heidegger's concern with Being to be essentially atheistic. A truly religious metaphysics is one, which is rooted in our pre-occupation with fellow human beings. "Hence metaphysics is enacted where the social relation is enacted – in our relation with men. There can be no 'knowledge' of God separated from the relationship with men. The Other is the very locus of metaphysical truth, and is indispensable for my relation with God. (*TI*: 78)". This bears out yet again what Levinas means by ethics as first philosophy – philosophy is rooted in ethics.[54] In contrast, the atheism deeply embedded in the dominant tradition of philosophy leads to what may be called a superficial humanism, which in his opinion, is profoundly anti-human, and to an individualism which is, in the end, hostile to real individuality.

3. *Hineni* and *Me, voici*

As already mentioned, Levinas does not wish to see his *oeuvres* as a contribution from Jewish philosophy; nor does he wish to see it as part of holocaust discourse. Nevertheless, this does not mean that his writings have not been influenced by Judaism and by the Talmudic tradition, of which he was a rabbi.[55] Indeed Putnam says that "Levinas is universalising Judaism (2002: 46)." This, perhaps, is to go too far but Putnam is right in drawing attention to that strain from Judaism which can be detected in Levinas's thought.[56] In

---

[54] Religion is distinct from philosophy and may bring its own peculiar consolations. As for religion, Levinas remained resolutely committed to Orthodox Judaism all his life.
[55] For a detailed discussion of Levinas and the Talmudic tradition, see Chalier (2002).
[56] See Putnam (2002): 52.

particular, Putnam understands Levinas to valorise the ethical content, at the expense of the religious content, of *hineni*, the Hebrew for "here I am" which in French, for Levinas, becomes "*Me voici*", as a witness of the infinite. Putnam cites two passages from Levinas to support his interpretation, the second of which reads:

> You are thinking: what becomes of the Infinity that the Title *Totality and Infinity* announced? To my mind the Infinite comes in the signifyingness of the face. The face signifies the Infinite. It never appears a theme, but in this ethical signifyingness itself; that is the fact that the more I am just the more I am responsible; one is never quits with regard to the Other. (2002: 53)

The fundamental obligation consists of *hineni* to the Other. It is not, as we have already outlined in general, and shall see later in greater detail, a question of grasping abstract principles of reason (like Kant), of acting on sympathy (like Hume), of intuiting moral obligations and goodness (like G. E. Moore or Plato), or of applying a master rule (like the principle of utility). Rather, it is grounded in one's relation to the Other as concrete, flesh and blood, individual that he/she is; the response is elicited by the respect for the alterity of the Other. Putnam is right to say: "I do not know any other ethical philosopher who has so powerfully combined the idea that ethics is based on the perception of persons, not of abstractions, with the idea that the ethical perception must fully respect alterity (2002: 55)." The ethical life consists of making oneself open and available to the neediness of others, an availability which is not dependent upon any prior contract, whether historical or fictional – the fundamental spontaneity of *Me voici*, therefore, does not arise in the way rights and duties are said to arise either in a Hobbesian, Lockean or Kantian context.[57] Levinas is against any philosophy, which insists that there can be no obligation in the absence of abstract justification or indeed of meaning. Regarding the latter, humankind recently confronted it in the twentieth century in the suffering during the Second World War and the holocaust. Levinas raises not merely the obvious matter of the suffering of the victims caused by the actions of the perpetrators, but especially on the responsibility of so-called innocent by-standers. If responsibility is simply understood in terms of reciprocity, then these by-standers are indeed innocent. But responsibility can and should also be understood, as Levinas wants to maintain, in terms of one's asymmetrical and non-reciprocal responsibility to and for the suffering of the Other.[58] We shall see later why this thesis of Levinas appears so difficult to grasp and indeed even absurd within the context of dominant Western moral philosophy today.

---

[57] This aspect will be more fully developed in the section to follow on Saintliness and Virtue Ethics, especially *via* an exploration of Victor Hugo's cosmic hero, Jean Valjean, in *Les Misérables*.
[58] See, for example, *OB*: 117, 196 for Levinas's emphasis on suffering.

4. Saintliness and Virtue Ethics

Perhaps one way of getting a handle on Levinas's ethical thought is to regard his key notion of infinite responsibility to others as an expression of **saintliness**, but not obviously in religious terms as normally understood theistically.[59] His conception of ethics as theology, as we have seen, is different from the traditional understanding of theology in the west; similarly, saintliness (holiness) for him is not ordained by any church, god or God, but informed by an inner compulsiveness which amounts to an obsession (though not an obsession in the psychological sense) – the face compels one to be responsible for the Other.[60] It also goes without saying that his notion has nothing to do with the tradition of canonisation based on the performance of miracles.[61]

However, the notion of secular saintliness and sainthood is not unintelligible. Such a status could be bestowed on a person who simply recognises the duty to help those who suffer and to do justice, even when the cost to him/herself may be great, when the person is not motivated by either gain/praise either of an earthly or heavenly kind, but who is simply compelled to act out of the humanity he/she recognises and sees in the other. It is a little surprising that Levinas seemed, as far as one can ascertain, to have overlooked a very powerful embodiment of this notion in French literature,[62] namely, in the cosmic role of Jean Valjean in Victor Hugo's masterpiece, *Les Misérables*.[63]

Three outstanding episodes in that *oeuvre* bear witness to it. At the very beginning of the novel, the bishop, M. Myriel, confronting the escaped convict, Valjean, "worked a miracle" upon the latter, transforming him from the embittered, hardened being that he was into a "secular saint". The bishop did not accomplish it by preaching at the man, by getting him to confess his so-called sins and to repent, or to say *Ave*s and *Glory Be*s as penance; he simply recognised that the humanity of the individual who landed on his doorstep demanded his help, and required to be "saved" from the clutches of the law, as Valjean had been caught with the silver stolen from the bishop's household. Instead, M. Myriel told the police that the silver was a gift; and after having dismissed the agents of law and order, he turned to Valjean and said in a low voice:

> "Do not forget, never forget that you have promised to use that silver to become an honest man."

Jean Valjean, who had no memory whatsoever of having ever made such a promise, remained silent. The bishop had laid emphasis on those words in pronouncing them. He continued with a kind of solemnity:

---

[59] The notion will be examined again later to defend it from criticisms in the context of supererogation and utopian thinking. For now, I am merely trying to present it in an embodied form via the character of Valjean as created by Victor Hugo, as well as to consider it in the context of virtue ethics.

[60] For Levinas's thoughts on obsession, see, for example, *OB*: 83, 90, 191, 197; see also Haar (1997).

[61] For instance, the Pope is keen to canonise Mother Teresa but even in spite of the new fast-track system for sainthood innovated by the Vatican recently, the good woman in question (who dedicated her life as a nun to helping the poor and the sick primarily in Calcutta) has still not yet performed that crucial second miracle for canonisation, which is now eagerly awaited. The Vatican has recognised that she has worked so far one miracle, which would entitle her, however, only to being beatified – see Bates (2002).

[62] Levinas acknowledged the influence of Russian literature (Pushkin, Dostoyesky and Tolstoy) and of English Literature (Shakespeare, especially *Macbeth* and *King Lear*) – see Mostley (1991), 11.

[63] Admittedly, Hugo was only concerned to depict the relationship between individuals in the light of this notion. It remains to be seen if it also has application in the public/political domain, a point which will be looked at later – in particular, see Third Part, section 1.

> "Jean Valjean, my brother, you no longer belong to evil, but to good. It is your soul which I have bought; I have drawn it back from dark thoughts and the spirit of perdition, and I have given it to God." (1995: 163)[64]

After his "redemption", Valjean made good in the world and became a successful respected member of society under an assumed name. He spent his wealth and position to do whatever good he could to ameliorate poverty and suffering whenever he confronted them, just as M. Myriel had done and had enjoined him to do. In particular, he attempted to save a young woman, a poor victim of society's hypocrisy, who had ultimately to turn to prostitution in order to save herself and her illegitimate child from hunger; and when she died, he continued his project of rescuing her daughter, Cosette, from the cruel suffering to which she was subjected as an abandoned orphan. Valjean's prolonged project may be said to be an obsessive one (in the Levinasian sense of the term).

The third episode concerns the struggle within his soul between the obsessive call of responsibility for the Other and the infinitely easier option of simply turning his back upon that duty – one day he came to hear that a poor innocent individual had been arrested, having been misidentified as Jean Valjean, the escaped convict and was to be tried for Valjean's own misdeeds in the eyes of the law, certain to be found guilty and sent to the labour camp. During that long night of his own Calvary:

> It seemed that he had just awakened from some sort of a sleep and that he found himself in the night sliding down a slope, standing up, quivering, trying in vain to hold himself back from the brink of an abyss. He saw distinctly in the shadow of an unknown being, a stranger, which destiny would take to be himself and push into the abyss in his place. That abyss would only close up if someone were to fall into it, either him or the other. (1995: 306)

But responsibility to the stranger meant that he must throw himself into the abyss, so that "in entering hell, he would become angel" while in "remaining in paradise, he would become devil (1995: 320)." The obsessive call of duty to the Other triumphed – the respectable and respected citizen denounced himself in court, declaring to the unbelieving audience around him that he, and not the poor person in the dock, was Jean Valjean. He had become a saint.

Hugo seems to have deliberately used religious language as we have seen.[65] He continues in this vein:

> Thus this unfortunate soul argued within himself in his agonising. Eighteen hundred years before this unfortunate man, amidst the olive groves which trembled before the fierce winds of infinity a mysterious being who contained within himself all forms of saintliness as well as having taken upon himself all manner of suffering on the part of humanity, had like him pushed aside with his hand the terrifying chalice which seemed to him to be full of shadows, and running over with darkness in the depth of skies full of stars. (1995: 321)

---

[64] The translation of this passage and the ones to follow is mine.
[65] In this Levinas and Hugo concur. Especially in *OB*, the former also deliberately uses words with strong religious connotations, like election, soul, inspiration, creation, expiation, sacrifice, exile, obedience, guilty, although like Hugo, he too, does not intend them to have their normal theological baggage.

In other words, Hugo sees the cosmic role of Valjean as the secular analogue of Christ. Just as Christ felt infinite responsibility for the souls of all humanity, Hugo's secular saint feels equally responsible for others (with the more human proviso that his saint would be expected to do only whatever he could to help ameliorate the suffering of others). What Hugo has depicted in his novel seems very close in spirit to Levinas's conception of infinite responsibility for others in all its obsessiveness.

Of late, in the literature of so-called Anglo-Saxon tradition of moral philosophy, a distinctive engagement in ethical theorizing has appeared, namely, virtue ethics, in addition to the more familiar Kantian ethics on the one hand and consequentialist ethics on the other.[66] However, the approach is not new, as it is the mode most frequently associated with Aristotle and moral theorists of the ancient Greek world.

> Many modern philosophers think of the moral life as a matter of relating properly to moral rules, but in the virtue ethics of the ancient world and in those few instances of virtue ethics one finds in modern or recent philosophy, the understanding of the moral or ethical life primarily requires us to understand what it is to be a virtuous individual or what it is to have one or another particular virtue, conceived as an inner trait or disposition of the individual. So the first thing we can say about virtue ethics in an attempt to distinguish if from other approaches is that it is *agent-focused.* (Slote (1997: 177)

In other words, virtue ethics is *aretaic*, not *deontic* in orientation.[67] In virtue ethics, ethical characterisation is made primarily in aretaic terms (such as "virtuous", "admirable", "morally good") while considering deontic epithets (rules, principles, moral law) either to be superfluous or derivative from the aretaic.

While it seems clear that Levinasian ethics has nothing in common with deontic ethics (either of a Kantian or of a consequentialist variety), it is not so obvious that Levinasian ethics does not bear some kinship to aretaic ethics.[68] That element of virtue ethics, which appears to resonate with Levinasian ethics, is the emphasis on inner strength.[69] As we have seen, what Jean Valjean has learnt from the saintly bishop, M. Myriel, is inner strength, both in doing justice and in doing benevolence. Take the latter – Slote holds that Nietzsche has touched on this point when Nietzsche (*Beyond Good and Evil*) cites the person who gives generously from a sense of superabundance, which goes beyond the usual egoism/altruism dichotomy.[70] The generous giver (Valjean when he became rich) is not promoting a "feel good" feeling in himself or a "feel good" image of himself; neither is he simply responding to the needs of the needy. It is that, of course, but it also involves something more – somewhat like Plato's Form of the Good, which informs the healthy soul and guides its conduct. In Levinasian ethics, it is a case, as we have seen, of *Me, voici*.

---

[66] See Baron, Pettit and Slote (1997).
[67] In this sense of "deontic", both Kantian ethics and consequentialist (utilitarian) ethics are deontic – they are both rule-oriented, though the basic rules of their respective systems are different. However, for a defence of Kant's moral philosophy as virtue ethics, see Louden (1992).
[68] The resemblance between Levinasian and aretaic ethics will be borne out in some detail in the later – sections 6.1 and 6.3. Some differences between Levinasian and Kantian ethics will be looked at in the section 6.1.
[69] See Slote (1997): 216-20.
[70] Slote (1997): 219.

A possible objection, which can be raised against the notion of inner strength, is that it might render the virtues of benevolence, compassion, caring or justice to be only derivatively admirable and morally good.[71] However, one may be able to distinguish a strong from a weaker application of the notion to moral thought and action – while the former may be susceptible to the criticism just mentioned, the latter may not. It is rather to say that moral perfection aims not merely at being benevolent or just, but at being also benevolent or just from inner strength. It is not to say that benevolence or justice is a secondary value, derivative from it. To act benevolently or justly *simpliciter* is to act in a morally desirable and admirable way; to act benevolently or justly from inner strength is, in addition, to act in accordance with moral perfection. While undoubtedly it is true that one might not always achieve moral perfection, the notion of moral perfection itself is not unintelligible. Perhaps, this weaker understanding of acting from inner strength is all one needs to invoke in defence of Levinas.

At this particular stage of my presentation of Levinasian thought, and in concluding this section of this part, I would, here, like to make a rather bold claim on behalf of the interpretation given so far of Levinas's conception of ethics as first philosophy and his *aretaic* characterisation of ethics in terms of saintliness/holiness: that it is a genuine new moral paradigm measured against the major traditional accounts of ethics in modern Western thought such as Kantianism, liberalism and utilitarianism. At this stage in the presentation of Levinas's thoughts, I can only make it baldly; however, as the chapter develops, I hope to make good the claim in some detail under two aspects – first, that it is a genuine new paradigm (see in particular section 7), and second, that it is the new paradigm which is relevant to the problems which face the world in the twenty-first century (see in particular Third Part , section 3). But, for the moment, I need to engage with some possible criticisms against the interpretation itself of Levinas's notion of infinite responsibility as presented so far.

5. How to Meet Some Criticisms

It is wise to labour the point once again that this is not a thesis devoted to Levinas. There is neither the time nor the space for such a comprehensive study; furthermore, its remit is not to defend or to render coherent his entire philosophy. However, as it wants to lean on his notion of infinite responsibility for the Other, it is necessary to address certain criticisms, which could be directed against it.[72] The concept is bound to be extremely problematic to any one immersed within the Anglo-Saxon philosophical tradition which defines the dominant conception of (individual) responsibility, both in morals and in law. The moral/political philosophers working within that framework have tended to ignore it. However, Richard Rorty, though not normally seen as a moral philosopher, does refer to it, but only to dismiss it in a few lines.[73]

---

[71] See Slote (1997): 219-20.
[72] This very limited attempt to defend Levinas must be taken in the spirit in which it is made, that is to say, totally independent of what Levinas himself might or might not have said, should he so wish to defend himself, of whether he might approve of this kind of exercise on his behalf. For a different kind of criticism than the sort raised here, see Haar (1997).
[73] See Rorty (1998): 96-97; it would be cited later on.

5.1. *Supererogation and Kantian Ethics*[74]

To see where some of the difficulties may lie, one must recall that embedded in standard moral philosophy, is the distinction between duty on the one hand and supererogation on the other. While it is morally obligatory to perform the former, it is not morally obligatory, though morally laudable, to perform the other. Those who engage in it are honoured with the label of moral 'heroes' or 'heroines' who have sacrificed themselves for the good of others. They are the 'good samaritans', those who have gone beyond duty to help others while putting themselves out or exposing themselves to considerable or great risks of danger. They are considered in that sense to be "abnormal", thereby creating the distinction between "normal" moral agents who are in the majority and "abnormal" ones who tend to be in the minority.

Increasingly over the last twenty years or so, in Britain, in any case, that number seems to be diminishing, judging by anecdotal accounts and news reports. For instance, a local free sheet in Manchester (*The Reporter*, 14 November 2002) carried a news item about an eighty-year old grandmother who was badly mugged by some teenaged girls while walking along a suburban street in the early evening; she appealed to a male passer-by for help who refused and walked away.[75] On the other hand, history of the second half of the twentieth century provides some sublime examples of supererogation. For instance, some gentiles in Nazi-occupied Europe risked their very lives to hide and/or help Jewish people, whether neighbours or total strangers, to escape to safety.[76]

However, much as one might praise or be moved to tears by such noble efforts of samaritanism, and much as one might bemoan or be upset by the lack of the samaritan spirit in more mundane instances where the effort and risk incurred in helping someone in distress or danger is no more than some inconvenience to those on the scene, it remains the case that both forms of samaritanism, mundane or sublime, are regarded as forms of supererogation within the dominant (Western) tradition of moral philosophy. There is just no moral duty to carry them out.[77] Yet Levinas's emphasis on responsibility for the Other implies the abolition

---

[74] It may be wise to remind the reader yet again that in this discussion (and throughout this chapter) the term, "Kantian Ethics" is used to refer to that ethical perspective in modern Western moral thought which has been influenced by Kant's ethical theory, and not necessarily uniquely to Kant's ethical theory in the narrow and strict sense.

[75] The decline of good samaritans in the UK could be put down to a variety of reasons: the feeling that it is often not safe to intervene, as one could be involved with violent behaviour, or that it would be futile to try to subdue some one potentially violent when other by-standers are not equally willing to join in to tackle the aggressor; owing to the change in ideological climate since 1979, more people than before tend to believe that rational egoism is the best policy to adopt – one turns away and leaves well alone whatever does not immediately affect one's own interests; in a society where the spirit of litigation is rapidly being entrenched, one could even be sued for whatever damage one might unwittingly cause to another in one's effort to help the victim. As a result, one finds today in Britain a greater reluctance to act as good samaritans even if the act involves little effort or risk, such as helping the mugged grandmother in question.

[76] See Gilbert (2002).

[77] However, if it is argued that these are not acts of supererogation but duties to others – that one is simply mistaken in holding that they are acts of supererogation – then the concept of supererogation runs the danger of being an empty category. What acts could possibly count as those of supererogation if not these? It would be incumbent on such critics to provide "genuine" instances of supererogation, to show how these differ significantly from the examples cited here, especially those which involve a very real risk of life to the "do-gooder". In the absence of convincing arguments to make their point, one would be entitled to conclude that the concept of supererogation has been rendered null and void. Yet if these critics regard themselves as Kantian (as opposed to being utilitarian) in spirit and outlook, then they would have undermined their own standpoint. However, this criticism would not apply if the would-be critics are utilitarians, as the utilitarian tradition does not need to recognise the distinction between duty on the one hand and supererogation on the other – for them, whether

of the deep-seated distinction between duty on the one hand and supererogation on the other. That is why Levinas's conception of responsibility is said to be infinite responsibility, and also, therefore, considered as unintelligible to those who adhere to the dominant conception of responsibility in western moral thought, such as Rorty. On the standard understanding of morality, failure to carry out a moral duty is morally reprehensible and in legal contexts, justifies the infliction of an appropriate penalty;[78] failure to carry out a supererogatory act, while still attracting some mild reprobation especially in instances where only inconvenience would be incurred in discharging such an act, is not regarded to be morally reprehensible in the way that failure to carry out a moral duty attracts moral/legal disapproval. On the other hand, to engage in such an act (whether minor or major) earns the agent moral praise and honour, as already mentioned. The Levinasian conception of responsibility forces one to look at this asymmetry anew.

From his perspective as interpreted here, it would be incoherent to draw a boundary between those acts which constitutes duties to others and those which are less than duties to others when in either instance, one's effort could end with the same result, namely, preventing harm to another. The aim of not laying a trap in the dark for another is precisely the same as the aim of getting medical help to another seriously injured by falling into such a trap; yet (a) why should the former constitute a duty and the latter a mere supererogation? (b) why suffer moral unease when there is failure to help another in distress, unless the failure to do so constitutes an act which hurts or injures another?

To raise questions like the above is to draw attention to the 'thinness' of the moral universe purveyed by the dominant account of responsibility. 'Thinness' here refers to the absolute minimum amount of moral engagement between human beings, which is necessary for society to cohere and to exist. To draw the boundary between self and others in this way would ensure minimal overlap and, hence, the maximal space for the self to operate and to 'do its own thing', protected, as much as possible, from being tangled with the lives of others. This would be in keeping with the notion of autonomy as well as the philosophy of individualism and liberalism.

It may be fair to say that modern Western ethical thought has focused, perhaps unfairly so to Kant's own complex thoughts, on the so-called notion of perfect duties to others.[79] We shall see why in a moment. To greatly simplify matters, Kant may be said to use two sets of distinction – perfect/imperfect duties on the one hand and duties to self/to others on the other – thereby creating four categories of duties: perfect duty to self (such as the duty not to commit suicide), imperfect duty to self (duty to develop and realise one's own potential),

---

one has a duty in any one instance depends entirely on good consequences outweighing bad ones overall. In the case of saving Jews from Nazi persecution, if one were to do a utilitarian calculation, it would probably turn out in some instances that overall, bad rather than good consequences would ensue; in the majority of instances, it would be very difficult even to envisage what the consequences could be given the extreme uncertainties surrounding the dilemma; and probably in a few cases, it might be possible to say definitively that good consequences would prevail.

[78] Note that in law (English law, at least), the general public has no legal obligation to assist another who is in distress. For example, in a swimming pool, one is not legally obliged to save someone who is drowning; however, the poolside supervisor/monitor does have a legal duty to save the drowning person, and should he fail to do so, that act of omission would amount to criminal negligence and render him liable to be charged with criminal manslaughter.

[79] This point is an important one to emphasise here. First of all, this very brief discussion of Kant's moral philosophy in terms of the Categorical Imperative and of duties is not meant to be, as it necessarily cannot be, thorough, systematic or exhaustive.

perfect duties to others (duties not to kill, maim or damage others, bodily and economically), imperfect duties to others (duty to help others to thrive and flourish).[80] Kant's efforts to clarify the Categorical Imperative, embedded in his philosophy of freedom through its various formulations, is complicated, not easy to set out briefly and is not without problems.[81] In moral deliberation, one must adopt the standpoint of a rational agent, and in so doing, arrive at an imperative which in turn applies universally to all rational beings.

In other words, reason dictates – according to the first formulation of the Categorical Imperative – that in deciding to act to carry out an end, the agent must act only on that maxim which when universalised would not involve the agent in a contradiction, that is, a maxim which one can will as a universal law – "*Act as if the maxim of your action were to become by your will a **universal law of nature*** (4: 4.21; Gregor (1998): 31)." Although the maxim is formal, yet far from being devoid of practical implications and content, it is commonly understood to yield very concrete injunctions, such as one has a duty not to break promises. Contradiction is involved as follows:

(a) To be a moral law, the maxim which forbids promise-breaking, must be universally binding.
(b) Should I wish to act against this moral law, such as to break a promise whenever it is to my advantage to do so, I would be making an exception of myself to the law.
(c) Yet, in granting this exception to myself, I must grant it to all others, as every moral agent, including myself, is a rational agent,
(d) But if every rational agent were to act as I do, that is, to make an exception of him/herself to the moral law, the institution of promise breaking will be undermined or abolished.
(e) Hence, I cannot universalise the maxim of my action – keep promises if and only if my own interests are advanced – without contradiction.
(f) And hence, the maxim – always keep promises – is universally binding, and therefore a moral law.

However, while it is relatively easy to justify this example of perfect duties to others under the first formulation, it does not seem to work quite so readily in the case of Kant's prohibition of suicide – perfect duty to self – as an instantiation of it. No contradiction appears to be involved in the same way as a contradiction is shown to be involved in the maxim about promise breaking, as set out in the note earlier. Suppose I will that I and every rational agent such as myself commit suicide. What would happen is that the whole of humanity would probably be wiped out (save those who do not qualify to be rational agents, such as the infantile and the very senile in mind). Absurd as the implication of such a universal maxim might be, no contradiction has been committed in proposing it. Absurdity may be a departure from rationality in some other sense of the term but it does not amount to a contradiction in this context. Furthermore, Kant has not given any other characterisation of the concept of rationality, save relying on its strongest form, namely, the principle of non-contradiction. So Kant has not demonstrated that prohibition against suicide is a moral law,

---

[80] For a recent thorough discussion of the detailed complexities of Kant's moral philosophy, see Sullivan (1989); and for an anthology of essays on the subject, see Chadwick (1992).
[81] See Sullivan (1989); for a shorter account, see Scruton (1982): 58-77; for a more critical account, see Walker (1978): 147-64.

and therefore, that suicide is invariably morally wrong. In any case, rational beings are more likely to propose a more nuanced maxim, such as: I will that I and rational agents like myself who are incurably/terminally ill and in extreme pain commit suicide or be assisted to do so. Kant might claim that there is a contradiction involved here, namely, that one would be committing oneself to the pursuit of happiness and at the same time to steps, which would render its further pursuit impossible. But such an attempt does not sound very convincing – happiness, after all, might well be found under these circumstances in what might be called a "good death", a death of which the rational agent is in full control, in full exercise of his/her autonomy. Such a maxim does not sanction suicide *tout court* but suicide under certain specific circumstances only. However, Kant's aim is to prohibit suicide in all forms and not to distinguish that class which we call euthanasia – one could say that Kant's formal use of rationality (*via* the principle of non-contradiction) is not sufficient here to generate a substantive norm of conduct.

Similarly, Kant's treatment of imperfect duty to self suffers from the same weakness. The maxim: "Let everyone neglect his talents" is perfectly universal. It might not be rational to will it as a moral law but not in the sense that as a universal maxim, it embodies outright contradictions. Furthermore, to say that one cannot (rationally) will to neglect one's talents since as a rational being one necessarily will that all one's power's be developed is unconvincing – the utterance amounts to a tautology unless further content were given to what is meant by 'rational being', 'necessarily will'.

However, Kant's category of imperfect duty to others is more amenable to the treatment he has in mind. The maxim: "Let no one ever help anyone else" is also universal. The contradiction amounts to this:

(a) All rational agents, myself included, necessarily will our own individual happiness.
(b) All rational agents, myself included, also necessarily will the means to achieve our respective ends.
(c) All rational agents, myself included, sometimes require the help of others and, thereby, necessarily will their help on such occasions.
(d) "Let no one ever help anyone else" is, therefore, incompatible with the conjunction: (a), (b) and (c).

This could be one reason why the category of perfect duties to others (which could, by and large, be translated into negative duties of the kind commonly formulated in terms of "thou shall not kill", "thou shall not steal", "thou shall not lie or break promises" etc.) receives more attention than the other three categories, in spite of the fact that the category of imperfect duties to others is more akin to the logic of perfect duties to others (as shown in the preceding note) than the remaining two categories of duties to self.[82]

Kant's notion of rationality, autonomy and freedom implies that every rational agent is "an end in himself", according to his second formulation – "*So act that you use humanity, whether in your own person or in the person of any other, always at the same time as an end,*

---

[82] That is why Kant's first formulation of the Categorical Imperative is said to provide the philosophical basis for the Golden Rule – do unto others what you would wish others to do unto you. See Ross (1954): 44-45; Scruton (1982): 70. For an alternative interpretation, see Sullivan (1989): 204.

never merely as a means (4:429; Gregor (1998): 38)." In other words, one must treat all rational agents never simply as means to one's own ends, but as ends in themselves.

As the first formulation has shown, the moral agent must regard the moral law as something universally legislated and binding; this point is reinforced in the third formulation, namely, that the will of every rational agent is "a universally legislative will" involving a "kingdom of ends" to which every agent subscribes in acting autonomously. It is sometimes formulated as follows: "Act as if you were through your maxims a legislating member of a Kingdom of Ends (Walker (1978): 158"; the original passage in Kant reads: "The concept of every rational being as one who must regard himself as giving universal law through all the maxims of his will, so as to appraise himself and his actions from this point of view, leads to a very fruitful concept dependent upon it, namely that *of a kingdom of ends* (4.433; Gregor (1998): 41)."

As I have just mentioned, the first formulation seems to fit best the category of perfect duties to others. The second formulation underpins Kant's notion of *persons* as opposed to *things* – while the latter is not rational, autonomous and free, the former is category is eminently so. Kant writes:

> Beings the existence of which rests not on our will but on nature, if they are beings without reason, still have only a relative worth, as a means, and are therefore called *things*, whereas rational beings are called *persons* because their nature already marks them out as an end in itself, that is, as something that may not be used merely as a means, and hence so far limits all choice (and is an object of respect). (4.428; Gregor (1998): 37).

This in turn serves to lay the foundation of the concept of right. Persons who come under the aegis of the Categorical Imperative are those beings who have rights to whom we owe duties. Respect for persons and rights go hand in hand, leading once again to an implied emphasis on the category of perfect duties to others.

In this light, the Kantian influence in shaping modern Western moral thought seems to have been confined to an emphasis on rights and respect as well as on the notion of perfect duties to others. This in turn may have led to a de-emphasis on benevolence, which may have been reinforced by Kant's privileging reason over passion. Benevolence is a sentiment or inclination, which may or may not reside in any one person on any one occasion. To act out of benevolence appears to be a chancy affair, depending on mood and circumstance. In any case, mere inclination or passion has no particular moral worth; moral worth lies in the ability of the rational human agent to resist inclination to which he/she is also prey – "It is a very beautiful thing to do good to men from love to them and from sympathetic goodwill, or to be just from love of order, but this is not the true moral maxim (*Critique of Practical* Reason (trans. Abbott): 249)." Thus the desire to live is mere instinct; however, the desire to continue to live in spite of all the odds, out of duty, not to commit suicide, constitutes moral worth.[83]

Furthermore, while Kant emphasises that one may not refuse to help others in need in so far as one can do so, that one may not in general be indifferent to the happiness of others, nevertheless, he is of the opinion that these moral duties need have no juridical counterparts.[84] In other words, he seems to imply that while they are morally laudable and even obligatory, and, indeed, that one should actively cultivate "love" of others – "moral love" in the sense

---

[83] See, for example, Scruton (1982): 74.
[84] Following Sullivan (1989): 71.

that one ought to feel genuinely benevolent to others irrespective of whether one likes them or cares for them personally – the relevant realm of their operation is inter-personal conduct between individuals, and not in the public domain, either civic/national and international.[85] However, as we shall see a little later, western societies of late on the whole have opted to recognise in law certain minimum obligations to secure the welfare of all its citizens; however, for societies/governments to recognise that similar obligations to others in need outside their national boundaries is more difficult to secure.

5.2. Supererogation and Common Sense Morality

However, at this point of the argument, I need to introduce a new element to complicate the picture so far outlined, which might further explain why it appears difficult for societies to recognise obligations to those in need outside their national boundaries. I have up to now in this chapter focused on the major (philosophical) normative systems which have informed and defined modern Western moral thought, namely, the Kantian, the liberal and (to some extent also) the utilitarian traditions, all of which in principle are universalising ethics – for the first, the Categorical Imperative applies to all those human beings who count as persons; for the second, the liberal principle is applicable to all normal adult human beings whose rational faculty could be assumed to be properly developed; for the third, the principle of utility covers all those beings (theoretically including non-human ones, but in practice in the main applied to humans only) who can suffer pain. However, in reality, historically and in political terms, their universalising aspect has not always been applied to those who may qualify in philosophical terms for consideration under their respective rubrics; given the historical and cultural differences between groups and societies, those who have been (or are) excluded have been (or are) perceived to be different from those included.

It appears that at the same time, in practice, these major traditions, within which the notion of individual responsibility is philosophically embedded, have also been checked by another current in modern Western society, which subscribes not so much to a universalising approach to ethics, as to a much older conception of duties to others, which may be called 'concentric'.[86] By this is meant, that duties to one's family constitute the innermost circle, and therefore, the most compelling; then to people who live within the national jurisdiction; then to so-called 'kith and kin' in the diaspora. In the past, the family usually included three generations, children, parents and grand parents. However, to day, the pattern has changed in the advanced industrial countries in the West and even elsewhere. In the past, duties to elderly parents were considered quite as compelling as duties to children and to husband/wives. Today, duties to the former are construed so minimally as to be virtually non-existent; a good

---

[85] On Kant's emphasis on moral love, see Sullivan (1989): 205-6. This then means at best private charity.

[86] The combination of the historically and culturally determined limitations in the application of the major universalising ethics may be seen in the following examples. For example, Kantian ethics took a rather long time indeed in modern Western societies to break through the concentric circle of males as far as voting was concerned, although it is clear that normal adult women do qualify to be persons in the Kantian sense of the term. Mill withheld the application of his liberal principle from the working classes of his day on the grounds that their rational faculty was under-developed owing to their lack of education. And as far as the utilitarian tradition is concerned, Bentham, to his credit did advocate the emancipation of slaves, but subject to orderly utilitarian requirements – that is to say, free your slaves and as many of them at any one time as was compatible with security, order, and indeed, economic contingencies. Although the formal act of emancipation occurred in the USA nearly two centuries ago, it remains true that even to this day, by and large, African Americans are still at a disadvantage in numerous spheres of life compared to their compatriots, in general, of European descent.

many may still have the residual feeling that they should get in touch a few times a year with their elderly parents or grand parents, such as on birthdays and at Christmas. The care of the elderly increasingly is no longer the responsibility of the immediate family but of institutions, whether paid for by the state or by the individual. The family increasingly is construed as the nuclear family – not only has the notion shrunk in scope and size but also has come, in some cases, to be regarded as a temporal thing which endures only until the children obtain the age of majority.[87] On the hand, recent developments on the environmental front have forced society and some theorists to consider the problem of duties to posterity and to debate the issue whether present generations owe obligations to future generations.[88]

As already mentioned, people, on the whole, recognise, one's moral and legal (minimum) obligations to others, especially fellow citizens, who live within the national jurisdiction, although many are none too keen to see too much of their taxes diverted to support services which are universally open to all or to those in need. However, with regard to people, outside one's national boundaries, no matter how needy, there is even less moral enthusiasm in general to divert taxes to help support them. Some governments may have set the laudable goal of devoting 1% - 2% of their GNP to foreign aid, but very few ever reach it. The UN is trying again; its Millenium Development Goals was adopted by the General Assembly in September 2000.[89] This attitude has been (or is) regarded as normal because traditionally all societies make a distinction between kith and kin on the one hand and total strangers on the other.[90] To the former in distant lands, one owes duties to help under certain circumstances, but to the latter, who do not share one's language/culture/history, one owes no such things. However, today, when the television brings instant images of want and suffering into one's living room, when man-made changes in climatic and other conditions are global in character, when economic relations between nations are increasingly drawn into a complicated world-wide network under the aegis of globalisation, etc., a change in attitude is being set in motion by certain individuals, NGOs, and even some governments to expand the notion of duties to others to include people in need who live outside one's national jurisdiction and who may not share one's language/culture/history.[91]

---

[87] One in three marriages in the UK, today, ends in divorce or separation. Some divorced parents even take the view that their duties to their offspring are at best confined to financial support only. However, the rate of re-marriage following divorce is also high. In this sense, a new kind of extended family has taken the place of the old; but the duties to step children are not in general construed to be as compelling as duties to one's own offspring.

[88] See, for instance, De-Shalit (1994).
The minimum time span is generally agreed to be a hundred years. It is difficult today to work out how many generations would occur over a period of a hundred years, as the pattern of child-bearing has altered so dramatically of late, especially now with medically-assisted reproduction of one kind or another in place.

[89] See UN's Millennium Development Goals (2000). See also the Pre-Budget Report of the Chancellor of the Exchequer, UK (2002). Gordon Brown has proposed to the G7 countries, the IMF and the World Bank, in the name of global justice, to double international aid to $100 billion dollars between 2002 and 2015 in order to meet the UN's millennium development goals. For an account of the mechanisms which Brown hopes to rely on to achieve the goal he has set out, see Elliott (2002).

[90] In some tribal societies in the past, not only was there no duty to help strangers in distress, there is, on the contrary, a positive duty to harm them, as strangers were usually the bearers of ill-will and aggression.

[91] The UK government in November 2002 announced a plan for a two-tier system for drug pricing which would make essential drugs available to the poor countries at cost price while the developed countries continue to pay for them at the rate charged by pharmaceutical companies. However, Clare Short's – Minister for International Development – initiative was/is expected to run into opposition from the US government and its pharmaceutical lobby. See Boseley (2002). And it has; in the month following, Dick Cheney, the US vice-president, at the WTO talks in Geneva ruled out a deal which would have allowed a full range of life-saving drugs to be imported into Africa, Asia and Latin America at cut-price costs. Acting at the behest of the drug

In other words, in today's culture, it remains on the whole to be the case that while one may be said to have some moral obligations to the needy who live in one's jurisdiction, who are one's kith and kin, who share one's history, language and culture, etc., one has no such duties to those who are outside these boundaries. At best it would be laudable to help such others, but that would be an act of supererogation and not duty. Given this orientation, it is convenient, on the whole, for affluent Western societies to leave the job of satisfying the needs of the poor and the sick living in the world's less developed economies to those who desire to perform acts of supererogation by supporting international non-governmental organisations such as Oxfam and Médecins sans Frontières

I have now briefly unpicked some of the strands which make up the moral consciousness and conscience in general in today's Western societies, traced some of them back to what may be called a sub-conscious selective borrowing, probably, of certain aspects of Kant's moral philosophy, reinforced by certain elements in so-called common sense morality, which may be said to make it easy for theorists to dismiss out of hand Levinas's notion of infinite responsibility for others. His notion is infinite for precisely the reasons already set out, that is to say, he rejects the distinction between family/kith and kin on the one hand and strangers on the other, between so-called perfect duties on the one hand and imperfect duties on the other, between (as Kant would understand it) reason on the one hand and inclination/passion on the other, between duty on the one hand and supererogation on the other, and thus he also rejects the asymmetry between moral praise for acts of supererogation on the one hand while withholding moral condemnation for failure to carry out such acts on the other. For Levinas, it appears that each and every one has one supreme duty, and that is, always to be responsible for others, to act out of benevolence to others. As we have seen, ethics as first philosophy for Levinas tolerates no exclusion – our moral duties are not confined to certain groups and to certain kinds of action only.

5.3. *Saintliness/Holiness or Moral Perfection: Is it so Absurd?*

In the following exchange, Levinas raises the notion of saintliness.

> Question: The self, as the ethical subject, is responsible for everything and everyone; one's responsibility is infinite. Is not this situation non-viable for the subject itself as well as for the other as I risk to terrorise it by my ethical will? Is there not then an ethical impotence in the will to do good?
>
> Levinas: I do not know if the situation is non-viable. It is not what one would call agreeable, certainly, it may not be pleasant, but it is the good. What is very important – I am able to support that without being myself a saint, nor do I pass myself off as a saint – it is the ability to say that the notion of being truly human, in the European sense of the term, comes from the Greeks and the Bible, and which understands saintliness as the ultimate value, as the unquestioned value. Sure, it is very difficult to preach that; it does not go down well to preach it and to do so may well incur the scorn of society as presently evolved. (*Entre-Nous* : 239) [My translation]

Supererogation may be said to be an aspect of **saintliness**. As shown earlier, while acts of supererogation/saintliness may be laudable, all the same, these notions are not part and parcel

---

companies, he wants to impose the narrowest possible interpretation of the Doha Declaration, and to confine price reduction only to drugs dealing with HIV/Aids, malaria, TB and a few other diseases unique to Africa

of morality or moral thinking as commonly practised or understood in modern Western societies. They do not constitute moral duties as such. To aspire to such sublime moral heights is perfectly laudable from the point of view of cultivating moral virtue or perfection in one's character; but it implies that not all moral agents are expected to follow such a path. It is analogous to the attitude of the Roman Catholic Church, at least in the past, to the religious vocation. While exhorting its young to enter the religious life, to embrace the vows of chastity, poverty and obedience, nevertheless, the Church is well aware that not every one is capable of being called or of following such a calling – those, who do, are honoured, but those, who do not, are neither blamed nor censured.

Saintliness or holiness is, therefore, a private calling for the few. Furthermore, to try to practise it outside the domain of the personal and the individual is a sign of obtuseness and inaptitude, which would produce more bad than good – after all, the way to hell is paved with good intentions. Such a spirit is behind the brisk dismissal by Rorty of Levinas:

> The notion of 'infinite responsibility' formulated by Emmanuel Levinas and sometimes deployed by Derrida ... may be useful to some of us in an individual quest for private perfection. When we take up our public responsibilities, however, the infinite and the unrepresentable are merely nuisances. Thinking of our responsibilities in these terms is as much of a stumbling-block to effective political organization as is the sense of sin. (1998: 96-97)

But is saintliness/supererogation as moral perfection such a useless or unhelpful notion in public political life? In the next part, it will be argued that in practice, certain events taking place around the world today show that, perhaps at long last, there are signs in the twenty first century, that some societies, some organisations and some governments are pushing hard to break down such a practice. However, this part of the chapter will examine and try to defend the notion against the kind of intellectual ridicule made by philosophers like Rorty of Levinas's version of saintliness or moral perfection in his notion of infinite responsibility to others.

To make sense of the notion of saintliness or moral perfection, one should simply regard it as an ideal towards which we ought to aspire and to execute in practice as much as it is possible in both the personal and the public domains. (However, for the purpose in hand, only the public domain will be looked at.) Such an enterprise is neither inherently absurd nor unsound in practice. In political philosophy proper, similar disdain is expressed about utopias and the idea of utopianism itself, although it does not prevent a massive literature on the subject from building up over the centuries by theorists all over the world.[92] It is true that utopias when put into practice have in general failed, and in some cases become distinctly distopian in character. But from this, one cannot simplistically infer that the very attempt to formulate it is either unintelligible or has no worth. The idea of utopia is analogous to the notion of truth in epistemology. Many epistemologists, too, have argued that the notion of truth is either incoherent and/or unachievable; however, that has not prevented other philosophers as well as scientists (of the natural world) from hanging on to some version of it,

---

but for which the drug companies do little or no research – see Elliott and Denny (2002); Denny (2003).

[92] Just to cite one limited example of the volume of work in this genre which is confined to one country alone in the course of only a hundred and fifty years of its history, see Claeys (1997). For recent critical assessments, see Kumar (1991); Kolnai (1995).

arguing that it is nevertheless indispensable in any attempt to give an account of the world around us. One very influential philosopher of science, Karl Popper, has talked about verisimilitude or approximation to truth as an indispensable epistemological goal in scientific theorising – even if we would never know the whole truth or know that we know the (whole) truth, nevertheless, it makes sense for us to strive to get at the truth and to say that one theory is closer to the truth than other, and in this way arrive at least at some truths, though necessarily partial.[93]

In the same way, one must have ideals, some of which are captured in utopian thought, to inform our social and political visions, or public life would be very impoverished indeed. Utopian ideals play the important role of providing a focus for a critique of extant society. In their absence, no truly radical criticism and departure from the *status quo* would be feasible. Utopias in concrete may be transient or be corrupted in practice, yet they appear to have the habit of leaving residues behind, with a kind of underground life, slowly permeating through the public consciousness eventfully to make itself felt, though not in the form envisaged by the utopian author himself. Take Charles Fourier (1772-1837) and his utopian vision as an example.[94] Those set up in America in his name did not last long, it is true, yet his idea of sexual emancipation for both men and women from what he saw as the unhealthy repression of sexuality on the part of Christianity – a crucial element of his social/political philosophy – finally only became accepted and mainstream in the 1960s.[95] In this sense, many so-called utopian ideas are only utopian because they are well ahead of their time, so much so that their contemporaries often, if not invariably, regarded their originators to be insane, a fate which Fourier suffered. In other words, in many instances, an ideal written off as utopian is simply one which has been enunciated before its time, and whose unwitting role seems then to be that of preparing the ground for its later reception. What appeared at first to be highly idealistic, in the sense of being impractical and unlikely to have mass appeal, becomes ultimately accepted by society in general and even commonplace. Like truth or approximation to it which acts as epistemological guide to the eventual emergence of theories which are more true than false, analogously, society informed by certain utopian ideals may be able to inch towards them, perhaps never fully achieving, though often successful eventually in partially instantiating them.

It is probably in a similar fashion that Levinas himself understands his notion of infinite responsibility for the Other. In an interview in 1988, he was reported to say:

> That is the great separation that there is between the way the world functions concretely and the ideal of saintliness of which I am speaking. And I maintain that this ideal of saintliness is presupposed in all our value judgements. ... There is a utopian moment in what I say; it is the recognition of something which cannot be realized but which, ultimately, guides all moral action. ... There is no moral life without utopianism – utopianism in this exact sense that saintliness is goodness. (1988a: 177-78)

---

[93] See Popper (1969) and Kuhn (1970). Kuhn, whether rightly or wrongly, is often construed as undermining the notion of truth in science in that book which first appeared in 1962.

[94] See Fourier (1841).

[95] This, however, is not to say that the existence of the utopian idea in itself is the only necessary and sufficient condition for its eventual (partial) instantiation. For example, two other conditions in the 1960s may also be mentioned regarding the change in attitude to sexual behaviour: the existence of effective contraception and the improvement in the economic situation of women.

Perhaps the moment for the utopian ideal of saintliness or moral perfection in the form of Levinas's notion of infinite responsibility to bear some fruit is about to arrive in the public domain, both nationally and internationally.

The transition to practical implementation could perhaps even be eased by a proposal to pare down the notion a little without undermining its essence. To see how this could be done, let us take a look at utilitariansim and a particular criticism often raised against it. Its overarching value is to maximise pleasure/happiness on the one hand and to minimise pain on the other – the former may be referred to as positive and the latter as negative utilitarianism.[96] The positive version is said to be unworkable for the simple reason that the notion of happiness or pleasure is considered to be slippery. After all, one person's pleasure is another person's poison; furthermore, one person may derive intense but another only mild pleasure from the same activity. Worse, the pursuit of happiness is elusive – upon achieving it, it seems to evaporate. Hence the goal of maximising pleasure in society is inoperable.[97] The negative version, however, does not suffer from these criticisms.[98] Although we may have no idea about what makes people happy, we have a much clearer idea as to what makes people miserable – to suffer from hunger, cold, great heat or thirst, to have no roof over the head, to endure (severe and sustained) pain from illness and disease, etc.[99] To minimise pain/suffering constitutes a coherent social vision, sufficient to generate a consensus as guide to policy-making in the public domain. If policy A adversely affects x number of people, yielding n units of pain, while policy B affects 10x adversely, yielding 10n units of pain, then choose policy A over B.

Analogously, Levinas's notion of responsibility for others may be a given a negative interpretation. While we definitely have a duty to others (irrespective of kith/kin, nationhood, race/culture/history), nevertheless, we may not have responsibility for their happiness, as we do not know what makes people happy (borrowing, for the moment, the language of utilitarianism). But all the same we do have a duty to reduce their poverty, suffering, their misery, as we know, by and large, what constitutes their unhappiness and their pain.[100] In this

---

[96] For a discussion of this issue, see Popper (1957): 158, 284 (note 2).

[97] One standard retort is to say that these criticisms are beside the point. One can ignore them by simply asking those who would be affected by a particular policy (over an alternative) how much pleasure (along a scale) each would derive, and add up all the units of pleasure to determine which is the better policy to pursue. However, this is not the place to delve into this particular set of problems.

[98] It does seem to invite the criticism that it entails the conclusion that one ought to kill everyone painlessly. However, this *reductio ad absurdum* would not apply to the negative version proposed here of Levinas's notion of infinite responsibility for the Other.

[99] Such deprivations are part of what is meant by poverty in the absolute sense of the term. However, it has been argued that poverty is never absolute, always relative – the former makes no sense. For instance, if poverty were to be understood in absolute terms only, one might have to conclude that no body (or very few people) in the advanced industrial economies today are poor, as the welfare safety net on the whole succeeds in preventing the unfortunate from falling into really dire straits. But all the same, such people constitute the socially excluded, with no money to buy and run a car, to buy expensive presents for their children, etc.; they are said to suffer from relative poverty. It is not part of the remit of this thesis to deny that the notion of relative poverty has application. However, it does reject the further thesis that the notion of absolute poverty is either unintelligible or does not exist in spite of the incontestable fact that absolute poverty in the world does exist – millions of poor people die because they cannot afford to buy the food to keep alive, of diseases induced by the lack of safe drinking water and/or adequate nutrition as well as by the lack of hygiene and/or proper medication.

[100] In environmental philosophy, the duty to posterity is understood in these terms. Regarding future peoples, we may not know what makes them happy, but we certainly know what would make them miserable – lack of clean air, clean water, unpolluted soil, to name just a few of the conditions the absence of which would render human life, if not totally impossible, at least unbearable – see Baier (1981).

way, although one may still have infinite responsibility for others (in the sense that none shall be excluded), the nature of the duty is somewhat more circumscribed, and therefore, more do-able. When this sense of being do-able is added to the other sense of being affordable in economic/financial terms, then there should be no inherent obstacle, both intellectual and practical, to discharging that responsibility to others.

Levinas's emphasis on the suffering of others lends weight to this suggested defence. As we have seen, he is against social exclusion, he talks about the neediness of others, the plight of the widow, the orphan, the weak, the sick, all demanding a response from us.

5.4. Rawls's Test of Reflective Equilibrium and Revolutionary Moral Ideas

Let me turn to another possible criticism of Levinas's radicalism, namely, that it lacks a certain merit often claimed for Kant's moral philosophy which, clearly, is not utopianist in character. On the contrary, the claim emphasises that the "greatness", "profundity", "relevance" of Kant's moral philosophy lie in part, if not wholly, in the fact that it captures the intuitions of common morality, and that it reflects and respects ordinary moral thinking.[101] This move may be made in conjunction with the methodological claim that in moral theorising the way open to us to test and refine a normative theory is to see how far it is compatible/incompatible with extant moral notions – the so-called method of reflective equilibrium as advocated by John Rawls.[102]

This part does not in any way wish to dispute that Kant's moral philosophy does possess the qualities normally attributed to it, nor to query *per se* the method of reflective equilibrium in moral theorising. All that I wish to do here is to draw attention to some points, which should not be forgotten. First that compatibility of theory with extant accepted notions, though legitimate, cannot be the sole criterion by which we judge the adequacy or otherwise of the moral theory. This is because morality is not static, but dynamic, in character. As already mentioned, what is considered to be mad, scandalously taboo-breaking at one point in time, may become moral orthodoxy some time in the future. Furthermore, there is an equally dynamic relationship between theory and practice – the former reinforces the latter. Kant might indeed have captured the moral intuitions of his society and his readers at the time he wrote and published, but because of the perceived compatibility between his theory and accepted morality, his moral philosophy could serve to reinforce and strengthen the practice.[103] If Kant's moral ideas are still relevant in the contemporary world, it is partly because of this effect, and also because they are primarily embedded in the philosophy of individualism, which remains the dominant ideology of today.

On the other hand, it would be irrelevant and pointless to invoke Rawls's test of reflective equilibrium to assess utopian moral ideas, as they do not, *ex hypothesi*, answer to anything in the extant corpus of moral notions and would, therefore, fail to correspond to the moral intuitions of society, so to speak. Obviously, they would not strike one as bearing the mark of "self-evident" truths. "Naturally", Levinas's notion of infinite responsibility for the Other, judged in this light, would have to be written off as "unintelligible", "incoherent", "impractical".

---

[101] See, for instance, Sullivan (1989): 4-6; Scruton (1982): 71-74.
[102] See, Rawls (1999) 42-5; 507-08.
[103] Society in general and theorists in particular tend to pick and choose what they want from a theory, an inevitable fate from which, as we have seen, Kant does not escape – except for perfect duties to others, no one bothers much with the other categories of duties he has distinguished.

6. TOWARDS A NEW PARADIGM

To conclude and to re-cap: I have identified and distinguished several senses of Levinas's notion of infinite responsibility. Responsibility is infinite because:

(1) it recognises no distinction between duty on the one hand and supererogation on the other;
(2) it does not recognise the distinction between perfect duties on the one hand and imperfect duties to others;
(3) it is inclusive, not exclusive, as it fails to recognise the distinction between family, kith/kin on the one hand and strangers on the other, between insiders (those who share the same history, culture, language, ethnicity) on the one hand and outsiders who do not. It urges one to recognise the humanity in the Other, in all others, not only in some, namely, those who are regarded as *persons* in the philosophical sense or kith and kin in the sociological sense. One should be the good samaritan and not pass by, indifferent to the life or death, pain and suffering of fellow humans;[104]
(4) one can distinguish between the positive and the negative senses of responsibility for others. While one concedes that it does not need to be understood in the former sense of doing whatever one can to render them "happy", one can, nevertheless, meaningfully discharge that duty in the reduced negative sense of doing what one can to relieve others of suffering and poverty, there being a clear consensus as to what constitutes misery.

As such, Levinas's notion may be said to be radical as it seems to challenge well-entrenched presuppositions especially in the Kantian tradition of Western moral thought, as well as of so-called common sense morality, which in turn enables one to understand why his notion is ignored in general or dismissed out of hand by those like Rorty, who care to comment on it, as either inherently absurd and/or impractical.

Furthermore, and more importantly, I have attempted to argue that Levinas philosophy can be construed as an attempt to construct a new moral paradigm which, contrary to the tradition of modern Western philosophy, follows from his view of ethics as first philosophy, an *aretaic* ethic based on secular saintliness/holiness, which is a radical departure from the dominant strands of moral philosophy, whether Kantian, liberal, or utilitarian (as we shall see later).

However, Levinas's radical challenge inevitably invites the charge of utopianism, and utopianism itself in turn is considered to be inherently absurd, and impractical. But is it? Levinas's brand may just be blazing the moral trail in the twenty first century.

Having mounted what I hope is a plausible theoretical defence of Levinas's philosophy in general and his concept of infinite responsibility for the Other in particular in this part, I shall attempt, in the next part to make a case for saying that it is not as lacking in applicability in practice as it might at first sight appear in at least one important domain which is the pre-occupation of this chapter, namely, that of corporate responsibility, both at the legal and moral levels. Furthermore, I hope to strengthen the defence of Levinas by arguing that his

---

[104] On one of the few occasions when Levinas refers to the Holocaust, he remarked: "The absence of concern for the other in Heidegger and his personal political adventure are linked (Levinas (1992)."

paradigm is not only new but that it is also relevant to meeting certain pressing problems which face the world today in the twenty-first century, particularly those posed by the enormous power and influence exercised by trans-national corporations.

III. LEVINAS AND CORPORATE RESPONSIBILITY: ONE CASE STUDY[105]

1. Corporate Legal Responsibility and Manslaughter

1.1. Background

In the last twenty years or so, the UK alone has seen an appalling loss of lives in a litany of disasters on the railways (Clapham, Southall, Paddington, Hatfield, Potters Bar); at sea (Zeebruggge/the Herald of Free Enterprise); on the river (Marchioness), in the workplace (Piper Alpha), etc. This has provoked over the years dissatisfaction with the apparent inability of the existing legal structure to render justice to the victims themselves and to their families for the negligence caused by the corporations involved in these disasters. The law appears impotent to find them guilty of manslaughter. The central difficulty as we have already seen in First Part lies in the apparent difficulty of identifying the directing mind/s of the company which could be said to have initiated the chain of causation, leading eventually to the loss of lives. As a result of this perceived difficulty, successful prosecutions in the history of English law can be counted on the fingers of two hands, and then, not in spectacular disasters like those earlier mentioned. [106]

The matter even seems or seemed to have troubled the present UK government. Jack Straw, the Home Secretary, supported by John Prescott, the Deputy Prime Minister, in the spring of 2000, announced imminent reforms to the law on involuntary manslaughter, a proposal already mooted by the law commission in 1994. Straw professed that he was outraged that corporations, or their directors, had got off so lightly over some very reckless and negligent things that they appeared to have caused.[107] The government let it be known that the law was closing in on those who persistently refused to take health and safety as a top priority issue, threatening those in charge of organisations, which continued to endanger lives (whether these be those of workers, customers or members of the public) with imprisonment.

The issue has become more and more pressing and complicated – many companies are trans-national (presenting another layer of difficulty, as can be seen in the Bhopal disaster in India), some have become bigger, while being fragmented at the same time because of privatisation, so much so that responsibility for safety is diffuse and divided between several related bodies. A bill, the Corporate Homicide Bill, was designed to sort out these matters.

On 18 April 2000, it was presented to Parliament, which envisaged that a corporation would be guilty of corporate killing if the cause of someone's death could be causally traced to a management failure. "Failure" was defined as "conduct falling below what can

---

[105] The case selected is: the disaster concerning the Herald of Free Enterprise which has already been introduced and analysed within the specific framework of First Part. This case is made to stand as proxy for the issues which may be raised under the respective notions of corporate legal (a) and moral (b) responsibility within the Levinasian framework.
[106] See First Part, section 2.2; also Mansfield (2002).
[107] In this matter, the situation even in the USA is better than in the UK – large corporations can face punitive damages and prison terms, and, ultimately, offending companies can be closed down.

reasonably be expected of the corporation, particularly if it fails to ensure the health and safety of persons employed or members of the public affected by its activities". The directing minds of a corporation are deemed to be the chairman, managing director, chief executive or secretary. However, the fate of this bill is at the moment unknown (May 2003); the Queen's speech at the opening of Parliament in 2002 failed to mention it. Rumour has/had it that a bill on health and safety would eventually be adopted which would deal with virtually the same issues as the Corporate Homicide Bill. But one expert has noted that the subject of corporate manslaughter appears not to be on the agenda of such a bill.[108]

More recently, the *Modernising Company Law* bill, published as a white paper in July 2002; but it, too, is not really concerned with the problems which pre-occupy the Corporate Homicide bill presented in April 2000. It does, however, in its proposed statement of duties, refer to another set of problems, namely, a company's need "to foster its business relationships including those with its employees and suppliers and the customers for its products or services", "its need to have regard to the impact of its operations on the communities affected and on the environment", and "its need to maintain a reputation for high standards of business conduct" as matters which directors are supposed to consider in their decision-making provided that a "person of care and skill would consider them relevant." [109]

This, in turn, overlaps to a limited extent with those concerns promoted by yet another bill, the Corporate Responsibility Bill whose second reading took place in June 2002. (This, too, failed to be mentioned in the Queen's speech at the opening of Parliament in 2002.) The bill has been drafted in response to the perceived failure of the voluntary approach to corporate responsibility. It seeks explicitly to expand the duties of directors beyond the usual narrowly-defined financial considerations to include environmental, social, and general economic impacts of a company's operations; in other words, to take into account not merely the interests of the share-holders, but of all its stake-holders, which include workers directly involved in its operations, residents in the neighbourhood of their activities, customers, consumers, etc. Directors of companies should also be required to disclose the social and environmental impact assessments of their activities.[110] Even more importantly, directors would be made liable for their own negligence and for the wilful misconduct of their companies in specified circumstances. Breaches of any provisions would amount to a criminal offence, and offences would be liable to imprisonment, not merely a fine, if judged appropriate.[111]

Legislation apart, however, there has been a move in the UK to promote corporate social responsibility (CSR), with emphasis on issues which may be summed up under such headings as the following: to prevent abuse of immediate workforce and those further on in the supply chain, to minimise damage to the environment, to refrain from doing business with oppressive regimes, to have respect for customers/consumers, to ensure that patent protection of a product does not prevent it from being made available in times of national emergencies. At

---

[108] See Mansfield (2002).
[109] See http:// www. dti.gov.uk/ companiesbill/ whitepaper. html
[110] Denmark and the Netherlands have already introduced mandatory environmental reporting, while Sweden and Norway demand some such reporting. France, too, wants mandatory social and environmental reporting, extending the provisions now already found in its *Bilan Sociale*. See Mayo (2002).
[111] See http:// www. corporate-responsibility.org. See also http://www. foe.org/ WSSD/sixreasons.html; http:// www.foe.org/ WSSD/positionpaper.html

the same time, share-holders and investors are urged to take advantage of the corporate governance on risk to make companies take seriously corporate responsibility for certain social (like child labour) and environmental issues.[112] The UK government itself is keen to emphasise the virtues of the voluntary approach in spite of its well-known drawbacks, although it may not be against regulation in principle.[113]

One must admit that so far legislative success has been elusive. But this does not mean that the issues have gone away. The world and society are rapidly changing, bringing in tow matters, which no government could wish away, and which any serious government must face up to; the law itself, therefore, must also change.

1.2. Levinas: The Saying and the Said

In the context of corporate legal responsibility, it seems to me that the most relevant of Levinas's notions is the distinction between what he calls **the Saying** and **the Said**.[114] So I must give a brief account of it.

In the last part, I have already raised the point that for Levinas the priority of ethics is based upon the primordiality of language. The pursuit of justice which is intrinsic to morality is tied up with language, and is to be understood through the distinction between the Saying and the Said.

In the context of the discussion here, one can argue that the Said contains everything that comes under a Code in the legal sense of the term, and the Saying is the speech that inspires the spirit of the law. In the context of a corporation and, according to French's terminology, the Said is the Corporation's Internal Decisions Structure (CID) and the Saying is the speech that inspires the (CID). (See First Part.)

But the Saying is always in excess of the Said as it is the condition of the possibility of discourse; however, there is always the threat of betrayal of the Saying by the Said. This is the reason why Levinas warns us that the social relation which supposes justice could be a more vulnerable relation than the face-to-face relation, or in other words, to forget the Saying is only to pretend to close the others in a collective frame, to reduce the human plurality to a multiplicity. At the level of corporations this reduction implies that the logic of the economic system – geared to capital accumulation and profits always with exponential growth and accountability to share-holders as its targets – in which corporations operate, would not readily go hand in hand with the Levinasian requirements of responsibility for the Other. But the precise virtue of approaching the matter from a Levinasian perspective is that the latter forces one to address the deficiencies of the theory of individual responsibility in the context of liberalism and of the market. Levinasian insights can help us to articulate the relevance of

---

[112] See Crowe and Porritt (2002).

[113] See its DTI Report – *Corporate Social Responsibility*, 2002 – http://www.societyandbusiness.gov.uk/2002/report/index.html# See also Stephen Timms (2002) – Minister for E-Commerce at the DTI, UK.

[114] *Otherwise Than Being* goes beyond *Totality and Infinity* (which conceives language as playing a central role in ethical relations because the encounter with the Other always involves speech) in maintaining that the exposure to the Other effected in saying is at the very core of ethical relations; language is neither condition nor source of Saying, but Saying itself. The Other who faces me awakens me to a dimension beyond the universe of beings and their Being. In speaking to somebody I transcend the realm of Being by accepting that my being is meant to be there for the Other: "To say is to approach a neighbour, 'dealing him signifyingness'. This is not exhausted in 'ascriptions of meaning', which are inscribed, as tales, in the said. Saying taken strictly is a 'signifyingness dealt the other', prior to all objectification; it does not consist in giving signs. (*OB*: 48)."

responsibility on the part of corporations to others beyond share-holders. One can say that a corporation's social interactions with others fall, at least, into four categories:

1. Interchanges between individual agents.
2. Corporations interacting with individual agents.
3. Corporations interacting with other corporations.
4. Corporations interacting with society.

As an example of the first category: Mr. Ruben, one of the managers of Body Shop and I meeting on a street of Manchester; the second: the Body Shop billing me for a kind of skin product and responding to my objections; the third: the Body Shop arranging to bank with the Co-op Bank instead of Barclays Bank; the fourth: the Body Shop creating a school for handicap children in Bangladesh.

Corporations in their relations and actions, as is obvious and already mentioned, have far more power and control over many others than individual agents because they, by and large, structurally constitute the situations in which individual agents have to operate and make choices. For instance, in a recent article in *The Guardian*, John Pilger (2001) wrote about the inhuman conditions and low wages in which people are forced to work and live, to be able to survive under the *dictum* of globalisation where big companies such as Gap or Nike exercise their power, depriving the workers of a free and dignified life.

However, the problem, as shown by the example of the Herald of Free Enterprise, is that corporations in the majority of the cases are typically insensitive to such matters and ignore them. Recall the several memoranda written by employees/officials warning the corporation of the risk of the excessive number of passengers, the lack of the indicator lights, the limited capacity of the ballast pump. The answer to these different warnings was the same, that is, pure indifference, which attests to the incapacity or unwillingness on the part of the corporation to make sense of them, to treat each case seriously and give it due attention.

In *Otherwise than Being*, Levinas presents the notion of justice as one with a double structure – justice as a question, and justice as a problem. From the asymmetrical point of view, the Other always has primacy, (*après vous, monsieur* or "after you, Sir"). One starts the analysis with the question: who goes in the first place? Who has primacy? In the case of corporations and taking into account what I have said previously about the four social interactions with others, the answer to this question is even more complex than in the case of individual agents. However, as an example, one can ask: is it more important to respond to the interests of the share-holders and the pressures of competition or to respond to the matter of the safety of passengers by improving the safety of the equipment with which the corporation runs its business? This question is a question of justice. The responsibility for the Other presupposes asymmetry, non-reciprocity, disproportion.

The state which gives the possibility for justice is not for Levinas the arbiter of power based on relations of force; it is not the state of the Leviathan. And to judge is not to subsume the particular case under a rule. The same can be said in relation to a corporation, whose particular interests should not be subjugated to corporate goals. In the specific case of the Herald of Free Enterprise, the good service to customers could not be neglected (especially in matters relating to safety) in the name of particular interests, namely the challenges of competition or the pressure of share-holders to increased profits. A corporation should be organised according to the principle of justice, which means what Levinas says, that if the responsibility for the Other "is the surplus of my duties over my rights", then the order of justice is one in which duties override rights.[115] A corporation is just in its relations when its social interactions are based on the inequality of the ethical relation; injustice begins when one loses sight of the alterity of the Other and forgets that the corporation is informed by my relation to the Other. Or as Levinas says, "this means that nothing is outside of the control of the responsibility of the one for the other (*OB*: 159)." — concern for the law, concern for justice, concern for the responsibility for the Other.

The domain of morality and legality are intimately linked in spite of their being distinct domains at the deep level which Mill's principle of preventing harm to others may be said to operate – based on individual freedom, Mill has argued that the aim of the law is to protect people against others, not against themselves. The position that Levinas sustains is quite different from such a position as his point of departure is not freedom, but responsibility. For him responsibility is given in the asymmetrical relation between the I and the Other. In saying this, he is not denying the need for law, which is not meant to relieve the agent of his/her responsibility for the Other, but to ensure that this responsibility does not transform itself to become injustice. This means that interpersonal responsibility is extended to all the others; the domain of the collective becomes visible in the face-to-face relation. The aim of the law is to do justice to all the others, without at the same time neglecting the asymmetrical relationship of the face-to-face.

We are not only responsible for the intended consequences but also for the unintended consequences of our actions, because the core of the Levinasian notion of responsibility is an infinite responsibility in the first person. *Me, voici* (here I am); not only for the Other but for all the absent others who look at me in the eyes of the Other.[116] Equality is the foundation of justice, but Levinasian justice is not distributive justice, based on equality as proportion, but based on an asymmetrical disproportion.[117] In this light it is possible to say that justice is always and simultaneously between two plans: the plan of the Saying and the plan of the Said; the plan of ethics and the plan of ontology.

It follows from what I have said in First Part about the (CID) in a corporation that a corporation chart is important. However, this chart is not valuable in itself and needs continuous questioning by the Saying, which means that in the complex net of interdependent and dependent relationships, a particular Other can not be privileged to the detriment of another, but that the relations should be based on justice. The law sets upon the Said, from which it is possible to judge. However, this Said, codified, thematically treated, intrinsically requires for completion the Saying, but this Saying is not an origin, it is pre-originary, and non-synchronised with the Said. It is in this paradoxical relation between the two plans, indifferent to each other and yet at the same time linked, that Levinas sees justice as a problem.[118] Against the peril of the degradation of justice, Levinas argues:

> In no way is justice a degradation of obsession, a degeneration of the for-the-other, a diminution, a limitation of anarchic responsibility, a neutralization of the glory of the Infinite, a degeneration that would be produced in the measure that for the empirical reasons the initial duo would become a trio. (*OB*: 159)

---

[115] See *OB*: 159.
[116] This point refers to the Levinasian notion of "the third" which will be discussed in some detail in section 2.1.
[117] To possible objections to this point, see as defence, Critchley (1992: 232).
[118] See *OB*: 161.

The peril of this degeneration can come not from equality but from equality reduced to uniformity, as equality, which is the basis of justice, does not forget the inequality of responsibility.

Justice in Levinas is against *conatus* or force, which has neither boundaries nor limits. According to Levinas the legal system in its formalism is inspired by this inequality. However, this inequality and this excess are not the origin of law, since the law presupposes synchrony between a principle and its consequence, between the general and the particular. Justice is and must be the domain of the visible, nevertheless, Levinas permanently calls our attention to the fact that before the law, there is the pre-original, an-archic responsibility for the others. If the law forgets this primacy of responsibility, it would transform itself to become a mere regulation of forces. This reasoning when applied to a corporation means that the corporation has responsibility for each party which has a relationship to it, such as its customers, and that such responsibility should not be defected by or undermined in the name of rules, pressures, economic growth or profits.

> Responsibility for the others or communication is the adventure that bears all the discourse of science and philosophy. Thus this responsibility would be the very rationality of reason or its universality, a rationality of peace. (*OB*: 160)

The central question in this discussion is the fact that justice is not viewed as a formal or abstract legality regulating society, with the mere aim of producing social agreements by reducing conflicts. A society regulated by abstract legality is without faces and friendship; in other words, it is a society without a true recognition of human diversity and difference, in which economic abstraction and reification are represented by so-called free and equal autonomous individual.[119] In Levinasian terms this is a society without proximity.[120]

But responsibility as proximity, doubtless, exerts an enormous demand on me as a moral agent. It leaves me with two stark options: either I answer the call of the Other and through it discover the real meaning of myself, or I completely turn my back on such responsibility thereby losing my true identity. Identity in Levinas is not acquired by free choices, but in the encounter with the Other as, "If I do not answer for myself, who will answer? But if I only answer for myself – will I still be myself?"[121] The same reasoning can be applied to corporations, which cannot be indifferent to the fate of the people with whom they have relations, as its identity is ultimately linked with the way that they are able to respond to the different and multiple calls of the Others as customers, share-holders, society, etc. Furthermore, "the tie with the Other is knotted only in responsibility." Thus, responsibility is the link between the agent and the Other, or, in more general terms, the source of the moral "ought". There is no authentic sociality apart from ethics, and there is no ethics apart from sociality. To say that responsibility is foundational for ethics and interpersonal relations is to say not only that responsibility is what links one agent inextricably to another, but also that the meaning of the otherness of the Other is given in responsibility.

Like the individual moral agent, it is through responsibility that the corporation is able to discover its true aim and meaning. Its identity is given in the One for the Other, in the way it responds to the call of others with whom it has relations. Such a perspective implies that

---

[119] On this point, see Critchley (1992).
[120] This notion will be looked at in some detail in section 2.1 to follow.
[121] Levinas (1972: 95).

ethics is an inherent part of economic and corporate life. It is not simply a consequence of actions good, bad or indifferent performed by the individuals who form part of this life, but also that such life is part of ethical life itself, which is all embracing and all pervasive from which no domain of human activities can be insulated. To be human is to be responsible in this demanding Levinasian sense. In repudiating or shunning it, executive business suits must necessarily lead dehumanised lives, pretending that the ethical has no remit within their professional existence.

For Levinas, "true society" is not constituted merely by values that individuals give to the social world, as the societies, in which the individuals are engaged, always precede the individuals and succeed to them. It imposes on the individuals objective and durable institutions within which the individuals take a place.

It is within institutions/corporations that we are placed in relation with other individuals, but the link which is established in the framework of an institution/corporation is organised "around something (*De L'Existance à L'Existant*: 62)," and as I have mentioned above, a corporation is organised around a (CID) structure, aims and projects. The contact between individuals is not direct but through a common interest, an idea, or a project, which sustains it. Therefore, one can say that each individual belongs to a determinable and objective context given the function or role that he/she occupies in a particular social structure, as I have mentioned in the case of the Herald of Free Enterprise. (See First Part .)

Society, according to Levinas, is not the mere product of the unintended consequences of individual actions. The individuals are not isolated entities, taken out of context, but beings shaped by society as well as determining, in turn, society itself. In the words of Levinas:

> Normally we are a "character": we are a professor at the Sorbonne, vice president of the Council of the State, son of Someone, everything which is in the passport, our way of dressing. ... And all signification, in the usual sense of the term, is related to a context. (*Étique et Infini* : 80-81)

Levinas, in his analysis of society, takes into consideration the work of Durkheim and identifies in it an "elaboration of the fundamental categories of the social ... starting from the main idea that the social cannot be reduced to the sum of individual psychologies (*Étique et Infini*: 17-18)." The individual is not an abstract de-contextualised being; he/she becomes a moral agent from the instant that he/she places his/her centre of behaviour outside him/herself and in this way his/her conduct indicates their necessary commitment to the Other and all others. Levinas appreciates the way that Durkheim considered the spiritual/moral dimension of the individual in its organicist dimension, in the sense that the society is a whole, constituted by distinct but interdependent parts. Levinas recognises in Durkheim a "metaphysician" of the social, because Durkheim is capable of demonstrating that society is structured as a totality, which presupposes that a social totality has its own reality, apart from that of the individuals that constitute it. The social totality defines the organisational systems of a social group, be these economic or legal. In the "social of Durkheim" Levinas recognises the value of the social totality, as a structured whole. For Levinas, the interest of Durkheim lies in the fact that for the latter, the coexistence of individuals within a social totality is not simply a bald fact, but that social totality makes possible the elevation of the individuals to morality. This presupposes that the individual and society are not separate and independent of each other, but that human action can only be understood within the complex nexus of relations and interrelations in a determined context.

By analogy and reinforcing what I have set out in First Part, this kind of Levinasian/Durkheimian reasoning would enable one to argue that a corporation would only become a truly responsible agent if it were to place its centre of gravitation outside its own narrow limited interests. It would also enable one to argue that a corporation is an entity with a complexity of relations in a particular context in relation to which it is possible to apply responsibilities (legal and moral) for its actions. As we have seen in First Part, the difficulties in attributing criminal responsibility to a corporation are not simply related to the inadequacy of the law as it stands, but also importantly to our cultural values, specifically shaped by the standard current notions of individual freedom and responsibility under which human actions are not viewed as being interrelated and interdependent, but as independent and unrelated. As a consequence, and as I have been maintaining all along in this study, our Western culture is based on individual values, with a prejudice against collective ones.

However, in spite of much possible agreement with Durkheim, Levinas, nevertheless, differs from and remains very critical of Durkheim. One of his main criticisms is directed against Durkheim's excessive confidence in social institutions/corporations, because from an Levinasian point of view:

> (totality), the State, politics, techniques, work at every moment on the point of having their center of gravitation in themselves, and weighing on their own account. (*OB*: 159)

From the point of view of totality the individuals are not considered on their own, but they are seen simply as elements of the system that overtakes them. Against Durkheim, Levinas does not look for the first element of morality in the elevation of the individual to humanity through his /her participation in the social totality, but in inter-individual relationship.[122]

The stress in the inter-individual relationship as the basis of morality leads Levinas to maintain a critical attitude towards social institutions, which, as such, are indifferent to the fate of individuals. It is precisely because the standard current account of corporations lacks this critical Levinasian attitude that the remit of their responsibility is distorted. Corporations play their own game, with their immanent logic, making sure they rationally manipulate all other parties to advance their own goals. When social relations are reduced to their mere institutional forms, we arrive at an anonymous world, or as Levinas says at an "in-humane neutrality (*De L'Existance à L'Existant*: 11)." It is this "neutrality" which is at the basis of the view that crimes perpetrated by a corporation are not crimes, but accidents. This is another reason why it is so difficult to attribute criminal responsibility to corporations, and it explains why in the case of the Herald of Free Enterprise, it was not possible to apply the charge of corporate criminality. (See First Part .)

Within their own limited parameters, corporations cannot be faulted, as long as they are faithful to their own immanent logic. The present difficulty of attributing criminal responsibility to corporations is precisely due to a tacit, if not explicit, acceptance of that

---

[122] "The social relation is not a relationship initially which goes beyond the individual, with something more than the sum of the individuals and superior to the individual, in the Durkheimian sense (*De L'Existance à L'Existant*: 161)." [My translation]

logic and framework, a deep-seated reluctance to question it from outside. Ironically, a Durkheimian understanding would simply reinforce such a *status quo*.

It is not the social totality on its own which Levinas critiques, but the totalization understood as an organisational system in which all forms of social existence are reduced to the limited logic of institutions/corporations. Although individuals do not disappear in the total order, their irreplaceable singularity is diminished, because a totalising system reduces every social relation to a simple form of participation in the social order.

In a corporation all relations are strictly dictated by an internal order and regulated by a standardised behaviour according to the ideology of the corporation or institution, and no deviation could be entertained. In the Sheen Report, it is mentioned that Captain Blowers of the Pride had written a memorandum drawing the attention of Mr. Develin, Director and Chief Superintendent to the peril of the lack of indicator lights. When Mr. Develin in turn showed the memorandum to his superiors offices, nobody paid any attention to it because it was not considered a priority, or more tellingly in the words of Mr. Alcindor, the deputy chief superintendent, the issue raised by the received memorandum was dismissed sarcastically: "Do they need an indicator to tell them whether the deck storekeeper is awake and sober? My goodness!!" But as things turned out, we know that the lack of indicator lights was a direct cause, if not the only possible cause, of the tragedy of the Herald.

The Levinasian critique of social totality resists the reduction of the social relation only to its objective and institutional expression. The aim of his critique is to alert liberal societies to the fact that totalization is not a deviation of the contingency of the political order but is a permanent threat. Levinas says:

> A society respectful of liberties would not simply have as a foundation "liberalism", objective theory of society, which argues that it works better when things are left alone. Such liberalism would make freedom depend upon an objective principle and not from the essential secret of lives. (*Éthique et Infini* : 73-74)

Levinas contends that no institution or corporation could by its own means limit the extension of its authority. Its boundaries come from the outside, from the *parole propre* (speech), the Saying as the confirmation of the agent's singularity and at the same time as the expression of my responsibility for the Other and all the others.[123] The Saying defines the possibility for each agent to speak for him/herself, and in this way be "personally present" in his/her speech.[124] Levinas holds that from the point of view of social order:

> Language would be equivalent to the constitution of rational institutions in which an impersonal reason which is already at work in the persons who speak and already sustains their effective reality would become objective and effective ... (*TI*: 217)

From the point of view of social order, speech rarely has a value on its own; it expresses other things, a particular interest and a social habit. It is by this fact that the logic of institutions/corporations has a tendency to dispossess the agents from their *parole propre*, with the aim to reduce language to a mere repetitive and monological role, to a social habit. A repetitive discourse is a discourse without interlocutors, because the interlocutors are

---

[123] See *TI*: 296.
[124] See *TI*: 296.

themselves represented as "moments". At this point one can say that corporate responsibility is exercised when the singularity of the speech of each agent is not systematically ignored in favour of the established order, but is seriously taken into account. This speech does not only translate the agent's desire to talk in its own name, but defines the social relation, distinct from that of institutions/corporations. In the words of Wilden this enables:

> (the) creativity of labor potential that makes each of us, not an abstract individual – not an economic abstraction exchanging human value for monetary exchange value, not a commodity in the economic machinery worth a specific, competitively defined, quantity of dollars per hour to a part of the system over which we have no control – but a qualitatively differentiated individual, inseparable in the long run from our dependence on complex and undefinable sets of nonexploitative communications and exchanges with our fellow human beings... (1978: 122)

To talk in one's own name, to exercise freedom of expression is to dare not to take refuge behind a recognised authority, and respond to the call of the Other. Speech is beyond the domain of the established order and establishes significations. On the one hand, it is the agent's manifestation of his/her power of rupture and on the other hand, it is the opening to unpredictable directions. Responsibility at whatever level – corporate or individual – is unconditional for the Other and all the others. To be responsible, as we have seen, is not a question of choice, but a question of a deep liberty, the liberty of taking the burden of the infinite responsibility for the Other - customer, employees, community, public at large, others.

The rupture with the established order instituted by speech allows the existence within public space of another type of social relation other than the relation reproduced by the logic of any one social order like that of a corporation. Speech disturbs order but does not propose another stable order in competition or in conformity with a given order. This disobedience of the logic of the social order is a radical protest but without connivance, because this protest does not have the ambition to install a new order; the only "ambition" is to give the first place to the Other.

As I have outlined in the last part, the face is speech addressed to the I who has the possibility to respond or not. The response makes the difference between an I who wants to be free to accept responsibility for the Other, or an I who is a prisoner of his/her own freedom, by refusing to take responsibility for the Other. The latter response is always a way towards violence, because it is a refusal to accept the alterity of the Other and to accept one's infinite responsibility for him/her. In the context of corporate legal responsibility, Levinas may be said to be inviting society to make corporations face up to their responsibility for the Other as well as at the same time to be inviting corporations themselves to accept such responsibility for the Other and, in so doing, to render themselves truly free.

2. Corporate Moral Responsibility

2.1. Levinas: Proximity and the Third

Within the context of today's global politics and economics, perhaps the most relevant Levinasian notions are those of proximity and of the third. So I need to set them out in brief outline.

For Levinas, I do not agree to live ethically with the Other. I am ordered to do so. The encounter with the Other is both singular and disquieting. He characterises the life of the human/moral subject as an answer to a calling – I become a human subject on the condition that I answer for everything and everyone. My responsibility for the Other is neither freely chosen nor actively desired. It is not an episode in my biography. Before I am even myself, I am responsible for the Other, absolutely and without repeal or further appeal.

Proximity is the term Levinas uses to refer to the immediacy on confronting the face of the Other. Proximity is felt as immediate contact which demands a response and hence, that it amounts to responsibility, that is to say the ability to respond.

> In proximity the absolutely other, the stranger whom I have "neither conceived nor given birth to " I already have on my arms, already bear, according to the Biblical formula, "in my breast as the nurse bears the nurseling". He has no other place, is not autochthonous, is uprooted, without a country, not an inhabitant, exposed to the cold and the heat of the seasons. To be reduced to having recourse to me is the homelessness or strangeness of the neighbour. It is incumbent on me. (*OB*, 91)

However, although it is true that *via* proximity and the face-to-face relation, the agent is called to an infinite responsibility, it is the notion of **the third** (*le tiers*) which constitutes the key to social justice.[125] Without universalization, how can the encounter of the Other be at the foundation of morality? Levinas answers this question by the notion of the third. The face to face does not establish a comfortable intimacy between myself and the Other. It shows me the existence of a huge world outside myself. At the same time as I discover the Other, the potential presence of innumerable others is also a reality to me. On the basis of this, the ethical relation may turn into a concern for social justice. Society is not founded on a unity of species, but on a multiplicity of Others, in which each Other is unique, resistant to classification; justice is, therefore, not founded on universal principles or on some social contract designed to tame the "natural instincts" of the "human species. This social justice is fraternity, but this fraternity is not synonymous with equality or some kind of symmetry between people, or even the certitude that they belong to a common genre. According to Levinas, this fraternity comes from the encounter with the Other's face.

> The third party looks at me in the eyes of the Other – language is justice. ... The epiphany of the face qua face opens humanity. The face in its nakedness as a face presents to me the destitution of the poor one and the stranger; but this poverty and exile which appeal to my powers, address me, do not deliver themselves over to these powers as givens, remain the expression of the face. The poor one, the stranger, presents himself as an equal. His equality

---

[125] "If proximity ordered only the other alone to me, there would have not been any problem, in any sense, even the most general of the term. The question would not have been arisen, not with regarding consciousness, nor self-consciousness. The responsibility for the other is an immediacy antecedent to questions, it is proximity. It is troubled and becomes a problem when a third party enters (*Autrement Qu'être*: 245)." (My own translation.)

within this essential poverty consists in referring to the *third party*, thus present at the encounter, whom in the midst of this destitution the Other already serves. (*TI*: 213)

With the introduction of the third, the asymmetry of the infinite responsibility for the Other is moderated and gives place to the possibility of an institutional political order. In *Otherwise than Being* (157), Levinas affirms that justice begins "with the third man" in the sense of the third party.[126] The third confronts us with the parameters that are present in the organisation of human plurality.[127] *Via* the third, my infinite responsibility for the Other is called to respond not only to the face which is in front of me but to all absent faces.

As already demonstrated in the last part, Levinas is against exclusion; the Other is characterized as stranger, foreigner, widow, orphan, namely those who are disadvantaged as outcasts or outsiders, who are needy and who suffer. Proximity compels not merely each and everyone of us in the mature economies to confront our responsibility to these others but also, especially those, who are identifiable within the CIDs of big companies with the power of policy-articulation and policy-execution, to discharge their responsibility by ignoring the safety of their customers and society at large. Individuals in the affluent economies cannot be said to be totally innocent in the role they might be playing in supporting the extant responsibility-denying policies of such corporations. Individuals themselves may not have money invested in them, it is true; however, on the whole, they make contributions to pension funds, or buy policies with insurance companies which in turn may invest the money in such corporations. When big corporations (in the case of the Herald of Free Enterprise the demands of several captains in their memorandums were neglected) proclaim that they cannot change their extant policies, otherwise, they would be short-changing their share-holders (to which group alone, corporations recognise legal and moral accountability), it is then also up to individuals to use their power as consumers and share-holders to put pressure on pension funds managers to avoid enterprises which deny their moral responsibility to other groups in the world at large, besides that of the share-holders. However, having said that, it remains the overwhelming case that power-holders themselves within big corporations must confront the challenge posed by the Levinasian notion of proximity. For Levinas, compassion fatigue is no excuse, but simply yet another evasion of the responsibility one bears for the Other.[128] Nor is human frailty and weakness to live up to moral ideals an excuse. For Levinas, as I have already argued, the pursuit of holiness/saintliness is at the core of his vision. Of course, as frail humans, we may rarely live up to the virtue of saintliness and its onerous demands – failure is not, however, an excuse for acquiescence but is simply the eternal call for further effort. To give up striving to implement the holy and the good is sheer cowardice. And for the CEOs and other relevant figures in corporate management to blame, in the main, share-holders for their responsibility-denying policies is "to cop out", to use a colloquial expression.

The moral force behind the notion of proximity reinforces that of the third, as the latter is " the whole of humanity, in the eyes that look at me (*TI*: 213)." In particular, it is that part of humanity, which suffers, that is looking at me in the eye. The key power holders of Western companies cannot pretend, given the evidence, that there is no direct causal link between their responsibility-denying policies and the suffering in front of their very eyes.

---

[126] For further discussion, see Bernasconi (1999), Purcell (1996), Faessler (1984).
[127] For further discussion, see Soares (2000).
[128] To borrow an expression from Sartre, this amounts to bad faith.

Morality accepts the Kantian dictum that "ought implies can" and Levinas is not an exception to this view despite his profound disagreement with the dominant tradition of philosophy and moral philosophy in modern Western thought. If a child were drowning in a river, but I literally cannot swim, (and assuming that my cries for help turn out to be useless as nobody was within earshot), then should the child drown, society cannot hold me morally responsible for not having saved the child; nor would I need to feel myself morally responsible and, therefore, guilty about the unfortunate death. However, imagine another scenario: I cannot swim but I'm sitting on the bank, near to the drowning infant and if I were to stretch out my hand, with no danger to myself whatsoever, I could have grabbed hold of the baby and saved her. But, in so doing, I would have messed up my brand new outfit. I failed to perform that simple act. As a result, the infant drowned. Here, the moral judgment would be the harsh one: I would have behaved less than impeccably, because it is not true in this case that I literally cannot save the child; it is simply the case that in my calculation, the child's life is worth less than the inconvenience/economic loss caused by ruining my clothes. Society rightly judges that this action is morally callous.

We now raise the question: "Could The Herald of Free Enterprise (financially) afford to prevent the accident?" If they literally cannot, then it follows from the Kantian dictum that such corporations would have no moral obligation to make those concessions. They would then be analogous to the person who did not save the child in the first scenario because s/he could not. However, the evidence available does not seem to support the analogy. Corporations claim that they cannot afford to depart from the *status quo*, because then they would become less profitable as enterprises, and therefore, less attractive to potential investors. However, and in the case of The Herald of Free Enterprise, as mentioned by the Report, five faults related to safety are the direct cause of the disaster. First, the pressure to leave the berth immediately after the loading. Second excessive number of passengers. Third, indicator lights – "there is no indicator on the bridge as to whether the most important watertight doors are closed or not." Fourth, ascertaining draughts: "The ship's draught is not read before sailing, and the draught entered into the Official Log Book is completely erroneous. It is not standard practice to inform the Master of his passenger figure before sailing. Full speed is maintained in dense fog". Fifth, the capacity of the ballast pumps. The existing pump took 1.30 minutes to empty the tanks, which meant that the ferry could not get back on to an even keel until it was well out to sea. A new pump would only have cost £25,000, but the Company regarded this as prohibitive.

"From top to bottom the body corporate was infected with the disease of sloppiness", said the Report on the disaster. The board of directors ignored the several recommendations about the safety management of their vessels.

This then means that their behaviour is analogous to the person on the river bank, who failed to save the drowning child under the second scenario. Just as the moral consensus in that case is a moral thumbs-down, similarly, the moral consensus about the attitude and conduct of corporation must be one of disapproval. In other words, the Herald of Free Enterprise can afford to act in a morally responsible manner but has chosen not to do so, and to turn its back on Levinas's the third, out of moral callousness.

3. Conclusion: Is There a Need for a Paradigm Shift after All?

If the defence of Levinas's notion of infinite responsibility for the Other, mounted in this part, at the level of practice in the domains of corporate legal as well as moral responsibility is at all plausible, then this would show that some steps in moral progress[129] in the twenty-first century could be made by leaning on the central Levinasian concept and some of its associated notions. The insight thus borrowed enables one to challenge and to transcend some of the severe limitations of the dominant concept of individual responsibility, deeply embedded in modern Western moral thought.

However, the entire project in this part and the preceding one of exploring and defending some of Levinas's key insights in moral philosophy has been premised on the argument that there is a need for a paradigm shift – see first part, section 4 and second part, section 6. The first part have tried to show the limitations of the philosophy of individualism and the theory of individual responsibility within which it is situated, by examining, in particular, the weaknesses (in spite of their strengths) of two particular traditions, namely, Kantianism and liberalism, for the issues and problems of responsibility as they have arisen in the kind of world we occupy today. But to make my arguments as persuasive as I can, I need to take another look at the call for a paradigm shift in our moral thinking by addressing briefly yet one more criticism which might be used to undermine or sidestep the project. This is to say that while the chapter might have cast some doubt on the theory of individual responsibility resting on Kantianism and liberalism, it has not so far looked at the claims of another great moral tradition in modern Western moral thought, namely, utilitarianism (apart from a few brief references to it *en passant*). If utilitarianism can be shown to be viable as a moral philosophy for our age of large and powerful corporations operating within the environment of globalisation, then there will be no need to turn to a new paradigm – revamping the old rival to Kantianism and liberalism would do the job. But can utilitarianism rise adequately to the occasion? I wish to argue that it does not.[130]

However, to avoid misunderstanding on this point, let me first of all point out that in the matter of responsibility, utilitarianism does seem to score in some limited respects over its traditional rivals and to embrace some of the virtues claimed on behalf of the Levinasian account. For instance, as already pointed out in Second Part, unlike Kantianism, but like my Levinasian interpretation of responsibility, it does not recognise the distinction between duty and supererogation, as duty is conceptually and morally dependent only on the maximisation of pain over pleasure. However, it remains the case that utilitarian calculation may lead to differing conclusions depending on who is doing the calculation, on the facts of the case as ascertained by the calculating agent, on the postulated foreseen and foreseeable consequences to alternative courses of action, on how far and how wide each utilitarian agent may care to "look" into the future. Apart from empirical imponderables which affect one's calculation, it is also the case that there are theoretical difficulties facing utilitarianism, such as the very well known problem of incommensurability between Bentham's different dimensions of pleasure (intensity of pleasure versus certainty, intensity versus extent, etc), whether one accepts

---

[129] The more neutral term "development" could have been used here. However, it is beyond the remit of this thesis to justify the use of the notion "progress" against those critics who hold that it is unintelligible to claim that there can be progress in moral matters.

[130] My task here is an extremely limited one; it is not its remit to examine both historically and critically the doctrine of utilitarianism in moral/social/legal philosophy.

cardinality or ordinality, the various competing formulations of utilitarian theory – act utility and rule utility, each with its own peculiar difficulties.[131] However, in spite of these inherent problems, one could say on its behalf that it has put its finger on a crucial variable, namely, that consequences of actions do play a role in moral/social/legal thinking, no matter how difficult it may be to identify and define them.

My attempt to defend Levinasian responsibility is similar to utilitarianism in so far as it also acknowledges consequential thinking to be pertinent, but unlike utilitarianism, I do not claim that it is the core of moral thinking. Hence I, too, appear to argue for a kind of analogue of "negative utilitarianism" – see Second Part, section 5.3. However, it would be not merely simplistic but totally wrong-headed to infer from the mere relevance of consequences to moral reflection and action that my account of Levinasian insights in the last part and the application of it to problems about legal/moral corporate responsibility in this part are sufficient to turn it into a form of utilitarianism, and for the following reasons:

1. As a theory of individual responsibility in the legal domain, the drawbacks of utilitarianism are well known. Its logical outcome is Wootton's model of strict liability, a model which dispenses with *mens rea*, indeed, ultimately with the notion of responsibility itself, or as Wootton advocates, to allow it to "wither away". Such a proposal undermines the fundamental notion of fairness in matters of culpability and punishment. On the other hand, the defence I have mounted here of Levinasian responsibility is perfectly compatible with the retention of *mens rea*.

2. However as far as individual moral responsibility is concerned, I have already briefly drawn attention to some of the difficulties in Second Part, so there is no need to repeat them here. In the domain of corporate behaviour *vis-à-vis* the example chosen in this study, it is by no means obvious that utilitarian reasoning would straightforwardly lead to the morally desired conclusion that The Herald of Free Enterprise could act differently. Like its Kantian/liberal rivals, utilitarianism is an offshoot of the philosophy of individualism; hence its theory of responsibility is also a theory of individual responsibility, as we have seen. As such, it, too, would consider the notion of collective/corporate responsibility to be unintelligible or absurd, and for exactly the same reasons (already set out) as those given by its traditional rivals. So most significantly of all, as it is a normative theory which springs from individualist roots, it cannot have anything to say about corporate responsibility, as its fundamental ontological commitment, like those of its traditional rivals, does not permit one to recognise that collective entities, like corporations to be real and to exist. It cannot, therefore, make sense of the notion of corporate moral and legal agency as it confines itself solely, in conformity with its own ontological and methodological requirements, to the recognition of individual agency alone.

---

[131] The literature is immense. Here is a very small sample: Bentham (1996); Smart and Williams (1973); Lyons (1965); Hodgson (1967); Sen and Williams (1982); Hardin (1988), Quinton (1989); Pettit (1993); Scarre (1996); Goodin (1995); Jones (1999); Hooker (2000)

For the reasons cited above, it does not look as if utilitarianism could fit the bill as the alternative paradigm to its traditional rivals in moral thinking in general and in the matter of responsibility in particular.[132] On the other hand, the interpretation and defence mounted in this chapter of Levinas's conception of moral philosophy together with its notion of infinite responsibility for the Other might stand a chance to be the genuine new paradigm that people on the ground may be groping towards. To sum up, I urge that it is a genuine new paradigm for the following main reasons:

1. It is *aretaic*, whereas Kantianism, liberalism and utilitarianism are deontic in the sense that they are rule-oriented[133] – see Second Part, section 4. Since the efforts of the early Greek philosophers, such as Aristotle, no major attempt has been made in Western (secular) moral thought to construct an *aretaic* account.[134] Levinas's conception of ethics as first philosophy and my interpretation of his particular concept of infinite responsibility for the Other lend some plausibility to the claim that his moral philosophy can be construed as such an attempt. It is a counsel for moral perfection based on secular saintliness/holiness: the moral agent seeks obsessively to be responsible for the Other and where the goodness of the agent's character/action has as its object the alleviation of suffering in others and all others. This concept of secular saintliness may look utopian; however, utopian ideas are the life-blood of moral visions.
2. Being *aretaic* in character and not rule-based, it issues no fundamental rules like the Kantian Categorical Imperative, or the liberal principle that actions which do not harm others physically or economically should neither be the object of legislation nor the concern of society, or the utilitarian axiom of maximizing pleasure over pain. In so far as one feels inclined to cast it in the form of a rule, it could be framed vaguely as: strive to be a saint, that is to say, strive to cultivate moral perfection in one's character and to live up to that ideal in one's efforts, to the best of one's ability in whatever circumstances the moral agent finds him/herself. However, it is probably best not to resort to the discourse of rules as rules distort the very character of virtue ethics. Of course, at the heart of such an ethic as of every other, there is a fundamental value or set of values; in the case of Levinas, it is secular saintliness/holiness. As it is not rule-oriented or maxim-based, it is not open to the sorts of objections which rules, such as the rule of utility, face when they are applied.
3. On the one hand, it shares the virtue with traditional theories of ethics such as Kantianism and liberalism as forms of universalising ethics. On the other, it differs from these as their respective scopes are still limited – Kantianism to the class of persons, liberalism to the class of normal adults. In this respect, it is more like (historical) utilitarianism, as it includes all human beings. However, as we have seen, it is also unlike Kantianism, but more like utilitarianism, in that it does not recognise the distinction between duty and supererogation.

---

[132] For the same reason, I have not addressed myself to the vast literature on the ethics of care, of the philosophy of welfare economics, etc., as these are all, in the main, offshoots of utilitarian moral philosophy.

[133] Act-utility is no exception. It, too, is rule-oriented, the rule being: in any proposed course of action, always maximise pleasure over pain.

[134] Of late, there has been a revival of interest in virtue ethics – see Baron, Pettit and Slote (1997). But no major systematic account has so far been constructed, as far as one can ascertain.

But these differences and similarities sink into relative insignificance when one grasps the crucial point that, unlike them all, it is not a theory of individual responsibility and is not embedded in the philosophy of individualism. Unlike the traditional individual models of responsibility, be these backed by Kantianism, liberalism or utilitarianism, it does not suffer from the drawbacks inherent in an individualist philosophical framework, which cannot make sense of the concept of corporate agency at all.

4. On the contrary, it is a theory of responsibility which sees ethics as the first philosophy, thereby turning its back, as Levinas argues, on the entire tradition of modern Western philosophy. The "I" which is the bearer of infinite responsibility for the Other can be identified with (a) individual agency as well as (b) corporate agency (as an instance of collective agency). However, in each context, the agency operates equally in an unmysterious way – in both, the agents involved are "flesh and blood" individuals, so to speak. In the case of the corporation, its agency is identified with certain "flesh and blood" individuals who occupy a certain position of power, of decision-making and decision-execution within its hierarchy. In virtue of their roles and positions as director general/chief executive officer, etc., it makes both conceptual and moral sense to hold them liable for the policies and activities of their corporations should they harm others. In this sense, the new Levinasian paradigm can enable us to work out an account of corporate/collective responsibility which goes beyond the traditional models of individual responsibility, models which have so singularly failed society so far, as according to them, it is conceptually and morally impossible for society to hold corporations both morally and legally responsible for their negligent behaviour and harmful activities. This is a lamentable failure in the increasingly globalised world of the twenty-first century in which trans-national corporations wield immense power and influence for good as well as for ill.

CONCLUSION

The chapter is an attempt to defend the notion of corporate responsibility from the usual objections mounted against it by its critics, usually from the standpoint of the theory of individual responsibility. The main strength of individual responsibility in the legal domain lies in the emphasis on mens rea, which ensures that no individual agent could be said to be culpable unless the harm is pre-meditated either directly (or wilfully) or indirectly (or knowingly by running the risk of causing the harm, as in recklessness). The exponents of the theory of individual responsibility tend to rely on this feature to criticise and undermine the notion of corporate responsibility in the legal domain. I have, however, tried to show that the notion of mens rea is not necessarily incompatible with that of corporate responsibility, provided the following points are borne in mind:

(a) To recognise that pre-meditation or direct intention is irrelevant, as it is obvious that no corporations could be convicted of wilfully murdering their victims – not even tobacco companies, which continue to manufacture and sell cigarettes, could be thus convicted, in spite of the fact that one could show that they know that their products could lead to disease and death in a good many cases.

(b) To recognise all the same that indirect intention obtains. Corporations may be said knowingly (indirectly) to intend the harm in the sense that they can foresee that harm would occur, but are prepared to run the risk in doing so. Tobacco companies know that harm would come to some of their customers but this does not prevent them from making and selling their poisonous products. In this sense, they could be convicted of recklessness. In the same way, Townsend Car Ferries Limited (later P & O Ferries) also could and did foresee that harm could and would very likely occur, yet the corporation continued to cut costs by failing to implement certain safety measures, ranging from the installation of indicator lights on the bridge and a second pump, abandoning the policy of taking on passengers above the official limit or working their staff to exhaustion owing to the very tight scheduling of the voyages, to querying the very design of the ro-ro ferry itself without bulkheads so that more cars could be accommodated, but which would lead to easier flooding when water entered the ferry, and to its eventual faster sinking.

(c) To recognise that gross negligence (which does not rely on mens rea) leading to death, though perhaps rightly objected to in some cases where individual defendants are involved, may be said to be appropriately applied in the case of a corporation. The reason is that, unlike an ordinary individual agent, the corporation possesses vast resources, which it deploys in researching the market, in designing its product or service, in calling on science and technology to do its bidding, etc. In other words, it answers perfectly to the legal fiction of the "reasonable man". As the "reasonable man", the corporation ought to have foreseen, could have foreseen the harm that ensued.

(d) To recognise that a corporation is a highly structured entity with its own explicit aims and objectives, freely chosen and endorsed, and with clearly worked-out strategies for implementing them. In other words, a corporation knows or ought to know exactly what it is doing, is not ignorant or unfocused. As such, it satisfies the description that it is rational, free and autonomous, in much the same way as an individual agent may be said to be rational, free and autonomous. To be free and autonomous does not, of course, mean that the agent, whether individual or corporate, may act without constraints whatsoever – for example, either type of agent has to act within the confines of the law.

However, what has been shown above may not be enough to silence the critics of corporate responsibility. So I have also examined the Humean understanding of cause.

The abstract or fictive individual is a totally ahistorical being, whose characteristics, psychological and even physical, are given in isolation from any social/external context. It is as if one were borne fully formed overnight, as Hobbes says, like mushrooms. Such a conception of the individual, conceived as causal agent, and perceived to be acting within a causal framework, which accepts implicitly the Humean analysis of cause, could, at best, end up assigning culpability to an individual agent working for a corporation, while leaving the corporation itself off the hook. The Humean model of cause may be said to be linear, that is to say, the causal arrow works only in one direction; it is the billiard ball model of causation where ball A moves ball B by hitting it, that is, to say by impact. In other words, A causes B to move (the effect), but B cannot in turn be said to have any causal impact on A — it cannot envisage that B, in moving, may bounce off the edge of the table to hit, in turn, A and to move it along. In contrast, the reciprocal (or non-linear) model of cause can envisage such happenings, which reflect more realistically the complex causal nexus, which obtains out there in the world, as it were. The instinct from the standpoint of the individual theory of responsibility wedded to an implicit Humean model of causation, for instance in the case of the sinking of the Herald of Free Enterprise, is to single out the failure of the assistant bosun to close the bow doors as the culpable agent for the ensuing deaths. As the causal agent is abstracted from the context in which he/she acts, the corporation's policies of maximising profits and, therefore, of reducing costs by cutting corners in safety measures and operations, are not regarded as significant, just as the edge of the billiard table is not part of the analysis of cause as pursued under the Humean model. The assistant bosun had fallen asleep at the time when he should have been shutting the bow doors; this was a reaction to the exhaustion brought on by the corporation's policy of saving labour costs. This lapse, on its own, would not necessarily have led to the sinking, but for the fact that the corporation had deliberately chosen not to implement (thereby behaving recklessly) the very simple safety measure of installing indicator lights on the bridge. However, if one were not adhering implicitly to the simplistic model of Humean causation and to the fictive account of the causal agent which stand behind the individual theory of responsibility, then it is not obvious why the corporation, Townsend Car Ferries Limited, should not have been found guilty of manslaughter, either on grounds of recklessness (which involves mens rea) or of negligence (which requires no mens rea).

The opponents of the notion of corporate responsibility, in adhering to methodological individualism, have also failed to appreciate two things:

1. That the notion of a collective entity like a corporation cannot be reduced to the mere behaviour of individuals (who are also abstract in character). Under methodological individualism, the corporation is simply an aggregate of such individuals. However, under the alternative analysis proposed, the corporation refers to an entity over and above a mere aggregation of abstract/fictive individuals. As we have also seen, the corporation has a tightly focused structure and organisation (CID) within which policies and strategies are articulated, formulated, discussed, discarded or endorsed and then implemented. Obviously, only "flesh-and-blood" individuals can articulate, formulate, debate, discuss, reject/endorse goals and the means for executing them. But these "flesh-and-blood" individuals are not fictive or abstract individuals — they are people acting within a certain social context, fulfilling certain functions, carrying out certain roles. Their mens rea when they act in such a manner can be assessed in the same way as the mens rea of any ordinary, humble "flesh-and-individual" called Joe Bloggs, when Joe Bloggs, for example, pressed on the accelerator, exceeded the speed limit recklessly, taking the risk of causing harm to other road users.

2. Under methodological individualism, social phenomena are explained as the accumulation of the unintended consequences of individual actions, and therefore, no one single individual agent could be blamed for the collective bad that might ensue. Again, the theory of individual responsibility implies a simple-minded view of causation, namely, that the only important type of action is the kind where one individual can single-handedly and, either deliberately or recklessly, bring about the

harmful bad consequence, such as when someone, who had lost his temper, deliberately drove the car over his neighbour and killed her, or took the risk of killing her by driving at her, but hoping that she would leap out of his way in time. But not all actions fall under this paradigm. Ex hypothesi, collective bads do not fall under it. Corporation A, which tips its toxic waste of type A into the stream, may not poison the stream when such an action occurs in isolation from other like actions, but if Corporation B also tips its toxic waste of type B into the stream, and if Corporation C similarly tips its toxic waste of type C into the stream, etc., the stream would be poisoned. Suppose that one were to pose the simple-minded causal question in turn regarding each of the corporations involved: does the tipping of its toxic waste cause the stream to be poisoned? The answer, each time, would be no. It is, after all, the accumulation of the unintended consequences of their individual acts of tipping their respective toxic waste, which brought about the stream being poisoned. (Furthermore, the various different types of toxic waste may synergistically cause poisoning of the stream on a greater scale than it would have been the case if they had all tipped out the same type of waste.) So adhering to the theory of individual responsibility would have let all the corporations involved off the hook. But corporations, as we have seen, have large resources and given access to these, the legal fiction of the "reasonable corporation" ought to apply. This is to say, that each of them ought to have foreseen that the tipping into the stream of its own toxic waste could cumulatively lead to the stream being poisoned, and therefore, could reasonably be held culpable if people died from drinking the water drawn from the poisoned stream.

My defence (in part) of the notion of corporate responsibility, therefore, does not depart radically from mens rea or the legal fiction of the "reasonable man", although it questions and rejects other significant baggage implicitly carried by the theory of individual responsibility, such as methodological individualism, its account of the fictive abstract individual, its rejection of collective entities as being real, its endorsement of the simple-minded Humean understanding of cause.

However, all this might not be sufficient on its own to bring about a change in the cultural ethos so steeped in such an "ideology". That is why I have enlisted the help of Levinas, borrowing some of his insights about his notion of responsibility to construct the outline of an alternative understanding of responsibility which can more comfortably accommodate the notion of corporate responsibility. The Levinasian approach is a comprehensive one about moral responsibility in general. Its central concept is infinite responsibility for the Other; the agent is responsible for the Other as well as for all others. Responsibility, for Levinas, is not a consequence of free choices but a given, to take care of the Other. In this sense, freedom does not come from either a social contract or as the result of the standardisation of (abstract/fictive) individual wills. Nor is it a virtue imposed on an individual of good will, but a happening which seizes one upon encountering "the face" of the Other.

In this sense, responsibility integrates not only the individual dimension of moral/legal responsibility, but also of collective responsibility in general, and corporate responsibility in particular, to cover both corporate legal responsibility and corporate moral responsibility. Corporations are responsible not only for the intended consequences of their actions but also for the accumulation of the unintended consequences of their actions, because the Levinasian notion of responsibility is an infinite responsibility in the first person; it is a responsibility without conditions, as one has an infinite and unconditional responsibility for the Other and all the others. This would imply that corporations take into account not only is own interests, but also those of the customers they serve, and of society at large. Corporations should be organised according to justice which, in Levinasian terms, means that duties to the Other override my rights. It is through responsibility that corporations are able to discover their true aim and meaning. Corporate responsibility is unconditional in the sense that to be responsible is not a question of choice, but one of deep liberty, the liberty of taking the burden of the infinite responsibility for the Other — customers, employees, the public at large, and those who suffer in the world (the victims of the extant responsibility-denying policies pursued by certain corporations, such as those in the Western pharmaceutical industry), etc. Corporate responsibility, understood from the Levinasian standpoint, would not reduce institutional relations to an anonymous world of neutrality; under it, harm caused by corporations would no longer be described or viewed as mere "accidents".

Corporations in a globalised world necessarily have an enormous responsibility. As B. Shipka says:

> For companies that truly have a vision of being global, the expansion of human minds and hearts is more than geographic expansion. ... A global business is a business – whether worldwide or not – that has a vision of questing toward wholeness – for itself, for the people within it, for the world at large.[135]

Against the myth of free, autonomous, fictive (or abstract) individuals which underpins the theory of individual responsibility, Levinas proposes an alternative account of responsibility based on asymmetry and interdependence between agents. Against a totalitarian, homogenous society, Levinas opens the way to a social pluralism, which has its sources in the disquiet provoked by the strangeness of the Other's face.

If my defence of the Levinasian philosophy of responsibility against certain criticisms were plausible, and if Levinas's understanding of responsibility were to permeate consciousness both at the individual and collective level, then there might be a chance that a society (as well as its legal system), such as is found in England and Wales, would change its perception of corporate responsibility regarding especially manslaughter in the law of homicide, and be able to accept both its intelligibility from the philosophical and legal standpoints as well as its desirability from the moral point of view.

The revolutionary ideas behind the Levinasian philosophy might have fallen on stony soil in the latter part of the twentieth century but there are emerging signs that it may yet, at long last, find fertile ground in the wider politics of the twenty-first century. This would then, hopefully, constitute progress, the manifestation of a new kind of moral vision, which reflects more adequately the contemporary order of globalisation than the philosophy of individualism and of individual responsibility, which has emerged during a historical era reflecting a world somewhat different from the one we increasingly come to occupy.

---

[135] Quoted by Roddick (2000): 27.

I have urged that society needs a shift of moral paradigm and that the Levinasian account of infinite responsibility for the Other, as presented and defended in this chapter – an attempt to forge an aretaic ethic based on secular saintliness/holiness – may be regarded as a genuine new paradigm.

BIBLIOGRAPHY

Baier, Annette, "The Rights of Past and Future Persons" in *Responsibilities to Future Generations*, edited by Ernest Partridge, Buffalo, New York, Prometheus Books, 1981.

Baron, Marcia, "Kantian Ethics" in *Three Methods of Ethics*, eds M. Baron, Philip Pettit & M. Slote, London, Blackwell Publishers, 1997.

Bates, Stephen, "Miracle Puts Mother Teresa on Saintly Path", *The Guardian*, 21 December 2002: 14.

Bayles, M, "Character, Purpose and criminal Responsibility", *Law and Philosophy*, 1, 5, 1982, pp. 5-20.

Bentham, Jeremy, *An Introduction to the Principles of Morals and Legislation* (The Collected Works of Jeremy Bentham), Oxford, Oxford University Press, 1996.

Bergman, David, *Disasters – Where the Law Fails – A New Agenda for Dealing with Corporate Violence*, London, Herald Families Association, 1993.

Bernasconi, Robert and David Wood, eds, *The Provocation of Levinas: Rethinking the Other*, London and New York: Routledge, 1988.

Bernasconi, Robert, "The Third Party – Levinas on the Intersection of the Ethical and the Political", *Journal of the British Society for Phenomenology*, vol. 30, no. 1, January, 1999, pp. 76-87.

Botbol, Mylène Baum, "Après vous Monsieur", *La Responsibilité – La Condition de notre Humanité*, Paris, Éditions Autrement – Séries Morales, no. 14, 1995, pp. 51-71.

Box, S., *Power, Crime and Mystification,* London, Tavistock, 1983.

Boyd, Colin, "Case Study – The Zebbrugge Car Ferry Disaster", *Business and Society – Public Policy, Ethics*, ed. by W. C. Frederick, J. E. Post and K. Davis, New York, McGraw-Hill, Inc., 1992.

Cadbury Committee, *Report on the Financial Aspects of Corporate Governance*, London, Gee Publications, 1992.

Cadbury, Adrian, "Developments in Corporate Governance", Unpublished Communication during the Symposium about Ethics in Portuguese Corporations, Lisbon, April, 1996.

Chadwick, Ruth F., ed., *Kant's Moral and Political Philosophy (Immanual Kant: Critical Assesments, Vol. 3)*, London, Routledge, 1992.

Chalier, Catherine, *L'Utopie de L'Humain*, Paris, Albin Michel, 1993.

—— , "Emmanuel Levinas: Responsibility and Election", *Ethics*, Royal Institute of Philosophy Supplement: 35, ed. Phillips Griffiths, Cambridge, Cambridge University Press, 1993, pp. 63-76.

—— , "Levinas and the Talmud" in *The Cambridge Companion to Levinas*, edited by Simon Critchley and Robert Bernasconi, Cambridge, Cambridge University Press, 2002.

Claeys, Gregory, ed., *Modern British Utopias, 1700-1850,* 8 Vols, London, W. Pickering, 1997.

Cohen, Richard A., ed., *Face to Face with Levinas,* Albany: State University of New York Press, 1986.
Clarkson, C. M. V, "Corporate Culpability", *Web Journal of Current Legal Issues*, 1982, pp. 1-16.
——, "Kicking Corporate Bodies and Damning Souls", *The Modern Law Review*, 59, 4, July, 1996, pp. 557-72.
Crainer, Stuart, *Zeebrugge: Learning from Disaster – Lessons in Corporate Responsibility,* London, Herald Families Association, 1993.
Critchley, Simon, *The Ethics of Deconstruction: Derrida and Levinas,* Edinburgh, Edinburgh University Press, 1992.
——, Introduction, *The Cambridge Companion to Levinas*, edited by Simon Critchley and Robert Bernasconi, Cambridge, Cambridge University Press, 2002.
Critchley, Simon and Robert Bernasconi, eds, *The Cambridge Companion to Levinas*, Cambridge, Cambridge University Press, 2002.
Crowe, Roger and Jonathan Porritt, *Government's Business: Enabling Corporate Sustainability*, London, Forum for the Future, 2002.
Danley, John, "Corporate Moral Agency", *A Companion to Business Ethics*, ed. by Robert E. Frederick, London, Blackwell Publishers, 1999, pp. 243-56.
Davies, Paul, 'Sincerity and the End of Theodicy: Three Remarks on Levinas and Kant', *The Cambridge Companion to Levinas*, edited by Simon Critchley and Robert Bernasconi, Cambridge, Cambridge University Press, 2002.
Davis, Colin, *Levinas: an Introduction*, London, Polity Press, 1996.
Davis, Nancy, "Utilitarianism and Responsibility", *Ratio,* Oxford, Basil Blackwell, Vol. XXII, 1980, pp. 15-35.
DeGeorge, R, "The Status of Business Ethics: Past, Present, and Future", *Journal of Business Ethics*, vol. 6 n. 3, 1978, pp. 56-67.
Denny, Charlotte, "Bush Blocks Deal Allowing Cheap Drugs for World's Poor", *The Guardian,* 19 February 2003.
Department of Trade and Industry (DTI), UK. *Corporate Social Responsibility Report, 2002.* URL: http://www.societyandbusiness.gov.uk/2002/ report/index. html# [25 November 2002]
De-Shalit, Avner, *Why Posterity Matters: Environmental Policies and Future Generations*, London, Routledge, 1994.
Dickens, William & James Flynn, "Great Leap Forward", *New Scientist*, April 21, 2001.
Donaldson, John, *Key Issues in Business Ethics*, London, Academic Press, 1989.
Donaldson, Thomas, *Corporations and Morality*, New York, Prentice Hall, 1982.
Elliott, Larry, "A Bond with the Poor of the World", *The Guardian*, 16 December 2002: 21.
Faessler, M., "L'Intrigue du Tout-Autre – Dieu dans la Pensée d'Emmanuel Levinas", *Les Cahiers de la nuit surveillée,* Verdier, Paris, 1984, pp. 119-45.
Fisse, Brent and Braithwaite, John, "The Allocation of Responsibility for Corporate Crime: Individualism, Collectivism and Accountability", *The Sydney Law Review*, vol. 11, 1988, pp. 468-513.
Field, Stewart and Jörg Nico, "Corporate Liability and Manslaughter: Should we be going Dutch?", *The Criminal Review*, 191, 1978, pp. 156-71.
Ford, David, F, "On Substitution", *Facing the Other; the* Ethics *of Emmanuel Levinas,* ed. Séan Hand, Richmond, Curzon Press, 1996.

Fourier, Charles, *Oeuvres Complètes de C. Fourier*, deuxième édition, Paris, Librairie Sociétaire, 1841.

French, Peter, *Collective and Corporate Responsibility*, NewYork, Columbia University Press, 1984.

——, *Responsibility Matters*, Kansas, Kansas University Press, 1992.

——, *Corporate Ethics*, London, Harcourt Brace College Publishers, 1995.

——, "Corporate Moral Agency", *The Blackwell Encyclopedic Dictionary of Business Ethics*, ed. by Patricia Werhane and R. Edward Freeman, London, Backwell, 1997.

Friedman, Milton, "The Social Responsibility of Business is to Increase Profits", *New York Times Magazine*, September 13, 1970, pp. 36-51.

Friedmann, F, " Does Business Have a Social Responsibility?", *Bank Administration,* April, 1971.

Gerwen, Jef Van, "Corporate Culture and Ethics", *Business Ethics – Broadening Perspectives*, ed. by J. Verstraeten, Leuven, Peters, 2000.

Gilbert, Martin, *The Righteous: The Unsung Heroes of the Holocaust*, New York, Doubleday, 2002.

Goodpaster, Kenneth and John Matthews, "Can a Corporation Have a Conscience?", *Harvard Business Review*, 1982, pp. 132-41.

The Guardian, Saturday, 11 November 2000, p. 4, "Tactless Corbett Says Sorry to Crash Families".

——, *The Guardian,* Monday, 22 January 2001, p.1, "Hatfield crash inquiry shelved".

——, *The Guardian* Monday July 30 2001, "Railtrack Faces Charge of Manslaughter".

Hardin, Russell, *Morality Within the Limits of Reason*, Chicago, University of Chicago Press, 1988.

Haar Michel, "The Obsession of the Other: Ethics as Traumatization" in *Philosophy and Social Criticism*, vol. 23, no. 6, 1997, pp. 95-107.

Harris, J. W., *Legal Philosophies*, Butterworths, London, 1997.

Hart, H. L. A., *Law, Liberty and Morality*, Oxford, Oxford University Press, 1963.

——, *Punishment and Responsibility – Essays in the Philosophy of Law*, Oxford, Clarendon Press, 1968.

——, "Positivism and the Separation of Law and Morals", Essay 2 in *Essays in Jurisprudence and Philosophy*, Oxford, Clarendon Press, 1983.

——, *Essays in Jurisprudence and Philosophy*, Oxford, Clarendon Press, 1983.

Hayat, Pierre, *Emmanuel Levinas – Éthique et Société*, Paris, Editions Kimé, 1995.

Herzog, Annabel, "Is Liberalism 'ALL WE NEED'? - Lévinas's Politics of Surplus", *Political Theory*, vol.30, no.2, April 2002.

Hodgson, D.H., *Consequences of Utilitarianism: A Study in Normative Ethics and Legal Theory*, Oxford, Clarendon Press, 1967.

Hodgson, Geoffrey, *Economics and Institutions: A Manifesto for Modern Institutional Economics,* Philadelphia, University of Philadelphia Press, 1988.

Hooker, Brad, Elinor Mason and Dale E. Miller, eds, *Morality, Rules and Consequences: A Critical Reader*, Edinburgh, Edinburgh University Press, 2000.

Horder, J, "Criminal Culpability: The Possibility of a General Theory", *Law and Philosophy*, 1, 5, 1993, pp. 193-215.

Hugo, Victor, *Les Misérables*, Vol. 1, Paris, Gallimard, 1995.

Jackall, Robert, *Moral Mazes: The World of Corporate Managers*, Oxford, Oxford University Press, 1988.

Jones, Charles, *Global Justice: Defending Cosmopolitanism*, Oxford, Oxford University Press, 2000.

Kant, Emmanuel, *Critique of Practical Reason and Other Works on The Theory of Ethics*, trans. by T. K. Abbott, London, Longmans, (1873) 1909.

——, *Critique of Pure Reason,* trans. N. Kemp Smith, London, Macmillan, 1929.

——, *Lectures on Ethics*, trans. by L. Infield, New York, Harper and Row, 1963.

——, *Critique of Practical Reason,* trans. by Mary Gregor, Cambridge, Cambridge University Press, 1997.

——, *Groundwork of the Metaphysics of Morals*, translated and edited by Mary Gregor, Cambridge, Cambridge University Press, 1998.

Kearney, Richard, 'Dialogue with Emmanuel Levinas' in *Dialogues with Contemporary Continental Thinkers*, Manchester, Manchester University Press, 1984.

Kemp, Peter, ed., *Emmanuel Levinas: Ethics of the Other,* a special issue of *Philosophy and Criticism*, vol. 23, no. 6, 1997.

Kieran, M, "Applied Philosophy and Business Ethics", *Journal of Applied Philosophy*, vol.12, no.2, 1995, pp. 175-87.

Kitson, A and Robert Campbell, *The Ethical Organization – Ethical Theory and Corporate Behaviour*, London, Macmillan Press, 1996.

Kolnai, Aurel, *The Utopian Mind and Other Papers: A Critical Study in Moral and Political Philosophy*, London, The Athlone Press, 1995.

Kuhn, T. S., *The Structure of Scientific Revolutions*, Chicago & London, University of Chicago Press, second edition, 1970.

Kumar, Krishan, *Utopianism*, Milton Keynes, The Open University Press, 1991.

Ladd, John, "Morality and the Ideal of Rationality in Formal Organizations", *The Monist*, October, 1970, pp. 483-500.

Laufer, W. S, "Corporate Bodies and Guilty Minds", *Emory Law Journal*, 43, 647, 1994, pp. 645-60.

Lee, Keekok, *A New Basis for Moral Philosophy*, London, Routledge & Kegan Paul, 1985.

——, *Social Philosophy and Ecological Scarcity*, London, Routledge, 1989a.

——, *The Positivist Science of Law,* Avebury, Aldershot, 1989b.

——, *The Legal-Rational State: A Comparison of Hobbes, Bentham and Kelsen*, Avebury, Aldershot, 1990.

Leigh, L. H, *The Criminal Liability of Corporations in English Law*, London, L.S.E. Research Monographs 2 Eidenfeld and Nicholson, 1969.

Levinas Emmanuel, *Totalité et Infini – Essai sur L'Exteriorité*, Paris, Biblio Essais, 1967.

——, *L'Humanisme de L'Autre Homme*, Paris, Biblio Essais, 1972.

——, *Autrement Qu'Être ou Au-Dela de l'Essence,* Paris, Biblio Essais, 1974.

——, *Noms Propres*, Paris, Biblio Essais, 1976.

——, *Du Sacré au Saint,* Paris, Minuit, 1977.

——, *Hors Sujet,* Paris, Biblio Essais, 1978.

——, *Éthique et Infini – Dialogues avec Philippe Nemo*, Paris, Fayard/Culture France, 1982.

——, "Paix et Proximité", *Les Cahiers de La nuit surveillée,* Verdier, Paris, 1984, pp. 339-46.

—, "Ethics of the Infinite", *Dialogues with Contemporary Continental Thinkers*, ed. Richard Kearney, Manchester, Manchester University Press, 1984.

—, *Ethics and Infinity*, Pittsburgh, Duquesne University Press, 1985.

—, "The Paradox of Morality: In an interview with Emmanuel Levinas", *The Provocation of Levinas*, ed. Robert Bernasconi and D. Wood, Routledge, New York, 1988a.

—, *En Découvrant L'Existance avec Husserl et Heidegger*, Paris, Vrin, 1988b.

—, *De L'Existance à L'Existant*, Paris, Vrin, 1990a.

—, *Difficile Liberté*, Paris, Biblio Essais, 1990b

—, "Socialité et Argent", *Cahier de L'Herme*, Paris, Biblio Essais, 1991a.

—, *Entre-Nous – Essais sur le penser-à-l'autre*, Paris, Bernard Grasset, 1991b.

—, *Totality and Infinity – An Essay on Exteriority*, trans. by Alphonso Lingis, London, Kluwer Academic Publishers, 1991c.

—, Interview in *Le Monde* (1992); reprinted in *Les imprévus de l'histoire*, Montpellier, Fata Morgana, 1994: 209. (See also Critichley and Bernasconi (2002): 13.)

—, "Transcendence et Intelligibilité", *L'Intrigue de L'Infini*, Paris, Flammarion, 1994.

—, *Quelques réflexions sur la philosophie de l'hitlérisme*, Payot, Paris, 1997.

—, *Otherwise than Being – Or Beyond Essence*, trans. by Alphonso Lingis, Pennsylvania, Duquesne University Press, 1998.

—, *Of God Who Comes to Mind*, trans. by Bettina Bergo, Stanford, California, Stanford University Press, 1998.

Llewelyn, John, *The Middle Voice of Ecological Conscience: A Chiasmic Reading of Responsibility in the Neighbourhood of Levinas, Heidegger and Others*, London, Macmillan Academic and Professional Ltd, 1991.

—, *The Genealogy of Ethics – Emmanuel Levinas*, Routledge, London, 1995.

Louden, Robert, "Kant's Virtue Ethics" in *Kant's Moral and Political Philosophy (Immaneul Kant: Critical Assessments*, Vol. III), edited by Ruth Chadwick, London and New York, Routledge, 1992.

Lucas, J.R, *Responsibility*, Oxford, Clarendon Press, 1993.

Lukes, Steven, "Methodological Individualism Reconsidered", ed. by Alan Ryan, *The Philosophy of Social Explanation*, Oxford, University Press, 1973.

Lyons, David, *Forms and Limits of Utilitarianism*, Oxford, Clarendon Press, 1965.

Mansfield, Michael, "Victims the Law Left Out", *The Guardian*, 20 November 2002: 19.

May, Larry, *The Morality of Groups: Collective Responsibility, Group-Based Harm, and Corporate Rights*, Indiana, University of Notre dame, 1987.

—, *Sharing Responsibility*, Chicago, University of Chicago press, 1992.

Mayo, Ed, "It's Time to Set Out Transparency Targets", *The Guardian,* 25 November 2002, *The Giving List*: 28-29.

McDonald, M, "The Personless Paradigm", *University of Toronto Law Journal*, 37, 1987, pp. 219-20.

Mostley, Raoul, *French Philosophers in Conversation*, London, Routledge, 1991.

Peperzak, Adriaan, *To the Other: An Introduction to the Philosophy of Emmanuel Levinas*, Indiana, Purdue University Press, 1993.

—, *Ethics as First Philosophy*, London, Routledge, 1995.

—, *Beyond – The Philosophy of* Emmanuel *Levinas,* Illinois, Northwestern University Press, Evanston, 1997.

Pettit, Philip, ed., *Consequentialism*, Aldershott, Dartmouth Publishing Company, 1993.

Perkins, Rollin, *Criminal Law*, New York, The Foundation Press, 1969.
Pike, Dag, "The Physics of Capsizing a Top-Heavy Ferry", *New Scientist*, March 12, 1987, p. 15.
Pilger, John, "Spoils of a Massacre", *The Guardian*, Saturday 14, July, 2001, pp. 18-29.
Popper, Karl, *Conjectures and Refutations*, London, Routledge & Kegan Paul, 1969.
—— , *The Open Society and Its Enemies,* Vol. 1, London, Routledge & Kegan Paul, 1957.
Posner, R, *Law and Legal Theory in England and America*, Oxford, Clarendon Press, 1996.
Purcell, M, "The Ethical Significance of Illeity (Emmanuel Levinas), *Heytrop Journal*, vol. 37, no. 2, April, 1996, pp. 125-38.
Putnam, Hilary, "Levinas and Judaism", in *The Cambridge Companion to Levinas*, edited by Simon Critchley and Robert Bernasconi, Cambridge, Cambridge University Press, 2002.
Quinton, Anthony, *Utilitarian Ethics*, London, Duckworth, 1989.
Rawls, John, *A Theory of Justice*, Oxford and New York, Oxford University Press, 1999.
Roddick, Anita, *Business as Unusual*, London, Harper Collins Publishers, 2000.
—— , *Globalisation – Take it Personally*, London, Harper Collins Publishers, 2001.
Rorty, Richard, *Achieving Our Country: Leftist Thought in Twentieth-century America*, Cambridge, Massachusettes, Harvard University Press, 1998.
Ross, Sir David, *Kant's Ethical Theory*. Oxford, Oxford University Press, 1954.
Scarre, Geoffry, *Utilitarianism*, London, Routledge, 1996.
Scruton, Roger, *Kant*, Oxford & New York, Oxford University Press, 1982.
Sheen Report, Department of Transport, Report of Court No. 8074. Formal Investigation of mv Herald of Free Enterprise, HMSO, London, 1987.
Smart, J.J.C. and B. Williams, *Utilitarianism: For and Against*, London, Cambridge University Press, 1973.
Smith, J. C, "Responsibility in Criminla Law", *Barbara Wootton – Social Science and Public Policy – Essays in her Honour*, ed. by Philip Bean and David Whynes, London, Tavistock Publications, 1986.
Smith, J.C & B. Hogan, *Criminal Law,* London, Butterworths, 1996.
Soares, Conceição, " Two Different Approaches to Ethics – A Challenge or a Solution to the Subject's Problems?", Unpublished Paper, presented at the Conference entitled, *Ethics in the New Millennium*, Ottawa, September, 2000.
—— , "Emmanuel Levinas e a Obsessão do Outro", *Didaskalia*, Lisboa, vol.XXX, 2000, pp.169-94.
Stiles, Peter, "Corporate Governance and Ethics", ed. by P. Davis, *Current Issues in Business Ethics*, London, Routledge, 1997, pp. 39-49.
Sullivan, G. R, "Express Corporate Guilt", *Oxford Journal of Legal Studies*, 15, 281, 19, 1995, pp. 281-92.
Sullivan, Roger J., *Immanuel Kant's Moral Theory*, Cambridge, Cambridge University Press, 1989.
Taylor, Charles, *Human Agency and Language,* Cambridge, Cambridge University Press, 1985.
Taylor, Richard, "Determinism and the Theory of Agency", *Determinism and Freedom in the Age of Modern Science*, ed. by Sidney Hook, New York, Collier Books, 1958.
Tebbit, Mark, *Philosophy of Law – An Introduction*, London, Routledge, 2000.
Theodore de Boer, "An Ethical Transcendental Philosophy" in Richard A. Cohen (ed.), *Face to Face with Levinas*, Albany: State University of New York Press, 1986.

Velasquez, Manuel, "Why Corporations are not Morally Responsible for Anything They Do", *Business and Professional Ethics Journal*, 2, 1983, pp. 1-18.

Walker, Ralph C.S., *Kant: The Arguments of the Philosophers*, London, Routledge and Kegan Paul, 1978.

Wells, Celia, 'Manslaughter and Corporate Crime', *New Law Journal*, vol. 139, 30 June, 1989, pp. 931-34.

——, "Corporate Responsibility", *Encyclopedia of Applied Ethics*, ed. by Chadwick London, Academic Press, vol.1, 1998, pp. 653-58.

——, "The Decline and Rise of English Murder: Corporate Crime and Individual Responsibility", *The Criminal Law Review*, December, 1998, pp. 788-801.

——, *Corporations and Criminal Responsibility*, Oxford, Oxford University Press, 2001.

Werhane, Patricia, *Persons, Rights and Corporations*, New York, Prentice-Hall, Inc. Englewood Cliffs, 1985.

Wilden, A, "Ecosystems and Economic Systems", *Cultures of the Future*, ed. by Maruyama and A. Harkins, The Hague, Mouton Publishers, 1978.

Chapter 9

RELEVANCE LOST IN CORPORATE RESPONSIBILITY RESEARCH: GETTING BEHIND THE SMOKESCREENS THROUGH ACADEMIA–NGO COLLABORATION

Niklas Egels-Zandén[*]

Centre for Business in Society
School of Business, Economics and Law at Göteborg University
Box 600, SE – 405 30 Göteborg, Sweden

ABSTRACT

Paraphrasing Johnson and Kaplan's (1987) well-known argument that management accounting research has lost its relevance, this chapter argues that research into corporate responsibility in developing countries faces a similar dilemma. Due to an unwillingness to consider alternative research methods, corporate responsibility research has lost its relevance in terms of being able to describe corporate practice accurately and credibly. Instead, corporate responsibility research has ended up describing the smokescreens (created by transnational corporations and their suppliers) that serve to hide actual factory conditions. To restore relevance to corporate responsibility research, this chapter proposes an alternative research method based on academia–NGO collaboration in collecting empirical data in developing countries. The pros and cons of the developed research method are discussed, as are possible ways to overcome the difficulties of academia–NGO collaboration. Finally, the chapter concludes by discussing how managers can use the developed method both to improve and scrutinize their own monitoring.

---

[*] Niklas.Egels-Zanden@handels.gu.se; +46-31-7862729 (telephone).

INTRODUCTION

In their well-known and provocative book, *Relevance Lost: The Rise and Fall of Management Accounting* (1987), Thomas Johnson and Robert Kaplan harshly criticized management accounting research for losing touch with contemporary corporate practice. They argued that academics interested in management accounting had been led astray by their narrow focus on traditional research paths, making them produce distorted input for management decision making. In brief, they argued that management accounting research – as well as management accounting practice – had lost its relevance because of its inability to provide an accurate representation of corporate practice.

While most academics would regard these arguments as too "black and white" (e.g., Noreen, 1987; Solomons, 1987; Ezzamel *et al.*, 1990; Segovia, 1990), Johnson and Kaplan's core idea does contain important insights. It identifies the general problem of academic research decoupling from corporate practice, confining itself to hypothetical intra-academia discussions rather than focusing on accurately representing corporate practice. This chapter argues that critical analysis of corporate responsibility research conducted in recent decades reveals that this general problem – albeit on a smaller scale than in management accounting research – also exists in corporate responsibility research. Such research fails to provide accurate representations of corporate practice in at least one central respect: transnational corporation (TNC) operations in developing countries. The loss of relevance in corporate responsibility research is particularly prevalent in studies of working conditions and workers' rights in developing countries.

Most corporate responsibility researchers would agree that the exploitation and mistreatment of workers in developing countries is among the most central contemporary corporate responsibility topics. With TNCs increasingly offshoring production to developing countries (e.g., Christerson and Appelbaum, 1995; Hathcote and Nam, 1999; Jones, 2005; Taylor, 2005), core corporate responsibility issues are being offshored as well. In fact, since the working conditions in these countries are substantially worse than those in Europe and the U.S.A. (e.g., Chan and Senser, 1997; Chan, 1998, 2000; Lee, 1998, 1999), not only are corporate responsibility issues moving offshore, but additional issues are emerging as well. However, this offshoring and outsourcing trend in corporate practice has proven difficult for corporate responsibility researchers to tackle. With most researchers based in the U.S.A. and Europe, access to empirical data is difficult. This is partly due to the need to travel to developing countries to collect data, but – more importantly and more difficult to overcome – it is also due to the problem of collecting credible data once researchers are actually present in developing countries. As several researchers have argued, the traditional way of collecting empirical data through official interviews and observations is unreliable in many developing countries, since the studied organisations have developed techniques for deceiving individuals collecting data in this way (e.g., O'Rourke, 1997; Graafland, 2002; O'Rourke, 2002; Winstanley *et al.*, 2002; Hemphill, 2004).

Corporate responsibility researchers have adopted two main strategies for handling this difficulty. First, central corporate responsibility topics in relation to developing countries have either been neglected or treated theoretically rather than empirically. Second, researchers have used inappropriate methods and based their conclusions on unreliable empirical data. Obviously, neither of these approaches is satisfactory, and both have led to a loss of relevance in corporate responsibility research. In this way, academics have become unable to provide accurate descriptions of current corporate practices in developing countries, or to provide reasonably correct information to inform corporate strategies.

To help revitalise corporate responsibility research and restore its relevance, this chapter outlines an alternative research method for collecting empirical data in developing countries. It does so by proposing that academics must partly relinquish the notion of collecting empirical data by themselves, in favour of an approach involving collaboration with organisations – in particular, non-governmental organisations (NGOs) – that have better access to reliable data. The suggested method has implications not only for academics, but also for corporate managers interested in getting behind the smokescreens created by firms in developing countries, to achieve an understanding of the actual working conditions at their own and their suppliers' factories. The discussion of the research method developed here will be illustrated throughout with examples from a recent collaboration between a Swedish research group, Swedish NGOs, and a Hong Kong-based NGO (Egels-Zandén, 2007).

METHODS USED IN PREVIOUS RESEARCH

This section does not review all previous research into corporate responsibility in developing countries. Rather, the focus is on illustrating a general point by reviewing empirical research into a specific and highly relevant strain of corporate responsibility research: research into working conditions at the factories of TNCs' suppliers in developing countries. The focus is on working conditions, because this is both a central corporate responsibility issue in developing countries and also likely a key area in terms of lost relevance. While corporate responsibility research has arguably lost relevance in relation to other aspects of TNC operations in developing countries, aspects such as operations in conflict zones (cf. Pegg and Wilson, 2003), the loss of relevance appears to be worse in relation to workers' rights and working conditions.

Following TNC outsourcing of production, suppliers have come to comprise central organisations for corporate responsibility researchers. Since it is more difficult for TNCs to control and influence their suppliers' operations than their own, the most pressing corporate responsibility issues in developing countries often reside in this setting. Supplier relations are also central to current TNC practices, since most TNCs currently assume responsibility for working conditions at their suppliers' factories (e.g., Emmelhainz and Adams, 1999; Kolk and van Tulder, 2002; Ählström and Egels-Zandén, 2007). This extension of TNC responsibility was a consequence of severe criticism from various stakeholders regarding the working conditions at the factories of TNCs' suppliers (e.g., Frenkel, 2001; van Tulder and Kolk, 2001; Roberts, 2003; Frenkel and Kim, 2004; Egels-Zandén and Hyllman, 2006).

In practice, codes of conduct have emerged as the dominant approach to operationalising TNCs' responsibility for workers' rights at their suppliers' factories (e.g., Kolk and van Tulder, 2002; Sethi, 2002; Radin, 2004). The only real alternative to codes of conduct is international framework agreements, but few TNCs have signed such agreements (Hammer, 2004; Riisgaard, 2005; Egels-Zandén and Hyllman, 2007). Hence, codes of conduct are the dominant way in which workers' rights at TNCs' suppliers are in practice governed.

Therefore, this section focuses on reviewing previous research into supplier compliance with TNCs' codes of conduct.

Previous research has used two main ways to acquire empirical data. First, most studies have relied on secondary data provided by the organisations monitoring compliance with codes of conduct (e.g., Murphy and Mathew, 2001; Graafland, 2002; Sethi, 2002; Winstanley *et al.*, 2002). Second, a few studies have relied on primary data collected via announced, official interviews with managers and employees (O'Rourke and Brown, 1999; Frenkel, 2001; Frenkel and Scott, 2002; Frenkel and Kim, 2004). Since monitoring organisations, like researchers, collect data through official (often announced), on-site interviews, the main difference between these two previously used methods concerns *who* collects the data, monitoring organizations or academics. Given that several researchers have criticised monitoring organisations for inadequate monitoring (O'Rourke, 1997, 2000, 2002, 2003; Burnett and Mahon, 2001; Florini, 2003; French and Wokutch, 2005), using academics to collect primary data seems to be the more reliable method.

However, both these methods share a severe credibility problem, in that they rely mainly on announced, official, on-site interviews. Several authors have questioned the use of such an interview setting for collecting reliable data (O'Rourke, 1997; Hemphill, 2004; Egels-Zandén, 2007), since suppliers have developed techniques for deceiving individuals collecting data this way. The most common such techniques identified in previous research are as follows: i) instructing employees what to say on monitoring occasions, ii) financially compensating employees for providing "correct" answers on monitoring occasions, iii) punishing employees for providing "wrong" answers on monitoring occasions, iv) hiding part of the workforce on monitoring occasions, v) forging salary lists, vi) forging time cards, and vii) forging employee contracts (Doig and Wilson, 1998; Frenkel and Scott, 2002; Graafland, 2002; Healy and Iles, 2002; O'Rourke, 2002; Winstanley *et al.*, 2002; Egels-Zandén, 2007).

To explore the importance of these deception techniques to the quality of obtained empirical data, I conducted a study of supplier compliance with TNCs' codes of conduct, based on anonymous, unannounced, unofficial, off-site interviews with employees at Chinese toy suppliers' factories (Egels-Zandén, 2007). The focus was on analysing code of conduct aspects such as working hours, financial compensation, insurance, child labour, and the existence of employee contracts. The study found that all suppliers violated some of the evaluated code of conduct standards, with over two-thirds of the suppliers not complying with most of the studied standards. The study's results suggested a significantly lower level of supplier compliance with codes of conduct than that identified in previous research based on either primary or secondary data (e.g., Frenkel, 2001; Frenkel and Scott, 2002; Graafland, 2002; Sethi, 2002; Winstanley *et al.*, 2002; Frenkel and Kim, 2004). Hence, the results presented in Egels-Zandén (2007) suggest that research relying on primary data collected by researchers, or on secondary data collected by monitoring organisations, actually describes the decoupled smokescreens created by suppliers rather than the actual conditions at suppliers' factories (cf. Meyer and Rowan, 1977). Thus, previous research into code of conduct compliance has become irrelevant when it comes to providing accurate descriptions of actual conditions at suppliers' factories.

Restoring the relevance of corporate responsibility research in developing countries, particularly in relation to working conditions, calls for alternative methodological approaches. The remainder of this chapter is focused on one such approach. This approach is not without caveats and is not the only potentially promising approach to getting behind code of conduct smokescreens in developing countries. It is just one possible approach, one that attempts to tackle the problems evident in previous research and serves as a first step towards revitalising corporate responsibility research.

THE PROBLEM OF ACCESSING CREDIBLE DATA

The main problem with the previously used research methods is that several actors have incentives to describe workplace conditions inaccurately. It seems that TNCs mainly take responsibility for working conditions in developing countries in order to repair or improve their legitimacy (cf. Meyer and Rowan, 1977; Pfeffer and Salancik, 1978; Ählström and Egels-Zandén, 2007). Hence, to TNCs the *appearance* of good working conditions is what is important, not *actual* good working conditions. Actual good working conditions likely even have negative effects on central purchasing criteria, such as purchasing price, since improved working conditions tend to yield higher production costs (cf. Lee and Lim, 2001; Liew, 2001; Cooney et al., 2002; Cooke, 2004). Similarly, supplier management has incentives to uphold an *appearance* of good working conditions while avoiding them in practice. Interestingly, employees also have incentives to create smokescreens, despite the fact that they would benefit from changes in working conditions. This is both because supplier management rewards them for providing incorrect information (and punishes them for providing correct information) and because employees fear TNCs would switch suppliers if the real working conditions at the supplier were revealed. Hence, researchers interested in describing working conditions in developing countries must overcome this information asymmetry by convincing those with reliable information – mainly supplier management and employees – to reveal it. This problem is not restricted to working conditions at suppliers' factories; for example, in describing conditions in conflict zones and at TNCs' own factories, researchers face similar problems with informants lacking incentives to reveal actual conditions (cf. Pegg and Wilson, 2003).

Of the involved parties – TNCs, supplier management, and employees – researchers will likely have greatest success convincing employees to provide adequate information: they possess most of the relevant information and stand to gain the most from improved working conditions. To ensure that this is the case, negative incentives in the form of punishments imposed by supplier management on employees must be decreased. This can only be done if employees are interviewed anonymously, and this in turn can only be achieved if the interviews are unofficial, off-site, and unannounced (cf. O'Rourke, 1997; Hemphill, 2004).

While the analysis of *what* must be done to obtain credible empirical data is relatively straightforward, it is more difficult to determine *how* exactly this is to be done in practice. To conduct anonymous, unofficial, unannounced, off-site interviews, the researcher must be "invisible" in the empirical setting: any traces of his/her presence would risk jeopardising employee anonymity, in turn making employees unwilling to reveal information regarding the actual working conditions. This "invisibility" not only entails familiarity with the local language, but also familiarity with the local culture, an appearance similar to that of the employees (in terms of race, sex, age, clothing, etc.), and an ability to move freely around the production facilities. The last aspect is particularly problematic in free trade zones and in countries, such as Myanmar, Sudan, and China, with restricted freedom of movement for foreigners. Here, access to the production milieus is restricted for foreigners, making it necessary for "invisible" researchers to enter these milieus without the knowledge of local governmental agencies. I would argue that few, if any, European or U.S. researchers possess the necessary characteristics and skills to achieve such "invisibility". Some local researchers can approach this ideal (see, for example, the work of Anita Chan, 1998, 2000, and C.K. Lee, 1998, 1999), but even these researchers have difficulties passing as insiders, and consequently risk jeopardising the employees' security and the credibility of the data.

To truly overcome these problems, it seems as though corporate responsibility researchers must abandon the idea of collecting empirical data themselves. For various, and sometimes good, reasons, most researchers have so far rejected this suggestion. First, for academics to relinquish their monopoly on collecting empirical data, would call into question their role as the experts of our time – a central and strongly embedded part of perceptions of academia. This ideological position has recently been challenged by several authors, and can be replaced by the idea that the researcher is just one of many actors who produce knowledge (e.g., Gibbons *et al.*, 1994; Callon, 1998; Leadbeater and Miller, 2004). Second, and more importantly, by allowing others to collect empirical data, researchers lose control over the data collection process, i.e., they lose control over procedures designed to ensure credible data. As any textbook of interviewing techniques will argue (e.g., Kvale, 1996), the skills of the interviewer are crucial for the credibility of the data gathered. Hence, by abandoning collecting data, researchers risk lowering the credibility of their research. Despite this criticism, corporate responsibility researchers have little choice but to follow the unexplored path of relinquishing part of the data collection process if their research is to regain its relevance and credibility in describing conditions in developing countries. Hence, the question is not *if* people other than researchers should collect the empirical data, but rather *who* these people should be.

ACADEMIA–NGO COLLABORATION

Identifying Appropriate Partners

Since the question is *who* rather than *if* people other than researchers should collect empirical data in developing countries, the central decision facing researchers interested in accurately describing conditions in developing countries is to identify appropriate partners with whom to collaborate. Ideally, these should be people who can pass as insiders in the research context, while still being experienced interviewers.

Many of the most pressing workers' rights issues exist in low-skill industries in which most employees are 18–25-year-old female migrant workers (cf. Frenkel, 2001). Hence, interviewers should ideally fit this profile in order to pass as "insiders", as well as having experience of working in similar conditions. While such individuals could potentially be found in both labour unions and NGOs, they are more likely to be found in the latter. This is possibly related to the traditional male domination of unions (e.g., Gallin, 2000; Hale, 2004; Povey, 2004; Prieto and Quinteros, 2004), and to the lack of union presence in many regions in developing countries (e.g., Chan and Ross, 2003; Valor, 2005). Of course, suitable interviewers could potentially also be found at local universities in developing countries, in the form of Ph.D. students or senior researchers. However, few local academics would have sufficient experience of working in or around production facilities to be able to pass as "insiders". If such researchers exist, they would obviously be desirable partners for the type of study outlined in this chapter.

In a recent study of workers' rights in Guangdong province in China (Egels-Zandén, 2007), the research group was unable to identify a local academic researcher capable of passing as an "insider", and instead found that the most appropriate interviewers were linked to an NGO, the Hong Kong Christian Industrial Committee (HKCIC). This NGO had a unique combination of extensive experience in interview studies in the studied region (AMRC, 1996, 1997; HKCIC and AMRC, 1997; HKCIC and CAFOD, 1999; HKCIC, 2000a, 2000b, 2000c, 2001, 2002; HKCSPT, 2003) and access to interviewers who had previously worked both as production workers in the region and as interviewers. Additionally, HKCIC's previous studies had been used to support factual claims in previous academic research (e.g., Chan, 1998; Snyder, 1999; Tracy, 1999; Langer, 2004). By collaborating with HKCIC, the research group was able to identify experienced interviewers who were able to pass as "insiders".

The study presented in Egels-Zandén (2007) demonstrates that it is possible to identify "invisible" interviewers, although this is often a time-consuming process. However, despite rigorous efforts to identify qualified interviewers, credibility problems are still associated with using non-academic interviewers who may possess a clear political agenda (cf. Pegg and Wilson, 2003). For example, the interviewers might influence employee responses in a direction supportive of future NGO campaigns (cf. Kvale, 1996). Hence, the next central step after having identified appropriate interviewers is to minimise potential interviewer effects.

Minimising Interviewer Effects

A first step in minimising interviewer effects is to standardise the interview. This is useful, since it allows the researcher to conduct test interviews with the interviewer, in which interviewer effect tendencies can be identified. In the study presented in Egels-Zandén (2007), standardisation was done by having the interviewer start each interview by providing a standardised description of the study, which informed the respondent of the purpose of the study (i.e., to study working conditions at the production unit), the affiliation of the interviewer (in this study, none of the informants had prior knowledge of HKCIC), and that the interview would be anonymous and not jeopardise the factory's contracts with its buyers (this last point is crucial and will be dealt with in more detail below). Following this introduction, the interviewer followed a predefined interview guide containing brief, specific, non-leading, and mainly open-ended questions (cf. Kvale, 1996; Bryman, 2004). The questions were factually focused on conditions at the factory, since interviewer effects are less prevalent in questions concerning factual matters rather than attitudes (Boyd and Westfall, 1965; Frenkel and Scott, 2002; Davis and Silver, 2003). While standardised interviews are preferable for minimising interview effects, they also impose a rigid structure on the interview situation. This could be problematic, since informant reluctance to reveal sensitive information could call for a more flexible approach. A balance must thus be struck between standardisation and context sensitivity. In Egels-Zandén (2007), this trade-off was handled by granting the interviewer the freedom to vary the order of the interview questions and to formulate additional follow-up questions.

Interviewer effects can also be minimised by allowing the researcher to analyse the complete interview data. However, this requires that the data be recorded and transcribed, something to which informants may be reluctant to agree. Such reluctance was indeed found in the study presented in Egels-Zandén (2007), so rather than recording the data, the interviewers were restricted to taking extensive notes during the interviews. Such restrictions obviously lower the transparency and credibility of the interview data and increase the potential for interviewer effects.

Through measures such as those outlined above, it is possible for researchers to minimise the interviewer effects stemming from the use of non-academic and less-experienced interviewers. There will obviously always be some undesirable interviewer effects stemming from the use of non-academic interviewers, effects that will lower the credibility of the data. However – and this is the main point of this chapter – such negative effects are much less serious than the negative effects of having the researchers themselves collect empirical data in these settings.

PITFALLS OF ACADEMIA–NGO COLLABORATION

The above discussion demonstrates that it is possible to identify appropriate NGO partners and minimise negative interviewer effects so as to obtain credible data. The question is then the type of relationships academics should form with NGOs. Academics can apply two main strategies when using NGOs to collect empirical data. First, NGOs could be commissioned merely to collect data and restricted from using any of the data for their own purposes. Second, a collaborative academia–NGO relationship could be formed in which both parties are allowed to use the collected data for their own purposes. While the second strategy involves more potential pitfalls, it entails two major advantages. First, it might be difficult to convince NGOs to collect empirical data without allowing them the option of using them; this is a practical difficulty that must be evaluated on a case-by-case basis. However, whenever NGOs are interested in collecting data without using them in their own campaigns, this arrangement would be preferred in terms of data credibility.

Second, and more importantly, NGOs can potentially bolster a central aspect of any study, namely, protecting the respondents. A crucial promise that must be made to a respondent before initiating an interview, is that his/her responses regarding the actual working conditions at the factory will not jeopardise the factories' contracts with its buyers. Hence, when European and American TNCs learn of the mistreatment of workers by their suppliers, they should not be allowed to switch suppliers, thus jeopardising the employment of the respondents. However, academics have limited abilities to ensure that this promise is followed through in practice, since they lack the capacity to force TNCs to act in certain ways. Certain NGOs, on the other hand, have media and consumer campaign channels that give them the ability to discipline TNC practices. This is clearly demonstrated by the numerous NGO campaigns that have led to TNCs assuming responsibility for workers' rights at their suppliers (e.g., Frenkel, 2001; van Tulder and Kolk, 2001; Roberts, 2003; Frenkel and Kim, 2004; Egels-Zandén and Hyllman, 2006). Hence, *collaborating* with NGOs provides a research group with the possibility of protecting respondent employment in a way that merely *commissioning* NGOs to collect data does not. Given the importance of protecting respondents, both from an ethical perspective and to ensure credible data, collaborating with NGOs is often more promising than commissioning them to collect data. There are, however, three main pitfalls in academia–NGO collaboration that must be overcome to achieve successful collaboration.

Transparency: Different Academia and NGO Needs

A first potential pitfall of academia–NGO collaboration is that academics and NGOs have different transparency needs. For NGOs participating in such collaboration, the central aspect of transparency is to reveal the names of the studied firms and usually of the respondents as well (cf. Spar and La Mure, 2003; Ählström and Egels-Zandén, 2007). This is seen as essential for launching NGO campaigns based on the results. Such transparency is not as essential for academics as for NGOs, since many academically published results are anonymised in any case. The tradition of anonymising the studied firms in academic research is based on the perception that firms are less willing to participate in studies if the described practices can be linked to them. Of course, firms' unwillingness to disclose detailed information is further strengthened by the threat that not only will their identities be revealed, but they might also become the targets of NGO campaigns if they participate in studies. Such NGO campaigns might also negatively affect relationships between researchers and firms, potentially jeopardising future collaboration with them.

Rather than emphasising transparency in terms of the names of involved actors, academics emphasise transparency in both the data collection and analysis processes, since these are central ways to achieve research credibility. Here, NGOs are less stringent than academics are in their transparency demands, and data collection and analysis is often done in an intuitive rather than structured fashion; for example, no interview guides are developed, interviews are not recorded, and the obtained data are analysed without using established methods. Although all these shortcomings could be corrected by involving academics, NGO practices are not only based on a poor understanding of scientific methods; they are also linked to an emphasis on the quick presentation of research results. The inadequacy of NGO transparency and of stringency in terms of data collection and analysis is related to their prioritisation of quickness over "accuracy" in producing results.

Speed: Quick versus Slow

Consequently, the second potential pitfall of academia–NGO collaboration is that NGOs and researchers often operate according to different "timelines", time seeming to move faster for NGOs than for researchers. This difference is symptomatic of two more general differences between academics and NGOs regarding i) access to financial resources and ii) the news value of studies. First, in terms of access to financial resources, researchers can preserve longer timelines, since they often base their research projects on long-term funding, for example, in the form of research grants or academic positions. Hence, there is little need for a particular study to produce quick results, and the focus is more on publishing in prestigious journals. For example, the often lengthy review and publication processes of academic journals are related to this relatively limited need to produce quick results. In contrast, NGOs usually compete for financial resources from individual supporters, and consistently must advertise their activities. The financial support that NGOs receive from governmental and/or private agencies is also usually reviewed yearly or even more frequently. In this way, NGOs are pressured to produce quick results from particular studies in order to be eligible for further financing and continued existence. Hence, for financial reasons, NGOs are pressured into producing results more quickly from a given study than academics are.

Second, in terms of the "news value" of a study, NGOs also operate according to shorter timelines than do researchers. As implied in the lengthy review and publishing processes of academic research, the focus is less on *current* empirical data than on general theoretical implications. Hence, the news value of an academic paper is only slightly related to when the empirical data were collected. In sharp contrast, the news value of an NGO report is largely a function of the newness of the empirical data. It is substantially more difficult to launch a successful NGO campaign based on one-, two-, or three-year-old empirical data than on recently collected data. This need for data newness is mainly related to a media and consumer focus on recent events, but also to the fact that studied firms could dismiss "old" data reports as irrelevant, since conditions may have changed since they were gathered. In sum, NGOs' need for an "empirical contribution" in the form of publishing current data and academics' need for a "theoretical contribution" in the form of more general implications lead them to operate according to different timelines. This difference can lead to frustration on the part of both academics ("NGOs move too quickly") and NGOs ("academics move too slowly"), and may harm the collaboration. This harm could well increase given the third pitfall, one that arises out of the difference between academics and NGOs regarding the use of jointly collected empirical data.

Data Use: Normative versus Descriptive

The purpose of NGO campaigns is to promote a normative agenda and to suggest changes to contemporary corporate practices. For example, NGOs could collect, and successfully have collected, empirical data regarding working conditions at TNCs' supplier factories, doing so to support campaigns pressuring TNCs to extend their responsibility for workers' rights at their suppliers' factories (e.g., Emmelhainz and Adams, 1999; Kolk and van Tulder, 2002; Sethi, 2002; Radin, 2004; Ählström and Egels-Zandén, 2007). Furthermore, successful media and consumer campaigns are built on a "black and white" presentation of data that points out, and sometimes even exaggerates, a study's central findings (cf. Whawell, 1998). Hence, NGOs strive to promote a normative change agenda based on a black and white presentation of recently collected empirical data, i.e., a "quick and dirty" research strategy.

In sharp contrast to this "quick and dirty" strategy, academics usually pursue a more descriptive agenda, trying to explain corporate practice rather than change it. As some researchers have noted (e.g., Freeman, 1999), the distinction between normative and descriptive is not straightforward. However, it is still a commonplace distinction in corporate responsibility literature, and I believe that in this context it identifies a central difference between academics and NGOs (cf. Swanson, 1999; Hendry, 2001; Kaler, 2003). A detailed academic descriptive analysis of an empirical phenomenon is also presented in shades of grey rather than in black and white, highlighting the roles of complexity, interpretation, and uncertainty in the collected data. As such, it is less well suited for media campaigns. On the other hand, thanks to the focus on nuance in academic research, the presented results are often perceived as more reliable than those produced by NGOs. Herein also lays a risk for academics collaborating with NGOs: NGOs have incentives to leverage the legitimacy of the collaborating academic institution, to increase the credibility of their interpretation of a study's results (cf. Meyer and Rowan, 1977; Suchman, 1995). Academics could find themselves unintentionally drawn into media campaigns orchestrated by their NGO partners, campaigns based on quickly produced normative analyses of jointly collected data. Such campaigns could well damage their, and their research institutions', reputations.

Overcoming the Pitfalls

Although problematic, the above described pitfalls can be overcome by carefully structuring the academia–NGO collaboration. One of the many different ways to overcome these pitfalls was developed in the study presented in Egels-Zandén (2007); the following description of this approach is intended to serve more as an example than as a universally applicable solution.

Initially, due to the importance of protecting the respondents, the research group decided to collaborate with a group of Swedish-based NGOs (in addition to the Hong Kong-based NGO collecting the data). It was decided that the Swedish NGOs and researchers could both use the collected data, but that the data use was to be split: the NGOs would pursue their normative campaign agenda based on their data interpretation, but without mentioning the research group's involvement, while the research group would pursue their more descriptive publication agenda. Of course, the researchers and NGOs collaborated during the data collection and analysis processes, but their presentations of the data were separated. In the end, the NGOs and researchers arrived at fairly similar interpretations of the study's results, the main difference being that the researchers were more cautious than the NGOs in interpreting unclear respondent answers. This separation of the data use protected the researchers from being drawn into the media campaign that followed the NGO publication of the study in the form of, for example, numerous newspaper articles and an hour-long debate on primetime national TV between NGO and firm representatives.

Naturally, the names of the studied firms were revealed in the NGOs' campaigns and publications, and this obviously led to legitimacy losses on the part of the corporations – an anticipated effect of publishing (and publicising) the study's results. The researchers were partly protected from involvement in this process, both by not being mentioned when the NGOs published the results and by the fact it was the NGOs that had initiated the contacts with the firms. Hence, the researchers neither had to use any of their corporate contacts to initiate the study nor risked damaging existing corporate relationships in the aftermath of the media "scandals". In this way, the NGOs' transparency needs were accommodated without negatively affecting the researchers'.

Finally, in terms of the academics' and NGOs' different timelines, this difficulty was overcome by separating the publication processes. The NGO report was published over two years before the academic publication of the study. It would have been impossible to release the publications simultaneously, given the NGOs' need for quick publication and the researchers' need for thorough analysis and time-consuming publication processes.

In this study, both the researchers and NGO representatives perceived that the collaborative structure of the project was successful, indicating that collaboration is possible despite the numerous potential pitfalls. The researchers gained access to interesting empirical data that has helped in restoring relevance to academic corporate responsibility research in developing countries. Moreover, they were able to participate in a study that potentially changed corporate practice without jeopardising their, and their research institutions', credibility. The NGOs received support in credibly collecting and analysing empirical data, and were able to help increase the academic community's awareness of working conditions in developing countries.

CONCLUSION

This chapter has described how corporate responsibility research has lost its relevance, by virtue of its inability to describe key contemporary corporate practices in developing countries. Furthermore, this chapter has demonstrated that this loss of relevance is a function of how academics collect empirical data, and that alternative research methods are needed to restore relevance, and credibility, to corporate responsibility research. One such alternative research method – academia–NGO collaboration – has been outlined, a method shown to be capable of gathering credible data. While promising, academia–NGO collaboration also presents potential pitfalls due to academia–NGO differences in terms of i) transparency needs, ii) timelines, and iii) data use, and the chapter has highlighted possible ways to avoid these pitfalls. The chapter has described a specific application of the outlined method, by which relevance is being restored to corporate responsibility research; the obtained results provide a very different description of corporate practice from that presented in research using traditional data gathering methods.

This chapter has focused on the academic implications of the developed research method. However, TNC managers interested in moving behind the smokescreens in developing countries are well advised to learn from the academic failure to describe corporate practice, since TNCs and their monitoring organisations tend to use methods that are similar to, or even less sophisticated than, those used by researchers to describe corporate practice (cf. Burnett and Mahon, 2001; O'Rourke, 2002; Florini, 2003; French and Wokutch, 2005). Consequently, there will continue to be constant media "scandals" regarding TNCs' inability to attain the corporate responsibility performance defined in their policy documents, since NGOs and unions will continue to use more appropriate methods for collecting empirical data than those of TNCs and their monitoring organisations. Even if TNCs wanted to accurately describe the working conditions at their and their suppliers' factories – and some TNCs genuinely seem to want to do this (cf. Ählström and Egels-Zandén, 2007; Egels-Zandén, 2007) – their methods render them incapable of doing so. Therefore, as long as TNCs continue to use their current monitoring methods, they will always have less accurate descriptions of working conditions in developing countries than those of NGOs and unions, making them unable to assess or change working conditions even if they wanted to.

However, for several reasons, unannounced, unofficial, and off-site interviews with employees might not be the best way to conduct TNC-led monitoring, so academia–NGO-led monitoring is likely not an alternative to regular TNC monitoring. However, via academia–NGO collaboration, TNCs could occasionally monitor their own monitoring, testing the adequacy of their current methods. Hence, rather than monitoring the *monitors* as such, for example, as Dara O'Rourke (2002) did in his study of monitors at PricewaterhouseCoopers, academia–NGO collaboration provides a method for TNCs to monitor the *monitoring*, i.e., to monitor the adequacy of the results of TNCs' own monitoring. In this way, TNCs could improve their own monitoring methods and potentially alter their own and their suppliers' corporate practices, minimising the risk of future media "scandals".

APPENDIX – INTERVIEW GUIDE[1]

1. *Personal Information*
    1.1. What is your name (optional)?
    1.2. How old are you?
    1.3. What department do you work in?
    1.4. Where are you from?
    1.5. How long have you been working in the factory?
    1.6. What are you employed as?
2. *Factory Information*
    2.1. What is the name of the factory?
    2.2. What products are produced in it?
    2.3. Who are the major clients of the factory?
    2.4. When are the factory's peak and low seasons? (Follow up: Specify months)
3. *Workforce information*
    3.1. How many workers are there in the factory? What is the male–female ratio?
    3.2. What different departments are there in the factory?
    3.3. What is the age range of employees? Mean age?
    3.4. At what age are workers recruited? (Follow up: Are there any workers under 16 years old working in the factory?)
4. *Wages, working hours, and vacation*
    4.1. Could you explain the organisation of working hours used at the factory? How many hours do you work per day/week? (Follow up: Please specify the differences between weekday and weekend hours, regular working hours and overtime, and peak and low season working hours)
    4.2. How many days off do you have per week/month?
    4.3. Could you explain the wage system of the factory? (Follow up: Does the factory use a piece-work rate or a time rate? Are there differences between departments?)

---

[1] The predefined follow-up questions are indicated in by either "If so" or "Follow up".

4.4. Is overtime compensation provided? If so, how?
4.5. What is the average monthly income of the workers? (Follow up: Please specify the differences between the peak and low seasons)
4.6. What happens if the factory does not have enough work for the workers in the low season?
4.7. Are workers guaranteed a certain minimum income every month?

5. *Employment*
    5.1. Does management sign a written contract with workers? If so, are you given a copy of the contract?
    5.2. What is the average length of the contract?
    5.3. Does the management provide health check-ups for workers? If so, how often?
    5.4. Can workers resign from the factory at will (observing the legal term of notice)?
    5.5. Does the factory ever fine or punish workers? If so, when?

6. *Insurance and welfare*
    6.1. Does the factory buy social insurance for its workers? (Follow up: Please specify whether this includes old age, medical, unemployment, and industrial injury insurance)
    6.2. If so, is anything deducted from wages for each type of coverage? If so, how much?

7. *Occupational safety and health (OSH) conditions*
    7.1. Could you tell us about the industrial accident situation in the factory?
    7.2. Does management pay compensation for injuries or occupational diseases related to work?
    7.3. Which department is most likely to have industrial accidents?
    7.4. Is a clinic provided at the factory? If so, how much does it charge for its services?
    7.5. Have you received any occupational training, either before or during employment?
    7.6. Is there any fire prevention training for new and current workers?
    7.7. Are there fire drills at the work place and in the dormitories? If so, how often?
    7.8. Do you know how to get to the fire exits if there is a fire?
    7.9. Is there any formal OSH training for new and current workers?
    7.10. What is the daily production quota in your department during peak season? What happens if you fail to meet the quota?

8. *Code of conduct auditing*
    8.1. Do any clients perform social audits inside the factory?
    8.2. If so, could you tell us how such an audit is conducted? (Follow up: How often do social auditors come? What would they check? Do they talk to workers? How does factory management prepare before the social auditors come?)
    8.3. Have you heard of codes of conduct? If so, how can workers access the details of the codes of conduct?
    8.4. Do you think that social audits can help improve factory conditions?

REFERENCES

Ählström, J., & Egels-Zandén, N. (2007). The Processes of Defining Corporate Responsibility: A Study of Swedish Garment Retailers' Responsibility. *Business Strategy and the Environment* (in press).

Asia Monitor Research Centre. (1996). *Labour Rights Report on Hong Kong Invested Toy Factories in China*. Hong Kong: Asia Monitor Research Centre.

Asia Monitor Research Centre. (1997). *Labour Rights Report on Hong Kong Invested Toy Factories in China No. 2*. Hong Kong: Asia Monitor Research Centre.

Boyd, H. W. Jr., & Westfall, R. (1965) Interviewer Bias Revisited. *Journal of Marketing Research, 2*(1), 58-63.

Bryman, A. (2004). *Social Research Methods*. Oxford: Oxford University Press.

Burnett, E., & Mahon Jr., J. (2001). Monitoring Compliance with International Labor Standards. *Challenge*, March-April, 51-72.

Callon, M. (Ed.) (1998). *The Laws of the Markets*. Oxford: Blackwell Publishers.

Chan, A. (1998). Labor Standards and Human Rights: The Case of Chinese Workers Under Market Socialism. *Human Rights Quarterly, 20*(4), 886-904.

Chan, A. (2000). Globalization, China's Free (Read Bonded) Labour Market, and the Chinese Trade Unions. *Asia Pacific Business Review, 6*(3/4), 260-281.

Chan, A., & Senser, R. A. (1997). China's Troubled Workers. *Foreign Affairs, 76*(2), 104-117.

Chan, A., & Ross, R. J. S. (2003). Racing to the Bottom: International Trade without a Social Clause. *Third World Quarterly, 24*(6), 1011-1028.

Christerson, B., & Appelbaum, R. P. (1995). Global and Local Subcontracting: Space, Ethnicity, and the Organization of Apparel Production. *World Development, 23*(8), 1363–1374.

Cooke, F. L. (2004). Foreign Firms in China: Modelling HRM in a Chinese Toy Manufacturing Corporation. *Human Resource Management Journal, 14*(3), 31-52.

Cooney, S., Lindsey, R., Mitchell, R., & Zhu, Y. (Eds.). *Law and Labour Market Regulation in Eastern Asia*. London: Routledge.

Davis, D. W., & Silver, B. D. (2003). Stereotype Threat and Race of Interviewer Effects in a Survey on Political Knowledge. *American Journal of Political Science, 47*(1), 33-45.

Doig, A., & Wilson, J. (1998). The Effectiveness of Codes of Conduct. *Business Ethics: A European Review, 7*(3), 140-149.

Egels-Zandén, N. (2007). Suppliers' Compliance with MNCs' Codes of Conduct: Behind the Scenes at Chinese Toy Suppliers. *Journal of Business Ethics* (in press).

Egels-Zandén, N., & Hyllman, P. (2006). Exploring the Effects of Union-NGO Relationships on Corporate Responsibility: The Case of the Swedish Clean Clothes Campaign. *Journal of Business Ethics, 64*(3), 303-316.

Egels-Zandén, N., & Hyllman, P. (2007). Evaluating Strategies for Negotiating Workers' Rights in Transnational Corporations: The Effects of Codes of Conduct and Global Agreements on Workplace Democracy. *Journal of Business Ethics* (in press).

Emmelhainz, M. A., & Adams, R. J. (1999). The Apparel Industry Response to 'Sweetshop' Concerns: A Review and Analysis of Codes of Conduct. *Journal of Supply Chain Management, 35*(3), 51-57.

Ezzamel, M., Hoskin, K., & Macve, R. (1990). Managing it All by Numbers: A Review of Johnson and Kaplan's 'Relevance Lost'. *Accounting and Business Research, 20*(78): 153-166.

Florini, A. (2003). Business and Global Governance: The Growing Role of Corporate Codes of Conduct. *Brookings Review, 21*(2), 4-8.

Freeman, R. E. (1999). Response: Divergent Stakeholder Theory. *Academy of Management Review, 24*(2), 233–236.

French, J. L., & Wokutch, R. E. (2005). Child Workers, Globalization and International Business Ethics: A Case Study in Brazil's Export-oriented Shoe Industry. *Business Ethics Quarterly, 15*(4), 615-640.

Frenkel, S. (2001). Globalization, Athletic Footwear Commodity Chains and Employment Relations in China. *Organization Studies, 22*(4), 531-562.

Frenkel, S., & Kim, S. (2004). Corporate Codes of Labour Practice and Employment Relations in Sports Shoe Contractor Factories in South Korea. *Asia Pacific Journal of Human Resources, 42*(1), 6-31.

Frenkel, S., & Scott, D. (2002). Compliance, Collaboration, and Codes of Labor Practice: The adidas Connection. *California Management Review, 45*(1), 29-49.

Gallin, D. (2000). *Trade Unions and NGOs: A Necessary Partnership for Social Development*. Geneva: United Nations Research Institute for Social Development.

Gibbons, M., Limoges, C., Nowotny, H., Schwartzman, S., Scott, P., & Trow, M. (1994). *The New Production of Knowledge: The Dynamics of Science and Research in Contemporary Societies*. London: Sage.

Graafland, J. J. (2002). Sourcing Ethics in the Textile Sector: The Case of C&A. *Business Ethics: A European Review, 11*(3), 282-294.

Hale, A. (2004) Beyond the Barriers: New Forms of Labour Internationalism. *Development in Practice, 14*(1–2), 158–162.

Hammer, N. (2004). International Framework Agreements: Overview and Key Issues. working paper presented at the *Industrial Relations in Europe Conference*, Utrecht 2004.

Hathcote, J., & Nam, I.-J. (1999). Advantages of Sourcing Apparel from China, Taiwan, South Korea and Mexico. *International Trade Journal, 13*(2), 157–185.

Healy, M., & Iles, J. (2002). The Establishment and Enforcement of Codes. *Journal of Business Ethics, 39*(1/2), 117-124.

Hemphill, T. (2004). Monitoring Global Corporate Citizenship: Industry Self-regulation at a Crossroads. *Journal of Corporate Citizenship, 14*, 81-95.

Hendry, J. (2001). Economic Contracts versus Social Relationships as a Foundation for Normative Stakeholder Theory. *Business Ethics: A European Review, 10*(3), 223–232.

Hong Kong Christian Industrial Committee. (2000a). *McDonald's Toys: Do They Manufacture Fun or More Exploitation?*. Hong Kong: Hong Kong Christian Industrial Committee.

Hong Kong Christian Industrial Committee. (2000b). *McDonald's Toys: Do They Manufacture Fun or More Exploitation? Follow up Report on Pleasure Tech*. Hong Kong: Hong Kong Christian Industrial Committee.

Hong Kong Christian Industrial Committee. (2000c). *Beware of Mickey: Disney Sweatshops in Southern China*. Hong Kong: Hong Kong Christian Industrial Committee.

Hong Kong Christian Industrial Committee. (2001). *How Hasbro, McDonald's, Mattel and Disney Manufacture Their Toys*. Hong Kong: Hong Kong Christian Industrial Committee.

Hong Kong Christian Industrial Committee. (2002). *Working Conditions of Soccer and Football Workers in Mainland China*. Hong Kong: Hong Kong Christian Industrial Committee.

Hong Kong Christian Industrial Committee and Asia Monitor Research Centre. (1997). *Working Conditions in the Sports Shoe Industry in China: Making Shoes for Nike and Reebok*. Hong Kong: Asia Monitor Resource Centre.

Hong Kong Christian Industrial Committee, & CAFOD. (1999). *Mulan's Sisters: Working for Disney is No Fairy Tale*. Hong Kong: Hong Kong Christian Industrial Committee.

Hong Kong Coalition for the Safe Production of Toys. (2003). *Unfair Trade for Unfair toys. .* Hong Kong: Hong Kong Christian Industrial Committee.

Johnson, H. T., & Kaplan, R. S. (1987). *Relevance Lost: The Rise and Fall of Management Accounting*. Boston, MA: Harvard Business School Press.

Jones, M. T. (2005). The Transnational Corporation, Corporate Social Responsibility and the 'Outsourcing' Debate. *Journal of American Academy of Business, 6*(2), 91–97.

Kaler, J. (2003). Differentiating Stakeholder Theories. *Journal of Business Ethics*, 46(1), 71–83.

Kolk, A., & van Tulder, R. (2002). The Effectiveness of Self-Regulation: Corporate Codes of Conduct and Child Labour. *European Management Journal, 20*(3), 260-271.

Kvale, S. (1996). *InterViews: An Introduction to Qualitative Research Interviewing*. Thousand Oaks, CA: Sage Publications.

Langer, B. (2004). The Business of Branded Enchantment: Ambivalence and Disjuncture in the Global Children's Culture. *Journal of Consumer Culture, 4*(2), 251-277.

Leadbeater, C. & Miller, P. (2004). *The Pro-Am Revolution: How Enthusiasts are Changing Our Economy and Society*. London: Demos.

Lee, C. K. (1998). *Gender and the South China Miracle: Two Worlds of Factory Women*. Berkely, CA: University of California Press.

Lee, C. K. (1999). From Organized Dependence to Disorganized Despotism: Changing Labour Regimes in Chinese Factories. *The China Quarterly, 57*, 44-71.

Lee, O., & Lim, J. (2001). Progressive Capitalism or Reactionary Socialism? Progressive Labour Policy, Ageing Marxism, and Unrepentant Early Capitalism in the Chinese Industrial Revolution. *Business Ethics: A European Review, 10*(2), 97-107.

Liew, L. H. (2001). What is to be Done? WTO, Globalisation and State-Labour Relations in China. *Australian Journal of Politics and History, 47*(1), 39-60.

Meyer, J., & Rowan, B. (1977). Institutionalized Organizations: Formal Structure as Myth and Ceremony. *The American Journal of Sociology, 83*(2), 340-363.

Murphy, D., & Mathew, D. (2001). *Nike and Global Labour Practices: A case study prepared for the New Academy of Business Innovation Network for Socially Responsible Business*. Bristol: New Academy of Business.

Noreen, E. (1987). Commentary. *Accounting Horizons, 1*(4): 110-116.

O'Rourke, D. (1997). *Smoke from a Hired Gun: A Critique of Nike's Labor and Environmental Auditing in Vietnam as Performed by Ernst & Young*. San Francisco, CA: Transnational Resource and Action Center.

O'Rourke, D. (2000). *Monitoring the Monitors: A Critque of PricewaterhouseCoopers (PwC) Labor Monitoring*. Boston, MA: Massachusetts Institute of Technology.

O'Rourke, D. (2002). Monitoring the Monitors: A Critique of Third-Party Labor Monitoring. In R. Jenkins, R. Pearson, & G. Seyfang (Eds.), *Corporate Responsibility and Labour Rights: Codes of Conduct in the Global Economy* (pp. 196-208). London: Earthscan.

O'Rourke, D. (2003). Outsourcing Regulation: Analyzing Nongovernmental Systems of Labor Standards and Monitoring. *The Policy Study Journal, 31*(1), 1-29.

O'Rourke, D., & Brown, G. (1999). *Beginning to Just Do It: Current Workplace and Environmental Conditions at the Tae Kwang Vina Nike Shoe Factory in Vietnam*. Boston, MA: Massachusetts Institute of Technology.

Pegg, S., & Wilson, A. (2003). Corporations, Conscience and Conflict: Assessing NGO Reports on the Private Sector Role in African Resource Conflicts. *Third World Quarterly, 24*(6), 1179-1189.

Pfeffer, J., & Salancik, G. R. (1978). *The External Control of Organizations: A Resource Dependency Perspective*. New York, NY: Harper and Row.

Povey, E. R. (2004). Trade Unions and Women's NGOs: Diverse Civil Society Organisations in Iran. *Development in Practice, 14*(1-2), 254-266.

Prieto, M., & Quinteros, C. (2004). Never the Twain Shall Meet? Women's organisations and trade unions in the *Maquila* Industry in Central America. *Development in Practice, 14*(1–2), 149–157.

Radin, T. J. (2004). The Effectiveness of Global Codes of Conduct: Role Models That Make Sense. *Business and Society Review, 109*(4), 415-447.

Riisgaard, L. (2005). Industrial Framework Agreements: A New Model of Securing Workers Rights?. *Industrial Relations, 44*(4), 707-737.

Roberts, S. (2003). Supply Chain Specific? Understanding the Patchy Success of Ethical Sourcing Initiatives. *Journal of Business Ethics, 44*(2/3), 159-170.

Segovia, J. J. (1990). Book Review: Relevance Lost: The Rise and Fall of Management Accounting. *Contemporary Accounting Research, 6*(2): 955-961.

Sethi, S. P. (2002). Standards for Corporate Conduct in the International Arena: Challenges and Opportunities for Multinational Corporations. *Business and Society Review, 107*(1), 20-40.

Snyder, F. (1999). Governing Economic Globalisation: Global Legal Pluralism and European Law. *European Law Journal, 5*(4), 334-374.

Solomons, D. (1987). Book Review: Relevance Lost. *Accounting Review, 62*(4): 846-848.

Spar, D. L., & La Mure, L. T. (2003). The Power of Activism: Assessing the Impact of NGOs on Global Business. *California Management Review, 45*(3), 78-101.

Suchman, M. C. (1995). Managing Legitimacy: Strategic and Institutional Approaches. *Academy of Management Review, 20*(3), 571-610.

Swanson, D. L. (1999). Toward an Integrative Theory of Business and Society: A Research Strategy for Corporate Social Performance. *Academy of Management Review, 24*(3), 506-521.

Taylor, T. (2005). In Defence of Outsourcing. *CATO Journal, 25*(2), 367–377

Tracy, J. (1999). Whistle while You Work: The Disney Company and the Global Division of Labor. *Journal of Communication Inquiry, 23*(4), 374-389.

Valor, C. (2005). Corporate Social Responsibility and Corporate Citizenship: Towards Corporate Accountability. *Business & Society Review, 110*(2), 191-212.

van Tulder, R., & Kolk, A. (2001). Multinationality and Corporate Ethics: Codes of Conduct in the Sporting Goods Industry. *Journal of International Business Studies, 32*(2), 267-283.

Whawell, P. (1998). The Ethics of Pressure Groups. *Business Ethics: A European Review, 7*(3), 178-181.

Winstanley, D., Clark, J., & Leeson, H. (2002). Approaches to Child Labour in the Supply Chain. *Business Ethics: A European Review, 11*(3), 210-223.

In: Business Ethics in Focus
Editor: Laura A. Parrish, pp. 247-258

ISBN: 978-1-60021-684-8
© 2007 Nova Science Publishers, Inc.

Chapter 10

THE EMPLOYMENT RELATIONSHIP – THE MEANING AND IMPORTANCE OF VOLUNTARINESS

Anders J. Persson[*]

Department of Philosophy and the History of Technology
Royal Institute of Technology, SE-100 44 Stockholm, Sweden

ABSTRACT

This paper explores the viewpoint that the voluntariness of the contracting parties in an employment relationship has substantial value. One overarching issue concerns the meaning of voluntariness in the employment context, and another issue is its normative importance. With respect to the former issue, the paper proposes conditions that are required for the contracting parties' voluntariness. However, I argue that exactly where the line should be drawn between voluntary and non–voluntary agreements in this context is indeterminate. Concerning the latter issue, the paper claims that even if we were able to draw such a line, it would tell us nothing about the voluntariness condition's normative importance, or about how much normative weight we shall assign to its fulfilment in the workplace context. Finally, the paper argues that the normative theory most suitable for support of the voluntariness condition is of a contractualist brand.

Keywords: contract of employment, contractualism, ethics, rights, utilitarianism, voluntariness

1. INTRODUCTION

An essential feature of employment contracts is that work should be voluntarily undertaken. This is also an entrenched part of the concept of free labour. The work contract relationship between a person and an employing entity can be described as a voluntary bargain between these parties. According to employment law as well as many other laws,

[*] Phone: +46 73018447; Fax: +46 8 790 95 17; ap@infra.kth.se

however, it is not legal to agree upon everything.[1] The core of these ideas rests on conditions concerning the contracting parties' voluntariness which put restrictions on both the form and the content of an employment relationship.

The aim of this article is to analyse a simple and quite uncontroversial statement, namely that the contracting parties' voluntariness in an employment relationship has substantial value, and due to that it should be ensured. One overarching issue concerns the meaning of that statement, and another is what normative importance we shall assign to it. This analysis will show that the contracting parties' voluntariness demands that certain conditions be fulfilled, but that it is indeterminate exactly where the line should be drawn between voluntary and non–voluntary agreements in this context. Concerning the latter issue, it is claimed that even if we were able to draw such a line, it would tell us nothing about the voluntariness condition's normative importance, or about how much normative weight we shall assign to the fulfilment of its conditions in the workplace context. Furthermore, it is argued that the best suited normative theory in support of the voluntariness condition is of a contractualist brand.

In Section 2 I briefly characterise the relationship between an employee and an employing entity. Section 3 discusses the meaning of the voluntariness condition and proposes sub–conditions for its validity. Section 4 investigates the voluntariness condition's normative status in relation to rights–ethicist, utilitarian and contractualist positions. A critical analysis of each position's capacity to support the voluntariness condition is developed, and it is argued that only a contractualist approach is suitable for this purpose. Section 5 contains my conclusions.

2. THE EMPLOYER–EMPLOYEE RELATIONSHIP

To begin with, a clarification of the relationship between ethical and legal matters may be useful. The legislative basis for the employment relationship is, of course, intimately connected to issues about what purpose employment is expected to serve in modern society. In this we can also see the connection between legal and moral issues, which David M. Beatty (1980) illustrates very clearly by an interesting argument. He claims that employment serves the purposes of being (1) the primary means by which society's productive output is generated, and (2) the vital means through which individuals' identity is shaped and expressed. He contends, however, that the prevailing contract theory of employment grants significance only to the former purpose, and therefore is at odds with our social intuitions and convictions about the nature of employment. In this respect legal contract theory concerning employment *ought* to be reformed, according to him. The "ought" here expresses no doubt a normative standpoint, and it is thus reasonable to conclude that issues of this sort primarily concern ethical considerations rather than legal ones.

In legal contexts the relationship between an employer and an employee is determined by several branches of labour law. "Individual employment relations" and the making, modification and termination of individual employment relations and the resulting obligations of the parties, as well as certain aspects of promotion, transfer, dismissal procedures and

---

[1] In addition to legal regulations, much of the contract's contents can originate in collective agreements with labour unions or in other forms of negotiations within companies.

compensation are all treated by labour law. From a historical perspective, the law on these matters was in several countries at one time described as the law of master and servant (Steinfeld, 1991). It implied a contractual relation in which one party agreed to be under the control of the other; the servant was bound to obey orders not only on what work he would execute but also on the details of the work and the manner of its execution. The master, on the other hand, had to pay a wage and grant certain minimum conditions for the worker's protection. As the law developed, various statutory incidents began to limit freedom of contract (Steinfeld, 1991). In most Western countries the individual employment relationship continues to be the subject matter of labour law, which contains a general legal framework for such contracts.

A general tendency in the modern development of labour law has been the strengthening of statutory requirements and collective contractual relations – often at the expense of rights and obligations created by individual employment relationships. The latter's remaining importance depends, of course, on the degree of personal freedom of both employer and employee in the given society. This in turn depends on, among other things, the current economic situation in the society in question.

To sum up, the "contract of employment" is mainly a legal concept that refers to a certain jurisdiction. The content of such legislation, covering paid work, varies between countries. It should also be noted that there are structural varieties in the relationships that are subject to such jurisdiction. Hence, in spite of the fact that both traditional wage-earner work (the so-called Fordist model is an example of this) and the work of self-employed entrepreneurs concern paid work, the important structural differences between them have to be reflected in labour law. Presently legal scholars discuss, among other things, how these different forms of relationships should best be accommodated in future legislation (Freedland, 2003). Such structural differences are certainly important and well worth elaboration also from an ethical point of view, but because my focus here is on what the parties can legitimately agree upon in general, structural issues of that kind will be seen in the rest of this paper as a separate issue. Furthermore, the analysis makes use of a convenient and common simplification: the company, the organisation, the person, etc., which stands in an employment relationship to an employed person, will be treated as a single entity, in short, the "employing entity." My treatment of the issue of what the parties in the employer–employee relationship can legitimately agree upon will be moral rather than legal; i.e., I will not investigate the contents of current laws but instead will discuss what moral rights and other moral considerations the laws in these areas should be based on.

3. VOLUNTARINESS – THE NATURE OF THE CONCEPTUAL PROBLEM

It seems reasonable to say that a demarcation criterion between slavery and "free labour" is the worker's voluntary decision to enter into, and his right to terminate, his relationship with an employing entity. Let us call this basic reference point for modern work legislation "the voluntariness condition." Given that the contracting parties' voluntariness has substantial value, and due to that it should be ensured, what, then, does it mean to voluntarily accept a certain job and its terms within the frame of the employment relationship? In order to answer this question we need to investigate what conditions should be fulfilled in order for a person to have made a voluntary decision in this context.

Such conditions can be formulated in different terms. Harald Ofstad (1961) has pointed out that they can be formulated in neurophysiological terms as well as in mentalistic or behavioural terms. In conformity with his exposition, a combination of the latter two alternatives seems to be best suited here, because "decision" should not imply that a decision must be narrowly directed only toward actions. Ofstad's suggestion is that a *decision* (to, for example, enter a contract of employment) must involve (a) that the person in question is aware of at least two different alternatives, (b) that a deliberation to some degree has taken place, and (c) that the person has arrived at a judgement whereby he commits himself to the chosen alternative (Ofstad, 1961, pp. 16–19). Let us call such a decision, in which these conditions are fulfilled, a *genuine decision*. An employee, E, and an employing entity, EE, have voluntarily entered into a relationship with each other only if the following condition is fulfilled: (1) *E's and EE's decisions are genuine decisions*.

For a decision to be voluntary, however, something more must be added. The condition above leaves open a wide array of circumstances when an individual's decision, due to facts about the individual in question, cannot be considered voluntary. Hence, for an action to be voluntary the agent should be competent (not an infant, not insane, not severely retarded, etc.). If this is true, a second condition on voluntary decisions in the workplace context is: (2) *Both E and EE have statuses as competent bargaining parties*.[2]

Furthermore, it has been proposed that the decision should not result from temporarily distorting states or circumstances (including impulsiveness, fatigue, intoxication, severe time constraint, powerful passion, pain, etc.) or from subtle manipulation (Feinberg, 1986). This gives rise to two additional conditions: (3) *E's and EE's decisions do not result from temporarily distorting states or circumstances*, and (4) *E's and EE's decisions do not result from subtle manipulation*.

Aristotle, for instance, claimed that voluntary actions are those performed neither under compulsion nor by reason of ignorance of the circumstances. Although reasonable as conditions for voluntary decision, Aristotle's suggestion concerning compulsion is problematic in application to the workplace context and also to other contexts. To begin with, "compulsion" may reveal itself in several forms. A decision can be forced of an evil less severe than the one threatened, or forced of a lesser evil than one expected from a natural source. Coercive offers and coercive pressures are other forms of compulsions that can disqualify a decision as voluntary (Feinberg, 1986). However, an essential condition for a decision (in the workplace context) to be voluntary is that (5) *E's and EE's decisions do not result from undue coercion*.

Aristotle's second condition, concerning ignorance of the circumstances, is even more problematic in application to the workplace situation. This is because ignorance of factual as well as likely circumstances and consequences would not lead to violation of the voluntariness condition according to this suggestion, while demanding that the (prospective)

---

[2] This condition may suggest that mentally retarded people not should be allowed to enter employment relationships, which would conflict with general moral opinions as well as jurisdiction in most countries. An established practice is to apply a combination of consent of the employee, consent of the guardian and special control of the society in question. Issues concerning how such cases ought to be handled are certainly important, but in the rest of this essay I will make a convenient simplification and treat the bargaining party as a single entity.

employee have full information about the work, its terms and the future overall working situation appears unreasonable. Because neither a full prediction of the future working situation nor knowledge about all facts about the work are tenable conditions for fulfilment of the voluntariness condition, ignorance of the circumstances must be admitted to a certain degree. In light of this a less strict interpretation of Aristotle's second clause is suggested: (6) *Both E and EE have information, to a sufficient degree, about the work, its terms, the likely future working situation and the other party's ability to fulfil his obligations.*

In conclusion: that an employee, E, and an employing entity, EE, in situation S voluntarily have entered into a relationship with each other may tentatively mean that the following conditions are fulfilled:

1. E's and EE's decisions are genuine decisions.
2. Both E and EE have status as competent bargaining parties.
3. E's and EE's decisions do not result from temporarily distorting states or circumstances.
4. E's and EE's decisions do not result from subtle manipulation.
5. E's and EE's decisions do not result from undue coercion.
6. Both E and EE have information, to a sufficient degree, about the work, its terms, the likely future working situation and the other party's ability to fulfil his obligations.

It is obvious that the application of these criteria to concrete employment cases may be very difficult. It is far from clear where exactly the line should be drawn between voluntary and non–voluntary agreements in this context. Furthermore, if Feinberg's (1986) claim that the model of perfectly voluntary choice is elusive is right, to what degree shall the conditions above be fulfilled in order to fulfil the voluntariness condition in the workplace context?

Because of these problems it may be more fruitful to avoid a binary division between voluntary and involuntary, and instead talk about decisions as more or less voluntary with reference to the criteria above, with maximally voluntary decisions at the one end and fully non–voluntary decisions at the other. Grave forms of slavery would thus be placed at the latter end, and decisions that meet all the criteria above land at the former.

This means that "voluntariness" is not, *pace* several libertarians, to be interpreted as a binary concept. The suggestion is instead that an agent's decision to enter an employment contract can be voluntary to different degrees. In the work contract context, important factors that impact the degree of voluntariness are different sorts of coercion or duress, disturbances in the agent's emotional life, positive/negative emotions toward business aims and job tasks and the potential employee's knowledge of the relevant aspects of the job and its tasks. Some of these factors are partly under the employer's control.

4. PREFERENCES VS. THE GOOD – THREE THEORIES

It is possible to describe a voluntary decision as one that reflects the individual's (integrated) preferences. Proponents of the voluntariness condition may insist on its primacy due to the value of an individual's existing preferences; such preferences have intrinsic value and their realization should therefore be ensured. Another stance, though, is that primacy should be accorded to the good of the individual rather than to his or her preferences. The value of the individual's pursual of his preferences in relation to his good or well–being can thus be accounted for in several ways: (1) The value of self–determination is seen as purely instrumental, and it can be derived from how conducive it is to the agent's good. (2) Self–determination is not a purely instrumental value to the agent's well–being, but has an intrinsic value and is more important than personal well–being. (3) Self–determination has intrinsic value but should be balanced against personal well–being because neither has priority over the other.[3]

It seems clear that paternalistic interventions are admitted according to the first interpretation, whereas the opposite will hold according to the second. The third can be seen as semi–paternalistic, because of its more limited potential to admit paternalistic interventions.

If we transfer this discussion to the employment context and its contracting parties, it appears far from obvious which of the three alternatives is valid. This seems to be the case even when the criteria for voluntary decision stated above are satisfied.

The voluntariness condition's normative status will differ according to different moral theories. Therefore it may be useful to consider what three different theories imply about the voluntariness of the employment contract's contents: the rights-ethicist, the utilitarian and the contractualist.

4.1. The Rights–Ethicist View

According to the rights–ethicist view, as developed, e.g., by Robert Nozick[4], individual rights are inviolable; people have fundamental rights that very strongly restrict how others are allowed to act toward them. Rational and autonomous agents have corresponding moral duties to respect other agents' rights. An important feature in this kind of theory is that negative rights are fundamental. You are, for example, not allowed to kill a person (given that the person does not want that), because then the person's right to life is violated. However, you do not violate any right of your fellow in omitting helping him to the effect that he dies. The latter case imposes no moral duties because there are no such things as fundamental positive rights, according to Nozick.

An essential right in most rights–ethicist theories is the right to one's property. I am allowed to do whatever I prefer to do with what I own (as long as I do not frustrate anyone else's rights). This means that we can transfer what we own to others, after which those to whom it has been transferred own what was transferred. Moreover, autonomous agents have unrestricted rights to make commitments with other autonomous agents.

---

[3] See Feinberg (1986). In addition he presents a fourth view according to which the relationship between self–determination and an individual's good is an invariant correspondence relation.

[4] It may appear far too narrow to describe the rights-ethicist view only in Nozick's version of it. Several other normative theories often are labeled as "rights-ethicist." The theories developed by, for example, W. D. Ross, J. J. Thomson and even Kant, constitute such examples. These theories may give a normative status to the voluntariness-condition different from the Nozickian version's. The latter version, however, is chosen here because it is the most straightforward one; in light of the Nozickian version of the rights-ethicist view it will be easier to grasp the general implications of voluntariness and employment contract contents from this normative direction, even if it is likely that some other version of the view better accommodates some of our moral intuitions.

In conclusion, from the rights–ethicist position it seems to follow that it is legitimate to make any type of agreement within the frame of an employment relationship, as long as no fundamental rights of the parties or other persons are frustrated. This means, among other things, that there is nothing special about this kind of relationship compared to other kinds of relationships within which agents make commitments with each other.

On its face the rights–ethicist view is perhaps the most natural candidate for strongly supporting the voluntariness condition, because, as mentioned above, the core of this view is that adults have unrestricted moral rights to make commitments with each other, without interference, as long as no rights are frustrated. However, it should first be noted that even the rights–ethicist has to face the challenge of specifying the preconditions for the exercise of such commitments as autonomous decisions. Above, we found that a concept of voluntariness that amounts to a matter of degree is preferable in the present context. Such a concept corresponds very badly with libertarian thought.

Given the assumptions that everyone owns his own person and body and that everyone has an unrestricted right to make commitments, an important problem emerges: the libertarian framework that Nozick suggests imposes very few limitations on what commitments agents can make. This has counter-intuitive consequences. Hence, as long as no rights are violated, agents are allowed to sell themselves as slaves.

> If we institute such a permanently voluntary general framework, are we not, to some extent, ruling out certain possible choices? [...] The comparable question about an individual is whether a free system will allow him to sell himself into slavery. I believe that it would (Nozick, 1974, p. 331).

This conclusion is certainly at odds with the widespread conviction that slavery is unacceptable. This does not, of course, necessarily mean that the conclusion is wrong. But the opposite of the right-ethicist's claim, that nobody can own a person or a person's body (not even the person himself), seems from an intuitive point of view at least equally plausible. Anyhow, in the Nozickian version of this view, the voluntariness condition as a demarcation criterion between slavery and free labour appears to be pointless; there is no problem with slavery, according to Nozick, as long as the agent in question voluntarily has agreed to it.

Even from a more restricted rights-ethicist position, e.g., one that does not allow selling oneself as a slave, it is hard to see that any general limitations on the employer–employee relationship will follow. The core of this view is that adults have unrestricted moral rights to make commitments with each other, without interference, for instance, by the state, as long as no rights are frustrated. The very core of the view is thus at odds with the idea that certain things will hold for contracts of employment in general and that there are certain contents which all such contracts ought to contain.

It can be argued that a reasonable conception of autonomy entails not only negative rights, i.e., freedom from external constraints on the individual's right to self-determination, but also positive rights, for example, access to economic opportunities and resources that make the agent's self–fulfilling decisions possible (Dworkin, 1981). Let us take an example to illustrate this point. A person living in an area with a scarcity of economic resources and job opportunities might lack substantial positive rights, which are necessary to fulfil the autonomy he requires. One of the conditions of voluntary decision, namely, that it does not result from undue coercion, would not be fulfilled in this example because one of the parties lacks choices that are normally realizable in a more competitive working environment. This argument, however, may not convince the straightforward rights–ethicist because of that theory's insistence that individual rights are exclusively negative.

In conclusion, a rights–ethicist position of Nozick's brand gives substantial weight to workers' (as well as other people capable of making decisions) right to make voluntary decisions. However, its potential to give substantial normative weight to the voluntariness condition in the employment contract is highly doubtful.

4.2. The Utilitarian View

The utilitarian view, as developed by celebrated philosophers such as Jeremy Bentham, John Stuart Mill, George Edward Moore and Henry Sidgwick, is the view that an action is morally right if and only if it produces at least as much utility for all (sentient beings) affected by the action as any alternative action the person could do instead.[5] According to act-utilitarianism, the most straightforward version of utilitarianism, the criterion of an action's rightness is that it maximizes utility.

Supposing that employment is defined by legal systems, then, according to the utilitarian view, the legally acceptable employment relationships are those that satisfy the utilitarian criterion of rightness. If we apply this view to the employer–employee relationship at least two possible versions of the utilitarian view are possible. First, the utilitarian view of employment could be that a legal system should be devised in such a way as to satisfy the utilitarian criterion of rightness; i.e., the relevant maximization of utility is only that of the people within the jurisdiction of the legal system in question. According to this view, the relevant consideration for the evaluation of a legal system is the amount of utility obtained by the people within its jurisdiction. This version is thus restricted to a certain jurisdiction. A second version of the utilitarian view is simply to interpret it more literally; the relevant consideration for the evaluation of a legal system is the amount of utility it produces – for all sentient beings, over the whole history of earlier and future sentient beings.

The first (restricted) view is not a utilitarian view in a proper sense. Nevertheless, in opposition to normative views that state fundamental rights and duties, it is consequentialist; what matters are the consequences of adopting and applying certain restrictions on the contents of the relationship between an employer and an employee.

The utilitarian view, whether it is restricted or unrestricted, may intuitively give some support to the voluntariness condition; it can be claimed that its fulfilment leads to overall best consequences. But this position is also impaired by difficulties. First, the value of voluntariness will be only an instrumental value, depending on how it contributes to the contracting parties' well–being. Voluntariness as such thus has no substantial weight, but can be outweighed by other values that better promote overall well–being. Second, we can never know whether preservation of the voluntariness condition is right or not, because a given legal system's total consequences cannot be calculated with any certainty. Furthermore, it is not feasible to list all possible legal systems, nor to single out any subset of them which are

---

[5] Two accounts of rightness seem to be possible according to this: "actualism" on one hand, meaning that the objectively right action would be that which actually does maximize utility, and "probabilism" on the other, that the subjectively right action would be that which maximizes expected utility.

better than the rest. As a result, it is impossible to know that the consequences of one system are at least as good (or better) than those of every alternative legal system. In spite of this we may often refer to good or bad consequences when defending the voluntariness condition. But all we can do, at best, is to make very rough and uncertain utilitarian evaluations of possible revisions of employment regulations in a given legal system. This may be very useful, but it is not what is required to provide foundations for the voluntariness condition's value in the workplace context.

4.3. Contractualism

The third theory to be considered with regard to the employer–employee relationship is contractualism. This term is rather ambiguous and has several connotations in normative ethics. The most well known modern form of contractualism is the one developed by John Rawls (in *A Theory of Justice*, 1971). According to Rawls' theory a social institution is morally justified, or fair, if it would be agreed upon by the people who are to live with it. The metaphor Rawls uses to describe the original position is "a veil of ignorance," behind which the parties to the contract do not know what their individual circumstances and individual characteristics are. We are told to assume that the participants have only a general social and psychological knowledge. Furthermore, we shall assume that their particular conceptions of the good are abstract, and that the parties are entirely self-interested and fully rational; this means that personal biases and particular bargaining positions cannot influence the agreements made "behind the veil." Because of these circumstances a contract made under such a procedure will be a fair one.

In a similar way, a system that regulates an employment relationship's contents will be fair and morally justified if it can be agreed upon behind a veil of ignorance. Another Rawlsian possibility of reaching that conclusion is that it is the outcome of a legislative process (in a well-ordered society) in accordance with a constitution that, in turn, satisfies the contractualist criterion.

The contractualist view seems to be the most attractive among the normative views discussed here, even if it too is impaired by some difficulties. According to Rawls, the (hypothetical) contract agreed upon depends upon how the contractual situation is defined and, most importantly, upon what beliefs, preferences and other psychological traits the parties to the contract are supposed to have. Concerning the value of voluntariness in the employment relationship between an employee and an employing entity, nothing in particular can be derived until these matters are fixed. And it is not apparent how they ought to be fixed; it may depend upon what the contract would be under different assumptions. Nevertheless, it seems reasonable to suppose that the parties will concentrate upon a basic constitution. This basic constitution may be such that necessary conditions for voluntariness in the employment relation would follow from assumptions about the constitution as a democratic one and Rawls' idea of primary goods. Of course, democratic decision making is not fully determined by constitutional rules because other factors, such as economic and technological developments, class structure, cultural biases and individual psychological facts about the decision makers also influence the outcome.[6] However, from the idea of primary social

---

[6] This point is emphasized by Lars Bergström (1999, p. 6).

goods, which are "...things citizens need as free and equal persons living a complete life; they are not things it is simply rational to want or desire, or to prefer or even crave" (Rawls, 2001, p. 58), it might be possible to derive the voluntariness condition. The "basic structure of society," that is, the way in which society's main institutions constitute one system of social cooperation, is, according to Rawls, the primary subject of political justice.[7] "Firms and labor unions [...] are bound by constraints arising from the principles of justice, but these constraints arise indirectly from just background institutions within which associations and groups exist, and by which the conduct of their members is restricted" (Rawls, 2001, p. 10). This idea may explain how the principles[8] emanating from "justice as fairness" regulate institutions and associations, for example, that are connected with employment relationships, indirectly from the special case of "the basic structure."[9]

If freedom of contract is to be defined as the scheme of contracting options in conjunction with the overall scheme of political and social institutions which best serves the two principles of justice, then it is reasonable to suppose that the voluntariness condition is a premise for such a scheme. According to Rawls, these institutions are assessed by the two principles of justice according to how they regulate citizens' shares of primary goods. One category of the primary goods suggested seems to specifically support the voluntariness condition, that is, "The social bases of self–respect, understood as those aspects of basic institutions normally essential if citizens are to have a lively sense of their worth as persons and to be able to advance their ends with self–confidence" (Rawls, 2001, p. 59).

Rawls stresses that the account of primary goods does not "rest solely on psychological, social or historical facts" (Rawls, 2001, p. 58). According to him, such facts presuppose a political conception of the person as free and equal, capable of being a fully cooperating member of society. *This*, political, conception is, according to Rawls, necessary to identify the appropriate list of primary goods. Primary goods are what free and equal people need as citizens and include freedom of thought, liberty of conscience, fair opportunities, reasonable expectations of income and wealth and so on (Rawls, 2001, pp. 58–59).

Rawls' idea is, furthermore, that the list of primary goods would follow from the fundamental idea of society as a fair system of cooperation. Given this premise and the implications Rawls draws from it via "the veil of ignorance," it seems reasonable to conclude that the voluntariness condition would also be implied by this. In other words, if Rawls is right, then the voluntariness condition can be derived from the idea of society as a fair system of cooperation and the list of primary goods which it produces.

---

[7] For Rawls, the basic structure is the domain of the two principles of justice.
[8] Rawls' revised version of the two principles of justice (in "Justice as fairness – A restatement") reads: "(a) Each person has the same indefeasible claim to a fully adequate scheme of equal basic liberties, which scheme is compatible with the same scheme of liberties for all; and (b) Social and economic inequalities are to satisfy two conditions: first, they are to be attached to offices and positions open to all under conditions of fair equality of opportunity; and second, they are to be to the greatest benefit of the least–advantaged members of society (the difference principle)" (Rawls, 2001, p. 42–43).
[9] In conformity with Rawls' vocabulary, such principles may be called principles of local justice (Rawls, 2001, p. 11).

5. CONCLUSION

In this paper I have argued that a simple and quite uncontroversial statement, namely, that the contracting parties' voluntariness in an employment relationship has substantial value, and due to that it should be ensured, conceals several difficulties. One overarching issue concerns this statement's meaning, and another is what normative importance we shall assign to it. Concerning the former, it is claimed (1) that to say that a person voluntarily has accepted a certain job and its terms within the frame of the employment relationship demands that all the following conditions be fulfilled to a certain degree: (a) E's (the employee's) and EE's (the employing entity's) decisions are genuine decisions; (b) both E and EE have status as competent bargaining parties; (c) E's and EE's decisions do not result from temporarily distorting states or circumstances; (d) E's and EE's decisions do not result from subtle manipulation; (e) E's and EE's decisions do not result from undue coercion; (f) both E and EE have information, to a sufficient degree, about the work, its terms, the likely future working situation and the other party's ability to fulfil its obligations. And, (2) that it is indeterminate where, exactly, the line should be drawn between voluntary and involuntary agreements in this context. Concerning the latter issue, it is claimed that (3) even if we were able to draw such a line, it would tell us nothing about the voluntariness condition's normative importance, or about how much normative weight we should assign to the fulfilment of its conditions in the workplace context. And finally, (4) the normative theory best suited to supporting the voluntariness condition is of a contractualist brand.

REFERENCES

Beatty, D. M. (1980). *Labour is not a Commodity.* In Reiter & Swan (Eds.), Studies in Contract Law. Toronto: Butterworths.

Bergström, L. (2000). Who Owns Our Genes? In *Proceedings of an international conference*, October 1999. Tallin, Estonia: The Nordic Committee on Bioethics.

Dworkin, R. (1981). What is Equality? *Part 2: Equality of Resources. Philosophy and Public Affairs,* 10 (283).

Feinberg, J. (1986). *Harm to Self: The Moral Limits of Criminal Law.* Oxford: Oxford University Press.

Nozick, R. (1974). *Anarchy, State, and Utopia.* New York: Basic Books.

Ofstad, H. (1961). *An Inquiry into the Freedom of Decision.* Oslo: Norwegian Universities Press.

Rawls, J. (1971). *A Theory of Justice.* Cambridge: Harvard University Press.

Rawls, J. (2001). *Justice as Fairness – A Restatement,* Cambridge: Harvard University Press.

Reiter, B. J. & Swan, J. (Eds.), (1980). *Studies in Contract Law*. Toronto: Butterworths.

Steinfeld, R. J. (1991). *The Invention of Free Labor: the Employment Relation in English and American Law and Culture,* 1350-1870. Chapel Hill: The University of North Carolina Press.

Swinton, K. (1980). *Contract Law and the Employment Relationship: The Proper Forum for Reform.* In Reiter & Swan (Eds.), Studies in Contract Law. Toronto: Butterworths.

Trebilcock, M. J. (1997). *The Limits of Freedom of Contract.* Cambridge: Harvard University Press.

Chapter 11

DO BUSINESS SCHOOLS' THEORIES NEGATIVELY INFLUENCE STUDENTS' ETHICAL POSITIONS?

Waymond Rodgers[*]
A. Gary Anderson Graduate School of Management,
University of California, Riverside, USA

Birgitta Påhlsson[†]
Högskolan I Borås
School of Business and Informatics, Sweden

Arne Söderbom[‡]
Högskolan I Borås
School of Business and Informatics, Sweden

ABSTRACT

This article develops and applies a decision making framework for understanding and interpreting ethical theories that impact the most on organizations. This framework classifies six major ethical positions that reflect issues in accounting and management courses. As such, the *Throughput Modeling* approach indicates how the ethical theory supporting the "rational choice theory can be influenced and perhaps enhanced by other ethical theories. In part, employees' behavior may be guided into improved ethical decision making that can be made defensible, and how special problems facing them can be dealt with via a decision-making pathway leading to an action.

---

[*] Waymond.Rodgers@ucr.edu
[†] Birgitta.Pahlsson@hb.se
[‡] Arne.Soderbom@hb.se

INTRODUCTION

Since our current students will be our future CEOs, CFOs, accountants, auditors, bankers, lawyers, managers or politicians, most of the future frauds, financial scandals, deceitful or misleading advertisements, among other consequences of unethical decisions, might be avoided with an adequate development of ethical education. Therefore, research on how to educate students on an ethical reasoning is absolutely essential for a healthy economy and a better society.

A dominant business school theory relates to the "ethical egoism" or rational choice decision making. This theory implies that one is better off by maximizing one's internally-driven utility function. Rational choice theory emphasizes the role of enlightened self-interest in individual decision-making deriving primarily from economic models. That is, individuals are viewed as adding up the benefits and costs of various courses of action. The rational choice perspective provides a language for describing how individuals' decisions are determined in business contexts, and is thus a natural methodology in addressing the students' behavior as reinforced by business school curriculum. However, while the rational choice view is adaptable to most business courses, it may not help students evolve through the aspects of moral reasoning, from perceptual moral sensitivity to judgment, and from the use of information in order to make moral decisions. This perspective does not consider contemporary public issues in problem-solving, which may be inadequate in an increasingly knowledge-based economy. For example, discussions of what might be considered as "personal" values such as cooperation, nurturance, and empathy are not incorporated in the rational choice view. The technological advances, global networks and vast amounts of information managed in even in the simplest of business dealings provide opportunities for ethical missteps. For instance, information technology (IT) central role is privacy, the ownership of personal data, and the obligations created by extended E-business partnerships. How have these controversies affected the ethical ability of IT managers and others involved with technology? What ethical issues, are business students struggling with in connection with cutting-edge IT? And where do employees go for guidance on ethically ambiguous situations? Recent articles (Alsop, 2005; Quelch, 2005) have explored how business students must be trained to develop a personal ethical compass and to apply ethics to business decisions in a variety of situations.

The purpose of this paper is to examine whether other competing ethical theories could complement, enhance or explain as much as the rational choice theory in business school curriculum. In other words, first, can several dominant "ethical reasoning" positions be effectively taught? Second, if so, what type of decision making model can effectively teach such value-laden analysis? Third, how several dominant ethical positions should be meaningfully incorporated into business courses? Fourth, would such incorporation accelerate ethical development of students/employees and lead to more ethical actions in organizations? Business schools curriculum, from several countries around the world, suggests that rational choice theory is embedded in required courses for students much more than other ethical based theories (Alsop, 2005). That is, the Aspen Institute and World Resources Institute's recent survey of nearly 100 Masters of Business Administration (MBA) programs around the world found that more than half require students to take courses on corporate responsibility, up from only one-third in 2001 (Alsop, 2005). We contend that the rational choice theory may be an important driver in determining how students and employees are influenced regarding their ethical actions towards others. A review of psychological scholarship indicates that business courses do not foster moral or ethical development in students in contrast to other educational experiences (e.g., Conry & Nelson, 1989; Rabouin, 1996). The next section imports a decision making model described as *"Throughput Modeling"* that addresses how a particular ethical behavior is the underlying driver for decisions. This modeling perspective is important in that teaching students to discern "ethical lapses" in one course, without teaching them how to frame problems and to process and analyze information, is a lot less than what is necessary. This section is followed by a discussion of six dominant ethical positions as reported by Rodgers and Gago (2001, 2003, 2004). Next, examples are provided for each of the six dominant ethical positions. Finally, conclusions and implications relating to the dominant ethical theory in business schools to other more relevant and socially responsible ethical theories are discussed.

THE THROUGHPUT MODEL

Some researchers (Dellaportas, 2006; Luthar & Karri, 2005) posit that ethical exposure could have a positive effect on students' perception about the linkage between ethical practices and business decisions. Apparently, the inclusion of ethical content in students' curriculum contributes to their knowledge and promotes ethics dilemma discussions. Making ethical decisions may provide individuals with a moral compass in order to determine what is ethically right or wrong. For this reason, students may be better equipped if they understand the cognitive processes and its different elements affecting their decisions.

Hence, we present a theoretical model that attempts to clarify the multiple ways in which ethical positions can influence students' behavior. This *Throughput Model* (Rodgers 1997) captures several different pathways and stages that can influence a decision at the individual or organizational level. Further, depending upon individuals or organizations' viewpoint, certain pathways may be weighted heavier than or dominate other pathways. Students can benefit from this model by observing what other pathways may need to be improved in order to modify their decisions. Finally, this novel approach enables us to complement several "ethical" positions with unique decision-making paths leading to a decision.

Throughput Modeling depicts the most influential pathways employed in arriving at a decision. That is, what we hold as valuable enters into our *perception*, and it can in turn influence our judgment and decision choice. Our *judgments* processes information sources, analyzes what is acceptable as information, what evidence we frame (i.e., perception), and is appropriate to answer questions about a particular part of reality are all influenced by what we hold as valuable (Rodgers & Gago 2001). Decision making in the *Throughput Model* is defined here as a multi-stage, information-processing function in which cognitive, economic, political, and social processes are used to generate a set of outcomes.

Perception involves the process of individuals framing their problem solving set or view of the world. Depending upon the task at hand, this framing involves individuals' expertise in using pre-formatted knowledge to direct and guide their search of confirming or disconfirming of incoming information necessary for problem solving or decision making. Rodgers (1997) argued that perception represents a person's expertise, classifying and categorization of information. For example, a supplier delivers products on a timely basis based upon the purchaser promise to pay cash. In some of the management literature data is considered as facts and *information* is processed, interpreted data (Alavi & Leidner, 2001). In addition, information is converted to knowledge once it is processed in the mind of individuals and knowledge becomes information once it is articulated and presented in the form of text, graphics words, or other symbolic forms. *Information* includes the set of managerial, economic, political, social, and environmental information available to a decision-maker for problem solving purposes. The *judgment* stage contains the process by which individuals' implement and analyzes incoming information (managerial, economic, political, social, and environmental), as well as the influences from the perception stage. From these sources, rules are implemented to weigh, sort, and classify knowledge and information for problem solving or decision-making purposes. Finally, in the *decision choice* stage an action is taken or not taken.

The stages of perception, information, judgment and choice are always present in decision making, however their predominance or ordering influences decision making. There are differences of opinion about how many stages and subroutines within stages exist and the order in which the stages occur. These concepts in the model proposed here appear with some consistency in the literature (Hogarth, 1987). This model represents a parsimonious way to capture major concepts about organizations. Further, it provides a more interpretative cognitive schema. That is, basic information processing modeling normally involves serial processing. We take this approach one step further by assuming parallel processing. That is we assume that there are many (often times simultaneous) pathways leading to a decision. Further, this decision-making model has been shown to be useful in conceptualizing a number of different issues important to organizations (Rodgers, 1997). It is particularly relevant for clarifying critical pathways influenced by ethical positions (Rodgers & Gago, 2001).

The conceptual model is presented in Figure 1. Arrows from one construct to another indicate the hypothesized causal relationships. In Figure 1, perception does not change the actual information, but influences an individual on what type, kind and magnitude of information will be selected for further processing. Also, information can influence, change, or alter an individual's perception based on the importance of the information (Rodgers 1997). Therefore Figure 1 presents perception and information as interdependent.

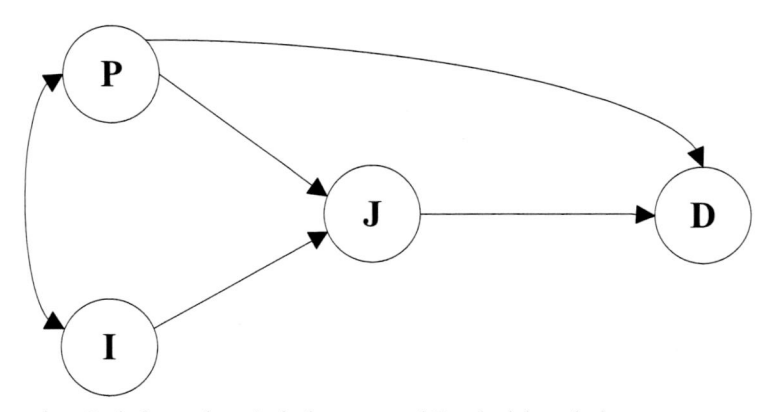

Where P= perception, I= information, J= judgment, and D= decision choice.

Figure 1. Throughput Modeling of Individuals' Decision Processes Diagram.

A point of clarification regarding the interdependence between perception and information is that the pathway shown as $P \rightarrow I$ represents a continuous forward and backward path (see Figure 1). Also, this pathway suggests that perception dominate information. Thus, when the path direction is $P \rightarrow I$, we suggest that *P dominates I* in an individual's actions toward reaching a decision. When the direction of the arrow is reversed: $P \leftarrow I$ implies that *I dominates P* and an individual's primary method of decision making is via information (Rodgers 1997).

To provide an empirical foundation for the six decision making pathways, Rodgers (1992; 1997) performed a covariance structural analysis with unobservable variables, based on a survey of loan officers' and novices' *perception, information, judgment,* and *decision.* The results of his calculation from his survey, the coefficients, represent the relations between the analyzed variables. A coefficient, r, is a number such that: $-1 \leq r \leq +1$. Overall coefficients, greater than 0.5, had more influence on a concrete pathway, whereas coefficients less than 0.5 had a weak effect on the variables associated with each pathway (Rodgers 1992, 1997).

Ethics Viewed in the Throughput Model

Throughput modeling begins with individuals stating their views of what should be done. The advantage of this approach is that it helps decision-makers understand why individuals have selected some information, which supports their position, and have ignored other information, which does not support their position. This approach helps uncover the observations and values that individuals rely upon when taking positions on issues. Also, the model is useful in depicting latter stages of processes, such as judgment, that are implemented in supporting individuals' positions.

Based on Figure 1, we can establish six general pathways:

$$P \rightarrow D \tag{1}$$

$$P \rightarrow J \rightarrow D \tag{2}$$

$$I \rightarrow J \rightarrow D \tag{3}$$

$$I \rightarrow P \rightarrow D \tag{4}$$

$$P \rightarrow I \rightarrow J \rightarrow D \tag{5}$$

$$I \rightarrow P \rightarrow J \rightarrow D \tag{6}$$

The *Throughput Model* draw attention to: (1) only 2 – 4 major concepts that are instrumental in arriving at a decision; (2) the order of a particular pathway (and its strength) will greatly influence the outcome of a decision; and (3) each decision making pathway relates to a particular ethical position. There are many philosophies, which are complex in nature. We discuss six prominent approaches depicted in the model's six general pathways.

The six ethical positions discussed below are ethical egoism, deontology, relativist, utilitarianism, virtue ethics, and ethics of care.

These six pathways are viewed as the most dominant and influential for decision making governed by particular moral perspectives (Rodgers & Gago, 2001). Although, it is important to note that other pathways in the described decision making model also contributes to the above ethical positions, but in a minor way. As discussed in Rodgers and Gago (2001) the corresponding pathway to each particular ethical view is the most dominant.

(1) $P \rightarrow D$ represents *ethical egoism position*, which stresses that individuals are always motivated to act in their perceived self-interest. Utility theory, which supports this position, was highlighted by von Neumann and Morgenstern (1947) in that they took cardinal utility theory and introduced game theory to economics and other social sciences. Game theory is the study of the ways in which strategic interactions among rational players produce outcomes with respect to the preferences (or utilities) of those players, none of which might have been intended by any of them.

The ethical egoism pathway of decision-making is made in a particular way that downplays non-supporting information or analysis. A circumstance is perceived and the decision is taken by downplaying previous judgment or information. Prevailing market and other social forces supported the idea that short run profit maximization was the solo raison d'etre of the firm (Daneke, 1985). Hence, ethical egoism in its purest form is the manifestation of maximizing shareholder wealth. In economics, the neoclassical marginal analysis regards the firm as a profit-maximizing unit (Cyert & Hedrick, 1972). The main point of this position is that shareholders differ from other constituencies since they are residual risk-bearers and they have unique problems of contracting that are best met by having control. The tenets of this position rest with the rational choice perspective in that the behaviors of individuals are causally depicted as outcomes determined by the maximization of individual objective functions.

$P \rightarrow D$ Example

Adam Smith (1776) argues that if we will leave self-interested people to seek their own advantage, the result, unintended by any one of them will be the grater advantage of all. No government interference is necessary to protect the general welfare. The relevant actions of a student can be viewed (P) as a self-interested person seeking his/her own advantage. This follows from the economic concept that maximizing one's utility is of the best interest of the individual when making a choice (D).

(2) $P \rightarrow J \rightarrow D$ depicts the deontology position that emphasizes the rights of individuals and on the judgments associated with a particular decision process rather than on its choices. For example, Kant (1996) argued that moral actions are based on a "supreme principle of morality" which is objective, rational, and freely chosen: the categorical imperative. That is, this decision-making position emphasizes that one's perception (P) is oriented by conditioning judgment (J) of the rules and laws before rendering a decision (D). In other words, the decision is induced by a judgment based on a perception of a circumstance. Further, deontology underscores the property rights perspective which answers puzzling business questions that occurs in corporate law. This corporate form of business organization

is justified on the grounds that it represents an extension of the property rights and the right of contract enjoyed by everyone. Ethical considerations come into play in difficult cases where the rules are unclear or in conflict. However, generalized rules of ethics may be unhelpful in counseling students. That is, students who know the rules of law, but have no mature personal beliefs about their own duty to obey them, have not been fully educated in ethical considerations.

P → J → D Example

Students might take a look at whether the decision itself contributes to "in general" the intent of a rule or law governing their behavior in a classroom setting. This requires identification (P) with the rule, and a subsequent analysis (J) of what comprises a "good" rule (D). These rules can be derived from their belief systems, those, which are derived from their memories, and those values that transcend it.

(3) *I → J → D* reflects the utilitarian position that is concerned with consequences, as well as the greatest good for the greatest number of people. Utilitarianism is based on collective "economic egoism". The judgment is based on information and the information conditions the decision. This position champions egalitarianism in the combined impacts of economic growth and civil development of social citizenship principles (Westergaard, 1984). That is, the civil development consists of person's liberty, freedom of speech, thought and faith, the right to own property and to conclude valid contracts, and the right to justice (Roche, 1987). Utilitarianism is an expansion of ethical egoism in that it is committed to the maximization of the good and the minimization of harm and evil to a society. Adam Smith (1776) stated over 200 years ago that "every individual is continually exerting himself to find out the most advantageous employment for what ever capital he can command. It is his own advantage, indeed, and not that of the society, which he has in view. But the study of his own advantage naturally, or rather necessarily, leads him to prefer that employment which is most advantage to the society." Further, Friedman (1970) argued that the purpose of the corporation is to seek profits for stockholders while acting in conformity with the moral minimum. Corporations may strive for profits as long as they commit no deception or fraud.

I → J → D Example

In a classroom environment, students would define an action as ethical only if it would produce the greatest good for the greatest number of relevant members. To do so, they must resolve two threshold issues: one, which sources of information and stakeholders of the community at issue are "relevant" (I)? And two, how does one define the "greatest good" (J) before rendering a decision (D)?

(4) *I → P → D* highlights the relativist position, which assumes that decision-makers use themselves or the people around them as their basis for defining ethical standards. A clash of values and interests, and tensions between what is and what some groups believe can prevent accommodations with other interested parties (Coser, 1957). Ethical relativism is the position that maintains that morality is relative to the norms of one's culture. An action that is right or wrong rests upon the moral norms of the society in which it is practiced. The same action may be morally right in one society but be morally wrong in another. For the ethical relativist,

there are no universal moral standards since standards that can be universally applied to all peoples at all times. The only moral standards against which an organization or society's practices can be judged are its own (Velasquez, 2006).

Relativism is a function of a company operating differently due to the rules or laws (or lack thereof) governing another country. The present information influences the perception and the immediate decision without a previous judgment. The information helps shape a company's perception to act in a particular manner. Therefore information is examined, the perception is framed and the decision is adopted. The relativism position dominated as companies began to emerge into multinational or global organizations with its home base centered in one country. The relativism position is that firm efficiency and wealth creation is shareholder wealth. Hence, the objective of the firm is generally expressed as shareholder wealth maximization (Modigliani & Miller, 1958). Relativism exists since many countries prohibit companies from committing deception or fraud at home; however, these countries take no action when deception or fraud acts are committed abroad. This affects otherwise honest people to justify their actions because they are not illegal.

$I \rightarrow P \rightarrow D$ Example

The first part of an analysis places the student as an actor in a particular environment (I). Their sensitivity (P) would be influenced by students discerning the facts within a condition, which will give the issue (D) its substance. That is students' fact-finding and investigation is often distorted or blinded by where the decision making takes place. This blindness is a failure to discern relevant facts and rigidity of factual development. Hence, cultural conditioning drives the ethical considerations at a particular time and place.

(5) $P \rightarrow I \rightarrow J \rightarrow D$ under scores the virtue ethics position, which is the classical Hellenistic tradition represented by Plato (427 BC – 347 BC) and Aristotle (384 BC – 322 BC), whereby the cultivation of virtuous traits of character is viewed as morality's primary function. Aristotle was quite explicit when he stated that a wicked person is responsible for his or her character. That is, not because he or she could now alter it but because he or she could have and should have acted differently early on and established very dissimilar habits and states of character. That is, the notion of an individual (citizen) as an entity in principle is capable of recognizing, knowing about, acting appropriately in respect of rights and duties (Marshall, 1964). In the virtue ethics position, a circumstance is perceived (P). A conscious look for information (I) is initiated. Based on the information a judgment (J) is made, which will support a decision (D). Virtue ethics position began to rise during the 1960s prompted by television and other mediums of advertising. The corporate image began to change to assume a disposition to act fairly but also a morally appropriate desire to do so. Popular social celebrities endorsed products and the corporate leaders appeared to have the traits of a virtuous character. However, shareholders still occupied center stage as the only stakeholder as opposed to employees, suppliers, customers, and the community.

$P \rightarrow I \rightarrow J \rightarrow D$ Example

The students' way of seeing and being in a particular situation is related to what Aristotle says about character. That is, first of all, it is a kind of perception based of good up-bringing (Solomon, 1999). Students become aware of and interpret a classroom situation (P), and then figure out what options are viable (I) to be analyze (J) before a decision is rendered (D). Let's assume a business student, who is the chairperson, displays an image (P) he "knows all the facts" regarding a particular subject to his entire studying group. He wants to make an impression to the members of his group since he is viewed as a knowledgeable person at his University. He selects an area or research (I) whereby others in the group have more knowledge about the subject matter, however is ignored. The group analyzes his work (J) and turns in the completed project (D) to the professor. The completed project receives a low grade. His group members are very upset that he portrayed himself as being the knowledgeable person in the group regarding the project.

(6) $I \rightarrow P \rightarrow J \rightarrow D$ represents the ethics of care position (stakeholders perspective), which focuses on a willingness to listen to distinct and previously unacknowledged perspectives. In other words a company must build solidarity among employees, suppliers, customers, shareholders, and the community. The ethics of care position recognizes the moral priority of caring for the particular others for whom we are responsible. This stakeholder position focuses on responsiveness to need, empathetic understanding, and the interrelatedness of people, rather than on individual rationality or universal moral rules. It emphasizes relations between people rather than the preferences or dispositions of individuals; it is thoughtful relations that are thought to have primary value. This position suggests:

1. Sensitivity to situations or dimensions of situations that involve abandonment, detachment, hurt, pain, or violations of intimacy;
2. Need to balance the needs of all parties, make them feel attached, and accept people for all their subtle distinctiveness;
3. Resolve conflicts by emphasizing procedures, consensus, wisdom, the logic of affect, and sensitivity to context; and
4. Commitment to non-violence, moral values, and the welfare of generations (Gilligan, 1982).

Ethics of care position states that existing important information (*I*) influences one's perception (*P*) of a circumstance. The influenced perceptions are judged (*J*) before rendering a decision (*D*). Also, ethics of care viewpoint emphasizes that not only shareholders have property rights but also employees, suppliers, customers, and the community. This presumptive equality among these groups is assumed to be enforceable in, their interactions and communications with each other (Schutz, 1964). Therefore, corporation actions result from the property rights and the right to contract every corporate constituency and not from those of shareholders alone. Also, Cornell and Shapiro (1987) advised that the firm value should include implicit claims to various constituencies and the costs to the firm of honoring these claims.

I→P→J→D Example
Students might consider how technology, gender, culture, and class (*I*) affect moral interpretations (*P*) of rules within their classroom setting. The students then analyze (*J*) ethical problems in light of their economic, social and historical context. For instance,

students may explore the rationale for the oaths taken by corporate managers, the regulations governing the rules, and the statutes governing corporate behavior.

EXAMPLES OF ETHICAL POSITIONS RELATED TO BUSINESS ISSUES

Students eventually employed by "Start up" companies may overlook one key element when assisting their companies off the ground. Ethical issues that often arise in the workplace may result in lawsuits that will drain their budgets or government penalties. Can several dominant ethical reasoning positions be effectively taught to avoid issues such as this? This section helps shed light on this issue by providing examples related to six dominant ethical positions. Some lessons of corporate ethical misconduct can be learnt by students being introduced to several different ethical positions in accounting, finance, information systems, marketing, operation research, organizational behavior, and strategy classes.

Ethical Egoism Position

An example from Skandia, a big international enterprise in the insurance business highlights the ethical egoism position. The chairman of Swedish Insurance Group Skandia resigned in December 2003 after a scathing investigation into the company's corporate activities poured light on an alleged culture of dishonesty and financial impropriety that undermined shareholders trust. The routines of internal audit and management control were not acceptable, bias was rampant in the financial reporting system, and the board was not acting in a professional way. The lack of management control, the "creative" incentive program and the favoring of jobs to relatives of the executives could be seen as expected outcomes determined by the maximization of individual objective functions, while not taking into account the negative effects on the stakeholders in general. Executives in Skandia can be said to have had a motivation to act in their perceived self-interest. Decision making downplayed or ignored non-supporting information or analysis. A circumstance was perceived (supporting individuals self interest) and the decision was made. This can be seen as an example of a rational choice perspective from an egoistic point of view.

Deontology Position

To obtain a rather stable income stream over years, income smoothing is the process of reducing reported profits of business during good periods and opposite increases them due to loss periods. This is an example of creative accounting whereby this type accounting rule inflates or smooth income flows. Also, when using artificial smoothing, different policies are used to shift income between different financial periods.

For example, Volvo Cars Ltd used tax consultants, lawyers and sometimes auditors according to the accounting rules for income smoothing. Although, they are known for world-leading work with better safety cars as their premium business concept, they also have been continuously engaged in large complex tax cases over the years. This has resulted in the company receiving very large tax deductions thereby causing a burden on society. They have developed a system of postponing taxes by carefully using highly qualified lawyers and tax consultants to achieve tax relief. Sometimes they win in court where in other cases they have lost. Volvo will benefit on income smoothing made possible from legal loopholes in the law. In the *Throughput Model*, Volvo's perception is centered on judgment were the law has legal loopholes for them to interpret before arriving at a decision.

Utilitarian Position

The rational goal model (Pfeffer, 1982) and the machine metaphor (Morgan, 1986) support the theory of the Economic Man as organizations' as rational controlling operations through factual information. One example from this viewpoint is the Swedish health system. Today we consider that a common ethical concept would be the work for the good and welfare of humankind. In the hospital treatment it is clear that priority is given to economic values. This rational perspective has resulted in "how many nursing sections are we going to close and how many hundreds and thousands beds shall be closed down for the public". The deductive reasoning is a cause and effect theme influenced from management accounting budgetary control. The unhealthy patients are in the debate that calls for a certain number of beds regarding bed reduction decisions.

This is an example of profit maximizing within the public sector run by a professional public administration. Objectivity and neutrality are forces that put organizations economic interests first and leaving humanitarian values behind. The *Throughput Model* starts with dominant information, taking the consequences of given budgets in consideration and then decide about the best economic alternative. Reliable and relevant information controls behavior (Häckner, 1989) when the financial structure is not sufficient.

Relativistic Position

There has been a series of discussions in the media pertaining to Swedish companies, Atlas Copco and Sandvik delivering drills for mining operations to companies in Ghana which have been accused of violating human rights and damaging the environment in the chase of gold. In this case Atlas Copco and Sandvik themselves have not been found to have violated human rights or caused damages to the environment, however the question remains is it ethical to be involved in a business that does, without taking any responsibility for trying to influence its business partners to fulfill the guidelines of Organization for Economic Co-operation and Development (OECD) about human rights etc.

Under the relativistic perspective Atlas Copco and Sandvik can justify their actions because they are acting formally correct, according to the law (with the objective of shareholders wealth maximization). These organizations do not feel responsible for the damage the mining companies in another country will create in their operation when using the drills from Sweden. In their decision they can be said to use the people around them as their basis for defining ethical standards. The relativistic position means that Atlas Copco and Sandvik perceive differently (negating the fact that the violation would not be acceptable in Sweden) due to the lack of rules/lack of control/lack of ethics governing the other country.

The present information (that is available) influences the perception and the immediate decision without a previous judgment of what effects the action will have on different stakeholders. Information is examined, the perception is framed ("the decision will not effect our business and shareholders wealth" and "It's not illegal or condemned in the country where the mining takes plays") and the decision is adopted.

Virtue Ethics Position

Automobile manufacturing companies identifies displaying what is usually the superior safety features for drivers, passengers, other road users and pedestrians. Both the Swedish car factories, Volvo and SAAB, have put safety first. They are good examples of two companies that have served as safety models for other automobile factories round the world. Volvo and SAAB shows in relation to all people and to their competitors that they are serious and also live up to their safety policy - they are trustworthy in their safety promises. Here, perception controls information in that Volvo and SAAB acts in relation to the morality rights and show, directed outwardly, that big policy decisions are in line of ethical safety. However, there is a de-coupling here meaning that the companies mentioned do work very convincingly with a safety policy, but in fact ignore the danger by continuously introducing new automobiles with stronger and stronger motors. Perhaps this may be motivated by an overall profit maximization corporate policy. This imply that higher speed kills and stronger and bigger motors pollute (fuel consumption are still high and has not significantly been reduced to lower levels in many years) and damage or alter nature and the environment. Consequently, people may be killed by speed harmed by a more polluted environment. Safety first represents a global corporate image that is not applied to wider safety thinking.

Ethics of Care Position

In the Body Shop International's Value Report, the company is said to combine business with values and good ethics showing social responsibility. Sustainability is a key word and the interests of "all" stakeholders (not only shareholders property rights) with a special focus on the demands of the customers, local and global environment, fairness in business and the work for human rights and animals rights. Involvement of employees, producers are also said to be important (equality among groups through interaction and communication). Disclosure, transparency and honesty are other keywords. In the report it is said that information is gathered from the customers/consumers about their demands and values and this information influence the perception on which judgment and decisions are made.

Another question is whether The Body Shop in each decision, acts from an ethical of care point of view. For example their vision is very interesting from a "media" point of view, meaning that the company doesn't have to put a lot of money in marketing due to the exposure in the media. (Business Idea/Vision/charter has a positive effect on shareholders value – rational thinking/profit maximization)

Another example is the "Ikea corporation way" with its Ikea Code of conduct, guidelines how to act in an ethical way and the auditing/control of the regulation. Ikea was earlier criticized for not having reacted on/taking action against employment of children in the production of rugs in India. After the critics Ikea's *changed position* (perhaps to protect its brand/image!), and is now highlighting ethical questions and is taking active part in the investigation of ethical behaviour in the local production companies in Asia.)

CONCLUSIONS AND IMPLICATIONS

If students and employees act in their own self-interest trying to maximize the utility for themselves (as the only stakeholder) the focus would be on decisions that will get them through an organizational setting in a smart and easy (efficient) way as possible, not caring about other stakeholders.

To pass the exams (with or without cheating) students may decide what to do that will benefit them the most, not considering the effects on other stakeholders. They may act towards the teacher in a way that favors their self-interest. For example, students may dress or behave in a specific manner in order to obtain favors from a professor. If a student happens to obtain information that would help him/her to improve a test score, he/she has a motivation to act in a perceived self-interest. The student will not share this information with other students (not acting in the best interest of the group). The decision-making downplays non-supporting information or analysis. A circumstance is perceived (supporting the individual's self interest) and the decision is taken.

Students' way of viewing and being in a situation may be very different, and this is where Aristotle claims that the question of character begins with how they perceive those circumstances. Yet another reason to expose students to the six dominant ethical positions tied to the *Throughput Model* can provide them with a constant education on how different positions can influence how they think and make decisions, which could harm a large number of people. For example, consider a student who knows that cheating on exams is not acceptable at his school. There are very specific rules governing the examination and the student will be suspended from school if caught. The student would not consider cheating under these circumstances. The student enrolls in a student exchange program, studying abroad for one semester. Knowing that this school is not as strict about cheating, his willingness to cheat increases. If caught the student will not be punished the first time it happens - just missing the test, having to do it again. The student adapts to the new circumstances, using the people around him as a basis for defining ethical standards. He will cheat until he has been caught in the courses he takes. The relativistic position means that the student acts differently due to the lack of rules/lack of control/lack of ethics governing the school abroad. The present information (the new environment) influences the perception and the immediate decision without a judgment. Information is examined, the perception is framed (adapting to new circumstances – cheating is not taken very seriously in the new school and will not effect the education) and the decision is adopted.

However, one of the bright lights for graduate school education is that some employers are now looking for students with a solid background in corporate social responsibility. That is, more companies are seeking MBA students who have taken courses and gained practical experience related to social and environmental responsibility. Further, in a Wall Street Journal-Harris Interactive business-school survey, 84% of the corporate recruiters said it is very or somewhat important that MBA students display "awareness and knowledge of corporate social responsibility (Alsop, 2005). Finally, many companies such as McDonald's, Gap, and Yahoo have begun forging close connections with the increasing number of business schools offering classes in social and environmental responsibility (Alsop, 2005). Hopefully, this trend can continue not only in graduate business schools, but also undergraduate schools of business.

The students who are trained in reflective and critical thinking would have a better chance to see the consequences of their actions for other stakeholders. To broaden the perspectives to a more ethical perspective, for example to study accounting or financial theories from different ethical positions, can improve the students' ability to become aware of:

1. Understanding what values are governing their perceptions;
2. Including the effects on all stakeholders in a business decision requiring students to be more analytical and thoughtful in addressing serious issues.

The students involved in a more dialogue-based education in a business curriculum (seminars; writing + dialogue + rewriting.) tend to be more open-minded and reflective, letting information influence their perception. To develop students awareness of what values/value system that governs their perception (and their judgment and decisions) must be important to "counteract" the influence of traditional classical economic theories, built on a rational economic thinking, in a business education. For example, an organization course in varying viewpoints of avoiding cruelty in action (towards stakeholders), based on experience and reflection would reflect an ethics of care perspective in this position.

In sum, more and more company executives are realizing that solving social problems is crucial to long-term business success and question whether maximizing shareholder value is an appropriate surrogate for serving society's needs. To this end, business schools can better equip their students by not just paying lip service to teaching ethics, but by including and evaluating different ethical positions in the business classes they offer. This approach may counter the effects of the dominant rational choice paradigm as depicted by ethical egoism in most of the courses offered in business. Finally, the *Throughput Model* can aid the process of selecting other dominant ethical positions as they relate to the use of framing a problem (perception), whether information is reliable and relevant for use, and analyses (judgment). That is, the *Throughput Model* helps us understand how major decision making concepts are underlined by dominant ethical positions such as ethical egoism, deontology, relativist, utilitarianism, virtue ethics, and ethics of care.

REFERENCES

Alavi, M. & Leidner, D.E. 2001. Knowledge management and knowledge management systems: Conceptual foundations and research issues, *MIS Quarterly*, 25, 107-136.

Alsop, R. 2005. Graduates trained to do good do well with recruiters. *The Wall Street Journal*, Tuesday, p. 30.

Aristotle. 1984. *384 BC – 322 BC. Complete works of Aristotle*. Princeton: Princeton University Press.

Conry, E.J. & Nelson, D.R. 1989. Business Law and Moral Growth. *American Business Law Journal*, 1: 20.

Cornell, B. & Shapiro, A. 1987. Corporate stakeholders and corporate finance. *Financial Management*, 16, 5-14.

Coser, L.A. 1957. Social conflict and the theory of social change. *The British Journal of Sociology*, 8, 197-207.

Cyert, R.M., & Hedrick, C.L. 1972. Theory of the firm: past, present, and future: an interpretation. *Journal of Economic Literature*, 10, 398-412.

Daneke, G.A. 1985. Regulation and the sociopathic firm. *Academy Management Review*, 10, 15-20.

Dellaportas, S. 2006. Making a Difference with a Discrete Course on Accounting Ethics. *Journal of Business Ethics*, 65, 391-404

Friedman, M. 1970. The responsibility of business is to increase its profits. *New York Times Magazine*, September 13, 1970.

Gilligan, C. 1982. *In a Different Voice.* Cambridge, MA: Harvard University Press.

Kant, I. 1996. *Religion and Rational Theology*, edited by Allen Wood and George Digiovanni. Cambridge: Cambridge University Press.

Luthar, H.K. & Karri, R. 2005. Exposure to ethics education and the perception of linkage between organizational ethical behavior and business outcomes. *Journal of Business Ethics,* 61, 353-368.

Marshall, T.H. 1964. *Sociology at the cross roads.* NY: Doubleday.

Modigliani, F. & Miller, M.H. 1958. The cost of capital, corporation finance, and the theory of investment. *American Economic Review*, 48, 261-97.

Morgan, G. 1986. *Images of organization.* Newbury Park, CA.: Sage Publications.

Pfeffer, J. 1982. *Organizations and Organization Theory.* Marshfield, MA: Pitman Publishing.

Plato. 1997. *427 BC – 347. Plato complete works*. London: Hackett Pub Co.

Quelch, J. 2005. A new agenda for business schools. The Chronicle of Higher Education, (B19).

Rabouin, E.M. 1996. Walking the talk: Transforming law students into ethical transactional lawyers. *De Paul Business Law Journal*, 1: 1-51.

Roche, M. 1987. Citizenship, social theory, and social change. *Theory and Society*, 16: 363-399.

Rodgers, W. 1992. The effects of accounting information on individuals' perceptual processes. *Journal of Accounting, Auditing and Finance,* 7, 67-96.

Rodgers, W. 1997. *Throughput modeling: Financial information used by decision makers.* Greenwich, CT: JAI Press.

Rodgers W. & Gago, S. 2001. Cultural and ethical effects on managerial decisions: Examined in a Throughput Model. *Journal of Business Ethics*, 31: 355-367.

Rodgers W., & Gago, S. 2003. A model capturing ethics and executive compensation. *Journal of Business Ethics*, 48: 189-202.

Rodgers W., & Gago, S. 2004. Stakeholder influence on corporate strategies over time, *Journal of Business Ethics*, 52: 349-363.

Schutz, A. 1964. *Collected papers* (vol. II). The Hague: Martinus Nijhoff.

Smith, A. (1776). *The wealth of nations* (ed. 1991) Prometheus Books.

Solomon, R.C. 1999. *A better way to think about business.* NY: Oxford University Press.

Velasquez, M.G. 2006. *Business Ethics: Concepts and Cases sixth edition.* Upper Saddle River, NJ: Prentice-Hall, Inc.

von Neumann J. & Morgenstern, O. 1947. *Theory of games and economic behaviour.* Princeton, NJ: Princeton Press.

Westergaard, J. 1984. Class of 84. *New socialist* Jan/Feb, 30-36.

Chapter 12

MISERY AS CORPORATE MISSION: USER IMAGERY AT THE NIGHTCLUB THE SPY BAR

Niklas Egels-Zandén[*]
Centre for Business in Society
School of Business, Economics and Law at Göteborg University
Box 600, SE – 405 30 Göteborg, Sweden

Ulf Ågerup[†]
Marketing Group, School of Business, Economics and Law at Göteborg University
Box 600, SE – 405 30 Göteborg, Sweden

ABSTRACT

Despite extensive corporate responsibility research into both *what* and *how* firms produce, research is lacking in one product category in which the *what* and *how* linkage creates questionable corporate practice – luxury products. Luxury is in some cases created by companies controlling the so-called user imagery of their customers, i.e., encouraging 'desirable' individuals to consume their products and obstructing 'undesirable' individuals from consumption. This chapter critically analyses the implications of this corporate practice based on a study of Sweden's most luxurious nightclub. The study's results show that the nightclub has organised its activities to allow categorisations of individuals into 'desirable' and 'undesirable' customers. Furthermore, the study shows that a creation of 'misery' for the vast majority of individuals (the 'undesirable') is essential for creating 'enjoyment' for the selected few (the 'desirable'). The chapter concludes by discussing implications for practitioners interested in altering this situation.

---

[*] +46-31-7862729 (telephone); Niklas.Egels-Zanden@handels.gu.se
[†] +46-31-93 23 29 (telephone); Ulf.Agerup@handels.gu.se

INTRODUCTION

When discussing a firm's corporate responsibility, two main issues arise. *What* products does the firm produce, and *how* does it produce these products? Researchers, as well as practitioners, have given much attention to the idea that some products are 'irresponsible' – most notably cigarettes, weapons, alcohol, and gambling products (e.g., Newton, 1993; Kinder and Domini, 1997; Elm, 1998; Havemann, 1998; Maitland, 1998; Brenkert, 2000; Green, 2000). For example, firms producing these products are often excluded from 'ethical' funds (e.g., Kinder and Domini, 1997). Similarly, much attention has been given to *how* products are produced. Lately, this debate has mainly been focused on human and workers' rights in production in developing countries. Hot research topics include the corporate embracement of codes of conduct (e.g., Frenkel, 2001; van Tulder and Kolk, 2001; Graafland, 2002; Winstanley *et al.*, 2002; Egels-Zandén, 2007), the signing of international framework agreements (e.g., Wills, 2002; Carley, 2005; Fairbrother and Hammer, 2005; Riisgaard, 2005; Anner *et al.*, 2006; Egels-Zandén and Hyllman, 2006, 2007), and corporate operations in controversial markets (e.g., Donaldson 1989, 1996; De George 1990, 1993; Donaldson and Dunfee, 1994; Carroll and Gannon, 1997; Schermerhorn, 1999). Despite the ample research into both *what* products firm produce and *how* they produce them, research is lacking in one product category in which the *what* and *how* linkage creates questionable corporate practice – luxury products.

A review of international publications on corporate responsibility in recent years clearly shows that luxury products are a neglected area of research. The likely reasons are that luxury products generally are not of 'irresponsible' nature (compared to cigarettes, alcohol, weapons, etc.), and that the quality demands and high price range often limit the abuse of human and workers' rights in production (cf. McWilliam and Siegel, 2001). Hence, since previous research has treated the *what* and *how* questions separately, luxury products have escaped its radar. However, this chapter argues that when treated together the *what* in luxury products (i.e., their exclusiveness) leads to problematic aspects of *how* the products are produced and marketed.

The purpose of this chapter is to address this gap in previous research by analysing the intersection between *what* and *how*. More specifically, we focus on the corporate practice of customer base management aimed at influencing the user imagery of the product, and critically analyse the implications of the practice. This is much needed, since previous marketing research into user imagery and luxury products has neglected the corporate responsibility aspects of this practice. Thus, corporate responsibility researchers have neglected the area of luxury products and user imagery, while marketing researchers have studied both luxury products and user imagery but ignored their corporate responsibility aspects. We base our analysis of user imagery on a study of Sweden's most luxurious nightclub – The Spy Bar. Our results show that corporate responsibility as well as marketing researchers are well advised to recognise the corporate responsibility aspects of luxury products and user imagery in future research, since the corporate practice entails critical issues for further academic and practitioner discussions.

LUXURY PRODUCTS AND USER IMAGERY

The core idea of 'luxury' is often taken to be that the product is attainable only for a limited range of consumers (e.g., Berry, 1994; Twitchell, 2002). However, recently there has been a shift in the clientele for luxury products with more affordable, although still expensive, alternatives for 'normal' people being launched (e.g., Twitchell, 2002; Allères, 2005). It is problematic to define 'luxury' precisely (e.g., Dubois *et al.*, 1995; Vigneron and Johnson, 1999), although most people in practice can categorise products into 'luxury' and 'non-luxury' products. In this chapter, luxury is defined as products that are widely desired and more expensive than what their utility motivates (cf. Berry, 1994; Twitchell, 2002). Hence, luxury products are primarily consumed because of their meaning to us rather than because of their utility. Consequently, brand-meaning creation is central to the creation of luxury.

Brand meaning is created partly through product design and market communication, but also through the communication between stakeholders in society (Balmer and Gray, 2000) in the form of, for example, public speech and print (Twitchell, 2002), word-of-mouth (Keller, 2003), and user imagery (Aaker, 1996). The idea of *user imagery* is that values are transferred to a brand through the people who are associated with it, i.e., that the brand meaning is dependent on those associated with the brand (cf. McCracken, 1989). This includes both companies' employees and the users of the product (Keller, 2000). Hence, consumers' perceptions of the brand users affect their perception of the meaning of the brand (Aaker, 1996; Schroeder, 2005; Brioschi, 2006). This relationship works in both ways. If 'desirable' individuals consume the brand it instils values of 'luxury' into the brand, and if 'undesirable' individuals consume the brand it has the opposite effect.

This idea of user imagery has led firms to invest in *ideal* users such as sponsored athletes, spokespersons, and people portrayed in advertising to promote the luxury of the brand (Aaker, 1996). The ideal users should not be confused with the target group for the brand, but should rather be seen as a reflection of the image that the firm wants to offer the target group (cf. Kapferer, 1994). In contrast to the ideal user who uses a brand because he or she is financially compensated for doing so, the *typical* users are those individuals actually using the brand (Aaker, 1996). In the same way as spokespersons, but arguably even more powerfully, these users instil the brand with values by conveying what can be seen as a visual word-of-mouth (cf. Twitchell, 2002; Keller, 2003). The focus in this chapter is on attempts to manage these typical users in order to improve the user imagery.

In essence, user imagery can be used as a tool to create a boundary between 'desirable' and 'undesirable' individuals. Framed in this way, it is clear that user imagery is based on the more general marketing ideal of identifying and targeting certain customer groups. Traditionally, this practice is referred to as positioning, which entails segmenting consumers into distinct but homogeneous target groups that require similar marketing mixes (e.g., Kapferer, 1994; Aaker, 1996; Keller, 2003). In these positioning strategies, any addition of customers not belonging to the target group is seen as a bonus – a *positive* side effect. However, when applying the user imagery logic, additional customers are seen as a *negative* side effect if they are from the 'undesirable' group. Since the consumers are perceived not only as income generators, but also as image creators, it is rational for purveyors of luxury to turn away potential consumers if their undesirable characteristics would taint the luxury brand's image. In other words, by employing customer base management to improve brand image, companies sacrifice short-term financial gain to create brand meaning. In creating brand meaning, user imagery plays a more central role for luxury products than for other product categories, since conventional branding activities are ineffective for luxury products (cf. Baker, 2006). Hence, brand meaning has to be created in alternative ways for luxury products, and companies have to rely more on influencing social discourses through tools such as user imagery than on traditional activities (cf. Twitchell, 2002).

The boundary creation between 'desirable' and 'undesirable' customers can be expected to affect a person's perception of herself. Several authors have shown that consumption is closely linked to the construction of identities (e.g., Levy, 1959; McCracken, 1986; Belk, 1988), and that this is especially so in consumption of luxury products (Berry, 1994; Vigneron and Johnson, 2004). Hence, by classifying an individual as a 'desirable'/'undesirable' consumer, companies influence individuals' identities. As will be shown in the study presented in this chapter, this influence can literally lead to matters of life or death. Despite these corporate responsibility implications, prior research into user imagery has neglected these aspects and solely focused on how firms strategically can employ user imagery to improve the brand personality (e.g., Aaker, 1996). Simultaneously, corporate responsibility research has neglected the topics of luxury and user imagery, leading to a lack of critical analysis of the implications of this type of corporate practice.

METHOD

To analyse how corporations strive to achieve user imagery through customer base management in luxury products, we make use of data from a study of Sweden's most luxurious nightclub – The Spy Bar. Data were collected via interviews, observations, and document analysis. The focus in the data collection was on studying the operations of the nightclub in relation to user imagery and customer base management. The Spy Bar is unusual in the sense that individuals from a security firm are the only individuals that the customers interacted with (except for bartenders and DJs). This is true also for the presentation of The Spy Bar on its webpage and in media articles in which the CEO of the security company – rather than the CEO of the nightclub – is the front figure for the nightclub. Thus, the nightclub has outsourced all significant interaction with customers to an independent security company. This has the effect that the head of security at The Spy Bar (also the CEO of the security company) is well known among the general public in Sweden. Given the importance of the security officers, they were the chosen focus in our data collection.

In total, 12 semi-structured interviews (lasting on average one hour) were made with the security officers (including the CEO) working at The Spy Bar. A handful of additional interviews were also made with representatives for The Spy Bar. These interviews were mainly used to provide a background understanding of the directives provided by The Spy Bar management to the security officers. Additionally, 15 semi-structured interviews (lasting on average 30 minutes) were made with customers inside The Spy Bar and potential customers queuing outside the nightclub.

In addition to interviews, observations were conducted during four evenings at the nightclub. During the observation study, the researcher closely followed the security officers' work and interaction with customers. In parts of the observation study, access was granted to the two-way radios used by the security officers. The observation study was focused on two central aspects of the security officers' work – the selection of customers outside the nightclub and the disciplining of customers inside the nightclub.

Finally, written documentation (in the form of web pages and media articles) was used as both input to interviews and as validation of the data received through observations and interviews. There were few inconsistencies between the data obtained in interviews and observations, but some between the data presented in the written documentation and the observations/interviews. In cases of inconsistencies, these were sometimes discussed with the security officers, and we based the descriptions presented below mainly on the data provided in the interviews and observations, since these seemed more reliable than the media articles and web pages.

The collected data were used to construct thick descriptions of the activities of the security officers. To validate the descriptions, they were sent to the CEO of the security company, who expressed no critique regarding the descriptions of their work. Based on these descriptions of the security officers' activities and the interviews with customers and The Spy Bar management, a 'typical' nightclub evening was constructed (as presented in the empirical section below). Evidently, there are problems in constructing a 'typical' nightclub evening, since nothing is 'typical' in corporate practice. However, this was perceived as the best way to present the empirical data in order to convey an understanding of a nightclub evening at The Spy Bar to the reader.

Night clubs belong to a specific category of luxury products. As shown by Allères (2005), luxury can be divided into different price levels. There is the inaccessible luxury level of yachts and mansions, the intermediate level of cars, watches, and hotels, and finally the accessible level where, although the products are more expensive than their substitutes, most people can afford to buy them should they wish to do so. This level covers, for example, champagne, perfume, and the empirical focus of this chapter: nightclub visits. In focusing on nightclub visits, i.e., on attainable luxury products, the purpose of this chapter is not to discuss the problems related to the first two types of offerings and, hence, to question the excluding nature of prices. Rather, the purpose of this chapter is to analyse those products that are attainable for most individuals. In these cases, the limitation has to be achieved in other ways than through prices, and as is shown in this chapter one way to achieve this is influencing user imagery via customer base management.

A 'TYPICAL' EVENING AT THE NIGHTCLUB THE SPY BAR

After midnight on a regular Friday evening, a large crowd stands outside a small entrance to a nightclub – The Spy Bar – in the city of Stockholm (the capital of Sweden). Separating the queuing individuals from the nightclub is a red rope, and inside the rope numerous security officers dressed in black suits control the queue, carefully selecting who should be allowed to enter the club. The queue is different from the traditional linear queue. It does not even look like a queue; rather, like an unstructured ocean of people. The head of the security officers (also the CEO of the security company) explains that this queue structure is generally referred to as a 'rainbow' queue, and that the purpose of the queue is to allow the security officers to freely select who is allowed to enter the nightclub without having to consider how long each individual has waited outside the club. The CEO mainly controls the selection of individuals himself, making him an influential and well-known figure in Swedish nightlife. He has, for example, been invited to go on tours around Sweden as a celebrity security officer.

While the selection procedure is extremely strict at this hour, it was easier to enter the nightclub earlier in the evening. Then, individuals were allowed to enter who now would not even come close to the 'desirability' status of the selected few that are allowed entrance. The security officers explain this by referring to the need for the nightclub to receive revenues throughout the evening, and that they have fewer individuals to select from early on in the evening. At this hour, the possibility to select individuals is seemingly endless. The management of The Spy Bar has defined the characteristics of those that are to be allowed to enter the nightclub, and the security officers do their best to implement these directives in practice. When asked what they are searching for in a customer, the security officers have difficulties providing a precise answer. Rather, they provide a list of characteristics to exemplify what they are after. Guests are to be celebrities, over 25 years of age, from the city centre, dressed in Gucci, trendy, financially wealthy, journalists, stockbrokers, real estate agents and/or CEOs. While those few with just the 'right' characteristics enter the nightclub quickly, the vast majority of guests wait outside for often over an hour, uncertain whether they will be allowed entrance. The length of the wait is also difficult to predict, since the 'rainbow' queue system provides no signals regarding whether, and if so when, a person will be allowed to enter.

The selection of individuals is a complex and sometimes ruthless process. The security officers establish contact with the visitors through body language and eye contact. Rarely, if ever, is there any verbal communication between the security officers and the visitors other than to inform someone to enter the nightclub or to impolitely answer visitors' attempts to persuade the officers to allow them entrance. Occasionally, the security officers signal (in a hardly noticeable way) to groups of individuals that they are to walk around the block and return without certain members of the group. Hence, the officers force groups to be split into the 'desirable' who will be allowed to enter and the 'undesirable' who will not.

Sporadically, celebrities arrive at the nightclub, walking past the crowd and straight into the club. This does not seem to surprise anyone. However, sporadically some individuals are allowed to enter the nightclub without fitting the expected characteristics of a Spy Bar customer. The queuing visitors quickly recognise this (they are often highly skilled themselves in judging the likeliness of others entering), and discussions start in the crowd. Some of these unexpected guests wear visible signs indicating that they are part of well-known criminal groups, while other unexpected guests seem to have a close relationship with some of the security officers (most often the CEO). Another surprising event to those in the queue is that some celebrities arrive highly confident of their chances to enter the club, but are denied entrance. This includes famous Swedish actors and Olympic winning sportsmen. Seemingly humiliated, these celebrities are forced to leave the queue and continue to another nightclub. Loud discussions start among the other queuing individuals, focused on understanding why these celebrities were not allowed to enter. Did the security officers not recognise them? Are the officers incompetent? Are they incapable of making a 'fair' selection?

The answer to why the celebrities were denied access to the nightclub is found inside the club. Here, the security officers are responsible for inducing the 'right' atmosphere to the nightclub. This mainly involves assisting guests and ensuring that no acts of violence occur throughout the evening, but it also involves disciplining individuals to behave in a 'correct' way. For instance, visitors standing in certain areas of the nightclub or attempting to climb onto the window-ledges are quickly and harshly reprimanded. If an individual, despite these reprimands, does not comply with the 'correct' behaviour, the security officers either make him/her leave the nightclub or restrict the individual's future entrance to the club. Such previous acts of 'incorrectness' (although of more severe nature) were the reasons for denying the above-discussed celebrities entrance to the nightclub.

In addition to disciplining customers inside the nightclub, the security officers are responsible for ensuring that only 'highly desirable' individuals are allowed entrance to the VIP areas within the club. The Spy Bar is thus really two, or even more, nightclubs, sharing little more than the same portal. In this way, the security officers' sorting of individuals into categories continues inside the nightclub as well.

About forty-five minutes before closing time, the security officers stop allowing individuals to enter the nightclub. However, this is not signalled to those in the queue, leading many to queue until the club closes. The evening ends with the security officers lining up outside the club, making sure that everything runs smoothly when the customers leave.

THE ROLE OF USER IMAGERY

The conducted study clearly illustrates that the security officers at The Spy Bar use customer base management to influence the user imagery and the nightclub brand in the desired direction. Hence, this study confirms the arguments and results of previous studies that corporations in practice use customer base management to influence user imagery (e.g., Aaker, 1996; Twitchell, 2002). In the case of The Spy Bar, this practice was explicitly demanded by The Spy Bar management and consciously implemented by the security officers. The security officers even regarded customer base management as one of the most – if not the most – important of their work tasks. As the CEO of the security company noted: "Popular nightclubs have strategically organised their activities in order to sort people into an A class and a B class. The entire organisation from the interior to the queue system is designed for this purpose." Furthermore, most security officers did not regard this as problematic or disturbing. Rather, it was seen as the common practice among luxurious nightclubs, a necessary strategy for creating the luxury status of the club.

The Spy Bar's focus on user imagery via customer base management should be seen in the light of the fact that the club had ample opportunities to select customers. Since a nightclub visit is an attainable luxury product (cf. Allères, 2005), most individuals can afford an evening at The Spy Bar and, given the perception of the club as the most luxurious club in Sweden, numerous individuals attempt to spend an evening at the club. However, the club is limited in size by the building it is occupying, so even if the security officers desired to allow all interested individuals to enter the club, this would be impossible. Hence, the club is in the rare situation that demand for its product vastly exceeds the supply and that the supply capability cannot easily be increased.

The security officers used customer base management to influence user imagery in two main ways. First, and most importantly, when selecting who should be allowed to enter the nightclub. The 'rainbow' queue system at The Spy Bar was an important tool for selecting who was allowed to enter. By creating a crowd of individuals outside the red rope that marks the division between inside and outside the nightclub, the security officers were able to continuously choose individuals who were perceived as 'desirable'. These 'desirable' individuals included royalties, 'celebrities', wealthy individuals, and 'cool' individuals. Importantly, an individual's spending capability was not the main criterion for the security officers' selections; rather, the officers attempted to identify an "appearance of luxuriousness". The 'undesirable' individuals, on the other hand, included overweight, poorly dressed, and 'ugly' individuals (especially if these were also immigrants and/or not from the city centre). These individuals were consciously restricted from entering the nightclub, regardless of their spending capability. In addition to the categories 'desirable' and 'undesirable', the security officers sorted individuals into a 'potentially desirable'/'not undesirable' category. This category filled a central role for the nightclub, to create a queue as large as possible outside the nightclub. Hence, the security officers consciously attempted to maximise the queue outside the club both to create an appearance of popularity, and to communicate that even the seemingly – to an outside observer – 'cool' and 'desirable' individuals in the queue were not 'desirable' *enough* to enter the nightclub. This practice can be understood as a negative user imagery message: these seemingly desirable individuals are not even qualified to be 'typical' users of The Spy Bar.

Second, in addition to the queue system, the security officers used customer base management inside the club. First, in a similar fashion as outside, there were restricted 'VIP' areas within the club, open only to especially 'desirable' individuals. Second, the security officers disciplined individuals inside the nightclub who did not act as a 'desirable' individual ought to act. This included evident behaviour such as acts of violence and sexual harassment, but also standing in certain parts of the nightclub and addressing the security officers in the 'wrong' way. Thus, besides being sorted into 'desirable' and 'undesirable' on the basis of mainly external attributes via different queue systems, individuals were sorted into 'desirable' and 'undesirable' through their behaviour inside the nightclub. 'Undesirable' behaviour occasionally led to individuals being forced to leave the club, but more frequently to being restricted in future attempts to enter the club. The sorting of individuals into 'desirable' and 'undesirable' continued throughout the customers' nightclub visit and affected their future classification. However, since there is not a perfect relation between 'desirable' external attributes and 'desirable' behaviour, some individuals who had 'desirable' external attributes were denied access to the nightclub due to behavioural aspects. For others who were unaware of the behavioural 'problems' of these individuals, this practice sent the message that the security officers were poorly skilled at recognising 'desirability', in turn potentially threatening the nightclub's user image.

MISERY AS CORPORATE MISSION

There are several implications of the security officers' classification of individuals into 'desirable' and 'undesirable'. First, the 'undesirable' individuals risk spending their weekend queuing outside the nightclub. It is common that individuals spend hours in the queue outside the nightclub, and still are not allowed entrance. Despite this, they return the next weekend to repeat the procedure. Since the 'rainbow' queue system restricts contact with the security officers, individuals receive no signals of whether they are to be allowed to enter the club or not. Hence, they may – and many in fact do – spend much of their weekend queuing outside The Spy Bar. Such behaviour can be considered desperate, suggesting a self-fulfilling process that might render them ever less desirable to the security officers who remember them.

Second, and even more important, the classification of individuals into 'desirable' and 'undesirable' not only influences individuals' weekend activities, but also their perception of themselves. Numerous authors have shown that consumption is closely linked to individuals' construction of their identities (e.g., Levy, 1959; McCracken, 1986; Belk, 1988), and that this is especially so in consumption of luxury products (Berry, 1994). Hence, to be classified as 'desirable' or 'undesirable' potentially affects individuals' perception of themselves. The vast majority of visitors to The Spy Bar are uncertain of their status when arriving at the nightclub, with only a handful confident of being allowed to enter the club. That most individuals are uncertain of their 'desirability' makes them susceptible to security officers' classifications. Our study's results also indicate that the security officers influence the visitors' perception of themselves –in both positive and negative ways. The few who are allowed to enter seem to experience improved self-confidence (at least temporarily) in perceiving themselves as successful individuals. On the other hand, the majority who are restricted from entering seem to experience diminished self-confidence (at least temporarily) in perceiving themselves as less successful than they had thought. In an age when individuals are increasingly uncertain of their identity and value (e.g., Gabriel and Lang, 2006), these 'desirability' signals plausibly have important implications for individuals' identities.

Moving from an individual to an organisational level, the links between the security officers' actions and individuals' identities provide an overall understanding of luxurious nightclubs' operations. As much as nightclubs are providing a service in the form of entertainment, they are also providing a service in ranking of individuals. The results of our study indicate that individuals do not mainly visit the nightclub for the music, drinks etc., but rather for the potential to feel 'desirable', 'successful' and 'exclusive'. However, in order for a selected few to feel this, the majority has to be categorised oppositely – as 'undesirable', 'unsuccessful' and 'ordinary'. This is achieved through creating a widespread queue of 'undesirable' individuals outside the club – individuals to whom the few 'desirable' can feel superior. Hence, while the mission of nightclubs is to create a feeling of 'successfulness' among the selected few, it is also to create a feeling of 'unsuccessfulness' or 'misery' among the vast majority of individuals interested in visiting the club. The nightclubs (and in the Spy Bar case the security officers) have become judges of our times, classifying individuals into an A and a B group while simultaneously promoting everyone's wish to be in the A group.

This categorisation of individuals as 'undesirable' is not always accepted by the undesirable, making them strike back. In the studied case, this resistance mainly took the form of verbal abuse of the security officers, but sometimes it also led to threats and acts of violence. When reflecting on these forms of resistance, the CEO of the security company said: "In practice, the 'rainbow' queue system leads to increased frustration and disorder among the guests – the opposite of the task of a security officer." Hence, the CEO of the security company was aware of the connections between their practices aimed at creating an exclusive user imagery and the resistance of the 'undesirable'. In extreme cases, the resistance has led to devastating consequences with frustrated 'undesirables', returning after being denied entrance to the nightclub, firing weapons into the queues and at the security officers. This has occurred several times in The Spy Bar area, although not directly at the nightclub itself. Hence, the practice of categorising individuals into 'desirable' and 'undesirable' customers to improve the user imagery can have severe implications, not only for the security officers but also for the individuals queuing outside the nightclub.

Cracks in the Façade

So far, the analysis of the role of user imagery at The Spy Bar has focused on the instances where security officers manage the customer base according to the nightclub's mission. However, there are also instances when this is not the case – when there are cracks in the façade. The most obvious such crack is that the 'desirability' of an individual seems related to when the individual attempts to enter the nightclub. A 'desirable' individual at 10-11 p.m. is often an 'undesirable' individual at 1-3 a.m. (not to mention at 4 a.m.). This is both because 'desirable' individuals only enter the nightclub scene after midnight, and because it is important for the profitability of the nightclub to receive revenues throughout the evening. This practice can be referred to as a 'geek tax' in the sense that, by entering the club early and spending money throughout the evening, otherwise 'undesirable' individuals buy themselves an entrance ticket to the club. However, the consequence of this practice is that 'undesirable' individuals are at the club later in the evening when the 'desirable' individuals arrive. Hence, the 'desirable' individuals are faced with 'undesirable' ones inside the club, potentially making them doubt the exclusiveness of the club and the 'success factor' of the clientele. Partly, the nightclub solves this by having VIP rooms, protecting highly 'desirable' individuals from mingling with 'undesirable' ones – but partly the 'problem' remains.

An additional crack in the exclusive user image façade is that the security officers allow some 'undesirable' individuals to enter despite an ample supply of 'desirable' candidates in the queue. This initially puzzling observation is partly explained by some of these 'undesirable' individuals having personal relations with the security officers. The security officers themselves would probably not have been classified as 'desirable' according to their own standards, and neither would their friends. However, since decision-makers are complex individuals (e.g., Sjöstrand, 1997), as well as boundedly rational (e.g., Simon, 1957; Cyert and March, 1963), they make decisions that are not necessarily in line with the corporate mission. The security officers sometimes prioritised assisting their friends over following the corporate mission, leading to 'undesirable' individuals being allowed to enter the nightclub. In addition to friends, other 'undesirable' individuals who still were allowed entrance belonged to criminal groups, and were given access to the nightclub in order for the security officers and the nightclub to avoid repercussions.

In sum, to enter the nightclub an individual has to be either 'desirable', or 'undesirable' but willing to pay a 'geek tax', or have a personal relationship with the security officers, or belong to a criminal group. Hence, there were several groups of individuals who, for different reasons, were allowed to enter the nightclub and who did not fit the characteristics of a 'desirable' individual. The practice of customer base management to improve user imagery seems, then, to be somewhat difficult to implement in practice, despite conscious attempts by The Spy Bar management. These cracks in the façade appeared to affect the user imagery negatively, with some individuals noting that the nightclub was not as 'exclusive' and 'successful' as they expected. Consequently, the instances of security officers' selection 'failures' negatively affected the nightclub's user imagery.

CONCLUSION

This chapter has shown that corporate responsibility researchers need to broaden their perspective and analyse the intersection between *what* products are produced and *how* they are produced, in order to capture central corporate responsibility issues. It has also shown that marketing researchers are well advised to include aspects of corporate responsibility in their analyses of user imagery. By addressing these gaps in previous research, the chapter has provided an initial study of the corporate responsibility implications of firms' customer base management strategies aimed at creating an exclusive user imagery. The study's results are distressing, indicating that some companies consciously organise their entire operations in order to sort individuals into 'desirable' and 'undesirable' categories. Furthermore, the employees sorting individuals often do not perceive this as problematic or unethical, despite being aware of the negative effects of their actions on the 'undesirable' individuals. They are just "doing their job".

Based on these results, the chapter has argued that exclusive nightclubs have two sides – one focused on entertaining the selected few and one focused on depreciating the vast majority. This 'enjoyment' and 'misery' of nightclubs are two sides of the same coin, with some people's 'enjoyment' being dependent on the 'misery' of others and vice versa. Indeed, the same duality may well be implied by the name of the nightclub The Spy Bar, since 'spy' is not only an English word meaning to see exclusive things, but also a Swedish word meaning 'to vomit'. More fundamentally, of course, it is a duality inherent in any society affluent and competitive enough to divide people into extreme winners and abject losers.

The conducted study has important implications for practitioners interested in altering the situation at exclusive nightclubs. First, the so-called 'rainbow' queue structure could be replaced by a regular queue system. This would shorten the time individuals spend in queues, force the security officers to inform and justify to each customer why he/she is not welcome, and decrease the frustration induced by the queue system. This fairly simple alteration in the operations of the nightclubs would significantly reduce the problems caused by the striving for an exclusive user image. Second, and more radically, the private security firms could be replaced by police officers, weakening the control of nightclub management on the selection and categorisation of individuals. Such a change would challenge the entire corporate organising for creation of an exclusive user imagery, compelling nightclub management to find alternative (and hopefully less problematic) ways of creating 'exclusiveness'.

ACKNOWLEDGMENT

We gratefully acknowledge the support of Michael Arvidsson, Johan Carlsson, Jacob Jonmyren, and Mattias Magnusson in collecting part of the data for this study.

REFERENCES

Aaker, D. A. (1996). *Building Strong Brands*. New York, NY: The Free Press.
Allères, D. (2005). *Luxe...: Stratégies, Marketing*. Paris: Economica.
Anner, M., Greer, I., Hauptmeier, M., Lillie, N., & Winchester, N. (2006). The Industrial Determinants of Transnational Solidarity: Global Interunion Politics in Three Sectors. *European Journal of Industrial Relations, 12*(1), 7-27.
Baker, R. (2006). *Top 10 Reasons Why Affluent Life Style Marketing is Essential Today*. Dallas: Premium Knowledge Group.
Balmer, J. M. T., & Gray, E. R. (2000). Corporate Identity and Corporate Communications: Creating a Competitive Advantage. *Industrial & Commercial Training, 32*(6), 256-261.
Belk, R. W. (1988). Possessions and the Extended Self. *Journal of Consumer Research, 15*(2), 139.
Berry, C. J. (1994). *The Idea of Luxury: A Conceptual and Historical Investigation*. Cambridge: Cambridge University Press.
Brenkert, G. G. (2000). Social Products Liability: The Case of the Firearms Manufacturers. *Business Ethics Quarterly, 10*(1), 21-32.
Brioschi, A. (2006). Selling Dreams: The Role of Advertising in Shaping Luxury Brand Meaning. In J. E. Schroeder, & M. Salzer-Mörling (Eds.), *Brand Culture* (pp. 198-210). New York, NY: Routledge.
Carley, M. (2005). Global Agreements – State of Play. *European Industrial Relations Review, 381*, 14-18.
Carroll, S. J., & Gannon, M. J. (1997). *Ethical Dimensions of International Management*. Thousand Oaks, CA: Sage.
Cyert, R. M., & March, J. G. (1963). *A Behavioral Theory of the Firm*. Englewood Cliffs, NJ: Prentice-Hall.
De George, R. T. (1990). *Business Ethics*. New York, NY: MacMillan Publishers.
De George, R. T. (1993). *Competing with Integrity in International Business*. New York, NY: Oxford University Press.
Donaldson, T. (1989). *The Ethics of International Business*. New York, NY: Oxford University Press.
Donaldson, T. (1996). Values in Tension: Ethics Away from Home. *Harvard Business Review, 74*(5), 48-62.
Donaldson, T., & Dunfee, T. W. (1994). Towards a Unified Conception of Business Ethics: Integrative Social Contracts Theory. *Academy of Management Review, 19*(2), 252-285.
Dubois, B., & Paternault, C. (1995). Observations: Understanding the World of International Luxury Brands: The "Dream Formula". *Journal of Advertising Research, 35*(4), 69-76.
Egels-Zandén, N. (2007). Suppliers' Compliance with MNCs' Codes of Conduct: Behind the Scenes at Chinese Toy Suppliers. *Journal of Business Ethics* (in press).

Egels-Zandén, N., & Hyllman, P. (2006). Exploring the Effects of Union-NGO Relationships on Corporate Responsibility: The Case of the Swedish Clean Clothes Campaign. *Journal of Business Ethics, 64*(3), 303-316.

Egels-Zandén, N., & Hyllman, P. (2007). Evaluating Strategies for Negotiating Workers' Rights in Transnational Corporations: The Effects of Codes of Conduct and Global Agreements on Workplace Democracy. *Journal of Business Ethics* (in press).

Elm, N. (1998). The Business of Unethical Weapons. *Business Ethics: A European Review, 7*(1), 25-29.

Fairbrother, P., & Hammer, N. (2005). Global Unions – Past Efforts and Future Prospects. *Relations Industrielles/Industrial Relations, 60*(3), 405-431.

Frenkel, S. (2001). Globalization, Athletic Footwear Commodity Chains and Employment Relations in China. *Organization Studies, 22*(4), 531-562.

Gabriel, Y., & Lang, T. (2006). *The Unmanageable Consumer*. London: Sage.

Graafland, J. J. (2002). Sourcing Ethics in the Textile Sector: The Case of C&A. *Business Ethics: A European Review, 11*(3), 282-294.

Green, R. M. (2000). Legally Targeting Gun Makers: Lessons for Business Ethics. *Business Ethics Quarterly, 10*(1), 203-210.

Havemann, C. (1998). Hawks or Doves? The Ethics of UK Arms Exports. *Business Ethics: A European Review, 7*(4), 240-244.

Kapferer, J.-N. (1994). *Strategic Brand Management: New Approaches to Creating and Evaluating Brand Equity*. New York, NY: The Free Press.

Keller, K. L. (2000). The Brand Report Card. *Harvard Business Review, 78*(1), 147-157.

Keller, K. L. (2003). *Strategic Brand Management: Building, Measuring, and Managing Brand Equity*. Upper Saddle River, NJ: Prentice Hall, Pearson Education Ltd.

Kinder, P. D., & Domini, A. L. (1997). Social Screening: Paradigms Old and New. *Journal of Investing, 6*(4), 12-19.

Levy, S. J. (1959). Symbols for Sale. *Harvard Business Review, 37*(4), 117-124.

Maitland, G. (1998). The Ethics of the International Arms Trade. *Business Ethics: A European Review, 7*(4), 200-204.

McCracken, G. (1986). Culture and Consumption: A Theoretical Account of the Structure and Movement of the Cultural Meaning of Consumer Goods. *Journal of Consumer Research, 13*(1), 71-84.

McCracken, G. (1989). Who is the Celebrity Endorser? Cultural Foundations of the Endorsement Process. *Journal of Consumer Research, 16*(3), 310-321.

McWilliams, A., & Siegel, D. (2001). Corporate Social Responsibility: A Theory of the Firm Perspective. *Academy of Management Review, 26*(1), 117-127.

Newton, L. (1993). Gambling: A Preliminary Inquiry. *Business Ethics Quarterly, 3*(4), 405-418.

Riisgaard, L. (2005). Industrial Framework Agreements: A New Model of Securing Workers Rights?. *Industrial Relations, 44*(4), 707-737.

Schermerhom, J. R. Jr. (1999). Terms of Global Business Engagement in Ethically Challenging Environments: Applications to Burma. *Business Ethics Quarterly, 9*(3), 485-505.

Schroeder, J. E. (2005). The Artist and the Brand. *European Journal of Marketing, 39*(11/12), 1291-1305.

Simon, H. E. (1957). *Models of Man*. New York, NY: Wiley.

Sjöstrand, S. E. (1997). *The Two Faces of Management: The Janus Factor*. London: Thomson Learning.

Twitchell, J. B. (2002). Living it up: Our Love Affair with Luxury. New York, NY: Columbia University Press.

van Tulder, R., & Kolk, A. (2001). Multinationality and Corporate Ethics: Codes of Conduct in the Sporting Goods Industry. *Journal of International Business Studies, 32*(2), 267-283.

Vigneron, F., & Johnson, L. W. (1999). A Review and a Conceptual Framework of Prestige-Seeking Consumer Behavior. *Academy of Marketing Science Review, 1999*(1).

Vigneron, F., & Johnson, L. W. (2004). Measuring Perceptions of Brand Luxury. *Brand Management, 11*(6), 484-506.

Wills, J. (2002). Bargaining for the Space to Organize in the Global Economy: A Review of the Accor-IUF Trade Union Rights Agreement. *Review of International Political Economy, 9*(4), 675-700.

Winstanley, D., Clark, J., & Leeson, H. (2002). Approaches to Child Labour in the Supply Chain. *Business Ethics: A European Review, 11*(3), 210-223.

In: Business Ethics in Focus
Editor: Laura A. Parrish, pp. 289-303

ISBN: 978-1-60021-684-8
© 2007 Nova Science Publishers, Inc.

Chapter 13

RESPONSIBLE COMMUNICATION AS AN INTEGRATOR: DISCOURSES LINKING VALUES TO ACTIONS

Tarja Ketola[*]
Associate Professor of Sustainable Development
University of Vaasa, Finland

ABSTRACT

Corporate responsibility incorporates economic, social and ecological issues, and sees these three areas as essential parts of business operations – not just separate charity gestures, which would earn society's acceptance to a company's real business. All business operations should be responsible. This means that the values, discourses and actions of the company should be consistent with each other. Coordinating and integrating these three levels of responsibility is a challenging task.

Empirical research shows that there is a wide gap between corporate values and actions, which companies tend to bridge with their discourses. However, often companies utilize these discourses to deny, excuse and justify those of their actions that are inconsistent with their values.

Based on empirical findings, there are at least three kinds of linking pin roles for discourses in companies that claim to value responsibility. Corporate discourses may be (1) *schizophrenic:* the discourses praise responsible values while deny and excuse irresponsible actions; (2) *desperate:* the discourses assert commitment to responsible values while justify irresponsible actions; or (3) *sublimating*: the discourses advocate responsible values and admit irresponsible actions in order to enable them to be turned into responsible actions.

This chapter argues that (1) schizophrenic and (2) desperate discourses exemplify irresponsible communication, which leads to separating corporate values and actions further apart while (3) sublimating discourses exemplify responsible communication, which leads to integrating values and actions into responsible business operations.

---

[*] tarja.ketola@uwasa.fi

Introduction

The purpose of this chapter is to study the role of corporate discourses as a linking pin between corporate values and actions. In particular, the aim is to show how responsible corporate communication can integrate corporate values and actions and turn them genuinely responsible. Three types of discourses will be identified. Two of them tend to result in corporate irresponsibility and one in corporate responsibility. The fundamental assumption behind this research is that, in addition to the three horizontal areas of corporate responsibility, economic, social and ecological, there are three vertical levels of responsibility: values discourses and actions. First these three levels of responsibility are introduced and the need to coordinate and integrate them is discussed. Second, it is maintained that there is a gap between corporate discourses and actions, which has much to do with organizational psychological defences. Most defences prevent companies from facing the irresponsibility of their actions, but there is one defence, sublimation, which allows concessive discourses and recovering actions. Third, it is argued that of the three linking pin roles of discourses, the first two push values and actions further apart while the third brings them together. Finally, it is concluded that virtue ethical values, sublimating discourses and matriarchal or ideal actions both attract and influence each other so that corporate values, discourses and actions can become responsible.

Three Levels of Responsibility: Values, Discourses and Actions

Corporate sustainability (CS) incorporates economic, social and ecological sustainability. Corporate responsibility (CR) with the same three aspects – economic, social and ecological responsibility – is a milestone on the way towards corporate sustainability. In responsible business, social and ecological issues are considered an essential part of business operations – not just separate charity gestures, which would earn society's acceptance to the company's real business. Ideally, all business operations should be sustainable.

In order to achieve this goal, the values, discourses and actions of the company should be consistent with each other. The first step is to coordinate corporate values, discourses and actions, so that they are line with each other. The second step, integrating these three levels of responsibility is a challenging task: a company's every action and every word should serve its values in a clearly demonstrated fashion. The company's whole business should be shining with its joyous values!

A. Corporate *values* are based on ethics of some kind or other. Many large companies state their values explicitly. Most of them do not wish stakeholders to think that these values are egoistic. For this reason, the stated lists of corporate values usually try to show that the company looks after the interests of all its significant stakeholders. These kinds of values that benefit both the company and its partners are utilitarian (origins in Mill 1861). Egoistic and utilitarian ethics are teleological, i.e., goal-oriented. Some companies feel that they have duties to fulfil in society; their values are based on duty ethics (Kant 1785). Some companies are concerned about the rights (Gewirth 1978) of different stakeholders and others emphasize justice (Rawls 1971). Duty, rights and justice ethics are deontological, i.e., motive-oriented.

Few companies base their values on virtues (Aristotle 348 B.C.) such as moderation, kindness, generosity, justness, loyalty, reliability and flexibility. Virtue ethics are human nature -oriented. Corporate values can thus be divided into three broad categories: egoistic/utilitarian values, duty/rights/justice values and virtue ethical values (Ketola 2005c).

B. Since many different stakeholders in society are joining in the debates, companies need to master several different kinds of *discourses*. For example, Halme and Takala (2003) divide nuclear power discourses into political power discourses, economic discourses and responsibility discourses, which are conducted both parallel and overlapping each other in society – and within companies.

Corporate discourses can be studied in many ways. Corporate annual reports, environmental, social and corporate responsibility reports, corporate brochures, press releases, web-pages and speeches given by executives and other corporate representatives can be analysed by anyone. Companies themselves can examine their discourses even more thoroughly because they can add to this material also their internal reports, minutes of meetings, discussions etc.

The responsible and irresponsible actions of a company can be compared to its discourses on the same topics. How do they match and how do they differ? Are discourses utilized to defend irresponsible actions and/or to exaggerate responsible actions or do they reflect the company's actions accurately? If there are major differences between actions and discourses or if the main purpose of discourses is to deny, excuse or justify actions, both the discourses and actions of this company need improvements. All corporate personnel naturally would like to be able to tell others about the responsible actions of their company, be proud of them. That is why the corporate actions must be raised to such a level of responsibility that the whole personnel can take pride in them and their company. The executives should dare to allow corporate discourses to focus on the critical evaluation of corporate actions and their improvement ideation as well as on the open and honest communication of proud-making responsible actions and humble-making irresponsible actions.

Furthermore, the role of corporate discourses is to link corporate values to corporate actions. Discourses are linking pins, which communicate the shared corporate values to all internal and external stakeholders, so that all units, departments groups and individuals all over the world commit themselves to implementing them in all their actions. Discourses should also work the other way by comparing every single corporate action to corporate values: are these actions useful, needed or absolute necessary for the implementation of the values? In essence, a company can use discourses to value its actions. In this way it can establish an order of preference, which can then be utilized to measure, compare and standardize the actions.

C. The responsibility level of corporate *actions* depends on the company's choices. There are eight different kinds of corporate responsibility alternatives to choose from: suicidal, plutocentric, anthropocentric, biocentric, technocentric, patriarchal, matriarchal, and ideal responsibility (Ketola 2006b). Suicidal companies minimize their economic, social and ecological responsibilities. Plutocentric prioritize economic responsibilities over social and ecological responsibilities. Anthropocentric companies give social responsibilities a preference over others. Biocentric companies emphasize ecological responsibility over economic or social responsibility. Patriarchal companies are traditional: they take both economic and social responsibilities. Technocentric companies take their economic and ecological responsibilities seriously but do not accept more social responsibilities than the law requires. Matriarchal companies find social and ecological responsibilities more important than economic responsibilities. Ideal companies maximize their economic, social and ecological responsibilities.

There seems to be a connection between the value basis a company chooses and the action alternative it chooses (Ketola 2005a). Companies with egoistic values are usually suicidal. Companies adopting utilitarian values tend to be plutocentric. Those companies, which practice duty/rights/justice values, are often either anthropocentric, biocentric, patriarchal or technocentric in their actions. Companies basing their values on virtue ethics are either matriarchal or ideal.

Discourses have an interesting role in between the values and actions. We shall see what kinds of discourses are attracted by different kinds of values and actions and how different kinds of discourses influence corporate values and actions.

When coordinating and integrating values, discourses and actions, the crucial task is to match them horizontally and vertically as table 1 illustrates. Coordinating and integrating corporate values, discourses and actions does not usually follow a linear path from creating shared values for the company, adopting them in discourses and putting them into action. The order may be quite different and the levels often become intertwined. For example, companies started to take ecological responsibility in the 1990s first at the discourse level (Lovio 1995). They began talking about it, responding to public concerns. The same happened with the re-emergence of social responsibility at the beginning of the 21st century.

According to a British business association, the Business for Social Responsibility, responsible business addresses the legal, ethical, commercial and other expectations that society has for business, and makes decisions that fairly balance the claims of all key stakeholders (Barthorpe and Gleeson 2004). They put it simply: what you do, how you do it, and when and what you say (BSR 2003). This definition of corporate responsibility takes account of actions and discourses but does not take values into account. Religions and philosophies can offer the missing link to values. The societal significance of religion crystallizes in its ability to give legitimacy to dominant or emerging values, so that all actors in society, companies included, will put them into effect in speech and action. Similarly, the words of philosophers weigh a great deal in social discourses. Both religious leaders and philosophers can bring an outsider's more objective view of the prevailing and desired state of corporate responsibility.

Discourses are not neutral but socially constructive. The discourses of ruling groups, such as political and corporate leaders, have the strongest power to mould society to their liking. In addition to philosophy and religion, social and natural scientific research has an important counterbalancing role in preventing political and/or corporate autocracy.

The corporate responsibility speeches and other discourses of companies may differ greatly from their values and actions. In their discourses with interest groups companies are happy to talk about their fine values, but they also try to defend themselves against the accusations that different interest groups put forth concerning their actions. For example, according to Fineman (1998) the business world has incorporated its superficially green values into its conventional business rhetoric.

Table 1. Matching the values, discourses and actions of economic, social and ecological responsibilities

	Values	Discourses	Actions	Match
Economic responsibility	Economic values	Economic discourses	Economic actions	**All levels of economic responsibility**
Social responsibility	Social values	Social discourses	Social actions	**All levels of social responsibility**
Ecological responsibility	Ecological values	Ecological discourses	Ecological actions	**All levels of ecological responsibility**
Match	**All values**	**All discourses**	**All actions**	**Matches of all**

Adapted from Ketola 2005c.

THE GAP BETWEEN CORPORATE DISCOURSES AND ACTIONS

The empirical studies conducted by Rhee and Lee (2003) show that there is a huge gap between corporate rhetoric and reality Corporate responsibility rhetoric changes faster than the corresponding reality. In the learning process reality tries to catch up with the rhetoric but since also rhetoric makes constant progress, the gap remains. Corporate initiative, top management leadership and external pressures from important interest groups have similar influence on both, but legitimacy pressures have greater impact on rhetoric and this deepens the gap. However, Rhee and Lee noticed that the "do the right thing" organization culture helps the responsibility reality to catch up the rhetoric.

Eden (1999) has discovered that companies and business associations resort to "expertise and rationality" rhetoric in their attempts to legitimize their evasion of responsibilities. They claim to be experts who understand the issues better than the laymen and who act rationally. Psychologically speaking these companies use the defence called intellectualization.

There are many psychological defence mechanisms that individuals and organizations use to protect themselves against anxiety caused by internal and external pressures. Organizational and managerial defences have been studied widely (e.g. Brown 1997, Brown and Starkey 2000, DeBoard 1978, Feldman 2003, Hirschhorn and Young 1991, Kets de Vries 2001, Kets de Vries and Miller 1984, 1991, Miller 1993, Morgan 1986). Organizations regulate their self-esteem through ego-defences. Defences are instrumental in protecting the moral integrity of the personality – whether individual or organizational – even at the expense of sacrificing the morality of actions. It is more important for (individuals and) organizations to feel that they are moral persons than to face the reality, i.e., the immorality of their actions.

Discourse analyses can point out the imbalances and problem points of discourses and amend the prevailing practices. By utilizing discourse analysis to identify the defences that companies use, it is possible to reach the root of the problem: companies are fooling themselves as well as others by denying, excusing and justifying their irresponsible actions. Having to be constantly on the defensive and possibly even acting against their individual values is an enormous mental stress for the managers and other personnel. Instead of having to resort defences in their discourses and spending plenty of time, money and energy on these debates, companies could spend the same time, money and energy to change their actions more responsible.

However, at the individual level, psychological defences are crucial for maintaining the wholeness of the ego and upholding the self-esteem through difficult times. The challenge is to allow the defences of individual members of the organization without letting the whole organization to regress to them.

Defence analyses have not yet been used to evaluate corporate responsibility discourses. In fact defences have been utilized in the corporate discourse analysis of a crisis situation (Ketola 2004), but not in every-day corporate responsibility rhetoric.

Managerial and organizational psychological defences have an important role in the slow, and often painful, change process towards a more responsible corporation. Swajkowski (1992) developed a matrix of four responses to accusations of organizational misconduct: refusals, excuses, justifications and concessions. The different psychological defences can be positioned into this matrix as figure 1 shows. This framework can be adapted to the analysis and evaluation of the corporate responsibility discourses of any kind of organization.

When an organization admits neither net harm nor responsibility for misconduct, it resorts to *refusals*. These refusals can take different forms: an organization may be in denial, it may repress misconduct into its unconscious, it may try to undo misconduct with tricks, or it may have omnipotent fantasies about its own greatness in order to forget its misconduct.

If an organization admits net harm but not responsibility for misconduct, it uses *excuses*. Splitting, projection, projective identification and regression are common excuses, with which an organization can claim that someone else is responsible for the occurrence. Idealization also wipes an organization clean of any misconduct. Isolation helps an organization to distance itself from both the incident and the accusers.

	Admits net harm? YES	Admits net harm? NO
Admits responsibility? YES	Concessions: -introjection -sublimation	Justifications: -rationalization -intellectualization -devaluing -reaction formation -object displacement -compensation
Admits responsibility? NO	Excuses: -splitting -projection -projective identification -regression -idealization -isolation	Refusals: -denial -repression -undoing -omnipotent fantasies

Figure 1. Organizational defences within four responses to accusations of organizational misconduct (Ketola 2004: 156).

Organizations, which admit responsibility for misconduct but do not admit that their misconduct has caused net harm, utilize *justifications*. Common justifications include rationalization, intellectualization and devaluing. In addition, through reaction formation an organization tries to hide its anger for having been caught. Through object displacement it can direct this anger to a third party, if it does not dare to use compensation to retaliate on the informer.

An organization uses *concessions* when it admits both net harm and responsibility for misconduct. Introjection is a helpless way of pleading guilty, but sublimation is a constructive form of concession that refines the primitive urges into repairing the wrong done and into reorienting towards future challenges.

Most companies wish to maintain an image of a responsible corporation (Ketola 2004, Rhee and Lee 2003). If this image is questioned either by internal or external stakeholders, certain forms of organizational behaviour, such as the use of psychological defences may become excessive. In these kinds of situations companies typically reveal their true nature, which they manage to hide under normal circumstances.

Bradford and Garrett (1995) conducted an empirical study on the impact of the four corporate responses on corporate image. In their research setting companies responded to accusations on unethical behaviour in four different situations: commission (company could provide evidence that it did not commit the alleged action), control (company could provide evidence that it did not have control over the occurrence), standards (company could provide evidence that inappropriate standards were used to evaluate the action) and agreement (company concluded that the allegations were valid). In all situations concessions had the best impact on corporate image.

Nevertheless, defences still have important roles to play in organizations. The organizational defences act as

-*bumpers* against companies becoming too conscious of the gap between the corporate reality and their rhetoric;
-subconscious *breaks* against too fast change demands;
-*batteries* in their preconscious effort to prepare for the change (Ketola 2006a).

Usually refusals act as bumpers, excuses as breaks and justifications as batteries, while concessions imply that a change towards a more responsible corporation is taking place.

THE LINKING PIN ROLES OF DISCOURSES BETWEEN VALUES AND ACTIONS

Discourses have a different role in different value/action alternatives that claim to be responsible. Figure 2 illustrates three different kinds of linking pin positions of discourses in each alternative.

(1) SCHIZOPHRENIC:

- EGOISTIC/UTILITARIAN VALUES: -advertise responsibility
- DISCOURSES: -praise values | -deny/excuse irresponsible actions
- SUICIDAL/PLUTOCENTRIC ACTIONS: -benefit the company

(2) DESPERATE:

- DUTY/RIGHTS/JUSTICE VALUES: -oblige to responsibility
- DISCOURSES: -assert commitment to values | -justify irresponsible actions
- PATRIARCHAL/TECHNO-/BIO-/ANTHROPOCENTRIC ACTIONS: -try to follow the values but in vain

(3) SUBLIMATING:

- VIRTUE ETHICAL VALUES: -virtues saa asis for responsible actions
- DISCOURSES: -advocate responsible values -admit irresponsible actions and sublimate them into responsible actions
- IDEAL/MATRIARCHAL ACTIONS: -are mostly responsible -improve from feedback

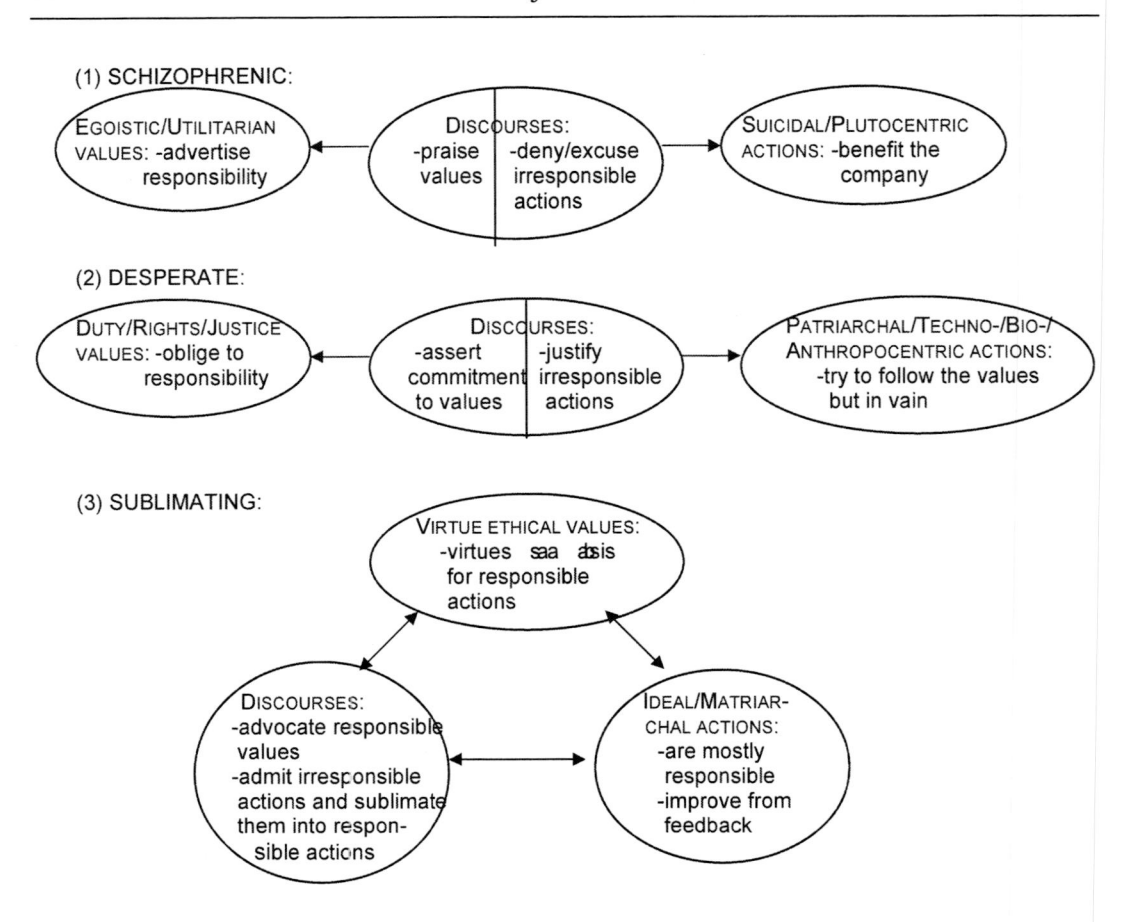

Figure 2. The relationships between values, discourses and actions in (1) schizophrenic, (2) desperate and (3) sublimating companies.

In a (1) *schizophrenic* company discourses are in a central position. The company uses discourses to praise corporate values it considers responsible. At the same time it utilizes discourses to defend with refusals and excuses its irresponsible actions. The discourses turn the company schizophrenic: on the one hand the defences drive the company to omnipotent fantasies about its level of responsibility and to idealize itself; on the other hand the defences drive it to deny, repress and undo all hard facts about its irresponsible deeds or to split and project the responsibility of its evil actions on others, so that it loses its sense of reality and begins to believe that it is acting responsibly. If the facts are undeniable, the last desperate defence is to regress or isolate itself to avoid responsibility.

For example, oil companies are enthusiastic advocators of their corporate responsibility. Their words are a far cry from their actions. Of the world's largest oil companies, *ExxonMobil,* has perhaps the worst reputation in ecological and social irresponsibility. Even compared to other major oil companies it has been characterized as Curly, the naughtiest of *Peter Pan*'s lost boys, who is always in trouble (Ketola 2005b) and the Beast of *Beauty and the Beast* (Rowlands 2000). Nevertheless, ExxonMobil has got corporate-wide ethical standards called Standards of Business Conduct, which consist of 16 polices including e.g., Ethics Policy, Political Activities Policy, International Operations Policy, Environment Policy and Safety Policy. Every year each and every ExxonMobil employee is obliged to sign a statement to affirm that s/he has not, to the best of his/her knowledge done anything that would violate the policies of this Standards of Business Conduct. In theory, this should lead to corporate responsibility as the actions of individual employees added together equal to corporate actions. In practice, the company's informal policies and practices press employees to act against some of the policies for the company's economic benefit. In this way ExxonMobil escapes corporate responsibility if it is caught in an irresponsible act. All responsibility falls on the individual employees.

A (2) *desperate* company is also at the mercy of its discourses. Its values oblige it to be responsible but its actions cannot fulfil this requirement as the values lack precise contents. For this reason the company tries with its discourses to assure others that it is following the values. At the same time it uses the discourses to justify irresponsible actions in order to make them look as responsible as possible in a given situation. The company tries to convince itself and others with justifications – rationalizations, intellectualizations, devaluing, reaction formations, object replacements and compensations – that it has done its best under the circumstances and better than others although it has not quite succeeded in reaching its values.

For example, many large companies that build factories in developing countries, where there is cheap labour and lower production costs, make their suppliers follow them there. For instance, the Finnish mobile phone company, Nokia, puts is suppliers in a difficult position with its tight purchase policies. One of Nokia's suppliers, *Perlos,* closed down its successful factory in Ylöjärvi, Finland, in March 2006 and laid off all its 600 employees there in order to get orders from Nokia. Nokia does not even ask for bids from Finnish factories, which forces its suppliers to transfer their production to developing countries. The suppliers have committed themselves to ecological and social responsibility values but they can follow them in practice neither in developed countries (shutdowns of eco-efficient factories, layoffs) nor in developing countries (eco-malignant factories, poor terms of employment and poor working conditions), which makes them desperate. Naturally, major companies such as Nokia are not desperate, but schizophrenic, in the way they excuse their actions of transferring both their own production and the production of their suppliers to low cost countries where there is little economic, social or environmental responsibility legislation to comply with.

In a (3) *sublimating* company values are the alpha and omega of corporate responsibility. They are based on universal virtues accepted by people all over the world. The company has truly committed itself to follow these values. In every situation it evaluates beforehand the responsibility level of all alternatives and chooses the most responsible alternatives for implementation. None of us is infallible, nor can we predict all consequences of our actions. The company immediately admits liability for those of its actions that turn out to be irresponsible. In every situation it looks for a chance to sublimate its primitive defence needs into virtuous, mending actions. In a sublimating company, responsible values, discourses and actions reinforce each other as a result of constant mutual feedback.

One example of a sublimating company is *Soya Ltd*, a tofu product company in Tammisaari, Finland. Soya Ltd was established in 1989. It produces different kinds of tofu products from organic soya beans. The company imports the soya beans from its Fair Trade partners in Brazil where gene manipulation of plants is illegal. The company has five employees in Finland. Its net sales are currently about 600.000 euros a year. The values of Soya Ltd do not include profit maximization or production efficiency maximization. Instead its basic values are: (a) employee satisfaction, (b) ecological production processes and (c) clean raw materials. (a) Soya Ltd's rationale is that since humans spend at least half of their waking hours at work, they should enjoy work and the work place. For that reason everyone is treated equally. There are no supervisors or clock time cards but employees agree upon the working hours on the basis on individual needs. (b) Soya Ltd uses geothermal energy in heating and collects all waste heat to return it back to the rock. The whole production process is as responsible as possible. One ecological problem remains there still unsolved: the final tofu products are packed in cardboard boxes so that they would not be damaged during transportation. (c) Finally, as mentioned before, Soya Ltd's main raw materials, organic soya beans, are imported economically, socially and ecologically sustainably through Fair Trade from small Brazilian farmers. All in all, Soya Ltd has truly committed itself to virtue ethical values and always tries to choose the most virtuous alternative in its operations. The company admits its failures and does its best to improve its performance. Hence Soya Ltd can be seen as a sublimating company, which could serve as a model for other small, medium-sized and large companies.

ExxonMobil has a long way to become a sublimating company. It could start with making the employees' commitment to its Standards of Business Conduct a virtue: employees should be encouraged to appeal to these standards if pressed to break them and be praised for it; the presser should be told off by the superior but also be allowed to sublimate for his/her irresponsible action. It is easier for ExxonMobil to become socially responsible than ecologically responsible, as its main raw material (crude oil), production processes and logistics, and core final products (fossil fuels) are inherently unsustainable. However, ExxonMobil can, if it wants to, change its line of business to renewable energy forms and turn itself from an oil company to a clean energy company.

Nokia could change its irresponsible actions to match its responsible values and stop excusing them in its discourses. It should instead harness its discourses to bridging its values and actions through constructive criticism. This is not as far-fetched as it seems: when Nokia made a videoed social responsibility inspection tour in one of its Chinese suppliers' factory in 2004, it allowed the film with all its revealing facts on the discrepancies between stated values and real practices to be shown on the Finnish national television. This kind of open and honest discourse can be expanded to Nokia's own actions. With such sublimating discourses Nokia's stated values on ecological and social responsibility could turn from rhetoric to reality.

Nokia's supplier, *Perlos*, should stop whining and choose from two paths to sublimation: either independence or demanding dependence. It can become more independent of Nokia, find other, more responsible customers, and if necessary, change its products and production processes to meet the needs of customers who have truly committed themselves to virtue ethical values. It would not be the first time a company changes its whole production concept to find more attractive markets. If Perlos cannot become independent of Nokia, it can in any case join the likeminded business, governmental and non-governmental organizations to press Nokia to meet its social and ecological responsibility standards. However, during summer 2006, Perlos laid off another 600 employees at its remaining Finnish units and in spring 2007 it decided to close down these units altogether, leaving another 1,400 people unemployed.

It is evident that (1) schizophrenic and (2) desperate discourses exemplify irresponsible communication, which leads to separating corporate values and actions further apart while (3) sublimating discourses exemplify responsible communication, which leads to integrating values and actions into responsible business operations.

CONCLUSION

There are intertwined connections between corporate values, discourses and actions. Basically a company's values should lead to same kinds of discourses and actions. A company's values usually evolve during the years, and this should influence its discourses and actions. In fact, it is often the changing discourses that gradually change the values and actions of a company: a company needs to respond to the pressures from its business environment and society at large by reflecting (or imitating) their discourses in order to gain their acceptance and maintain its licence to operate.

Most companies are *reactive*: they simply react to pressure. *Proactive* companies anticipate the changes needed by analysing the discourses in their business environment and by drawing conclusions of their predicted outcomes. *Entrepreneurial* companies change their actions before any societal discourses are powerful enough to be heard. These companies are very sensitive to the weak signals in society's changing values. They want to lead the change. *Creative* companies are not dependent on the outside world – they have their own internal values, discourses and actions, which, at their best, make them champions.

I have developed a model, illustrated in figure 3, which describes the relationships between corporate values, discourses and actions (Ketola 2005c). According to this model, certain kinds of values lead to certain kinds of discourses, which again lead to certain kinds of actions. The model is a simplification in the sense that does not take account of the intertwined relationships between values, strategies and actions in which each of them can influence each other. The basic message of the model is simply that I egoistic values lead to refusing discourses which ultimately lead to suicidal actions; II utilitarian values lead to excusing discourses which lead to plutocentric actions; III duty/rights/justice values lead to justifying discourses which lead to patriarchal or anthropocentric or technocentric or biocentric actions; and IV virtue ethical values lead to either introjective discourses which lead to matriarchal actions or to sublimating discourses which lead to ideal actions.

The model argues that the only responsible value alternative for companies is the virtue ethical values. Virtuous values can lead to either introjective or sublimating corporate discourses. Introjective discourses internalize the evil, i.e., the social and ecological irresponsibility of the current (business) world, and attempt to correct the wrongs by focussing on solving social and ecological issues. In the current market economy (which has prevailed only for a couple of decades and may not last), matriarchal actions that give social and ecological responsibilities a priority over economic responsibilities are often unrealistic. Therefore, in this day and age ideal actions that take equal account of economic, social and ecological responsibilities are the realistic responsible alternative in which sublimating discourses are possible and most welcome to further this threefold responsibility.

Sublimating discourses mean responsible communication, which leads to responsible business operations. There is no room for hiding behind words. Just as the title of this chapter argues, responsible communication is an integrator: discourses link values to actions.

VALUES:	DISCOURSES:	ACTIONS:
I. Egoistic ethical values: -use-value benefits to the company	**Refusals:** (1) denial (2) repression (3) undoing (4) omnipotent fantasies	**Suicidal:** -no economic, social or ecological responsibilities
II. Utilitarian ethical values: -use-value benefits to the company and its partners	**Excuses:** (5) splitting (6) projection (7) projective identification (8) regression (9) idealization (10) isolation	**Plutocentric:** -only economic responsibilities
III. Duty/rights/justice ethical values: -duty and right to protect humans and nature -justice to all beings	**Justifications:** (11) rationalization (12) intellectualization (13) devaluing (14) reaction formation (15) object replacement (16) compensation	**Patriarchal:** -economic and social resp. **Anthropocentric:** -social responsibilities **Technocentric:** -economic and ecological responsibilities **Biocentric:** -ecological responsibilities
IV. Virtue ethical values: -justness -generosity -kindness -moderation -loyalty -flexibility -reliability	**Concessions:** (17) introjection (18) sublimation	**Matriarchal:** -social and ecological responsibilities **Ideal:** -economic, social and ecological responsibilities

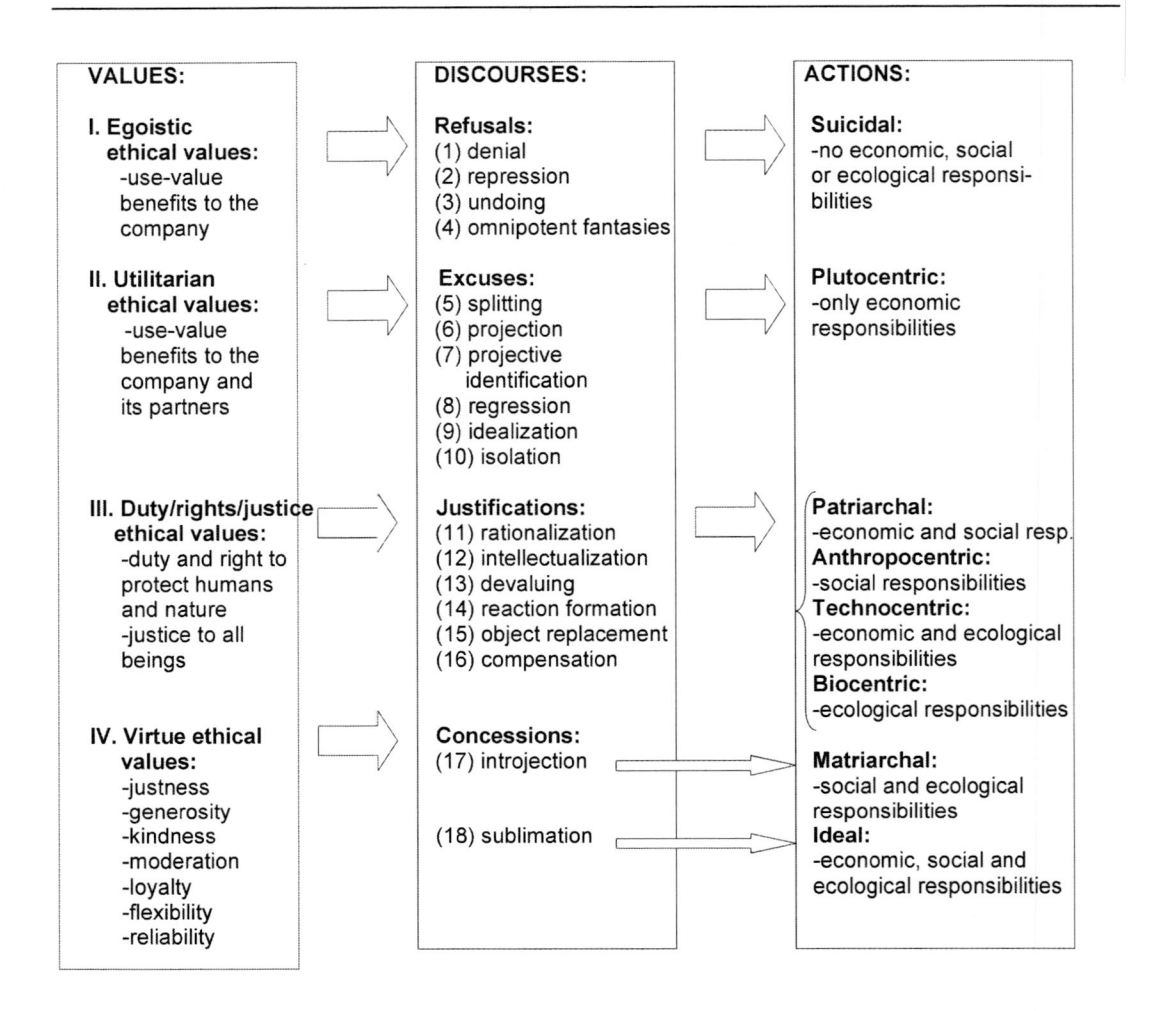

Figure 3. A holistic corporate responsibility model (Ketola 2005c).

Most companies do not yet follow virtue ethical values, but egoistic, utilitarian or duty ethical values. Most companies do not yet use sublimating discourses, but refusals, excuses and justifications. Most companies do not yet take ideal actions, but suicidal, plutocentric, technocentric or patriarchal actions (it is the environmental groups, social charities, some co-operative companies and some small and medium-sized companies (SMEs) who take biocentric, anthropocentric and matriarchal actions, respectively.)

It does not matter where these companies begin their change: they can start from values, discourses or actions. If they manage to change one, the others will inevitably follow because of both internal and external pressures to harmonize the three levels. In the long run it would be very stressful for the staff to be committed to one kind or values and have to speak and/or act differently. In the short term, these conflicts of values, discourses and actions take place, though, and I have studied these phenomena in another article (Ketola 2007). Also our contemporary society is very keen on monitoring corporate behaviour: many stakeholders quickly detect any discrepancy between companies' values, discourses and actions and express their dissatisfaction with such unethical conduct loud and clear.

As said before, the change often starts from corporate discourses and spreads then to both directions, to corporate values and to corporate actions. How to turn the discourses sublimating then? It requires open and honest communication and plenty of trust between the company and its stakeholders. Sublimation has two stages: concession and corrective action. Concession is extremely difficult for both organizations and individuals because admitting responsibility attacks the ego they have all their lives inflated in their dream to become godlike. The psychological defences serve to protect this dream from the reality.

The language of ethics is condemning, which makes it even more difficult to admit failure and responsibility. In Fineman's (1998) view, the morality of companies is usually evaluated by the cognitive language of reason, which cannot respond to the conflicting emotions companies and their staff experience. Fineman's (1996) empirical study on managers of six supermarkets pointed out how ecological and other responsibility pressures create among managers enormous surges of emotions ranging from pride to shame, fear to defiance, caution to rage and cynicism to enthusiasm.

Unfortunately, cognitive and behavioural aspects have overshadowed the emotional aspects in organizational research and practical management. It would be important for managers, staff and external interest groups to learn about defences. Such understanding could help them to find a shared language, which takes emotions into account and makes it easier to admit responsibility – which speeds up the corrective action part of sublimation. A shared language enables the development of a shared line of action. By adopting a new language and line of action companies could avoid the vicious circle of mistakes, which in turn would decrease human suffering caused by anxiety from the overuse of defences.

Organizations force their members into multiple defence exploitation in which many defences are employed simultaneously. When these do not erase the problem, even more defences are recruited until no honourable way out can be found, and the egos of the organization and its members collapse (see an example in Ketola 2004). If companies understand how the ego defences work, they can lower their personnel's reporting threshold of mistakes. The external interest groups could for their part ease the fate of those companies that immediately admit their mistakes relative to those who deny, reason or justify them.

Discourse analyses teach us a great deal about the psychology of corporate culture. Defences expressed in corporate discourses pinpoint the issues that are difficult to different companies, as the defences unconsciously chosen by each company reflect the ways characteristic of that company to deal with problems. This knowledge enables the company to find ways of preventing the negative effects of those defences on responsible business actions. Companies often use a lot of words to defend their irresponsible actions and the tone of their defence speeches, press releases and reports is negative, even aggressive. Becoming conscious about the subconscious messages of their words helps companies to transform their discourses into concessive, even positive words. Then they do not need to deny their actions or invent excuses or justifications for them. By admitting the possibility that they may be wrong, companies gain sympathy from their interest groups who willingly cooperate to find just solutions which benefit all parties.

In other words, the discourses of companies do not necessarily have to defend their current actions; instead the discourses can be harnessed to build more responsible actions. Words can become deeds. And these can turn into a set of shared values cherished by all the internal and external stakeholders of the company.

REFERENCES

Aristotle (348 B.C.). *Ethics*. In J. Barnes (Ed.) (1988). *The complete works of Aristotle.* Princeton: Princeton University Press.

Barthorpe, S. & Gleeson, J. (2004). Implementing corporate social responsibility through the framework of the considerate constructors scheme. *Conference proceedings,* 1–10. *Corporate Social Responsibility and Environmental Management Conference,* University of Nottingham, 28–29 June 2004.

Bradford, J. L. & Garrett, D. E. (1995). The effectiveness of corporate communicative responses to accusations of unethical behaviour. *Journal of Business Ethics,* 14 (11), 875–892.

Brown, A. D. (1997). Narcissism, identity and legitimacy. *Academy of Management Review,* 22 (3), 643–686.

Brown, A. D. & Starkey K. (2000). Organizational identity and learning: A psycho-dynamic perspective. *Academy of Management Review,* 25 (1), 102–120.

BSR (2003). Business for social responsibility, http://www.bsr.org. Visited on 15.06.2006.

DeBoard, R. (1978). *The psychodynamics of organizations.* London: Tavistock.

Eden, S. (1999). 'We have the facts' – How business claims legitimacy in the environmental debate. *Environment and Planning A,* 31 (7), 1295–1309.

Feldman, S. P. (2003). Weak spots in business ethics: A psycho-analytic study of competition and memory in "Death of a salesman". *Journal of Business Ethics,* 44 (4), 391–404.

Fineman, S. (1996). Emotional subtexts in corporate greening. *Organizational Studies,* 17 (3), 479–500.

Fineman, S. (1998). The natural environment, organization and ethics. In M. Parker (Ed.), *Ethics and organizations* (pp. 238–252). London: Sage.

Gewirth, A. (1978). *Reason and morality.* Chicago: Chicago University Press.

Halme, P. & Takala, T. (2003). Vastuullinen suhtautuminen ydinvoimaan – diskurssianalyyttinen tutkimus (Responsible attitude towards nuclear energy – A discourse analytic study). *Liiketaloustieteellinen aikakauskirja (The Finnish Journal of Business Economics),* 3, 495–517.

Hirschhorn, L. & Young, D. R. (1991). Dealing with the anxiety of working: Social defences as coping strategy. In M. F. R. Kets de Vries (Ed.), *Organizations on the couch: Clinical perspectives on organisational behaviour and change* (pp. 215–240). San Francisco: Jossey-Bass.

Kant, I. (1785). *Grundlegung zur Metaphysik der Sitten.* (Hier: mit Ein Kooperativer Kommentar von O. Hoffe, 1999. Frankfurt am Main: Klostermann).

Ketola, T. (2004). Eco-psychological profiling model: An oil company example. *Corporate Social Responsibility and Environmental Management,* 11 (3), 150–166.

Ketola, T. (2005a). *Vastuullinen liiketoiminta – Sanoista teoiksi. (Responsible business – From words to actions.)* Helsinki: Edita.

Ketola, T. (2005b). From 7 dwarfs to 4 lost boys: 10-year follow-up study of the largest oil companies' environmental policies. *Conference proceedings. Business Strategy and the Environment Conference,* Leeds University, 5–6 September 2005.

Ketola, T. (2005c). A holistic corporate responsibility (CR-) model. *Conference Proceedings:* Track: 6. Ethics and Organizational Processes/Practices. *European Academy of Management Conference,* Munich, 4–7 May 2005.

Ketola, T. (2006a). Corporate psychological defences: An oil spill case. *Journal of Business Ethics,* 65 (2), 149–161.

Ketola, T. (2006b). From CR-psychopaths to responsible corporations: Waking up the inner sleeping beauty of companies. *Corporate Social Responsibility and Environmental Management,* 13 (2), 98–107.

Ketola, T. (2007). Yritysvastuu: Arvot, sanat ja teot linjassa. (Corporate responsibility: Values, words and actions in line.) In *Vastuullinen liiketoiminta ja monitieteellisyys (Responsible business and interdisciplinary research).* Publications of the Turku School of Economics, Series KR, forthcoming.

Kets de Vries, M. F. R. (2001). *Struggling with the demon: Perspectives on individual and organizational irrationality.* Madison, Connecticut: Psychosocial Press.

Kets de Vries, M. F. R. & Miller, D. (1984). *The neurotic organization.* San Francisco & London: Jossey-Bass.

Kets de Vries, M. F. R. & Miller, D. (1991). Leadership styles and organizational cultures: The shaping of neurotic organizations. In M. F. R. Kets de Vries (Ed.), *Organizations on the couch: Clinical perspectives on organisational behaviour and change* (pp. 243–263). San Francisco: Jossey-Bass.

Lovio, R. (1995). Yritykset ja ympäristö: ongelmien ratkaisusta uusiin ongelmiin (Companies and the environment: From problem-solving to new problems). In I. Massa & O. Rahkonen (Eds.) *Riskiyhteiskunnan talous – Suomen talouden ekologinen modernisaatio (Risk society's economy – Finland's economy's ecological modernization)* (pp. 143–159). Helsinki: Gaudeamus.

Mill, J. S. (1861). *Utilitarianism.* (Here: Ed. by R. Crisp, 1998. Oxford: OUP)

Miller, D. (1993). The architecture of simplicity. *Academy of Management Review,* 18 (1), 116–138.

Morgan, G. (1986). *Images of organization.* London: Sage.

Rawls, J. (1971). *The theory of justice.* Oxford: OUP.

Rhee, S-K. & Lee, S-Y. (2003). Dynamic change of corporate environmental strategy: Rhetoric and reality. *Business Strategy and the Environment,* 12 (3), 175–190.

Rowlands, I. (2000). Beauty and the Beast? BP's and Exxon's positions on global climate change. *Environment and Planning C: Government and Policy,* 18 (3), 339–354.

Swajkowski, E. (1992). Accounting for organizational misconduct. *Journal of Business Ethics,* 11 (5/6), 401–411.

INDEX

A

academic settings, 50, 62
academics, 228, 229, 230, 232, 233, 234, 235, 236, 238
accelerator, 217
access, 54, 163, 218, 228, 229, 232, 233, 235, 238, 240, 253, 278, 281, 282, 284
accidents, 50, 164, 165, 206, 219, 240
accountability, 18, 19, 154, 160, 201, 210
accounting, xi, 4, 5, 8, 90, 95, 98, 99, 100, 101, 107, 146, 227, 228, 259, 268, 269, 272, 273
accreditation, 51, 67
acculturation, 33, 46
accuracy, 40, 235
achievement, 22, 23, 34, 128, 145, 146
acquisitions, 101
administrators, 55, 58, 59, 60, 61, 64, 65
adolescents, 30, 39
adulthood, 145
adults, 2, 4, 128, 157, 214, 253
advertisements, 31, 260
advertising, 30, 266, 277
Africa, 76, 192
African American(s), 34, 35, 38, 46, 191
age, 1, 2, 3, 4, 5, 6, 7, 8, 26, 28, 29, 30, 38, 42, 43, 56, 65, 80, 84, 91, 99, 102, 104, 124, 138, 144, 171, 192, 212, 231, 239, 280, 283, 299
agent, 17, 18, 19, 23, 70, 73, 74, 75, 155, 157, 162, 164, 169, 172, 174, 176, 179, 184, 187, 188, 189, 190, 203, 204, 205, 206, 207, 208, 209, 212, 214, 215, 216, 217, 218, 250, 251, 252, 253
aggregates, 161
aggregation, 161, 217
aggression, 192
aging, 60, 68
alcohol, 162, 276

alternative(s), x, xi, 14, 32, 76, 97, 118, 150, 161, 173, 174, 189, 196, 212, 214, 217, 218, 219, 227, 229, 230, 238, 239, 250, 252, 254, 255, 269, 277, 278, 285, 291, 292, 295, 297, 298, 299
altruism, ix, 113, 115, 117, 119, 121, 122, 123, 127, 130, 131, 184
analytical framework, 153
anger, 295
animals, 157, 270
anxiety, 293, 301, 302
apparel, 34, 37
appendix, 101
Arab countries, 43
argument, xi, 117, 118, 119, 120, 159, 191, 212, 227, 248, 254
Aristotle, 73, 80, 184, 214, 250, 266, 271, 272, 291, 302
arithmetic, 170
articulation, 210
Asia, 192, 241, 242, 243, 270
assessment, 9, 44, 60
assets, 18, 156
assignment, viii, 49, 50, 51, 52, 53, 54, 55, 56, 57, 58, 59, 60, 61, 62, 99
assumptions, 163, 253, 255
asymmetry, 178, 187, 193, 202, 210, 219
athletes, 277
attachment, 83
attacks, 60, 301
attention, 1, 29, 35, 39, 54, 100, 108, 109, 130, 136, 144, 160, 163, 165, 167, 180, 187, 189, 197, 202, 204, 207, 213, 263, 276
attitudes, 10, 44, 45, 108, 136, 137, 142, 147, 148, 164, 233
auditing, 100, 103, 129, 240, 270
Australia, 93
Austria, 44
authentication, 100
authority, 18, 19, 28, 97, 100, 155, 207, 208

automobiles, 270
autonomy, 19, 54, 153, 154, 155, 176, 178, 180, 187, 189, 253
availability, 121, 127, 181
avoidance, 33, 130
awareness, 3, 19, 55, 59, 61, 90, 123, 128, 176, 238, 271, 272

B

baggage, 7, 183, 218
Bangladesh, 202
bankers, 260
bankruptcy, 158, 179
bargaining, 250, 251, 255, 257
barriers, 54
basic needs, 61
basketball, 155
batteries, 295
behavior, vii, ix, xi, 1, 2, 3, 9, 13, 17, 18, 19, 20, 27, 28, 29, 31, 32, 33, 34, 35, 36, 37, 38, 39, 40, 41, 42, 43, 44, 45, 46, 47, 80, 86, 93, 97, 98, 113, 115, 117, 119, 120, 121, 123, 125, 126, 129, 130, 131, 133, 136, 138, 142, 143, 144, 147, 148, 259, 260, 261, 265, 267, 269, 273
behavioral intentions, 43
Belgium, 11, 46
belief systems, 265
beliefs, 2, 33, 40, 42, 44, 45, 46, 47, 71, 120, 255, 265
bias, 101, 102, 103, 105, 125, 132, 133, 268
Bible, 193
binding, 188, 190
biodiversity, 22, 24
biotechnology, 22
birth, 209
blame, 20, 75, 154, 155, 164, 167, 210
blindness, 266
blocks, 54
blood, 154, 156, 157, 159, 171, 173, 181, 214, 215, 217
bloodstream, 162
board members, 23
borrowing, 152, 153, 193, 196, 218
bounds, 117
boys, 296, 302
brain, 160
brand image, 41, 278
Brazil, 242, 297
breaches, 44
breathing, 171
Britain, 37, 44, 172, 186
BSR, 292, 302

Buddhism, 37
bureaucracy, 97
Burma, 287
business education, 272
business environment, 2, 108, 126, 145, 299
business ethics, vii, ix, 5, 11, 29, 67, 68, 90, 91, 113, 114, 115, 116, 117, 118, 119, 120, 121, 122, 123, 124, 125, 126, 127, 130, 131, 132, 133, 302
buyer, 73, 74, 76, 77, 169
by-products, 22

C

campaigns, 31, 41, 233, 234, 235, 236, 237
Canada, 93
candidates, 159, 284
capital accumulation, 201
capitalism, 26, 86, 117, 118, 119, 120
case study, xi, 53, 80, 122, 132, 150, 151, 153, 243
cast, 168, 174, 212, 214
categorization, 262
Catholic Church, 194
causal relationship, 169, 173, 262
causation, 168, 169, 170, 173, 199, 216, 217
certainty, 212, 254
chain of command, 96
channels, 76, 94, 96, 97, 234
charitable organizations, 146
charities, 300
chicken, 83
child labor, 28
childhood, 145
children, 82, 123, 128, 168, 191, 192, 196, 202, 270
China, vi, 135, 136, 138, 144, 147, 231, 233, 241, 242, 243, 287
chlorine, 60
Christianity, 37, 195
circulation, 171
citizenship, 123, 133, 265
civil society, 22
classes, viii, 50, 52, 54, 80, 83, 84, 191, 268, 271, 272
classical economics, 115
classification, 176, 209, 282, 283
classroom(s), 9, 15, 265, 266, 267
classroom environment, 265
clean air, 196
clean energy, 298
clients, 22, 54, 55, 56, 70, 71, 101, 104, 108, 109, 148, 239, 240
close relationships, 129
closure, 46
cluster analysis, 136, 137, 141, 148

clusters, 137
coal, 22
codes, vii, 18, 229, 230, 240, 276
coding, 125
coercion, 4, 98, 163, 250, 251, 253, 257
cognition, 43
cognitive ability, 82
cognitive development, 9, 45, 82, 90
cognitive process, 85, 261
coherence, 173
collaboration, xi, 227, 229, 235, 236, 237, 238, 239
college students, 39
colleges, 51, 137
collusion, 100
commerce, vii
commodity, 208
communication, xii, 18, 41, 54, 56, 60, 83, 90, 97, 129, 131, 177, 204, 270, 277, 280, 289, 290, 291, 298, 299, 301
communication systems, 60
communitarianism, 80
community, viii, 1, 13, 14, 15, 50, 51, 52, 55, 57, 58, 60, 62, 63, 64, 66, 123, 128, 146, 157, 163, 208, 238, 265, 266, 267
community service, 163
compassion, 14, 185, 210
compatibility, 119, 120, 121, 197
compensation, 15, 147, 159, 165, 230, 240, 249, 273, 295
competence, 133
competition, ix, 113, 115, 117, 119, 120, 121, 127, 128, 129, 131, 202, 208, 302
competitive advantage, 23
competitive conditions, 122
competitive markets, 115
competitiveness, 26
competitor, 174
complement, 260, 261
complexity, 26, 206, 237
compliance, ix, 17, 113, 126, 161, 230
components, 73, 160
comprehension, 174, 178
compulsion, 250
concentrates, 152
concentration, 116, 117, 119, 120, 121
conception, 26, 152, 173, 174, 182, 184, 185, 187, 191, 214, 216, 253, 256
conceptual model, 22, 262
concrete, 19, 166, 178, 181, 188, 195, 251, 263
conditioning, 264, 266
confessions, 73
confidence, viii, 50, 57, 62, 176, 206, 256, 283
confidentiality, 99

conflict, 126, 229, 231, 250, 264, 273
conformity, x, 34, 97, 135, 150, 208, 213, 250, 256, 265
Confucianism, 123, 128
confusion, ix, 69, 70, 81
Congress, 148
congruence, 95
conscientiousness, 17
consciousness, 45, 152, 174, 177, 193, 195, 209, 219
consensus, 196, 198, 211, 267
consent, 250
conservation, 34, 41
constraints, 62, 171, 178, 180, 216, 256
construction, 22, 278, 283
consultants, 268
consumers, vii, 24, 27, 28, 29, 30, 31, 32, 33, 35, 36, 37, 38, 39, 40, 41, 42, 44, 45, 46, 47, 114, 120, 122, 123, 127, 128, 129, 130, 131, 133, 200, 201, 210, 270, 277
consumption, vii, xii, 22, 27, 28, 30, 44, 46, 124, 270, 275, 278, 283
contingency, 44, 207
control, vii, 21, 44, 46, 93, 94, 95, 98, 100, 101, 102, 107, 125, 138, 157, 160, 162, 166, 174, 189, 202, 203, 208, 229, 232, 249, 250, 251, 264, 268, 269, 270, 279, 285, 295
conviction, 160, 164, 253
coping strategy, 302
corporate finance, 272
corporate governance, vii, 3, 13, 17, 18, 132, 158, 201
corporate life, 205
corporate scandals, 86
corporations, vii, viii, x, 2, 15, 19, 30, 31, 69, 70, 100, 149, 151, 153, 154, 155, 156, 157, 159, 160, 162, 163, 164, 165, 166, 167, 172, 173, 199, 201, 202, 204, 205, 206, 207, 208, 210, 211, 212, 213, 215, 218, 219, 237, 278, 281, 303
correlation, 102
correlation analysis, 102
correlations, 4, 104
cost saving, 128, 130
costs, 22, 23, 30, 41, 56, 63, 116, 117, 127, 128, 131, 152, 192, 216, 217, 260, 267
counsel, 167, 214
counseling, 264
coupling, 270
coverage, 240
covering, 94, 249
crack, 284
creativity, 208
credentials, 4
credibility, 95, 230, 232, 233, 234, 235, 237, 238

credit, 83, 169, 191
crime, ix, 69, 70, 160, 161, 163, 165, 167
criminal behavior, 126
criminality, 206
criminals, 28, 44
critical analysis, 228, 248, 278
critical thinking, 1, 59, 61, 272
criticism, 174, 185, 186, 195, 196, 197, 212, 229, 232, 298
CRR, 43
crude oil, 298
crying, 82
cultivation, 14, 266
cultural differences, 37, 45, 191
cultural values, 47, 206
culture, 6, 7, 13, 18, 19, 33, 35, 41, 42, 43, 46, 96, 136, 150, 156, 162, 167, 175, 179, 180, 192, 193, 196, 198, 206, 231, 265, 267, 268, 293, 301
current account, 206
curriculum, 15, 51, 59, 60, 90, 260, 261, 272
customers, xii, 13, 14, 15, 22, 39, 114, 116, 129, 146, 156, 158, 160, 199, 200, 201, 202, 204, 210, 216, 219, 266, 267, 270, 275, 277, 278, 279, 281, 282, 284, 298

D

danger, 186, 211, 270
data collection, 124, 232, 235, 237, 278
data gathering, 238
data processing, 155
death(s), 52, 55, 62, 63, 153, 156, 159, 162, 165, 169, 189, 198, 200, 211, 216, 217, 278
decision makers, 255, 273
decision making, vii, viii, xi, 3, 5, 7, 9, 10, 11, 14, 15, 27, 28, 29, 32, 33, 35, 38, 39, 40, 41, 42, 44, 45, 46, 51, 69, 75, 77, 91, 95, 101, 228, 255, 259, 260, 261, 262, 263, 266, 272
decision-making process, 96, 162
decisions, 1, 2, 6, 15, 17, 29, 44, 54, 55, 61, 75, 80, 85, 94, 110, 111, 147, 155, 159, 178, 250, 251, 253, 254, 257, 260, 261, 269, 270, 271, 272, 273, 284, 292
decoupling, 228
deductive reasoning, 269
defendants, 216
deficiency, 177
definition, 22, 70, 71, 72, 97, 292
degradation, 203, 204
delinquency, 46
delivery, 81
demand, 169, 200, 204, 281
demographic characteristics, 9, 42

demographics, 43, 84
denial, 39, 80, 153, 294
Denmark, 22, 200
deontology, vii, 14, 15, 263, 264, 272
Department of Health and Human Services, 68
dependent variable, 2, 102, 104, 106
desire(s), 14, 23, 72, 136, 144, 157, 158, 174, 179, 190, 193, 208, 256, 266
destruction, 94, 97, 98, 136
detachment, 267
detection, 18
developed countries, 192, 297
developing countries, xi, 227, 228, 229, 230, 231, 232, 238, 276, 297
developmental psychology, 86
deviation, 7, 141, 207
diet, 168
differentiation, 131
dignity, 3
direct cost(s), 63
direct observation, 23, 154
directives, 278, 280
disaster, viii, 49, 51, 52, 53, 54, 55, 56, 57, 58, 59, 60, 61, 62, 63, 64, 65, 66, 67, 151, 152, 163, 164, 165, 166, 167, 172, 199, 211
discipline, vii, 234
disclosure, 94
discomfort, 170
discourse, 176, 177, 178, 180, 201, 204, 208, 214, 292, 293, 294, 298, 302
discriminant analysis, 141
discrimination, 109
disorder, 284
dispersion, 86
displacement, 295
disposition, viii, 27, 31, 39, 45, 184, 266
dissatisfaction, 199, 300
distress, 170, 171, 186, 187, 192
distributive justice, 203
divergence, 177
diversity, 204
division, 2, 40, 160, 175, 251, 282
divorce, 192
DNA, 18
doctors, 6
Doha, 193
dominance, 130
donations, 127, 128, 129, 131
doors, 151, 165, 166, 171, 172, 211, 217
dream, 301
drugs, 72, 156, 192
dumping, 162

duties, vii, 109, 158, 164, 166, 171, 181, 186, 187, 188, 189, 190, 191, 192, 193, 194, 197, 198, 200, 203, 219, 252, 254, 266, 290

E

earnings, 13, 129, 131
eating, 30
economic behaviour, 273
economic growth, 204, 265
economic incentives, 90
economic institutions, 133
economic resources, 253
economics, 23, 26, 80, 115, 173, 209, 264
ecosystem, 15
education, viii, 1, 2, 4, 5, 6, 7, 8, 9, 11, 17, 41, 47, 49, 50, 51, 52, 64, 65, 67, 91, 108, 109, 132, 145, 191, 260, 271, 272, 273, 287
educational process, 6, 15
educational system, 8
educators, viii, 5, 6, 49, 52, 80
egalitarianism, 265
ego, 293, 294, 301
egocentrism, 175
egoism, vii, ix, 14, 15, 32, 113, 115, 117, 177, 178, 184, 186, 260, 263, 264, 265, 268, 272
elaboration, 205, 249
elderly, 128, 129, 191
election, 183
email, 49
emancipation, 191, 195
emergence, 195, 292
emergency preparedness, viii, 49, 64, 65, 68
emergency response, 57, 58, 64, 65
emerging markets, 45
emotions, 43, 157, 301
empathy, 17, 260
employees, vii, xi, 3, 5, 6, 7, 13, 14, 15, 22, 30, 31, 40, 41, 51, 56, 62, 74, 80, 86, 94, 102, 107, 109, 110, 136, 137, 138, 142, 144, 145, 146, 148, 154, 160, 162, 163, 165, 166, 200, 202, 208, 219, 230, 231, 232, 239, 259, 260, 266, 267, 270, 271, 277, 285, 297, 298
employment, xi, 14, 31, 99, 234, 240, 247, 248, 249, 250, 251, 252, 253, 254, 255, 257, 265, 270, 297
employment relationship, xi, 247, 248, 249, 250, 253, 254, 255, 257
encouragement, 71
energy, 293, 298, 302
engagement, 62, 184, 187
England, 151, 153, 172, 219, 225
Enlightenment, 150
enthusiasm, 192, 301

entrepreneurs, 132, 249
environment, 2, 13, 14, 19, 22, 24, 26, 30, 41, 46, 82, 107, 110, 117, 122, 124, 126, 128, 130, 145, 159, 168, 173, 200, 201, 212, 254, 266, 269, 270, 271, 303
environmental awareness, 33, 42
environmental factors, 168
environmental impact, 22, 200
environmental issues, 124, 201
epidemic, 68
epidemiology, 52
epistemology, 180, 194
equality, 203, 204, 209, 256, 267, 270
equilibrium, 23, 197
equipment, 202
erosion, 15
Estonia, 257
ethical issues, vii, 15, 29, 32, 43, 45, 54, 59, 61, 62, 63, 68, 81, 82, 86, 124, 131, 260
ethical standards, 2, 8, 14, 265, 269, 271, 296
ethics, vii, viii, ix, x, xi, 1, 3, 5, 9, 10, 11, 13, 14, 15, 17, 18, 19, 21, 23, 25, 26, 27, 29, 30, 33, 36, 38, 40, 41, 42, 43, 44, 45, 46, 47, 49, 50, 51, 52, 55, 61, 62, 63, 67, 68, 79, 80, 81, 82, 90, 91, 101, 113, 114, 115, 116, 117, 121, 122, 123, 124, 127, 128, 130, 132, 133, 136, 146, 150, 152, 174, 176, 180, 181, 182, 184, 185, 191, 193, 198, 201, 203, 204, 205, 214, 215, 247, 255, 260, 261, 263, 264, 266, 267, 269, 270, 271, 272, 273, 290, 292, 301, 302
ethnicity, 46, 198
ethology, 173
Europe, 172, 186, 228, 242
European Union, 172
euthanasia, 189
evacuation, 52, 55, 56
evening, 186, 279, 280, 281, 284
evil, 136, 145, 148, 183, 250, 265, 296, 299
evolution, 26, 163
exclusion, 193, 210
excuse, xii, 210, 289, 291, 294, 295, 296, 297, 300, 301
execution, 210, 215, 249
exercise, 53, 54, 55, 56, 60, 63, 97, 152, 185, 189, 202, 208, 253
experimental design, 95
expertise, 19, 261, 293
exploitation, 120, 128, 228, 301
exposure, 60, 201, 261, 270
external constraints, 253
external environment, 22
external locus of control, 138
external validity, 125

eyes, 183, 203, 209, 210

F

facilitators, 53, 75
factor analysis, 139, 140, 141
failure, 74, 76, 151, 159, 166, 171, 172, 177, 187, 193, 200, 210, 215, 217, 238, 266, 301
fairness, 17, 54, 123, 213, 256, 270
faith, 37, 153, 210, 265
family, ix, 30, 55, 57, 58, 64, 66, 79, 81, 82, 84, 123, 151, 191, 192, 193, 198
family members, 55
family relationships, ix, 79
farmers, 119, 298
fat, 156
fatigue, 210, 250
fear, 75, 98, 107, 138, 163, 231, 301
feedback, 53, 297
feelings, 14, 35, 36, 39, 176
feet, 170
females, ix, 4, 5, 6, 30, 79, 84, 99
fidelity, 14
film, 298
finance, 268, 273
financial resources, 235
financial support, 192, 236
financing, 236
Finland, 10, 289, 297, 303
firms, xii, 2, 4, 5, 7, 21, 23, 24, 101, 107, 114, 117, 121, 123, 126, 127, 128, 129, 130, 131, 132, 133, 157, 229, 235, 236, 237, 275, 276, 277, 278, 285
flexibility, 291
flooding, 216
focusing, xi, 52, 54, 55, 107, 132, 150, 151, 228, 279
food, 30, 55, 61, 128, 131, 196
Football, 243
Ford, 179, 221
foreign aid, 192
forests, 129
formal education, 2, 4
fossil, 298
fossil fuels, 298
framing, 133, 261, 272
France, 21, 22, 200, 223
fraud, 4, 30, 44, 100, 107, 265, 266
free choice, 157, 204, 218
free trade, 231
freedom, 90, 153, 155, 175, 176, 178, 179, 188, 189, 203, 206, 207, 208, 218, 231, 234, 249, 253, 256, 265
friends, 39, 284
friendship, 14, 204

frustration, 236, 284, 285
fuel, 270
funding, 235
funds, 15, 100, 158, 210, 276

G

G7 countries, 192
gambling, 276
game theory, 264
GDP, 156
gender, 1, 4, 5, 6, 7, 8, 9, 29, 38, 42, 65, 84, 101, 147, 267
gender differences, 5, 9, 38
gene, 168, 297
generation, 46, 128, 131
genes, 168
genetic endowment, 168
genre, 194, 209
Germany, 133
gestures, xii, 289, 290
gift, 146, 182
girls, 186
glass, 167
global climate change, 303
global networks, 260
globalised world, xi, 150, 174, 215, 219
globalization, 15
GNP, 192
goals, 3, 8, 18, 35, 121, 156, 158, 159, 161, 169, 192, 202, 206, 217
God, 37, 153, 180, 182, 183, 224
gold, 269
goods and services, viii, 27, 29, 31
governance, 13, 14, 15, 18, 158
government, x, 8, 56, 114, 150, 157, 158, 159, 167, 172, 191, 192, 194, 199, 201, 264, 268
graduate students, 85
grants, 235, 248
gravitation, 206
Great Leap Forward, 221
greed, 136, 157
grief, 161
gross domestic product, 156
groups, viii, 4, 6, 7, 9, 13, 22, 29, 32, 34, 43, 50, 52, 53, 56, 60, 62, 95, 99, 102, 114, 123, 142, 157, 191, 193, 210, 256, 265, 267, 270, 277, 280, 284, 285, 291, 292, 300
growth, 23, 42, 91, 109, 158, 169, 201
Guangdong, 233
guardian, 250
guidance, 260
guidelines, 14, 23, 62, 107, 126, 269, 270

guilt, 36, 39
guilty, 71, 73, 152, 153, 159, 162, 165, 166, 183, 199, 200, 211, 217, 295

H

hands, 59, 160, 172, 199
happiness, 189, 190, 196
harm, viii, ix, 33, 54, 67, 69, 70, 71, 72, 73, 74, 75, 76, 77, 80, 94, 100, 153, 158, 159, 162, 165, 187, 192, 203, 214, 215, 216, 217, 219, 236, 265, 271, 294, 295
harmony, 80
health, viii, 49, 50, 51, 52, 53, 54, 55, 56, 57, 58, 59, 60, 61, 62, 63, 64, 65, 66, 67, 68, 138, 159, 165, 171, 199, 200, 240, 269
health care, 51, 53, 54, 57, 58, 59, 61, 62, 63, 64, 65, 66, 67, 68
health care professionals, 63
health services, 55
heat, 55, 196, 209, 298
heating, 298
hedonism, 34
height, 168, 178
high school, 30
hip, 178
hiring, 5, 14
Hispanic population, 54
Hispanics, 54
HIV, 193
holding company, 18
homelessness, 209
homicide, x, 149, 152, 159, 167, 173, 219
honesty, 29, 30, 42, 145, 270
Hong Kong, 44, 148, 229, 233, 237, 241, 242, 243
hospitals, 67
hostility, x, 111, 150
hotels, 279
House, 111
households, 33
human actions, 206
human agency, 157
human behavior, 17
human intentionality, 157
human nature, 19, 291
Human Resource Management, 241
human rights, 269, 270
humanism, 180
humanity, 182, 183, 184, 188, 189, 198, 206, 209, 210
Hurricane Katrina, viii, 49, 50, 55, 56, 62, 67, 68
hurricanes, 68
husband, 191

hygiene, 196
hypocrisy, 183
hypothermia, 151
hypothesis, 96, 104, 106, 111

I

idealism, 34, 35, 36, 37, 38, 41
identification, 23, 26, 46, 68, 160, 161, 163, 164, 179, 265, 294
identity, 102, 175, 176, 178, 179, 204, 205, 248, 283, 302
ideology, 9, 34, 42, 44, 46, 173, 197, 207, 218
imagery, xii, 275, 276, 277, 278, 279, 281, 282, 284, 285
images, 14, 192
imbalances, 293
IMF, 192
Immanuel Kant, 225
immigrants, 33, 38, 39, 282
imperialism, 175
implementation, 3, 18, 21, 127, 155, 196, 291, 297
imports, 261, 297
impotence, 193
imprisonment, 159, 163, 164, 199, 200
impulsiveness, 250
in situ, 251
incarceration, 159, 163
incentives, 231, 237
incidence, 17, 30
inclusion, 261
income, 30, 41, 42, 130, 137, 144, 145, 240, 256, 268, 277
income smoothing, 268
independence, 298
India, 199, 270
indication, 167
individual action, 157, 169, 205, 217
individual character, 94, 255
individual characteristics, 94, 255
individual differences, 136
individual rights, 252, 254
individualism, 150, 157, 173, 180, 187, 197, 212, 213, 215, 219
individuality, 102, 178, 180
industriousness, 17
industry, 1, 4, 5, 6, 7, 8, 81, 108, 109, 124, 126, 128, 131, 167, 172, 219
ineffectiveness, 117
inequality, 203, 204
inertia, 23
infinite, x, xi, 150, 152, 153, 174, 176, 178, 180, 181, 182, 184, 185, 187, 193, 194, 195, 196, 197,

198, 203, 208, 209, 210, 212, 214, 215, 218, 219, 220
inflation, 30
information asymmetry, 231
information processing, 262
information technology, 260
inheritance, 168
injuries, 165, 240
innovation, x, 109, 110, 113, 118, 127, 130, 132
input, 25, 228, 279
insane, 195, 250
insight, 43, 84, 152, 212
inspiration, 136, 183
instability, 166
instinct, 190, 217
institutions, viii, 45, 69, 192, 205, 207, 208, 237, 238, 256
instruction, 51, 60
instructional methods, 50
instructors, 50, 51, 80
insurance, 210, 230, 240, 268
integration, 96
integrity, 17, 109, 154, 293
intelligence, 168
intensity, 37, 212
intentionality, 156, 157, 178
intentions, 43, 71, 72, 102, 157, 158, 162, 167, 194
interaction, 13, 38, 45, 110, 120, 168, 270, 278
interaction process, 120
interactions, 115, 119, 122, 133, 202, 203, 264, 267
interdependence, 219, 263
interest groups, 96, 292, 293, 301
interference, 253, 264
internal controls, 100
internet, 163
interpersonal relations, 204
interpretation, 97, 124, 126, 133, 181, 185, 189, 193, 196, 212, 214, 237, 251, 252, 273
interrelatedness, 267
interrelations, 206
intervention, 6, 167
interview, viii, 4, 18, 27, 32, 124, 125, 195, 224, 230, 233, 234, 235
intimacy, 209, 267
intoxication, 250
intrinsic value, 251
investment, 24, 25, 273
investors, 13, 15, 201, 211
invisible hand, 169
Iran, 244
Islam, 37
isolation, 54, 170, 216, 218

J

Jamaica, 1
Japan, 114, 123, 128, 129, 130, 131, 132, 133, 168
Jews, 155, 187
job satisfaction, 137, 138, 144
jobs, 19, 146, 268
journalists, 280
judges, 211, 283
judgment, 2, 3, 17, 97, 260, 261, 262, 263, 264, 265, 266, 269, 270, 271, 272
jurisdiction, 191, 192, 193, 249, 250, 254
justice, 5, 6, 42, 94, 152, 153, 169, 173, 177, 182, 184, 185, 192, 199, 201, 202, 203, 204, 209, 210, 219, 256, 265, 290, 292, 299, 303
justification, 75, 177, 181

K

Kantian philosophy, 176
Keynes, 223
killing, 167, 200, 218
knowledge-based economy, 260

L

labo(u)r, 156, 175, 183, 185, 201, 208, 217, 230, 232, 247, 248, 249, 253, 256, 297
lack of control, 269, 271
land, 179, 251
language, 99, 103, 154, 158, 177, 183, 192, 193, 196, 198, 201, 208, 209, 231, 260, 280, 301
Latin America, 192
law enforcement, 60, 96
laws, 14, 27, 28, 117, 118, 119, 120, 126, 130, 161, 247, 249, 264, 266
lawyers, 6, 166, 260, 268, 273
layoffs, 297
leadership, 3, 17, 18, 82, 90, 157, 293
learning, viii, 50, 51, 53, 54, 57, 59, 60, 62, 63, 66, 67, 68, 80, 82, 90, 91, 100, 293, 302
learning process, 293
learning styles, 53
legal issues, 121, 126
legality, 203, 204
legislation, 165, 214, 249, 297
liberalism, 150, 185, 187, 202, 207, 212, 214, 215
life cycle, 9
life satisfaction, 137, 138, 144
lifetime, 30
likelihood, 24, 47, 70, 71, 72, 76, 77, 94, 95, 101, 102, 104, 105, 106

limitation, 40, 85, 204, 279
linear model, 168, 169, 170, 171, 172, 173
linen, 94
linkage, xii, 2, 261, 273, 275, 276
links, 23, 129, 131, 205, 283
litigation, 186
local community, 118
local government, 232
localization, 86
location, 96
locus, 44, 138, 180
logistics, 298
long run, 208, 300
long-term memory, 68
love, 3, 14, 136, 145, 146, 147, 148, 153, 177, 190, 191
loyalty, 15, 17, 36, 41, 46, 96, 128, 291
LSD, 142
LTC, 60
lying, 20

M

Macedonia, 137, 148
Machiavellianism, 29, 35, 42, 43, 46
machinery, 208
Mainland China, 243
majority group, 101
malaria, 193
males, ix, 4, 5, 6, 30, 79, 84, 99, 191
malfeasance, 54
management, x, xi, 1, 3, 5, 6, 7, 8, 11, 17, 21, 23, 26, 31, 51, 52, 61, 67, 76, 77, 98, 100, 107, 111, 113, 114, 123, 124, 126, 127, 128, 129, 130, 131, 132, 136, 146, 147, 148, 151, 152, 164, 166, 200, 210, 211, 227, 228, 231, 240, 259, 262, 268, 269, 272, 276, 277, 278, 279, 280, 281, 282, 285, 301
management practices, 127
manipulation, 35, 100, 101, 102, 104, 108, 250, 251, 257, 297
manslaughter, x, 149, 153, 156, 159, 160, 162, 163, 164, 165, 166, 167, 173, 187, 199, 200, 217, 219
manufacturer, 22
manufacturing, 73, 270
manufacturing companies, 270
marginal product, 24
marginalisation, 165
market(s), ix, 19, 24, 41, 42, 44, 46, 108, 109, 113, 114, 115, 116, 117, 119, 120, 121, 122, 123, 124, 126, 127, 128, 129, 130, 131, 133, 156, 158, 169, 202, 216, 264, 276, 277, 298, 299
market concentration, 127, 129
market economy, 121, 133, 299

market segment, 122
market share, 129, 130, 131
marketing, 3, 5, 9, 25, 29, 31, 41, 42, 44, 45, 47, 114, 127, 128, 129, 130, 131, 268, 270, 276, 277, 285
marketing mix, 277
marriage, 192
masculinity, 33
materialism, 39
matrix, 294
maturation, 80
mature economies, x, 149, 210
measures, 1, 5, 17, 20, 124, 136, 161, 162, 163, 165, 166, 216, 217, 234
meat, 83
media, 31, 96, 107, 160, 164, 234, 236, 237, 238, 239, 269, 270, 278, 279
medication, 61, 196
membership, 101, 127, 158
memory, 56, 176, 182, 302
men, 4, 5, 6, 7, 86, 136, 180, 190, 195
merchandise, 146
MES, x, 135, 136, 140, 145
messages, 301
metaphor, 255, 269
methodological individualism, 154, 217, 218
Mexico, 242
Middle East, 33, 38, 39
mining, 269
minority, 186
misunderstanding, 152, 212
mobile phone, 146, 297
modeling, 60, 261, 262, 263, 273
models, 29, 32, 42, 44, 80, 115, 119, 121, 171, 215, 260, 270
modern society, 248
modernity, 157
modernization, 303
modules, 54
money, viii, x, 20, 27, 32, 39, 47, 135, 136, 137, 138, 141, 142, 143, 144, 145, 146, 147, 148, 157, 196, 210, 270, 284, 293
monopoly, 178, 232
mood, 18, 190
moral behavior, 9
moral code, 80
moral development, 1, 2, 4, 6, 28, 38, 42
moral judgment, 1, 2, 8, 13, 211
moral reasoning, 1, 2, 3, 4, 5, 6, 7, 8, 9, 28, 81, 110, 260
moral standards, 126, 265
morality, 9, 14, 20, 43, 153, 176, 187, 193, 194, 197, 198, 201, 203, 206, 209, 264, 265, 266, 270, 293, 301, 302

motion, 168, 192
motivation, 19, 20, 138, 147, 148, 268, 271
motives, 36, 40
movement, 15, 151, 231
multidimensional, 136
multiplicity, 179, 201, 209
murder, 155
music, 283
Myanmar, 231

N

Nash equilibrium, 24
nation, 76, 156
nation states, 156
natural disasters, 50
natural environment, 22, 302
negative attitudes, 137, 138, 142
negative consequences, 106
negative emotions, 251
neglect, 189
negotiating, 100
nerve, 160
Netherlands, 200
network, 26, 192
NGOs, x, 150, 192, 229, 232, 234, 235, 236, 237, 238, 242, 244
niche market, 120, 128, 129, 130, 131
Nietzsche, 184
Norway, 200
nuclear family, 192
nurses, 4, 9, 10, 55
nursing, 4, 8, 9, 52, 53, 58, 60, 62, 64, 65, 67, 68, 269
nursing home, 52, 53, 58, 60, 62, 64, 65, 67, 68
nurturance, 260
nutrition, 196

O

obedience, 18, 183, 194
objectification, 201
obligation, 62, 153, 181, 187, 211
observations, 115, 121, 228, 263, 278, 279
obstruction, 94, 160
OECD, 269
oil, 22, 296, 298, 302, 303
oil spill, 303
Oklahoma, 27
old age, 240
older people, viii, 50, 51, 52, 53, 55, 56, 57, 58, 62, 63, 64, 66

omission, 73, 172, 187
openness, 34
opportunism, ix, 36, 113, 115, 117, 118, 121
opportunity costs, 63
optimism, 127
organization(s), vii, ix, xi, 2, 3, 5, 6, 7, 10, 11, 13, 14, 15, 17, 18, 22, 24, 25, 26, 45, 46, 47, 51, 52, 57, 58, 63, 64, 65, 66, 70, 77, 93, 94, 95, 96, 97, 98, 100, 101, 106, 107, 108, 109, 110, 111, 132, 136, 144, 146, 154, 155, 194, 230, 259, 260, 261, 262, 264, 265, 266, 269, 272, 273, 293, 294, 295, 298, 301, 302, 303
organizational behavior, 2, 147, 268
organizational culture, 4, 18, 303
orientation, ix, 3, 5, 6, 7, 21, 23, 24, 26, 37, 80, 90, 113, 114, 115, 116, 117, 119, 120, 121, 122, 126, 127, 129, 130, 131, 133, 144, 152, 178, 184, 193
otherness, 176, 177, 205
output, 24, 248
outsourcing, 228, 229
overload, 97
overtime, 239, 240
overweight, 282
ownership, 169, 260

P

Pacific, 241, 242
packaging, 127, 130
pain, 189, 191, 196, 198, 212, 214, 250, 267
paradigm shift, 212
parallel processing, 262
parents, 123, 191, 192
Parliament, 200
parole, 207, 208
partnership(s), vii, 21, 22, 31, 260
passive, 60, 81, 82
pathways, 15, 261, 262, 263
pedagogy, ix, 79, 80, 82, 86, 90
peers, 100, 101, 102
penalties, 30, 130, 268
pensions, 74
perception(s), viii, 2, 7, 10, 31, 36, 37, 40, 41, 42, 43, 50, 57, 62, 67, 90, 101, 102, 110, 147, 160, 178, 181, 219, 232, 235, 261, 262, 263, 264, 266, 267, 269, 270, 271, 272, 273, 277, 278, 281, 283
perfect competition, ix, 113, 115, 119
permit, 97, 213
personal autonomy, 150
personal qualities, 14
personal relations, 14, 284, 285
personal relationship, 14, 285
personal values, 34, 41, 46

personality, 35, 128, 154, 278, 293
personality characteristics, 35
philanthropy, 121, 123, 125, 127, 129
philosophers, 152, 184, 185, 194, 214, 254, 292
pitch, 70
planning, viii, 50, 52, 55, 56, 61, 62, 68, 71, 169
plants, 73, 297
Plato, 136, 181, 184, 266, 273
plausibility, 214
pleasure, 196, 212, 214
pluralism, 219
plurality, 201, 210
poison, 162, 196, 218
police, 159, 163, 165, 167, 182, 285
political power, 291
politics, 157, 176, 206, 209, 219
pollution, 24, 126, 169
poor, 55, 144, 164, 168, 182, 183, 192, 193, 196, 209, 235, 297
population, 60, 61, 63, 125, 168
Portugal, 149
positive attitudes, 3, 38, 137
positive relation, 3
positive relationship, 3
poverty, 183, 194, 196, 198, 209
power, ix, x, 33, 34, 76, 93, 94, 95, 98, 99, 101, 104, 106, 108, 115, 116, 117, 119, 120, 121, 138, 144, 146, 149, 156, 157, 160, 161, 166, 168, 178, 189, 199, 202, 208, 210, 215, 291, 292
power relations, 95
prediction, 251
preference, 1, 4, 46, 56, 84, 291
prejudice, 206
premiums, 128
preparedness, viii, 49, 50, 51, 52, 53, 54, 55, 56, 57, 58, 59, 60, 61, 62, 63, 64, 65, 66, 67
president, 205
pressure, 23, 24, 94, 114, 123, 144, 151, 160, 166, 171, 172, 202, 210, 211, 299
prestige, x, 149, 157
prevention, 18, 30, 31, 43, 44, 240
price competition, 131
prices, 29, 30, 39, 41, 42, 279
primacy, 175, 202, 204, 251
primary data, 230
prior knowledge, 233
privacy, 72, 260
privatisation, 172, 199
probability, 24
probe, 110, 124
problem solving, 14, 62, 260, 261, 303
producers, 270
product design, 128, 129, 131, 277
production, 24, 25, 70, 118, 121, 130, 131, 175, 228, 229, 231, 233, 240, 270, 276, 297, 298
production costs, 231, 297
production quota, 240
production technology, 118, 121
profession(s), 4, 6, 11, 18, 19, 62
profitability, 114, 116, 118, 121, 122, 127, 131, 284
profit(s), 3, 19, 20, 23, 24, 25, 28, 32, 39, 42, 123, 127, 129, 144, 158, 166, 172, 201, 202, 204, 217, 264, 265, 268, 269, 270, 273, 297
program, 5, 18, 52, 61, 63, 66, 99, 121, 123, 129, 130, 131, 268, 271
property rights, 264, 267, 270
proposition, 23, 76, 77, 128, 157
psychoanalysis, 179
psychologist, 10
psychology, 81, 86, 168, 173, 301
psychopaths, 303
public administration, 269
public awareness, 41
public domain, 191, 194, 196
public health, 53, 59, 60, 61, 62, 67
public sector, 51, 63, 269
public service, 19
pumps, 152, 172, 211
punishment, 28, 159, 163, 164, 165, 213
P-value, 58

Q

qualifications, 109
qualitative research, 114, 121, 124, 125, 126
quantitative research, 124, 125
query, 197
questioning, 203
questionnaires, x, 41, 83, 85, 135

R

race, 179, 196, 231
radar, 276
range, vii, ix, 56, 58, 64, 65, 102, 104, 113, 125, 163, 192, 239, 276, 277
rating agencies, 22
rationality, ix, 113, 114, 115, 119, 121, 123, 126, 127, 130, 133, 154, 178, 180, 188, 189, 204, 267, 293
raw materials, 297
reaction formation, 295, 297
reading, 99, 100, 125, 200
real estate, 280

reality, 90, 161, 168, 175, 191, 205, 207, 209, 261, 293, 295, 296, 298, 301, 303
reasoning, ix, 1, 2, 3, 4, 5, 6, 7, 8, 9, 11, 28, 51, 79, 81, 82, 162, 204, 206, 213, 260, 268
recall, 156, 186
reception, 195
reciprocity, 153, 178, 181, 202
recognition, 43, 62, 146, 150, 155, 167, 177, 179, 195, 204, 213
reconstruction, 133
recycling, 33, 42
reduction, 22, 127, 193, 201, 207, 269
reflection, 213, 272, 277
reforms, 199
regression, 294
regulation(s), ix, 23, 86, 113, 119, 122, 126, 130, 201, 204, 242, 248, 255, 267, 270
regulators, 96
rejection, 218
relationship(s), ix, 7, 8, 9, 17, 18, 19, 23, 26, 29, 31, 32, 33, 34, 35, 36, 37, 38, 40, 41, 42, 43, 45, 46, 79, 80, 81, 82, 84, 85, 86, 110, 114, 123, 129, 155, 158, 163, 168, 169, 173, 175, 177, 180, 182, 197, 200, 203, 204, 206, 234, 235, 237, 247, 248, 249, 250, 251, 252, 253, 254, 255, 256, 257, 277, 280, 296, 299
relationship marketing, 45, 129
relatives, 268
relevance, xi, 114, 150, 153, 197, 202, 213, 227, 228, 229, 230, 232, 238
reliability, 42, 85, 124, 291
religion, 37, 44, 180, 292
religiosity, 29, 37, 42, 47
religiousness, 37
renewable energy, 298
repair, 231
repression, 195
reproduction, 192
reputation, 107, 200, 296
research design, 81, 125
reserves, 127
residues, 195
resilience, 55
resistance, x, 95, 98, 150, 152, 160, 175, 283
resolution, 5, 111
resource management, 147
resources, x, 41, 52, 54, 57, 58, 62, 63, 64, 65, 66, 95, 98, 107, 149, 156, 158, 159, 216, 218, 235, 253
responsiveness, 267
retail, ix, 30, 34, 39, 41, 44, 45, 46, 113, 114, 122, 124, 130
retaliation, 96, 98, 107

retention, 213
retirement, 81
returns, viii, 27, 31, 39, 68, 175
rewards, 231
rhetoric, 90, 292, 293, 294, 295, 298
right to life, 252
rigidity, 266
risk, 18, 144, 160, 164, 165, 186, 193, 201, 202, 215, 216, 217, 218, 231, 232, 237, 239, 264, 283
role playing, 5
Romania, 43
routines, 268
rubrics, 191
rural areas, 54

S

sabotage, 96
sacrifice, 39, 55, 178, 183, 278
safe drinking water, 196
safety, 60, 128, 151, 152, 159, 160, 162, 164, 165, 166, 167, 172, 186, 196, 199, 200, 202, 210, 211, 216, 217, 240, 268, 270
sales, 39, 47, 70, 71, 72, 146, 297
sample, 2, 6, 7, 34, 35, 36, 38, 39, 42, 82, 84, 95, 124, 132, 137, 140, 141, 143, 213
sampling, 124, 125, 132
sanctions, 107, 117, 159
Sarbanes-Oxley Act, 107
SARS, 68
satisfaction, 41, 137, 138, 144, 145, 147, 148, 297
saturation, 125
savings, 22, 131
scandal, 82, 95, 107, 158
scarcity, 253
scheduling, 216
schema, 170, 262
scholarship, 261
school, 4, 30, 51, 68, 80, 81, 84, 202, 260, 271, 272, 273
schooling, 6
scientific method, 235
scores, 1, 2, 4, 7, 20, 34, 35, 36, 37, 38, 39, 41, 57, 102, 104, 136, 266
search(es), 23, 29, 72, 151, 261
searching, 280
Second World, 153, 181
secondary data, 230
security, 31, 34, 191, 232, 278, 279, 280, 281, 282, 283, 284, 285
selecting, 272, 279, 282
self-confidence, 283
self-consciousness, 209

self-control, 17
self-employed, 249
self-enhancement, 34
self-esteem, 293, 294
self-interest, ix, 4, 14, 20, 80, 113, 115, 117, 118, 121, 122, 123, 127, 130, 155, 156, 178, 255, 260, 264, 268, 271
self-regulation, 19
semi-structured interviews, 124, 278
sensitivity, 6, 81, 233, 260, 266, 267
separation, 192, 195, 237
September 11, viii, 49, 50, 62
series, 1, 124, 158, 171, 269
sex, 231
sexual behaviour, 195
sexual harassment, 282
sexuality, 195
shame, 301
shape, 151, 164, 266
shaping, 5, 18, 190, 303
shareholder value, 80, 272
shareholders, vii, 14, 15, 21, 22, 24, 25, 70, 166, 173, 264, 266, 267, 268, 269, 270
shares, 156, 167, 214, 256
sharing, 75, 281
shelter, 56, 61, 68
short run, 264
sign(s), 101, 178, 194, 201, 219, 240, 280, 296
signals, 280, 283, 299
silver, 182
simulation, 91
Singapore, 148
skills, 51, 57, 67, 98, 107, 232
skin, 202
slavery, 249, 251, 253
slaves, 191, 253
smoothing, 268, 269
social audit, 240
social change, 273
social construct, 80, 90
social context, 217
social contract, 62, 179, 209, 218
social desirability, 100, 101, 102, 104, 125, 132, 133
social exclusion, 197
social group, 205
social institutions, 26, 206, 256
social justice, 54, 209
social network, 43
social order, 179, 207, 208
social phenomena, 169, 217
social problems, 272
social psychology, 147
social relations, 178, 206

social responsibility, vii, 13, 15, 17, 123, 124, 129, 133, 134, 200, 270, 271, 291, 292, 297, 298, 302
social sciences, 151, 264
social structure, 205
social support, 37
social theory, 273
socialization, 3, 9, 45
society, x, xii, 14, 24, 25, 27, 28, 39, 51, 80, 86, 94, 96, 123, 136, 144, 149, 150, 151, 153, 155, 157, 163, 169, 173, 179, 183, 186, 187, 191, 193, 195, 196, 197, 201, 202, 204, 205, 207, 208, 210, 211, 214, 215, 219, 220, 248, 249, 250, 255, 256, 260, 265, 268, 272, 277, 285, 289, 290, 291, 292, 299, 300, 303
soil, 22, 156, 196, 219
solidarity, 72, 178, 267
South Korea, 242
sovereignty, 178
Spain, 137, 148
specialisation, vii
species, 177, 209
spectrum, 17
speculation, 128
speech, 177, 200, 201, 207, 208, 265, 277, 292
speed, 151, 165, 166, 211, 217, 270
spirituality, 37
spontaneity, 169, 176, 181
stability, 81
staffing, 54
stages, 1, 4, 9, 10, 28, 81, 90, 124, 261, 262, 263, 301
stakeholder analysis, 26
stakeholders, vii, 10, 14, 21, 22, 23, 24, 44, 114, 115, 116, 118, 119, 120, 121, 122, 127, 128, 129, 130, 131, 229, 265, 267, 268, 269, 270, 271, 272, 277, 290, 291, 292, 295, 300, 301
standard deviation, 2, 56
standards, 13, 14, 18, 20, 29, 51, 67, 100, 119, 126, 127, 130, 131, 145, 159, 200, 230, 265, 284, 295, 298
stars, 183
statutes, 108, 267
stigma, 159
stock, 156
strain, 180, 229
strategies, x, 15, 26, 30, 31, 40, 41, 42, 57, 58, 64, 66, 149, 156, 158, 159, 161, 216, 217, 228, 234, 273, 277, 285, 299
strength, 184, 185, 215, 263
stress, x, 5, 51, 52, 63, 123, 135, 206, 293
structuring, 237
student group, 56

students, viii, ix, x, 4, 5, 9, 28, 30, 35, 36, 37, 38, 40, 42, 43, 44, 47, 49, 50, 51, 52, 53, 54, 55, 56, 57, 58, 59, 60, 61, 62, 63, 64, 65, 66, 67, 79, 80, 81, 82, 83, 84, 85, 86, 90, 91, 135, 137, 138, 142, 144, 233, 260, 261, 264, 265, 266, 267, 268, 271, 272, 273
substitutes, 279
substitution, 178
Sudan, 231
suffering, 181, 183, 184, 192, 196, 197, 198, 210, 214, 301
suicide, 187, 188, 190
sulphur, 118
summer, 298
superiority, 144
supervision, 145, 166
supervisor(s), 72, 74, 76, 187, 298
suppliers, xi, 13, 14, 15, 22, 200, 227, 229, 230, 231, 234, 236, 238, 239, 266, 267, 297, 298
supply, 155, 200, 281, 284
supply chain, 201
support services, 192
support staff, 60
surplus, 24, 25, 203
surprise, 172, 280
surrogates, 90
survival, 86
sustainability, 13, 290
sustainable development, 22
Sweden, xii, 200, 227, 247, 259, 269, 275, 276, 278, 279, 281
switching, 33, 39
symbiosis, 22
symmetry, 209
sympathy, 14, 181, 301
synergistic effect, 170
synthesis, 26, 44, 46
systems, 18, 167, 173, 184, 191, 205, 254, 268, 272, 282

T

tactics, 41
Taiwan, 147, 242
talent, 146
tanks, 152, 211
target population, 63
targets, 201, 235
tax deduction, 268
taxonomy, 22, 33, 44
Taylorism, 133
teachers, 4

teaching, viii, 4, 10, 49, 50, 52, 53, 54, 57, 58, 59, 60, 62, 64, 65, 66, 67, 68, 80, 90, 91, 261, 272
teaching experience, 52, 57, 58, 64, 66, 80
team members, 60
technological change, 25
technological developments, 255
technology, 24, 25, 82, 118, 155, 216, 260, 267
telephone, 76, 227, 275
television, 33, 192, 266, 298
tenure, 1, 3, 6, 7, 8, 99, 101
terminally ill, 189
terrorism, 50
textbooks, 21
theft, 30, 158
thematic responses, 60
theory, ix, x, xi, 4, 9, 11, 17, 19, 22, 23, 25, 26, 45, 46, 47, 80, 81, 82, 90, 93, 121, 125, 150, 151, 152, 154, 155, 157, 160, 161, 162, 163, 167, 169, 173, 186, 195, 197, 202, 207, 212, 213, 215, 217, 218, 219, 247, 248, 252, 254, 255, 257, 259, 260, 264, 269, 273, 297, 303
thinking, 1, 4, 39, 61, 80, 82, 181, 182, 194, 197, 212, 213, 214, 270, 272
Third World, 241, 244
threat(s), 50, 201, 207, 235, 283
threshold, 170, 265, 301
time, 3, 6, 15, 19, 44, 52, 55, 60, 62, 63, 72, 73, 76, 85, 86, 87, 98, 99, 103, 111, 115, 124, 131, 136, 137, 138, 145, 146, 151, 153, 157, 158, 161, 164, 166, 167, 168, 169, 170, 171, 172, 173, 178, 185, 189, 191, 192, 195, 197, 199, 201, 203, 207, 208, 209, 217, 218, 230, 232, 233, 235, 238, 239, 249, 250, 266, 271, 273, 281, 285, 293, 296, 297, 298
time constraints, 55
tobacco, 215
tofu, 297
top management, 5, 126, 161, 293
tourism, 90
toys, 243
trade, 22, 52, 63, 159, 165, 233, 244
trade union, 165, 244
trade-off, 52, 63, 233
tradition, 34, 123, 150, 152, 174, 176, 180, 182, 184, 185, 186, 191, 198, 211, 212, 215, 235, 266
traffic, 54, 169, 172
training, vii, viii, 5, 6, 14, 17, 31, 50, 51, 56, 57, 59, 61, 64, 65, 66, 67, 99, 240
traits, 14, 17, 18, 169, 255, 266
transcendence, 34, 41, 176, 177
transgression, 95, 96, 107
transition, 196
translation, 54, 175, 176, 183, 193, 206, 209
transnational corporations, xi, 227

transparency, vii, 13, 234, 235, 237, 238, 270
transport, 166, 169
transportation, 50, 54, 56, 60, 298
trend, 228, 271
trial, 94, 165
triangulation, 125
trust, 15, 17, 19, 23, 45, 145, 268, 301
Turkey, 41
turnover, 56, 127, 147

U

uncertainty, ix, 33, 69, 70, 237
undergraduate, ix, 36, 37, 40, 52, 79, 81, 83, 84, 85, 271
unemployment, 30, 240
unhappiness, 196
unions, 232, 238, 248, 256
United Kingdom(UK), x, 45, 113, 132, 133, 149, 150, 153, 158, 172, 186, 192, 199, 200, 201, 221, 287
United Nations(UN), 192, 242
United States, 74
universality, 204
universe, 81, 174, 187, 201
universities, 51, 232
university students, x, 34, 38, 135, 136, 137, 138, 142, 143, 144, 147
users, 217, 270, 277, 282

V

vacuum, 164, 169
validation, 279
validity, 42, 85, 124, 125, 248
values, vii, xii, 3, 9, 18, 28, 34, 45, 54, 57, 80, 82, 86, 101, 102, 108, 109, 163, 205, 206, 214, 254, 260, 263, 265, 267, 269, 270, 272, 277, 289, 290, 291, 292, 293, 296, 297, 298, 299, 300, 301
vandalism, 31
variable(s), 1, 7, 8, 29, 96, 102, 104, 105, 106, 137, 213, 263
variance, 7, 125, 141
variation, 22, 99
vehicles, 151
vein, 157, 183
vessels, 152, 164, 211
vice-president, 192
victims, vii, 27, 28, 163, 166, 181, 199, 215, 219
Vietnam, 243, 244
violence, 96, 208, 267, 281, 282, 284
violent behaviour, 186

vision, 18, 22, 55, 177, 195, 196, 210, 219, 270
vocabulary, 154, 256
voice, 1, 9, 90, 108, 177, 182
voting, 191

W

wages, 31, 202, 240
waking, 298
Wales, 153, 219
walking, 186, 280
war, 168
warrants, 100
waste management, 22
watches, 279
waterways, 172
weakness, 93, 100, 189, 210
wealth, 121, 183, 256, 264, 266, 269, 273
weapons, 276, 284
wear, 32, 110, 170, 280
web, 82, 279, 291
web pages, 279
websites, vii
welfare, 5, 28, 191, 196, 214, 240, 264, 267, 269
welfare economics, 214
well-being, 20, 28
Western countries, x, 150, 249
wholesale, 97
winning, 138, 143, 144, 280
wives, 191
women, 4, 5, 6, 7, 9, 85, 90, 93, 108, 191, 195
work climate, 2, 5, 7, 8, 11, 111
work environment, 19, 106
work ethic, 137, 138
workers, 62, 67, 68, 86, 199, 200, 202, 228, 229, 232, 233, 234, 236, 239, 240, 254, 276
working conditions, 63, 228, 229, 230, 231, 233, 234, 236, 238, 297
working hours, 172, 230, 239, 298
workplace, xi, 14, 45, 95, 165, 199, 231, 247, 248, 250, 251, 255, 257, 268
World Bank, 192
writing, 151, 272
wrongdoing, viii, ix, 69, 70, 73, 94, 95, 96, 97, 98, 100, 101, 102, 104, 106, 107, 108, 111, 161, 162, 165
WTO, 192, 243

Y

yield, 84, 188, 231